CYCLE OF SEGREGATION

CYCLE OF SEGREGATION

Social Processes and Residential Stratification

Maria Krysan and
Kyle Crowder

Russell Sage Foundation
New York

The Russell Sage Foundation

The Russell Sage Foundation, one of the oldest of America's general purpose foundations, was established in 1907 by Mrs. Margaret Olivia Sage for "the improvement of social and living conditions in the United States." The foundation seeks to fulfill this mandate by fostering the development and dissemination of knowledge about the country's political, social, and economic problems. While the foundation endeavors to assure the accuracy and objectivity of each book it publishes, the conclusions and interpretations in Russell Sage Foundation publications are those of the authors and not of the foundation, its trustees, or its staff. Publication by Russell Sage, therefore, does not imply foundation endorsement.

Library of Congress Cataloging-in-Publication Data

Names: Krysan, Maria, author. | Crowder, Kyle, author.
Title: Cycle of segregation : social processes and residential stratification / Maria Krysan and Kyle Crowder.
Description: New York : Russell Sage Foundation, [2017] | Includes bibliographical references and index.
Identifiers: LCCN 2017029335 (print) | LCCN 2017032595 (ebook) | ISBN 9781610448697 (ebook) | ISBN 9780871544902 (pbk. : alk. paper)
Subjects: LCSH: Social change—United States. | Social stratification—United States. | Segregation—United States.
Classification: LCC HN59.2 (ebook) | LCC HN59.2 .K79 2017 (print) | DDC 303.40973—dc23
LC record available at https://lccn.loc.gov/2017029335

Text design by Suzanne Nichols.

RUSSELL SAGE FOUNDATION
112 East 64th Street, New York, New York 10065
10 9 8 7 6 5 4 3 2 1

The ghetto is self-perpetuating, for by separating the white child from the Negro child we hand on to both our own dear delusions of race. We are now trapped in a situation where we must push for a miscellany of tortuous techniques, from pairing to busing, designed to integrate schools which serve segregated neighborhoods, both black and white. These schools must pretend that Americans live in one world and not two, but the children know better because they know their neighborhoods. The bus from the Negro ghetto in Evanston, Illinois, comes every morning to Lincolnwood elementary school, and the white children on the playground shout, "Here comes the colored bus!"

Neighborhood segregation is thus the sour grape that sets each new generation's teeth on edge. Right now we are creating another generation of Americans committed in their bones to segregation, not because we are formally teaching it (in many homes and schools we are teaching just the opposite), but because we are living it.

—National Committee Against Discrimination in Housing,
How the Federal Government Builds Ghettos

Contents

List of Illustrations |

About the Authors |

MARIA KRYSAN is professor in the Department of Sociology and the Institute of Government and Public Affairs at the University of Illinois at Chicago.

KYLE CROWDER is Blumstein-Jordan Professor of Sociology at the University of Washington.

Acknowledgments |

THIS BOOK IS the culmination of years of telephone conversations, emails, and meetings between the two authors. Kyle planted the seed. The ideas, data, and arguments were nurtured, modified, developed, and cultivated by these countless exchanges. And the book finally came to pass because of Maria's persistence. From start to finish, this was a collaboration; both authors contributed equally to the manuscript.

We are deeply indebted to thoughtful contributions to this work from many generous colleagues, all of whom helped us develop and strengthen the ideas and our presentation of them. Our collaborator, Michael Bader, deserves special thanks for his intellectual contributions over many years and especially for a careful read of an early draft that gave us insightful restructuring advice. In addition, we are particularly grateful to Stew Tolnay and several anonymous reviewers who also read early drafts of the book and pushed us to refine our arguments. We thank Erin Carll, Chris Hess, and Max Cuddy who provided careful research assistance.

The research in this book was supported, in part, by a grant to the authors from the National Science Foundation (Grant #1324039), and from a Eunice Kennedy Shriver National Institute of Child Health and Human Development research infrastructure grant, R24 HD042828, to the Center for Studies in Demography and Ecology at the University of Washington. The 2003 in-depth interviews and focus groups were a collaboration between Maria and Mick P. Couper, Reynolds Farley, and Tyrone Forman. These, and the 2012 in-depth interviews, were made possible by funding from the Office of Social Science Research, Campus Research Board, and the Institute for Research on Race and Public Policy (IRRPP), all at the University of Illinois at Chicago (UIC). A team of then-graduate students at UIC, including Rhonda Dugan, Vickey Velazquez, Jody Ahlm, Patrick Washington, and Melissa Abad conducted the interviews, and UIC's Survey Research Laboratory recruited respondents and provided needed facilities for the data collection. IRRPP also provided crucial fellowship support and a writing retreat for Maria; and in April 2015, the Schragg Family Fellowship provided support for Maria to spend a week of writing-in-residence at the University of Washington.

Kyle is deeply indebted to the members of the Context Working Group at the University of Washington—including Jerry Herting, Hedy Lee, Stew Tolnay and a host of brilliant graduate students—for countless enlightening conversations about neighborhood dynamics and the drivers of segregation. He is also exceedingly thankful for the endurance of his wife, Robin, and sons, C.J. and Finn, for their unwavering support, grounding, and humor as we worked on this book. Finally, special thanks goes to Kyle's mother, Karen, for providing early and consistent reminders of the importance of racial justice.

Maria is grateful to: the graduate student members of UIC's Neighborhoods, Housing, and Urban Sociology reading group who were a source of energy and a sounding board; the faculty and staff in the Department of Sociology who are a great intellectual community engaged in scholarship that makes a difference (special thanks to Tara Gordon-Williams and Jennifer Michals for helping protect Maria's time); Paula Dempsey, the amazingly helpful sociology librarian at UIC; and the many housing agency and non-profit professionals (especially Rob Breymaier and the Oak Park Regional Housing Center) she has interacted with through her work at the Institute of Government and Public Affairs. They have kept her grounded in the realities of segregation, the processes that perpetuate it, and the efforts to upend it.

At key moments in the writing of this book, Maria was able to take writing retreats both near and far (at the invaluable suggestion of Michelle Boyd) only because of the generosity of her daughter's grandparents, godmothers, and godsister. Carole and Jim Krysan, Michelle Harris, Carmelle Jackson, and Amanda Reid swooped in and helped care for the best daughter ever, Katerina. In addition to patiently awaiting the completion of this book, Katerina also provided her mom with inspiration, grounding, hope for the future, and "bubble charts" (not to mention taking on the role of special assistant to our editor, Suzanne Nichols, who also patiently awaited the arrival of this manuscript—and provided expert guidance along the way). Many colleagues (especially Larry Bobo), family (Damian, Sharon, Pat, Claudia), and friends (shout out to the balcony parents at TOPS) supported Maria in this effort in ways large and small throughout the years of its evolution; but Maria owes special recognition to Amanda Lewis, for always knowing what to say, having endless tricks for keeping the process moving along, and for always believing in her. Finally, Maria is grateful to Reynolds Farley, who through his scholarship and cheerful mentorship set her on the path to studying segregation; and to Howard Schuman who, by his example and through his training, gave her the tools to do so.

Part I | Segregation Then and Now

Chapter 1 | The Historical Roots of Segregation in the United States and the Need for a New Perspective

IN THE DEBATE leading up to the passage of the Fair Housing Act in 1968, Senator Edward Brooke of Massachusetts offered a concise summary of the then-current state of segregation:

> We make two general assertions: (1) that American cities and suburbs suffer from galloping segregation, a malady so widespread and so deeply imbedded in the national psyche that many Americans, Negros as well as whites, have come to regard it as a natural condition; and (2) that the prime carrier of galloping segregation has been the Federal Government. First it built the ghettos; then it locked the gates; now it appears to be fumbling for the key. Nearly everything the Government touches turns to segregation, and the Government touches nearly everything.[1]

At the time, Brooke was reflecting on the fact that black Americans faced an almost insurmountable set of housing policies and practices intentionally designed to restrict their housing opportunities and maintain the geographic separation of blacks and whites. Across the country, blacks were confined—through legal statute, local practices, and violence—to the poorest and most underserved parts of metropolitan areas as residential segregation reached its apex.

Certainly, much has changed since 1968. Although it offered only feeble enforcement provisions, the Fair Housing Act officially outlawed discrimination by race and provided an important legal tool for dismantling de jure systems of American apartheid. Moreover, recent decades have seen

3

dramatic softening of racial attitudes and the emergence of a significant black middle class. Populations in most metropolitan areas of the country have also become increasingly diverse, helping to at least complicate the traditional black-white systems of social stratification. All of these changes have helped to erode residential segregation in many metropolitan areas and led to the emergence of many stably integrated neighborhoods.

At the same time, much of what Senator Brooke said nearly a half-century ago still applies today. Segregation remains virtually unchanged in many of our largest, most populated metropolitan areas and is still stubbornly high in most places where large groups of racial and ethnic minorities live. Although a glimmer of hope is provided by recent Affirmatively Furthering Fair Housing (AFFH) directives from the U.S. Department of Housing and Urban Development (HUD) that municipalities do more to enhance residential opportunities, the federal government has remained "fumbling for the keys to the gate," failing to maintain a modicum of consensus on the necessity and method to dismantle the complex set of discriminatory forces that help to maintain segregation, much less seriously tackle the Fair Housing Act's mandate to affirmatively further desegregation. And segregation appears to be just as entrenched in the national psyche as it was decades ago; most Americans, and many legal actors, seem to have simply come to accept that cities and their suburbs are organized around racial lines to a degree that resembles a natural order.[2]

Also consistent with Senator Brooke's description of "galloping segregation," there remains a substantial amount of momentum behind the on-the-ground residential processes that drive segregation. To be certain, the drivers of segregation have changed, but racial and ethnic groups still exhibit starkly different patterns of residential mobility, typically remaining in, and moving between, largely separate sets of neighborhoods.[3] As a result, racially stratified patterns of residential advantage and disadvantage are passed on from one generation to the next, and despite substantial population churning, segregation is continually replicated and sustained from decade to decade within most metropolitan areas.[4]

Most importantly, as was true at the time of Brooke's testimony, segregation retains a key role in the maintenance of broader systems of stratification. Neighborhoods occupied by racial and ethnic groups are not only geographically separate but qualitatively different, so that members of different groups face dramatically different life chances as a function of differential exposure to educational and employment opportunities, pollution and other physical threats, crime, and social disorganization. There is strong evidence that these racial disparities in neighborhood opportunity structures—all rooted in persistent segregation—contribute in substantial ways to sharp racial differences in education, income, wealth, health, and general well-being.

For those interested in explaining the maintenance of racial stratification and the inner workings of cities, an important question has persisted: in the context of significant social change, demographic shifts, and improvements in the economic plight of at least some racial and ethnic minority groups, how can we explain the considerable and sustained momentum of residential segregation by race? In recent decades, this question has been the subject of thousands of articles and books, most of which have focused on three main explanations for the maintenance of segregation. According to the first explanation—and the one most widely adopted in the general public—residential segregation reflects group differences in racial residential preferences. That is, members of different groups end up living in separate residential spaces because they prefer to live near their own group. In contrast, the second theoretical explanation holds that segregation reflects the persistence of racial and ethnic differences in socioeconomic resources. Here the idea is that individuals sort themselves into neighborhoods based on their ability to pay for the most attractive residential options; so, for example, black Americans end up living in separate and more disadvantaged locations because they have lower average levels of education, income, and wealth than do whites. Finally, the third popular explanation focuses on the persistence of subtle but insidious forms of discrimination—including biased zoning provisions, discriminatory lending practices, the geographic concentration of subsidized housing, and a variety of other exclusionary and non-exclusionary forces—that effectively restrict the residential options of members of some groups.

Although all of these factors are surely important, we argue that a different set of forces—less clearly articulated in the existing literature—are important in maintaining the momentum of segregation. Our central argument is that while segregation in America was created out of a series of conscious efforts to ensure separation of the races, it is now maintained not just by overt segregationist efforts, socioeconomic differences, and racial preferences, but also by the social and economic repercussions of segregation itself.

The central goal of this book is to outline a new theoretical lens—the *social structural sorting perspective*—through which we might understand the forces that continue to drive the cycle of residential segregation. As we will argue, this theoretical frame has three central features that distinguish it from traditional perspectives on segregation. First, it starts from the realization that segregation is maintained through the continual reinforcement of racially disparate mobility decisions, and that understanding the momentum of segregation requires explicit attention to the processes through which members of different racial and ethnic groups search for, and select from, different residential options. Second, the social structural sorting perspective focuses on the fact that individuals approach the housing search with considerable biases and perceptual blind spots, the operation of which contradict implicit assumptions in our traditional perspectives about how processes of racial residential sorting operate. Third, this new perspective focuses on the ways in which segregation by race has become self-perpetuating, driving systems of economic stratification, shaping neighborhood perceptions, circumscribing social networks and systems of neighborhood knowledge by race and ethnicity, and creating patterns of mobility and immobility that differ sharply across racial and ethnic groups. In essence, the perspective suggests that residential moves are structurally sorted along racial lines, with individuals' perceptions and knowledge of residential options shaped by lived experiences and social interactions within a racially segregated social system. The racialized patterns of mobility and immobility that emerge from these structural conditions continually reproduce the system's segregated social and spatial structure. As a result of these self-perpetuating forces, segregation has declined much more slowly than might be expected based on changing patterns of economic stratification, shifting racial attitudes, and the abatement of the most overt forms of exclusionary discrimination. Variations in these forces also help to explain why segregation has declined sharply in some metropolitan areas but remained virtually unchanged in others.

To set the stage for building this new theoretical frame, we begin with a brief description of some of the main political, economic, and social forces that, historically, created segregation in metropolitan areas and the evolution of these forces since the passage of the Fair Housing Act. We then discuss the need for new ways of thinking about the problem of segregation in light of the fact that it is maintained even in the face of broader integrative forces, and in ways that are not adequately explained by existing arguments. As we will argue, the need for a new conceptual framework goes hand in hand with a need for new methods and analytical tools to describe and study segregation and its causes. Because the processes we highlight have largely been ignored in the literature on segregation, much of the evidence for our new approach comes in the form of unexplained patterns and is circumstantial. We then draw out a set of policy implications based in the idea that real progress toward desegregation and equality of neighborhood-based opportunity structures is impossible without recognition and systematic dismantling of these self-reinforcing processes. We will conclude by suggesting how research approaches must be retooled in order to fully test the new framework presented in the book and develop a stronger understanding of the drivers of segregation and its self-perpetuating nature.

SEGREGATION'S INTENTIONAL ROOTS: THE POLICIES THAT SET THE GALLOP IN MOTION

Although segregation has a long history in America, the extreme forms of neighborhood-based racial isolation that characterize many of our cities really emerged in the middle decades of the twentieth century.[5] As has been well documented by Douglas Massey, Nancy Denton, and others, this intensification of segregation in increasingly diverse metropolitan areas was affected by a multitude of racially biased community practices, policies, and public projects, all consciously designed to separate racial and ethnic groups into distinct residential spaces.[6]

During the initial buildup of neighborhood segregation, efforts to restrict black access to white neighborhoods were overt and fully sanctioned by local governments. In the early stages of the Great Migration, for example, many cities and towns of the North restricted the residential options of black residents with zoning laws expressly designating neighborhoods as all-white or all-black. During the 1920s and 1930s, community and neighborhood organizations increasingly employed protective covenants and "codes of ethics" to compel property owners to maintain segregation by refusing to sell or rent to black home-seekers. When those strategies failed to maintain the desired residential color line, local residents employed violence and intimidation to expel black pioneers in white neighborhoods and to deter future interlopers.

A series of federal policies in the ensuing decades exacerbated the impact of these local measures and provided a legal endorsement of efforts to maintain residential separation of racial groups.[7] Most overt were the explicit efforts to maintain segregation in public housing. As Richard Rothstein has pointed out, even the most liberal supporters of the original New Deal programs never envisioned that public housing would be integrated; from an early stage, federally funded public housing projects were designed for either black or white residents, not for a mixture of these groups. Public housing projects were intentionally and consciously placed in neighborhoods already dominated by one group or the other.

Perhaps more wide-ranging and ubiquitous were the effects of the lending rules adopted by the Federal Housing Administration (FHA) at its inception in 1934. These rules explicitly barred lending that might foster integration. Specifically, the FHA adopted "redlining" strategies that designated neighborhoods with more than a few black residents as risky locations for federally insured loans. At the same time, loans to individuals that would allow for the "ingress of undesirable racial or nationality groups" into the neighborhood were prohibited.[8]

The combination of these rules had several key effects. The designation of black and integrated neighborhoods as "hazardous" prompted the flight and avoidance by white residents, who, at any rate, were only able to gain federally guaranteed loans in all-white neighborhoods. Meanwhile, the combination of rules effectively prevented blacks from obtaining federally secured loans; they could not get loans in white neighborhoods because their presence would upset the existing "racial integrity" of the area, and they could not secure loans in integrated or black neighborhoods since such areas were considered too risky for FHA protection. In fact, in the first three decades of the FHA, only 2 percent of all federally insured home loans went to nonwhite applicants. An additional pernicious impact of these rules was that black neighborhoods were essentially cut off from investment. In effect, these federal rules severely limited opportunities for integration and confined the growing black population to city neighborhoods that were increasingly isolated and increasingly disinvested. Importantly, this isolation of the black population away from the white population was the conscious and intended purpose of these policies.

FHA lending rules were important but certainly not the only federal policy that solidified racial segregation in the middle of the twentieth century. Not to be underestimated is the role of the federal government, with help from local partners, in financing and facilitating the separation of black and white populations across city-suburb lines. In the face of growing prosperity and the combination of increasing population diversity and housing shortages in many American cities, the federal government in the middle decades of the twentieth century adopted measures to facilitate the redistribution of the white population to outlying areas. The 1956 Federal-Aid Highway Act—originally billed as a public safety measure—established the federal Highway Trust Fund, which diverted federal tax dollars to the creation of the first interstate highway system. As it developed, this highway system dramatically reduced the effective commuting distance into and out of central cities, opening up vast expanses of previously inaccessible land for development. Taking advantage of these opportunities, developers adopted new methods for mass-produced housing, spawning the first real suburban subdivisions, all with state and federal funds paying for roads, sewers, schools, and other infrastructure. Federal rules already in place helped builders fill these developments by guaranteeing millions of private mortgages for new white suburbanites. Mortgage programs through the FHA and the Veterans Administration (VA) allowed new home-buyers to purchase a home with very little money down and a monthly payment that was, in many cities, lower than the average monthly rent for a smaller unit in the central city. As Kenneth Jackson and many others have related, aggressive marketing, often with explicit racial overtones, helped to define a move away from increasingly diverse cities and to the suburbs as a standard component of the American dream.[9]

For tens of millions of white families in the postwar period, this dream became a reality, but explicit racial bias in federal lending policies continued to restrict opportunities for black home-seekers and provided a crucial endorsement of local segregationist policies. During this period, the vast majority of suburban developments had restrictive covenants, and many cited FHA rules directly to justify this discrimination.[10] At the same time, federal lending guidelines severely limited opportunities to secure loans for property in central-city neighborhoods, helping to throw these neighborhoods into a downward, self-reinforcing spiral of disinvestment and deterioration that made them undesirable to those with the means to afford alternatives.[11] Thus, the growing population of African Americans was continuously confined to deteriorating and increasingly isolated central-city neighborhoods, a problem exacerbated by the fact that public housing serving the poorest African Americans continued to be placed almost exclusively in the poorest, most racially isolated parts of most cities.[12]

By the 1960s, inequality of housing and neighborhood context was recognized as a central pillar of racial stratification and a key target of the civil rights movement. Yet, only after the civil unrest following the assassination of Dr. Martin Luther King Jr. in 1968 was the Fair Housing Act enacted, making discrimination in the housing market illegal, including the discriminatory policies that the FHA had relied on for years to maintain segregation. Subsequent amendments to the law, coming through executive order, required state and local governments to develop plans to "affirmatively further" fair housing goals by identifying discriminatory practices and other barriers to integration, developing plans to demolish these impediments, establishing strategies to actively promote patterns of development that would offer opportunities for integration, and monitoring the effectiveness of these efforts.[13] The U.S. Department of Housing and Urban Development, the successor to FHA, was tasked with monitoring compliance with these provisions and withholding federal funds to state and local governments that failed to develop—and make good progress on—these plans.

Yet the uneven implementation and poor enforcement of the Fair Housing Act since its passage has clearly reflected the weak commitment of policymakers to utilize the law to end the segregation that federal, state, and local policies had played such a strong role in creating. State governments and the federal government have relied on irregular and often ineffective methods to detect discrimination and require evidence of a lengthy pattern of blatant discrimination before meting out what typically amount to fairly minor sanctions.[14] Moreover, HUD has often failed to hold state and local governments to their responsibility to "affirmatively further fair housing," showing a persistent willingness to continue to provide development funds even to locations with poor records in this regard.[15] Between new HUD rules and a surprising Supreme Court ruling in June 2015, there are now signs of reaffirmation of the affirmative-integration aspect of the law. These events were met with cries from some that such requirements are tantamount to social engineering, an ironic twist given decades of federal and local policy designed to engineer and reinforce segregation.[16]

The central point is that modern forms of segregation have not emerged out of benign patterns of residential choice or individual resources, as is assumed in popular explanations, nor are the roots of segregation "unknowable," as has sometimes been claimed by justices of the Supreme Court.[17] In reality, modern segregation has its roots in conscious decisions and public policy. Local, state, and federal agencies undertook strategies that intentionally separated blacks and whites and limited opportunities for integration. It was on this legal scaffolding that the segregationist activities of millions of individual actors—builders, real estate agents, lenders, local governments, neighborhood groups, and individual residents—hung their own discriminatory strategies, completing an impressive set of multilevel factors that bolstered and maintained segregation even as our metropolitan areas became increasingly diverse.

THE CONTEMPORARY SCENE AND THE NEED FOR A NEW PERSPECTIVE

A common narrative today is that the discrimination that limited residential opportunities for African Americans and other people of color is in the past. Certainly, since the passage of the Fair Housing Act, the levels of the most overt forms of discriminatory treatment have declined.[18] Yet barriers to residential access remain. Audit studies continue to highlight the persistence of fairly traditional forms of discrimination, including racial steering, higher application rejection rates, and higher rates of nonresponse from landlords and real estate agents dealing with home-seekers of color. Also important are what the sociologist Vincent Roscigno and his colleagues refer to as non-exclusionary forms of discrimination: poor treatment that does not technically exclude individuals from gaining access to a particular neighborhood but that nevertheless creates hostile living conditions that individuals are likely to factor into their housing decisions.[19] Moreover, there is ample evidence that segregation is bolstered by discriminatory features of urban development strategies and biased housing market dynamics, such as local zoning ordinances that exclude low-income and minority populations from large segments of the metropolitan area and continued concentration of publicly subsidized housing and voucher holders in poor and racially isolated areas.[20] Moreover, government policies and infrastructure decisions continue to spawn the displacement of low-income and minority households from integrated areas, and predatory lending practices still concentrate subprime loans in minority-populated areas, creating the context for the disproportionate concentration of foreclosures in these areas and generating patterns of neighborhood change that have, at the very least, slowed the decline of segregation.[21]

Given these dynamics, it might be tempting to believe that segregation would disappear if we somehow did away with the racial biases built into our housing markets and urban development strategies—that is, if we eradicated discrimination in the housing market, fully enforced the Fair Housing Act, and ended public policies that help to maintain segregation. Reality, of course, is much more complicated. In fact, there is ample evidence that, once established, the deep segregation that characterizes many metropolitan areas tends to perpetuate itself with no overt discrimination required. This is not to say that modern forms of discrimination play no role in the maintenance of segregation. Available evidence clearly indicates otherwise. However, even in the absence of intentionally segregationist policies, residential stratification by race would surely persist well into the future, owing to a host of factors that maintain segregation—on a daily basis and at the individual level—in ways that are not fully appreciated in existing research on the topic.

Many of the most important social forces shaping residential stratification remain hidden from view because they shape segregation indirectly through other, seemingly benign features of residential sorting. Segregation is so deeply entrenched in our metropolitan areas that it has, in many ways, become self-reinforcing. That is, the separation of different racial and ethnic groups into distinct and qualitatively different residential spaces produces sharp racial differences in sociodemographic characteristics and life experiences that, in turn, shape profound racial differences in residential search processes and neighborhood outcomes. The resulting racial stratification in patterns of residential mobility and immobility continually perpetuates residential stratification into subsequent generations and across time, even in the absence of overt efforts to maintain the residential color line. We suggest that although the stability of segregation over time has the appearance of inertia, the underlying processes are dynamic—involving the continual mobility of people within and between neighborhoods—and so the image of momentum is more apt, since segregation is maintained by the churning forward of racially disparate residential mobility patterns. Our challenge is to understand why these dynamic individual-level processes continue a way as to reinforce segregation. Indeed, illuminating these self-reinforcing features of segregation is crucial if we are to develop stronger explanations of residential stratification and advance public policy to address its multidimensional effects.

The virtual blindness of existing research to the self-perpetuating features of segregation suggests the need for a new conceptual frame through which to view the drivers of segregation. In developing the social structural sorting perspective, we move beyond ardent adherence to traditional explanations of residential stratification. This new perspective draws attention to the fact that *social* dynamics, including the operation of social networks, life course experiences, residential histories, daily activities, and media exposure, shape individual patterns of neighborhood knowledge and perceptions, and that these patterns, in turn, create the decision-making *structure* that results in neighborhood selections and residential outcomes.

Again, the social structural sorting perspective starts with the well-established assumption that racial residential segregation is maintained by racially disparate patterns of mobility and immobility, and with the less-accepted recognition that these patterns of mobility reflect individuals' perceptions of the quantity, quality, and accessibility of residential options in their housing market. In so doing, it calls into question the implicit assumptions of existing segregation research: that people weigh the relative costs and benefits of all the possible options along a range of characteristics (convenience, safety, cost, attractiveness, and so on) and make the optimal selection from these options. The operation of this cost-benefit analysis as the cornerstone of the residential selection process is a fairly standard, albeit largely implicit, assumption of the traditional explanations of segregation. In essence, these arguments assume that to the extent that discriminatory institutional barriers allow, individuals sort themselves into neighborhoods that match their economic means and residential preferences.

Drawing on insights from geography, sociology, decision sciences, economics, and psychology, the social structural sorting perspective deviates from traditional theories in terms of assumptions about the extent to which this residential sorting is based on complete and reliable information about various residential options and in terms of the kind of decision-making processes that are used. Moving away from naive rational-action models that assume complete information and fully logical utility-maximization, the social structural sorting perspective suggests that residential decision-making occurs in stages that are socially embedded, and it rests heavily on the heuristics—essentially cognitive shortcuts—that individuals use to streamline and simplify decisions about where to search for housing. The perspective points to social processes through which these heuristics are developed and, in particular, how neighborhood racial composition may develop as a key component of the cognitive shortcuts people use in searching for housing. This more nuanced picture of residential decision-making suggests that racial residential segregation is maintained not just because members of different races are simply sorted into separate neighborhoods—based on some combination of economic resources, preferences, and discrimination—while drawing on a complete list of options. Rather, members of different racial-ethnic groups are, in many ways, operating in drastically different residential worlds and therefore choosing from racially distinct sets of neighborhood options.

Importantly, the social processes shaping residential decision-making are deeply entrenched in broader systems of racial stratification. Partly reflecting the influence of residential segregation, social interactions tend to be racially circumscribed in ways that create substantial differences in both neighborhood knowledge and neighborhood perceptions. As we will argue, segregation tends to perpetuate itself by creating residential histories for members of different racial and ethnic groups that intersect only marginally; by circumscribing daily interactions to distinct social spaces; and by shaping the geographic location of social networks in ways that limit experiences in, and knowledge about, neighborhoods containing other groups. Thus, the social structural sorting perspective provides a framework for understanding why, even in the face of apparent declines in economic disparities, racial animus, and discrimination, segregation is declining only slowly over time in many—though not all—of our nation's large metropolitan areas.

It is important to note that existing literature provides important clues about the dynamics implicated in the social structural sorting perspective. For example, Robert Sampson's seminal work highlights the potential importance of social networks in shaping mobility flows between neighborhoods—flows that continually reinforce segregation by race.[22] Other recent research demonstrates the importance of kin location in residential decision-making processes, pointing to one of the key forces through which racially residential stratification is perpetuated from one generation to another.[23] In addition, there is significant evidence of racial differences in the residential processes that continually reinforce segregation, including pronounced variations in patterns of neighborhood knowledge, as well as strong evidence that residential searches are much more restricted than is typically assumed in existing literature.[24]

Although now dated, empirical studies of housing searches conducted in the 1970s and 1980s also provide crucial insights into the complexity of searches, including their multistage nature, the reliance on limited information, and the sources and kinds of information that are used in different stages.[25] More recently, Elizabeth Bruch and her colleagues have pulled together insights from decision sciences and market research, and provided an innovative conceptual apparatus related to how people make complex decisions, including housing and neighborhood selection. They offer a "cognitively plausible" framework for considering decision processes in diverse contexts, including online dating and neighborhood sorting.[26] It is the goal of this book to articulate the importance of these dynamics, and the racial differences therein, for broader patterns of segregation by drawing together these clues into a coherent theoretical framework and placing them within the context of residential stratification processes.

THE PLAN FOR THE BOOK

In the remaining chapters of this book, we articulate the social structural sorting perspective, discuss the evidence related to this new theoretical framework, and explore implications for social policy and future research. In chapter 2, we set the stage with a closer look at variations in patterns of segregation across metropolitan areas and the residential mobility patterns that drive these differences, as well as the social, economic, and political consequences of these patterns. Here we pay close attention to the extent to which variations in residential outcomes can be explained by the factors implicated in traditional theoretical arguments of segregation. More importantly, we focus on the questions left unanswered by this now vast research on the causes of racial residential stratification.

In part II of the book, we lay out the core features of the social structural sorting perspective. First, in chapter 3, we argue that understanding residential stratification requires attention to the various stages of the residential selection process—a process to which traditional arguments are largely blind. By focusing on the residential selection process—and neighborhood selection and housing searches in particular—we bring into clearer focus the shortcomings of the narrow understanding of the traditional theories that have been so readily adopted in past research. In chapter 3, we also describe the diverse sources of the qualitative and quantitative evidence we use to investigate our theoretical arguments.

In the remaining chapters of part II, we focus on specific social processes that affect the stages of the neighborhood selection and housing search processes and, by extension, shape residential segregation. Chapter 4 focuses on the role of social networks in shaping individuals' knowledge about, and perceptions of, various neighborhood options in the metropolitan area, and the impact of these indirect exposures on residential decision-making. We also examine the extent to which the location of social networks affects actual residential patterns, and racial differences therein, in ways that bolster residential segregation by race. In chapter 5, we examine how residential history and daily activities shape individuals' perceptions of neighborhoods in the metropolitan area and, by extension, the decisions they make when searching for and selecting neighborhoods and housing. Here we focus on how sharp racial differences in residential experiences across the life course help to perpetuate residential segregation by shaping the context of subsequent moves. In chapter 6, we draw on principles of decision sciences and psychology to develop a more complete picture of the residential decision-making process. Building on the scaffolding articulated by Bruch and her colleagues, this description highlights the profound impacts on residential stratification of the reliance on decision-making heuristics in the context of the racially disparate patterns of neighborhood knowledge and perceptions described in chapters 4 and 5. These are ways generally ignored in past research on the topic.

Part III reviews the current state of knowledge about each of the traditional theoretical perspectives and reexamines them through the lens of the social structural sorting perspective. Specifically, we reassess the role of economic resources (chapter 7), racial residential preferences (chapter 8), and discrimination (chapter 9) in the residential decision-making process and, specifically, in patterns of neighborhood perceptions and knowledge. Our purpose is not to negate the importance of discrimination, preferences, and economic factors for understanding patterns of segregation. Rather, we point to the complex roles of these forces, which have been too simply depicted in existing debates about segregation. We suggest that while economics, preferences, and discrimination have typically been described as representative of distinct and competing explanations, they operate on the residential selection process in complex and often overlapping ways. Specifically, they are neither mutually exclusive nor exhaustive explanations of segregation; by applying our social structural sorting perspective to each of them, we reveal even more clearly the shortcomings of existing approaches.

In the final section of the book, we bring the insights of the previous chapters together and illustrate the cycle of segregation at the core of this framework. That is, we describe how these drivers of segregation work together to create a self-perpetuating system. To do this, we articulate the implications of our framework in terms of theories of segregation, methods for studying it, and policies for dismantling it.

Because our framework draws attention to new ways to understand both the old and the altogether new dimensions of segregation, these fresh insights into the drivers of segregation might be translated into innovative ideas about social policy. In chapter 10, we argue that our more nuanced understanding of the forces that keep the cycle of segregation moving also affords a broader range of policy levers that might effectively interrupt the legacy effects of segregation, affect greater residential equality, and help to loosen a key linchpin in the maintenance of broader systems of stratification. We propose these with appropriate caveats related to the circumstantial nature of our evidence, but draw heavily on studies of existing policies that align with this approach and propose fresh ones as well.

With respect to the theoretical implications of our framework, we describe how group differences in economic resources, neighborhood preferences and perceptions, experiences of (and reactions to) discrimination, daily activity spaces, kin location, access to information, and social networks are all affected by segregation in ways that continually reinforce racially differentiated patterns of mobility. All of these individual and neighborhood repercussions of segregation affect the profound racial differences in mobility processes and outcomes, which, in turn, continue the cycle of segregation. These reciprocal factors help to maintain the momentum of segregation, explain the slow pace of change, and maintain dramatic variations across metropolitan areas in terms of a trajectory toward integration, so that segregation remains stubbornly high in some of our largest metropolitan areas, which also contain the lion's share of our minority populations.

Although the central tenets of the social structural sorting perspective are consistent with a good deal of past research and supported by our qualitative and quantitative evidence, many of the implications of the theory are difficult to assess with current sources of data. Thus, chapter 11 describes the research implications of the perspective. Here we highlight the ways in which the basic premises of the model alter how we adjudicate the relative efficacy of existing theoretical arguments and interpret our results. We also outline a significant set of questions raised by the perspective and describe the unconventional sources of data that will be necessary to answer these questions. The central theme is that, in light of the underappreciated forces that help to drive segregation—including the complex interactions between forces implicated in conventional arguments, as well as forces completely outside of these traditional arguments—social scientists must drastically revise the standard approaches to studying group differences in residential outcomes, processes of neighborhood change, and broader patterns of segregation. By extension, the more complex and nuanced picture of how people come to live in certain types of places should change how we think about residential selection in the assessment of neighborhood effects. Accomplishing these goals will require a considerable amount of work to collect and analyze new qualitative and quantitative data that will permit tests of arguments about the complexities and trajectories of residential stratification.

Chapter 2 | Patterns and Consequences of Segregation in the United States

IN A RECENT comprehensive study, the economists Edward Glaeser and Jacob Vigdor argue that while segregation became a defining feature of urban space during the twentieth century, average levels of residential segregation across metropolitan areas have declined substantially in the past five decades, racial and ethnic diversity has increased in urban neighborhoods, and the number of neighborhoods occupied exclusively by a single group have become increasingly rare. These observations lead them to conclude that we have reached the "end of the segregated century."[1] This general sentiment has been echoed by several other notable scholars who point to declining levels of segregation in many metropolitan areas as a hopeful indicator of growing residential integration and, presumably, increasing racial equality.[2]

In this chapter, we rely on data from the U.S. Census Bureau and other sources to reassess these trends in segregation and related patterns of neighborhood change. In this grand-scale overview, we examine segregation patterns back to 1980—the census year at which the data reliably differentiate between black, Latino, and Asian groups—and therefore focus on the set of 331 metropolitan areas (referred to hereafter as the "core metropolitan areas") that were designated by the Census Bureau for the 1980 census and retained that designation through the 2010 census.

PATTERNS OF SEGREGATION

Figure 2.1 traces the average levels of segregation from 1980 to 2010, across the 331 metropolitan areas that were defined as of 1980.[3] At each census date, segregation is measured using the unweighted average of the standard

17

Figure 2.1   Trends in Residential Segregation from Non-Hispanic Whites, 1980–2010

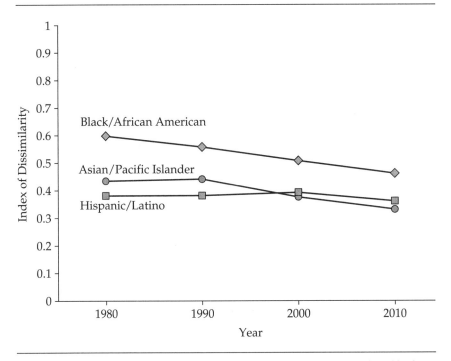

Source: Authors' calculations from the 1970–2010 Neighborhood Change Database (Geolytics 2014).

index of dissimilarity, which measures how evenly a pair of populations are distributed across the neighborhoods of a metropolitan area.[4] A perfectly integrated metropolitan area, with each neighborhood (here census tracts) containing shares of each racial-ethnic group that matches their share in the overall metropolitan area, would have a score of 0. A completely segregated metropolitan area, in which no members of a group share their neighborhoods with members of the comparison group, would have a score of 1. A common rule of thumb, advocated by the sociologists Douglas Massey and Nancy Denton, is to think of metropolitan areas with index of dissimilarity scores of 0.60 and higher as highly segregated, those with segregation scores between 0.30 and 0.60 as moderately segregated, and those with scores below 0.30 as having low levels of segregation.[5]

Several conclusions emerge from this figure. First, as described in the optimistic view, segregation is declining: for African Americans, Latinos, and Asian Americans, average levels of residential segregation from whites were lower in 2010 than in 1980. This trend toward greater integration is reflected in recent research highlighting the increasing diversity of metropolitan neighborhoods.[6] Consistent with the depiction offered by Glaeser and Vigdor, the relative number of all-white neighborhoods in these metropolitan areas has declined sharply in recent decades. Specifically, in 1980 there were 35,409 neighborhoods—representing about 60 percent of all neighborhoods—in the 331 core metropolitan areas that were at least 90 percent white. By 2010, only 14,214 of these original mostly white neighborhoods were still at least 90 percent white. Similarly, the number of metropolitan neighborhoods that were at least 90 percent black declined from 1,889 to 1,787 in these core metropolitan areas over the same time period.[7] All of this evidence provides ample fuel for the sentiment that the kind of racial residential isolation that helped to maintain broader systems of inequality in decades past is disappearing.

Yet the trends revealed in figure 2.1 and the patterns underlying them also provide considerable reason for concern. Despite declines in recent decades, the average level of segregation from whites of all three groups remains moderate (as defined by Massey and Denton). Even as of 2010, the average level of segregation from whites was 0.33 for Asians, 0.36 for Latinos, and 0.46 for blacks.[8] Thus, for example, nearly half of all black residents in the average metropolitan area would have to move to a different neighborhood in order to achieve an even distribution of the black population across the neighborhoods of the metropolitan area.

Furthermore, despite declining average dissimilarity scores and reductions in the relative number of exclusively white and exclusively black neighborhoods, the composition of most metropolitan neighborhoods has remained largely unchanged for decades. This durability of neighborhood racial-ethnic composition is reflected in figure 2.2, which displays changes in the racial composition of neighborhoods in our core metropolitan areas between 1980 and 2010. To maintain comparability of neighborhoods over time, we define neighborhoods here using 2010 census tract boundaries and utilize census data that has been normalized to allow for direct comparisons of racial composition in 1980 and 2010.[9] We focus on these most recent decades because census data for earlier census years is not sufficiently detailed about the racial composition of neighborhood units.[10] Following the strategy employed by the sociologist David Fasenfest and his colleagues, seven different types of neighborhoods are differentiated: predominantly white, predominantly black, predominantly other-race, mixed white and other-race, mixed white and black, mixed black and other-race, and mixed multiethnic.[11]

Figure 2.2   Changes in the Racial Composition of U.S. Neighborhoods, 1980–2010

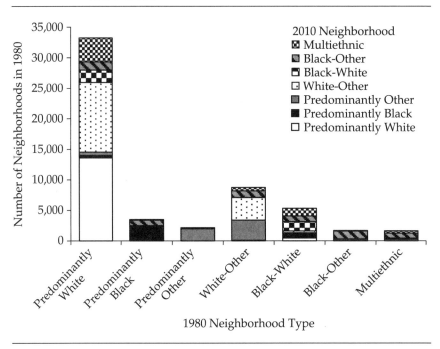

1980 Neighborhood Type

Source: Authors' calculations from the 1970–2010 Neighborhood Change Database (Geolytics 2014).

Notes: Calculations are for census tracts in 331 metropolitan areas defined in both 1980 and 2010. Neighborhood types are defined as:

"Predominantly white": A tract that is 80 percent or more white and 10 percent or less *each* of black, Hispanic/Latino, Asian, and other race.

"Predominantly black": A tract that is 50 percent or more black and 10 percent or less *each* of white, Hispanic/Latino, Asian, and other race.

"Predominantly other": A tract that is 50 percent or more Hispanic/Latino or Asian and 10 percent or less black.

"White-other": A tract that is between 10 and 50 percent Hispanic/Latino or Asian and 10 percent or less black.

"Black-white": A tract that is between 10 and 50 percent black, 40 percent or more white, and 10 percent or less Hispanic/Latino or Asian.

"Black-other": A tract that is 10 percent or more black, 10 percent or more Hispanic/Latino or Asian, and 40 percent or less white.

"Multiethnic": A tract that is 10 percent or more black, 10 percent or more Hispanic/Latino or Asian, and 40 percent or more white.

Figure 2.2 reveals that even as overall segregation is declining, there is strong continuity in neighborhood racial composition. For example, in 1980 just over 59 percent of all neighborhoods (33,225 of 56,294) in the core metropolitan areas were at least 80 percent white and had low concentrations of all other groups. By 2010, thirty years later, 59 percent of these predominantly white neighborhoods (19,653 of 33,225) had taken on enough nonwhite population to be considered racially mixed (less than 80 percent white or containing sizable shares of at least one other group). This also means, of course, that more than 40 percent of these all-white tracts retained their predominantly white composition even as of 2010, and even in the face of dramatic diversification of metropolitan populations. During this same period, 544 neighborhoods were added to the list of predominantly white places, with tracts that had a white-black composition in 1980 exhibiting by far the highest likelihood of transition to predominantly white by 2010.[12] Fueling the optimism about the end of residential isolation, the number of predominantly white neighborhoods has declined substantially in recent decades (33,225 in 1980 to 14,116 in 2010).[13] However, these *overwhelmingly* white neighborhoods—in which the average concentration of white residents is over 92 percent, far exceeding their representation in virtually all metropolitan areas—still represent more than one-fourth (14,116 of 56,294) of all neighborhoods in the core metropolitan areas.

Also noteworthy is the fact that, while many predominantly white neighborhoods have become more diverse over time, this diversity has come primarily through the addition of Asian, Latino, and "other-race" residents, including those reporting more than one race. Of those tracts that were predominantly white in 1980 but had a different composition by 2010, well over half (11,393 of 19,653, or 58 percent) had transitioned to the white-other category through the increase of Latino, Asian, and other populations. In fact, nonblack minority growth accounted for over 60 percent of the average diversification of previously all-white neighborhoods. Overall, white residential exposure to African Americans remains stubbornly low, as evidenced by the relative scarcity of black-white neighborhoods: even as of 2010, only 6.7 percent of all metropolitan census tracts comprised strong shares of both blacks and whites.

The durability of neighborhood racial composition is even more striking in predominantly black neighborhoods, which have tended to remain racially isolated for decades. Glaeser and Vigdor highlight the fact that gentrification has started to erode racial segregation by, at least temporarily, bringing diversity to some of the most isolated and disadvantaged metropolitan neighborhoods.[14] However, while examples of this dynamic can certainly be found, recent research has indicated that racially isolated black neighborhoods are the least likely to undergo such diversification.[15] In fact, fully two-thirds (67 percent) of predominantly black neighborhoods in the core metropolitan areas in 1980 remained predominantly black as of 2010, with an average concentration of African Americans in these neighborhoods over 88 percent. Indeed, there were more tracts (731) that saw their black population concentrations rise above 90 percent during this period, outstripping the number (629) that dropped below the 90 percent isolation mark.

Moreover, among those formerly isolated black neighborhoods that have diversified in recent decades, diversification has rarely been through the addition of a substantial white population. A more common trajectory has involved the addition of members of fast-growing Asian and Latino groups. For example, tracts that were predominantly black in 1980 saw, on average, increases of about 5.5 percentage points in the local concentration of Latinos. In contrast, the already low white representation in predominantly black neighborhoods declined by an average of about 2.4 percentage points between 1980 and 2010. As a result of these compositional changes, most of the predominantly black neighborhoods that transitioned to a different type between 1980 and 2010 (888 of 1,152, or 77 percent) moved into the black-other category (see figure 2.2). In addition, more than 15 percent (838 of 5,341) of the tracts that were white-black in 1980 became predominantly black by 2010, losing an average of about 21 percentage points in their white shares during this period. Thus, despite declining average levels of segregation over the past few decades, relatively isolated black neighborhoods have remained an indelible feature of metropolitan America. Overall, sharp increases in neighborhood diversity, while important, appear to be the exception to the rule of compositional stability. Even in the context of constant residential mobility at the individual level and rapidly diversifying metropolitan populations, the vast majority of neighborhoods have retained their racial composition for decades, and neighborhood diversification that involves white and black residents sharing neighborhoods appears to be especially rare.

As a result of this entrenchment of neighborhood composition, reductions in aggregate levels of segregation have not been matched by increasing levels of exposure between groups within residential neighborhoods. These trends in exposure to neighborhood diversity are displayed in figure 2.3. This figure is based on tract-level data from the U.S. census, normalized to avoid problems related to changes in the geography of neighborhoods between 1980 and 2010 and weighted by the size of each group's population to convey the average concentration of Asian, black, white, and Latino neighbors in the tracts occupied by members of these broad racial-ethnic groups living in one of the 331 core metropolitan

Figure 2.3   Average Neighborhood Composition by Individual
Race-Ethnicity, 1980 and 2010

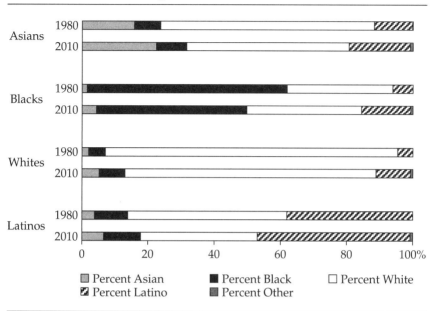

Source: Authors' calculations from the 1970–2010 Neighborhood Change Database (Geolytics 2014).

areas. The figure highlights the fact that, despite declines in the average black-white index of dissimilarity in recent decades, blacks' residential contact with white neighbors has barely grown. Specifically, in 1980, the average black resident of our core metropolitan areas lived in a neighborhood in which 31.9 percent of the residents were non-Latino white; by 2010, this average exposure of African Americans to white residents had increased to 34.7 percent. At the same time, the average concentration of black population in the neighborhood occupied by the average white resident increased from 5.1 percent in 1980 to 7.9 percent in 2010.

It is certainly true that both blacks and whites have become less isolated in recent decades. For African Americans, the average level of exposure to black neighbors dropped from 60.4 percent to 45.4 percent in the past thirty years. Similarly, the concentration of non-Latino whites in neighborhoods occupied by the average non-Latino white resident dropped from 88.3 percent in 1980 to 75.6 percent in 2010. However, this decreasing isolation of whites and blacks is mainly due to increasing contact with

fast-growing Asian and Latino populations rather than increasing exposure to each other; for both blacks and whites, the average exposure to
Latino and Asian neighbors more than doubled between 1980 and 2010.
At the same time, residential isolation among these growing Asian and
Latino populations increased. By 2010, the average Latino resident in our
core metropolitan areas lived in a census tract in which 46.2 percent of the
residents were also Latino, up from 38.1 percent in 1980. During this time,
the average tract percentage Asian for the average Asian American in our
core metros increased from 15.9 percent to 22.5 percent.

Finally, most troubling is the fact that the declines in segregation that
have fueled so much optimism among some have been highly uneven, and
modest at best, in those places where the size of the minority population is
largest. For example, between 1980 and 2010, just half of the 331 metropolitan areas saw declines in Latino-white segregation of more than a couple
of percentage points.[16] Similarly, in only 159 of the 331 metropolitan areas
did the level of Asian-white segregation decline by more than 10 percent
between 1980 and 2010. And significantly, segregation actually increased
in many of the metropolitan areas in which Asian and Latino populations
have grown the most in recent decades. For example, in those areas experiencing greater-than-average Latino population growth, average Latino-
white segregation increased by an average of 11 percent between 1980 and
2010. This includes the increasing segregation occurring in the newer metropolitan areas and smaller cities that have become new destinations for
growing Latino and Asian populations.[17]

Declines in black-white segregation also varied sharply across metropolitan areas, as shown in figure 2.4. In this figure, each bubble represents
a metropolitan area, and the location of each bubble reflects the correspondence between the level of black-white segregation in 1980 (on the horizontal axis) and the level of black-white segregation in 2010 (on the vertical
axis). The size of each bubble corresponds with the total size of the black
population in 2010. Here we contrast 2010 to 1980 to get an assessment of
declines in segregation across several decades. (Changes between 1990 and
2010 are, of course, more modest.)

Several conclusions emerge out of figure 2.4. First, it is worth noting that
in comparison to Asian-white and Latino-white segregation, black-white
segregation declined in a much larger share of metropolitan areas: 303 of
the 331 core metropolitan areas appear below the diagonal line in figure 2.4,
indicating a lower level of black-white segregation in 2010 than in 1980.
However, in 28 of the metropolitan areas, black-white segregation actually
increased between 1980 and 2010, and in another 46 metropolitan areas
black-white segregation remained virtually unchanged, declining by less
than 10 percent of its 1980 value. In fact, as indicated by the high clustering

Figure 2.4   Black-White Segregation in 1980 and 2010 for 331 Core
Metropolitan Areas

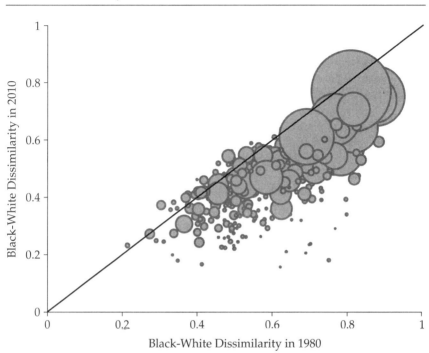

Black-White Dissimilarity in 1980

Source: Authors' calculations from the 1970–2010 Neighborhood Change Database (Geolytics 2014).

of cases around the diagonal line, most metropolitan areas retained levels of black-white segregation in 2010 that were remarkably close to their level three decades earlier.

A closer look at these levels and trends in segregation suggests a distinction between three types of metropolitan areas.[18] The first type includes those metropolitan areas that show signs of relatively rapid integration. Generously, these *integrating metros* declined in black-white segregation between 1980 and 2010 at a rate faster than the declines in the average metropolitan area.[19] Just under half of the metropolitan areas—149 of 331—fit this simple criterion, including a number of smaller metropolitan areas such as Omaha and Savannah, but also, notably, some larger metros such as Seattle and Dallas. By 2010, the average level of black-white segregation ($D_i = 0.39$)

was well in the moderate range, according to Massey and Denton's well-accepted thresholds.[20]

A second type of metropolitan area includes those in which black-white segregation declined more slowly than the average across all metropolitan areas, but where the level of black-white segregation in 1980 was already below the high-segregation threshold advanced by Massey and Denton.[21] In this group of 97 *persistently moderate* metropolitan areas, which includes places like Sacramento, Raleigh, and Topeka, the average level of black-white segregation dropped by only four points (from $D_i = 0.47$ to $D_i = 0.43$) between 1980 and 2010.

Finally, a third group includes 85 metropolitan areas in which black-white segregation was high in 1980 (average $D_i = 0.71$) and had declined at a slower-than-average rate by 2010. This set of *legacy metros* (so-called for their persistent segregation) includes a wide range of large and small metropolitan areas—from Little Rock and Shreveport to Baltimore, Philadelphia, San Francisco, and Chicago. In these legacy cities, the average level of black-white segregation ($D_i = 0.61$) was above Massey and Denton's highest threshold even as of 2010.

These three types of metropolitan areas are distinguished by a number of factors beyond their levels and trends in segregation, but perhaps most important is that the areas where black-white segregation declined most dramatically are those areas containing the smallest black populations.[22] For example, Missoula, Boulder, and Bellingham—the three fastest-integrating metropolitan areas in the country—had a total of just over 61,000 African American residents in 2010. In contrast, several legacy metros, including Chicago, Detroit, and New York—where segregation is very high and has barely changed for decades—had more than 1 million black residents in 2010. In fact, the number of black Americans living in the 85 persistently segregated legacy metros in 2010 was nearly three times higher than the total number living in the 149 integrating metropolitan areas (21.4 million versus 8.1 million).

The bottom line is that, while the average level of segregation has declined since 1980, these reductions have been driven primarily by diminishing segregation in places containing few African Americans. As a result, a relatively small share of the black population benefited from the larger declines in segregation. As of 2010, a full 24 percent of the black population in the core metropolitan areas were in areas in which black-white segregation declined by less than 10 percent between 1980 and 2010, and 52 percent were living in areas where the black-white dissimilarity score remained in the high range. In fact, the *average* level of metropolitan segregation experienced by individual African Americans in 2010 was still near 60 percent—still within the high range as designated several decades ago. Thus, despite reports to the contrary, residential segregation by race and ethnicity is far from dead in most metropolitan areas. Although recent trends provide plenty of room for optimism, these positive signs are overshadowed by the fact that segregation has been continually reinforced across the decades and remains a defining feature of the residential experiences of the vast majority of metropolitan residents.

WHY SEGREGATION MATTERS

The persistence of residential segregation by race is worthy of our attention primarily because it is so inextricably tied to broader systems of inequality. Despite the passage of significant civil rights legislation, the past half-century has seen remarkably little reduction in pronounced racial gaps in health or socioeconomic well-being. Racial and ethnic differences in high school completion remain pronounced, and the likelihood of attending college—especially the country's elite colleges—remains substantially lower for African Americans and Latinos than for whites.[23] The unemployment rate has remained about twice as high for blacks as for whites across the past sixty years, and this gap appears to be largely impervious to broader economic shifts. Racial and ethnic differences in median household income have also remained stubbornly consistent over the past fifty years, while wealth inequality has actually grown, especially since the 1990s. In comparison to white children, black children are more likely to be born into poverty and are substantially less likely to escape poverty in adulthood.[24] In 1960, black men were about five times more likely than white men to be incarcerated; fifty years later, they were six times more likely.[25] Finally, while racial differences in life expectancy have narrowed in recent decades, significant gaps remain, and African Americans continue to be substantially more likely than whites to suffer from heart disease, asthma, and multiple types of cancer.[26]

Although the persistence of multifaceted racial inequality reflects a combination of political, economic, and social forces, there is little doubt that residential segregation is a central driver of the disadvantage felt by African Americans and members of some other groups. The direct influence of segregation on these problems is not always apparent. Segregation's impact is often more distal and therefore more insidious, playing out indirectly by shaping drastic disparities in the material conditions of neighborhoods occupied by members of different races. Here we describe some of these differences in neighborhood context and review some of the key literature on the effects of these disparities on group differences in health, economic opportunities, and exposures across the life course.

Racial and ethnic differences in a few of these neighborhood conditions are illustrated in figure 2.5. This figure utilizes tract-level data from

Figure 2.5   Racial Disparities in Average Neighborhood Characteristics, 2000–2010

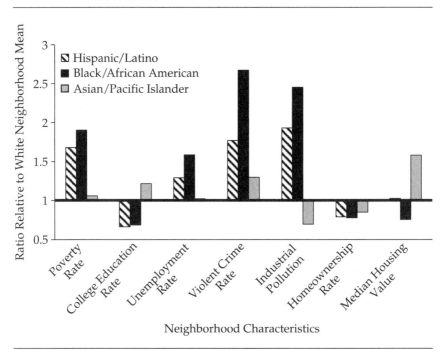

Neighborhood Characteristics

Source: Authors' calculations from the 1970–2010 Neighborhood Change Database (Geolytics 2014), the National Neighborhood Crime Study (Peterson and Krivo 2010b), and the Environmental Protection Agency's Toxic Release Inventory (EPA 2012).

several sources, including the U.S. Census Bureau, the Environmental Protection Agency (EPA), and the National Neighborhood Crime Study (NNCS). Because the tract-level data we use are weighted by the number of members of specific racial and ethnic groups in the tract, these figures can be interpreted as the average tract characteristics experienced by the members of each group. Following past research, we focus on tract-level characteristics linked to the strength of the local tax base, educational attainment, family formation behavior, and other individual-level outcomes.[27] To highlight the magnitude of racial differences in neighborhood conditions, figure 2.5 displays the average tract characteristics experienced by non-Latino blacks, non-Latino Asians, and Latinos as ratios of the average conditions faced by whites.

The key takeaway from figure 2.5 is simple: members of different racial and ethnic groups not only continue to occupy separate residential spaces but occupy spaces with fundamentally different physical, economic, and social characteristics. Perhaps most pronounced are dramatic differences in exposure to poverty and other features of socioeconomic disadvantage. Blacks and Latinos live in neighborhoods with poverty rates nearly twice the rate experienced by the average white metropolitan resident. Blacks and Latinos also live in areas with substantially lower concentrations of college-educated adults. The average unemployment rate is about 60 percent higher in neighborhoods occupied by African Americans, and 30 percent higher in neighborhoods occupied by Latinos, than in the average neighborhood for whites.

Importantly, the patterns revealed in figure 2.5 actually understate the racial and ethnic differences in neighborhood socioeconomic context, for three reasons. First, not only do African Americans and Latinos occupy neighborhoods with much higher levels of joblessness, but their access to quality jobs in surrounding areas—outside of the immediate neighborhood—has actually deteriorated in recent decades. Thus, despite increasing suburbanization of racial minorities, the neighborhoods with the highest concentration of minorities have also seen the greatest declines in access to jobs.[28] Second, figure 2.5 shows differences in average neighborhood conditions at just a single point in time. While these snapshot differences are large, what is even more damaging is the fact that, because of the persistence of segregation, African Americans and Latinos are much less likely to escape poor neighborhoods and therefore are much more likely to experience extended spells of exposure to high neighborhood poverty and related disadvantage.[29] Third, these racial differences in tract poverty, joblessness, and other census-based characteristics are accompanied by sharp racial and ethnic differences in exposure to harder-to-measure neighborhood features, including collective efficacy, network-based social capital, and the stability of local institutions.[30]

This concentration of socioeconomic disadvantage in black and Latino neighborhoods, which is well documented, is clearly linked to patterns of segregation by race.[31] As Massey and Denton forcefully argue, residential segregation establishes the context in which the ramifications of the economic dislocations that tend to hit African Americans hardest are felt disproportionately in the most racially isolated neighborhoods of the city.[32] In fact, racial residential segregation appears to be the single biggest factor in explaining racial differences in exposure to neighborhood poverty and socioeconomic disadvantage.[33] The sociologists Glenn Firebaugh and Chad Farrell show that Hispanic-white and, especially, black-white disparities in neighborhood poverty and income have narrowed since 1980, but remain large.[34] The gap is largest in places with higher levels of segregation, a fact that highlights the role of segregation in maintaining neighborhood inequality.

In several ways, residential segregation is also implicated in the concentration of crime, mainly through its connection to the concentration of poverty and structural disadvantage in minority neighborhoods. As the sociologists Ruth Peterson and Lauren Krivo put it, "The racial-spatial divide uniquely situates neighborhoods with distinct ethno-racial compositions in terms of the local conditions that encourage (or discourage) and control (or fail to control) crime."[35] In their comprehensive study, Peterson and Krivo summarize voluminous social research indicating that the shortage of economic opportunities in the most disadvantaged neighborhoods gives rise to crime as a way to make economic ends meet or gain status that cannot be attained through conventional means. At the same time, this disadvantage undermines the development of the kind of social capital and collective efficacy that would allow communities to thwart crime.[36]

Finally, the disinvestment in minority neighborhoods, accompanied by housing decline and structural deterioration and exacerbated by the Great Recession of the late 2000s, helps to create the physical conditions in which crime can thrive.[37] Together, these and related mechanisms produce extreme concentrations of crime in the most disadvantaged neighborhoods to which, because of persistent segregation, black and Latino populations remain highly exposed. The impacts of these dynamics are reflected in figure 2.5. The average level of neighborhood violent crime experienced by the average African American is over two and a half times higher than the average experienced by whites, and Latinos experience rates of violent crime that are about 77 percent higher than the average for whites. Thus, residential segregation tends not only to increase overall levels of crime in cities but to concentrate this crime in areas occupied by black and Latino populations.[38]

By concentrating blacks and some other minorities in the most structurally disadvantaged neighborhoods, segregation also contributes to dramatic racial disparities in exposure to environmental hazards. Figure 2.5 shows, for example, that the average neighborhood concentration of air pollution is over 2.4 times higher for African Americans, and 1.9 times higher for Latinos, than for whites.[39] Racial segregation also produces sharp racial disparities in access to healthy food choices in the neighborhood of residence and in exposure to neighborhood crime and other sources of environmental stress, and it even significantly affects decisions about the provision of services and the availability of health care.[40] Through its impact on this environmental inequality, segregation has important implications for profound and persistent racial disparities in health.[41] In fact, there is good evidence to suggest that segregation is associated with a wide range of negative health outcomes for black and Latino populations, including diabetes, cancer, cardiovascular disease, obesity, preterm birth, self-rated health, and life expectancy.[42] Recent research indicates a strong link between segregation and both levels of and racial disparities in overall mortality rates.[43]

The repercussions of segregation for economic opportunities are similarly dire: by relegating blacks and other highly segregated groups to the poorest neighborhoods, segregation has profound impacts on opportunities for socioeconomic advancement. Most directly, segregation undermines economic advancement by isolating blacks from job opportunities and access to the social networks that provide opportunities for employment and higher earnings.[44] As a result, high levels of residential segregation at the metropolitan level tend to increase rates of black poverty and income inequality across racial lines.[45]

Beyond the effect on employment and annual income, segregation's impact on differential neighborhood contexts also has important implications for racial differences in wealth. As shown in figure 2.5, African Americans and Latinos, in comparison to whites, reside in neighborhoods with lower rates of homeownership and, at least for African Americans, substantially lower housing values.[46] These segregation-related differences in local housing conditions, along with persistent group differences in homeownership, are a primary driver of large and growing racial disparities in wealth accumulation.[47]

Segregation's effect on racial disparities in wealth appears to have been exacerbated by the crash of the housing market and ensuing recession after 2005. Most directly, segregation created the context for sharp racial disparities in the financial risks associated with the Great Recession and resulted in the disproportionate concentration of housing foreclosures and related dislocations in neighborhoods occupied by blacks and Latinos.[48] As a result, black and Latino homeowners were hardest hit by the collapse of the housing market. Latino and black homeowners were about twice as likely as white owners with similar financial characteristics to experience foreclosure.[49] Those who retained their homes saw the value of their investments driven down by high concentrations of foreclosures and related structural deterioration in their neighborhood and surrounding areas.[50] Consequently, the already large racial gap in wealth grew dramatically over the last ten years: as of 2013, the median net value of assets among white families was about $265,000, compared to under $29,000 for black families.[51]

Perhaps more troubling is the effect of persistent segregation on life chances for children. Residential segregation across neighborhoods helps to maintain high levels of school segregation, with dire and demonstrable consequences for the racial educational achievement gap.[52] With the abandonment of busing and other efforts to counteract the effects of persistent neighborhood segregation, the proportion of black children attending racially isolated schools has actually increased since 1980, and this racial isolation at the school level tends to coincide with profound inequality in school funding and structural conditions.[53] The implications for educational outcomes are clear: higher levels of residential segregation produce larger racial gaps in academic test scores and substantially reduce the chances that black children will graduate from high school or college.[54]

Given these dynamics, it should come as little surprise that, by stifling the social mobility of large shares of metropolitan populations, segregation has profound impacts on broader patterns of inequality. As the sociologist Patrick Sharkey has clearly demonstrated, neighborhood stratification emerging from segregation provides a key mechanism through which family advantage and disadvantage are transmitted from one generation to another.[55] Where segregation remains high and African American and Latino families are relegated to neighborhoods characterized by underfunded schools, weak job opportunities, dangerous streets, and sequestration from valuable forms of social capital, the likelihood of upward social mobility for black children is severely diminished. The economist Raj Chetty and several colleagues recently documented that the ability of children to move up the economic ladder to occupy positions above the station of their parents is substantially lower in metropolitan areas in which racial residential segregation remains the highest.[56]

It is important to note that the inequality generated and maintained by segregation has costs that extend well beyond those borne by segregated racial and ethnic minorities. To be sure, there are general social costs that come from generating disparities in life chances that contradict the philosophical notions of meritocracy that are central to the national ethos.[57] More concretely, the inequality that emerges out of segregation has broader economic impacts and is implicated in the creation of costly social problems. For example, given the connection between inequality and economic growth, high levels of segregation may stifle opportunities for more robust economic development by undermining the economic productivity and wages for tens of millions of Americans and by generating demand for social programs designed to provide basic needs for the poorest populations in the poorest neighborhoods.[58] To this point, there is strong evidence that the educational disparities that emerge from segregation have reduced the nation's gross domestic product by trillions of dollars. In similar ways, segregation forces metropolitan areas to divert funds to the social dislocations that emerge from racial isolation and the concentration of poverty. The higher levels of racial and economic inequality that emerge from segregation are, for example, positively associated with spending on law enforcement.[59]

No less important are the broad social and political costs of segregation. In addition to diminishing interracial contact that might foster greater racial tolerance, persistent segregation and the inequality it spawns provide the structural backdrop to episodic unrest in urban centers.[60] More generally, segregation tends to reduce individual trust and levels of volunteerism and thwarts the effectiveness of community development efforts while also undermining political cooperation.[61]

Thus, there is strong evidence that residential segregation by race continues to exert strong and multifaceted impacts on the life chances of segregated populations. Despite declines in average levels of segregation and the increasing prevalence of multiethnic neighborhoods, members of different groups tend to remain exposed to fundamentally different opportunities as a function of their qualitatively unequal neighborhood environments. The consequences of this residential stratification for segregated minorities are vast and well documented. But the consequences of segregation extend well beyond those felt by segregated minorities. The more insidious effects of segregation are on the broader social, political, and economic health of the country. In light of this, developing a more complete understanding of the factors that maintain residential segregation is an important endeavor. Recent claims that we have reached the "end of the segregated century" threaten to divert our attention away from the multifaceted and persistent impacts of segregation.

OUR INCOMPLETE THEORIES OF SEGREGATION

While segregation and its impacts are alive and active, the study of segregation is largely catatonic. At the very least, our collective attempts to understand the root causes of segregation have fallen into a kind of intellectual malaise, characterized by the overly simplistic and completely automatic application of a few simple theoretical arguments. Virtually all of the massive body of research on the patterns and drivers of segregation is informed by some combination of three canonical theoretical arguments: the spatial assimilation model, the place stratification perspective, and preference-based arguments. The first of these, the spatial assimilation model, argues that residential outcomes are primarily determined by access to socioeconomic resources.[62] Accordingly, residential differentiation by social class emerges as individuals match their own socioeconomic status with that of their neighborhood, using their human capital and other endowments to purchase residence in the most desirable neighborhoods. In emphasizing socioeconomic characteristics as the main predictors of mobility between lower- and higher-quality neighborhoods, the economic model suggests that residential segregation emerges out of large racial and ethnic differences in socioeconomic resources.[63] Blacks and whites, for example, occupy separate residential spaces simply because, on average, blacks have fewer economic resources with which to buy their way into neighborhoods similar to those occupied by whites.

In contrast, the place stratification perspective explains residential segregation and the relegation of people of color to resource-poor neighborhoods as the result of discrimination in the form of differential treatment at the individual level, institutionalized biases, and discriminatory public policy. The place stratification perspective, developed largely in reaction to the shortcomings of the assimilation argument, maintains that racially disparate residential outcomes and the aggregate patterns of segregation they create are the result of the desire of more privileged groups to distance themselves from the less privileged. Most notably, whites' aversion to sharing residential space with minority neighbors is said to motivate discriminatory practices by real estate agents, landlords, mortgage lenders, and neighborhood residents that essentially block minority households from gaining access to neighborhoods occupied by whites and, more generally, from converting their socioeconomic resources into advantageous residential contexts.[64] Similar forces allow for the maintenance of discriminatory zoning, policies related to the development and redevelopment of public housing, redlining, predatory lending, and other institutional and policy forces that both limit the residential options of minority households and destabilize minority neighborhoods. Thus, according to this perspective, even minority households with the economic resources to buy their way into the highest-quality neighborhoods have limited opportunities to do so.

Finally, the explanation for segregation that may resonate best in public discourse is the idea that racial differences in residential outcomes reflect group differences in residential preferences. According to this argument, segregation persists because members of different racial and ethnic groups simply choose to reside in areas dominated by their own group. Certainly, there is strong evidence that, despite shifts toward more liberal racial attitudes, whites retain a strong preference for neighborhoods in which a strong majority of their neighbors are also white. According to this perspective, householders make their decisions about whether to leave a neighborhood, and which neighborhood destination to choose, based largely on the correspondence of a neighborhood's racial composition with their preferences for the composition of neighborhoods. The residential preferences of members of most nonwhite groups are a bit more complex. Available evidence suggests that members of many Latino and Asian groups hold negative stereotypes about blacks and express a limited willingness to move into predominantly black areas.[65] Like whites, blacks express the strongest preferences for neighborhoods containing large concentrations of own-race neighbors and a reluctance to be the extreme numerical minority in mostly white neighborhoods.[66] Many black survey respondents also express somewhat negative attitudes toward Latinos and Asians, and ethnographic research often points to black animosity toward other minority groups settling in predominantly black neighborhoods.[67] However, in comparison to whites, blacks express considerably greater tolerance for integration, preferring neighborhoods with considerably more nonblack neighbors than the neighborhoods that blacks reside in.[68] The link between preferences and actual residential outcomes is rarely observed.[69] Nevertheless, group differences in stated residential preferences leave open the possibility that segregation and resulting disparities in neighborhood conditions reflect group differences in residential preferences.[70]

As we discuss in subsequent chapters, there is ample research to suggest that the dynamics implicated in each of these "big three" theoretical arguments contribute to the maintenance of racial residential stratification. Nevertheless, our steadfast and exclusive reliance on them and our routine application of these theories in research have hampered our ability to develop a stronger understanding of the processes through which segregation is maintained.

One problem associated with the dominant theoretical arguments, at least as they have been applied in segregation research, is that the forces implicated in these theoretical arguments are often treated as competing, distinct, and exhaustive, so much so that weak evidence in a study for one theory is interpreted as support for another of the theories. For example, if racial differences in the neighborhood attainment patterns that shape segregation persist after controls for group differences in socioeconomic conditions, the typical conclusion is that the remaining differences reflect some combination of discrimination and group differences in preferences.[71] As we will argue, this tendency to view existing arguments as competing and additive undermines any ability to recognize the ways in which preferences, discrimination, and economic forces interact and complement one another in the maintenance of residential segregation. This standard approach also closes off the assessment of more complex, but no less important, forces that maintain residential segregation.

Perhaps more problematic is the tendency in past literature to focus exclusively on the links between the forces implicated in the traditional theories and residential *outcomes*. The typical strategy for employing "the big three" in studies of residential stratification is to assess the extent to which residential segregation, racial differences in neighborhood location, and underlying patterns of inter-neighborhood mobility can be explained by taking into consideration group differences in economic resources, preferences, or experiences of discrimination. Missing from this focus on outcomes is a clear articulation of the ways in which key forces operate to shape the *process* through which residential outcomes are achieved. For example, based on past research, it is difficult to know whether the link between socioeconomic resources and the likelihood of living in, or moving to, a relatively advantaged location reflects the influence of resources on the definition of potential residential options, the tools and strategies used to investigate and assess these options, or simply the ability to pay for housing in particular locations. This failure to focus on the various stages of the neighborhood selection and housing search process leaves our dominant theoretical arguments underdeveloped, lacking the specificity necessary to understand the potentially complex roles of economics, discrimination, and preferences in shaping residential processes, much less to develop effective policy approaches to address the resulting stratification.

One important repercussion of the lack of attention to the processes of neighborhood selection and housing search is a tacit adoption of highly dubious assumptions about how individuals make residential decisions. Research on the causes of segregation and underlying patterns of residential sorting is rooted in the underlying assumption that all individuals know about, and consider, a common set of residential options as they make decisions about whether and where to move. We assume that, to the extent allowable by their economic resources, rational individuals assess all available neighborhood options and choose the neighborhood in the area that best matches their residential preferences, although—at least according to proponents of the stratification perspective—some individuals are prevented from accessing their preferred neighborhoods by some discriminatory force. Accordingly, the racial differences in residential outcomes that continually reinforce residential segregation are assumed to reflect some combination of group differences in resources, preferences, or discriminatory treatment. In order for this process to operate as we assume, individuals must know about and assess the affordability and social conditions of the neighborhood options in the market and make rational choices among them. Moreover, we typically assume that each residential decision, including whether and where to move, can reasonably be treated as a fresh, rational assessment, with little attention to the ways in which past residential experiences and mobility decisions may shape subsequent moves.

This typical adherence to a rational-choice perspective and a present-time orientation obscures many subtler factors that play a large role in shaping broader systems of residential stratification. As the sociologist Robert Sampson has pointed out, some of the most influential determinants of residential sorting are social and structural forces that are largely invisible to the actor, the operation of which is inconsistent with the simple depiction of rational actors choosing the optimal residential location after a careful assessment of all options.[72] For example, the typical application of the traditional theories leaves little room for potentially crucial racial and ethnic differences in knowledge and perceptions of residential options and shows no recognition of the ways in which these perceptions and knowledge flow from variations in residential histories, daily experiences, social networks, and other variations in the mobility process. In fact, as we will argue, there is strong evidence to suggest that knowledge about neighborhood options varies significantly by race-ethnicity in ways that may produce highly disparate residential outcomes.

Overall, our dominant theories of segregation fail to recognize that knowledge about various community options is likely to differ among individuals, by virtue of their daily experiences and personal biographies—which themselves are often a function of racialized geographic systems—in level, quality, and content. To the extent that these daily and historical experiences vary by race-ethnicity, group differences in knowledge and perceptions of communities throughout the region are likely to emerge. As a result, members of different racial-ethnic groups may conceive of the residential spaces of the housing market in drastically different terms and contemplate dissimilar sets of residential options when they make decisions about whether and where to move. These dynamics would serve to perpetuate segregation in ways that are wholly unappreciated in existing theoretical arguments. Part II of this book lays out the foundation of our social structural sorting perspective.

Part II | The Social Structural
Sorting Perspective

Chapter 3 | A New Lens on Segregation: Understanding How People End Up Living Where They Do

A STRONGER UNDERSTANDING of the processes through which segregation is perpetuated generation after generation requires attention to *not only* group differences in economics, preferences, and experiences of discrimination—forces implicated in traditional theories of segregation—*but also* the more subtle factors that affect how people end up living where they do. To do that, we need to understand that neighborhood selection processes are complex and shaped importantly by experiences and knowledge of the larger metropolitan area. Thus, racial disparities in knowledge of, experience with, and perceptions about metropolitan communities themselves are probably generated by racial-ethnic differences in daily activities and geographic experiences that arise out of segregated patterns of social-spatial interaction. Although these forces might interact with, affect, and result from economic differentiation, experiences with discrimination, and racial attitudes—factors at the center of existing theoretical arguments related to residential segregation—they constitute a set of potentially influential independent factors that shape where people end up living. These factors are at the core of our *social structural sorting perspective,* to which we now turn.

THE NEIGHBORHOOD SELECTION AND HOUSING SEARCH PROCESS

We contend that most studies of segregation overlook the need for an explicit and sociologically informed model of neighborhood selection and housing search. In their most basic form, the traditional explanations assume a very simple model: individuals, using their vast knowledge of

41

the neighborhoods making up the housing market, identify those that meet their residential preferences and attempt to buy their way into the area with the best combination of features, with some individuals blocked from achieving their top choice by discriminatory treatment. To date, debates in the literature tend to focus on the relative roles of economics, preferences, and discrimination rather than the assumptions about the housing search process on which the argument rests. Our purpose is to use the lens of the neighborhood selection and housing search process to examine the social factors shaping one aspect of housing outcomes—the perpetuation or erosion of segregation. By doing this, we illuminate a broader set of factors that shape where people end up living and provide a complementary and more complete understanding of how discrimination, preferences, and economics operate to shape patterns of segregation.

In short, current debates about the drivers of segregation and underlying patterns of mobility pay too little attention to how people end up living where they do. In addition to virtually ignoring what we know from geography, psychology, decision sciences, and consumer behavior research about how residential—and other complex—decisions are made, the current approaches also fail to take into account the rootedness of residential decisions in social processes, interactions, and networks. In this way, the scholarly approach to residential mobility and the segregation it drives has not only ignored housing search and decision-making scholarship but also been a-sociological. Instead, the tendency is to conceptualize neighborhood selection and housing search processes through the same economic decision-making lens used to understand the selection of any other commodity—namely, that individuals faced with the prospect of choosing a new place to live (1) collect and assess (complete) information on all possible options, and then (2) attempt to maximize their utility by choosing the residential outcome that best fits the balance of their residential preferences, priorities, and resources. Save for the intense institutional barriers that limit options for some, the process is assumed to be not too different from that used to choose a smartphone, a pair of jeans, or a car.

But the process of collecting information about, and choosing, a neighborhood is fundamentally different than the processes involved in choosing any other commodity. Indeed, neighborhoods are such an integral part of our lived experiences from a very early age—defining our daily activities, shaping our opportunity structures, and affecting our perceptions of the social world—that we are constantly collecting information that can affect our residential decision-making: we learn about neighborhoods through residential experiences, daily activities, and interactions with other people both past and present. Because these are all inherently social processes, our knowledge of neighborhoods and housing options accumulates over our lifetime through interactions with family, friends, and coworkers, as well as with a variety of social institutions.

Moreover, the decision-making process itself is also distinctive. When it comes time to choose a new place to live, many of us focus on a specific set of potential neighborhood destinations without much concerted thought. We just search in the places that we already know are good and ignore those we "know nothing about." For others, the selection and search process might involve additional investigation of potential destinations, such as a comparison of school quality or crime rates. But even then, these information-collection exercises are likely to involve the comparison of a limited set of potential destinations, and both the places we are considering and the information we collect about them may be heavily shaped by our daily experiences, our residential histories, and information we have gleaned from social networks. In this way, the decision-making process is inherently social and involves many factors that do not fit neatly into a standard economic decision-making model. Delving into these explicitly social dynamics provides the opportunity to better understand the residential sorting process and raises potentially important implications for understanding the forces that shape its outcome.

The failure to attend to how these social factors shape the residential location process becomes clear when we again consider the model that underpins most of the existing debates about segregation. First, the assumption is that people searching for housing have perfect knowledge of their options—options that fit their preferences or meet their budget—and that this knowledge is unrelated to race-ethnicity. And second, it is assumed that they use this information to weigh and balance neighborhood and housing features and preferences to select the one that best fits their needs. But there are multiple scholarly disciplines that have both empirical data on how people actually search for housing and sophisticated models of decision-making that contradict this image. Until recently, segregation scholars have ignored both of these bodies of research. Although dated, the empirical studies of housing searches conducted in the 1970s and 1980s provide crucial insights into how searches are undertaken, such as their multistage nature, their reliance on limited information, and the sources and kinds of information that are used.[1] And Elizabeth Bruch and her colleagues have pioneered the introduction of insights from decision sciences and marketing into sociology in general and housing processes in particular to draw attention to what the neighborhood selection process actually looks like, offering what they call a "cognitively plausible" framework.[2] We rely on these insights from housing search scholarship and decision sciences to anchor our discussion of how racialized neighborhood selection and housing search processes either perpetuate segregation or could, conceivably, be inflection points at which segregation is interrupted.

In the next section, we summarize the key insights about how people end up living where they do that are offered by the decades-old housing search studies as well as by decision sciences—especially as advanced by Bruch and her colleagues.[3] This description provides the scaffolding upon which we then build out our core argument about how both these features of housing and neighborhood selection processes and the sources and kinds of information and perceptions that feed into them are fundamentally racialized in a way that perpetuates segregation.

Searches Happen in Stages

One of the most important insights from research on housing searches is that the image of the utility-maximizing decision-maker as a human computer who gathers up all the information, assesses the costs and benefits in a regression-like manner, and then makes a decision is incorrect. Insights from complex decision-making theory and specific studies of housing searches offer a number of corrections to this model, beginning with the core observation that a housing search unfolds in stages.[4] In the first stage, people decide to search in particular neighborhoods, communities, or geographic locations. In the second stage, they search for and identify the specific units within that smaller set of neighborhoods, communities, or other geographic areas that they will consider.[5]

Thus, when people search for housing—and indeed, when they embark on many other complex consumer choices, such as buying a car—they first make decisions related to the general target area. Car-buyers ask themselves: *Should I buy a minivan, a truck, or a sports car?* A home-buyer asks: *Which neighborhoods or communities should I consider?* As such, people first construct what we refer to as their "consideration set"—that is, those communities or neighborhoods where they will focus more concerted attention and within which they will seek out specific units or homes to consider. Through this winnowing down, housing searchers collect fuller information only on homes and apartments located in the communities in their consideration set. Completing this first stage makes the second stage, when people research and consider particular units, far more manageable.[6] This is the same task that a car-buyer completes when first deciding to buy a minivan rather than a truck or a sports car. Once that decision is made, the car-buyer can gather information about specific models and makes of minivans to determine which one she wants to purchase, and she can ignore everything about trucks, sports cars, SUVs, and sedans, there being no need to learn all about, for example, the different models of trucks that

Ford offers since trucks are outside her consideration set. So too do housing searchers seek information about available housing units only within their targeted neighborhoods.

It is clearly the first stage of a housing search that has the most profound consequences for segregation because this is when the spatial parameters of a search are cast in stone.[7] Of course, there is every possibility that during an active search the housing searcher will revisit the content of the consideration set, thus reminding us that the search process is dynamic. But in general, the rigidity of those spatial parameters means that racial differences in the definition of the consideration set will produce drastic racial differences in locational outcomes at the end of the search.[8] It becomes of primary importance to understanding how segregation is constructed and reconstructed that we understand how searchers define their consideration set—that is, what they do, or rely on, in the first stage to decide in which geographic areas, communities, or neighborhoods they will conduct a more detailed search.

For the purposes of our social structural sorting perspective, we amend what is often depicted as a two-stage search process by adding an explicit pre-search stage (which is implicit in models of housing searches). We highlight this "stage" in order to draw attention to one of our core arguments: that searchers do not enter the process as a blank slate with no information whatsoever about the communities and neighborhoods in their metropolitan area.[9] And importantly, to fully understand the cycle of segregation, we need to understand what factors shape the information and perceptions people carry with them into a search. Thus, the pre-search "stage" is not so much a stage of a search as a reference to the accumulation of a lifetime of direct and indirect experiences, exposures to media, and interactions with social networks that constitute what people know about the metropolitan area in which they live. This pre-search stage— which happens when a person is *not* contemplating a residential move or decision—is the outcome of ongoing social processes that themselves are deeply racialized and, as such, will have consequences for segregation.

In addition to being a multistage process, a housing search has two other features to which scholars have also drawn attention: the extent of housing-related information that people have, and how people process and use that information to make a decision.

Searchers Have Limited Information

In the 1970s, the marketing professor Donald Hempel conducted a comprehensive, survey-based study of the home-buying process in two housing markets in Connecticut. A researcher interested in consumer behavior,

Hempel aimed to understand the information (both content and sources) that people draw upon in the process of making this important consumer decision. He made the critical observation that searchers do not have complete knowledge of the market. Indeed, understanding where and how people get the information they use to make their decisions, he argues, is tremendously significant: since that information is incomplete and not always accurate, what becomes crucial is the *perceived reality* of the housing market. As he notes, understanding where information comes from is crucial, given the significance of the perceived reality of the housing market:

> The buyer's perception of the housing alternatives which are available in the market and of their relative desirability is strongly influenced by the information obtained through searching. . . . The workings of a housing market cannot be effectively understood without considering the channels of information that intervene between the household and the market.[10]

Hempel's extended discussion of the housing market—from the marketer's perspective—clearly explicates again that the assumption of perfect knowledge is faulty, and he highlights the importance of understanding home-buyers' processes and the information they rely upon. As he puts it:

> Market activity cannot be explained adequately without considering the state (level) of information within the market. Both buyers and sellers react to the "market" that they *perceive* as a result of information that has been obtained from a variety of social and commercial sources. . . . The information variable is usually assumed into nonexistence or reduced to insignificance in the development of market models. The notion of a perfect market system involving flows of complete information is useful as a theoretical framework. . . . Such models are also useful as standards for comparison by which the value of perfect information can be measured in terms of the differences in behavior that occur under both idealized and realistic market conditions. But it is clear from the research evidence . . . that buyers are not equally informed, nor do they have equal opportunity to become informed.[11]

Thus, an understanding of the information and perceptions of the actors is crucial—and recognizing the sources of this information and perceptions and any differences in them is essential as well. Decisions that searchers make and the evaluations upon which they make them are not based on the kind of substantial information about the full set of residential options available in the housing market implied by the rational-choice model and as characterizes the implicit models of the housing search process used by most analysts of the causes of residential segregation. Rather, as Hempel notes, we must understand a searcher's perceived reality of the housing market. This includes both whether a searcher knows a place and what impressions of it they have. We know from common sense and research that people do not know about all possible options in a large metropolitan area. One illustration of the lack of complete knowledge comes from the sociologists Maria Krysan and Michael Bader, who showed Cook County residents a map that included forty-one communities in the Chicago metropolitan area.[12] On average, they "didn't know anything about" thirteen of them. To "mere recognition," we add how much information a searcher has and its accuracy; together, these factors capture the searcher's perceived reality of the housing market.

The information people have that shapes their perceived reality of the housing market is of crucial importance to how they end up living where they do. Studies of housing search processes highlight the variety of information sources a searcher might use, including both formal sources—housing professionals, newspaper listings, the Internet—and informal sources such as family, friends, coworkers, and neighbors. The information can also be gathered actively, such as when a searcher makes explicit attempts in the first and second stages of a housing search to determine which places to consider and to find available units within them. But there is also a tremendous amount of passive information gathering—largely what we refer to as "pre-search." This information is gathered before a housing search is undertaken and is accumulated through the lifetime and in daily exposure to places and accounts of places in person, through the people one knows, and through exposure to the media in all its forms. Housing search research from the 1970s and 1980s pointed to the significance of indirect information, what Terence Smith and colleagues refer to as "general beliefs and attitudes" about neighborhood characteristics and the heavy reliance on personal knowledge of the city, and informal social— as opposed to commercial—information sources.[13] All of this reinforces the idea that there is a great deal of passive or indirect information that factors in and filters out certain places before an active search even begins. This passively acquired information is the "stuff" that people hear about neighborhoods from their friends, family, and other acquaintances. It is what people "pick up" simply by living life in a particular metropolitan area, what they "take for granted" about where the good (and bad) places are to live. In in-depth interviews about parents' decisions about housing and schools, qualitative scholars have shown the role of passively acquired knowledge in winnowing out large swaths of possible neighborhoods and zeroing in on a small handful to consider.[14]

Both the sources of the information that people rely upon to construct their understanding of communities and neighborhoods in their area and the passivity of this process (the pre-search) are captured by one of the Chicago residents we interviewed for this study. Aaron was a twenty-six-year-old suburban homeowner who, after describing his impressions of a number of communities in the Chicago metropolitan area, was asked: "Where do you get your information about these places?" His pithy and straightforward explanation captures the essence of our argument about the social factors that shape community information acquisition and points to the possibility that this information is not acquired systematically and intentionally: "From what I see. Mostly the news. My friends. I don't know. I don't write it down, where I get it from. It just kind of compiles in this big ol' noggin right here," he said, pointing to his head.

This answer covers most of the information sources identified by housing search scholars, but also suggests something important about how the information is acquired. Namely, the process is amorphous, informal, unstructured, and probably somewhat subconscious. People do not go through their lives taking notes about places; rather, they assemble the information simply through their "use of the city." Thus, when people begin a formal housing search, they are not a blank slate in terms of information about neighborhoods and housing. They have been gathering information all their life through exposure to the media, lived experiences, and relations with people who provide them with direct and indirect information. This pre-search shapes, we suggest, the actual search when it is undertaken.

Turning to the more active stages of a housing search, there is clear evidence that people rely on different information sources in the different stages. For example, Duncan Maclennan and Gavin Wood found in their study of the Glasgow housing market that informal information sources were critical in the first stage (what they call "area orientation"). As they observed:

> Personal knowledge based on regular use of the city and the advice of friends and relatives were markedly more important than in other search phases. However, . . . even at this phase area related information was also gleaned from newspapers and estate agents. Households were asked to indicate . . . the relative importance of channels in the search phase . . . and personal knowledge, newspapers, and friends and relatives were the important "orientation" sources of information.[15]

But their subjects' identification of available units (stage 2) showed very different patterns: few people said "personal knowledge" or "friends and relative" were important at this stage; instead, it was newspaper advertisements that were crucial.[16]

The important point is that housing searches turn importantly on the content of knowledge—and not only is knowledge incomplete, but different sources come into play at different stages. Therefore, to understand how people end up living where they do, and how segregation is perpetuated, we need to understand the social factors that feed information into each stage of the housing process and the racial differences therein. Of primary importance are both lived experiences (a key contributor to prior knowledge as a source of information) and social networks. These will be further explored and elaborated in chapters 4 and 5.

It is important to clarify that we are not the first to observe that housing decisions happen under conditions of imperfect information. For example, William A. V. Clark and Robin Flowerdew explain: "The searcher is never aware of the complete set of opportunities, and does not know if the use of a different information channel might bring to light better alternatives than he or she has already located."[17] Our point is that decades of segregation scholarship have been focused on the three traditional theoretical perspectives of economics, discrimination, and preferences and have largely overlooked the idea of the incomplete—and socially constructed—information that is used by people when they make residential decisions. Such work has not typically engaged seriously the question of how people actually end up living where they do, although recent conceptual and quantitative work by Elizabeth Bruch and her colleagues and qualitative studies of housing choice voucher holders by Stefanie DeLuca are examples of a turn in this direction.[18] It is the goal of this book—and the emphasis of the social structural sorting perspective—to build on this foundation and demonstrate how the lens of the housing search and neighborhood selection process can bring to light more complex and subtle factors that perpetuate segregation. The hope is that this book will encourage segregation scholars to grapple with the implications of the social structural sorting perspective more directly.

Searchers Are Not Robots

A crucial observation about housing decisions that stems from decision sciences—and that has been advanced recently by Bruch and her colleagues—is that many decisions, including those about housing, are complex because there are many more alternatives as well as much more information about those alternatives than people can absorb. Particularly in large metropolitan areas, it is unreasonable to assume that a searcher assesses all the characteristics of every neighborhood in the process of identifying a consideration set. So how do people make this decision task more manageable?

One possible answer is that individuals evaluate each option based on multiple criteria and then pick the one that scores the "highest" in some weighting or tallying system. This process would be compensatory—that is, when considering a particular housing unit, a high score on one feature (large lot size) could compensate for a low score on another feature (longer commute to work), and so this unit may be selected over another unit with a high score on the selected unit's low-scoring feature (a shorter commute). This example epitomizes the rational-choice model of human decision-making, but scores of studies and theories about human decision-making would conclude that it probably does not accurately characterize what people do when choosing a residence. Of most significance in the area of segregation research, Elizabeth Bruch and Joffre Swait have articulated and tested a sophisticated model of neighborhood sorting that is more "cognitively plausible" than this naive rational-choice model. They provide innovative and compelling evidence for an alternative model that relies on the multistage search process articulated by housing search scholars, assumes incomplete information, and involves a screening process that draws on heuristics. In what follows we highlight the key components of the Bruch-Swait model that are most important to our focus on the drivers of segregation, drawing on their work and also the original decision sciences principles on which it is based.[19]

Rather than use a rational-choice model, decision scientists suggest that we think about neighborhood selection and housing choices as a process of elimination or filtering out.[20] First filtered out from consideration (by default) are places that the searcher has never heard of (though he or she may become exposed to new location options through formal channels, such as a real estate agent). Then, among those places that are recognized, the searcher starts to rule out options that fail to meet a minimum cut-off value on a key attribute. After applying the initial rule (a particular evaluation criterion), if too many options remain, the searcher moves to the second most important attribute and considers whether each remaining option meets it or not. For example, if proximity to work is important, then any neighborhoods or communities beyond a certain distance from work will be crossed off the list from the outset. Then, within the set of communities that are close enough to work, the searcher may eliminate those communities that are too expensive. This process of elimination may end with two or three neighborhoods or communities that make it to the second stage of the search.

With the choice set dramatically reduced by eliminating many options based on a few evaluation criteria, the searcher can reasonably move on to the second stage: identifying specific housing options within the more manageable number of possible communities. It is in the second stage when searchers, drawing on a broader range of unit and neighborhood characteristics, may look like utility maximizers, assigning scores and weights to different units and attributes. Importantly, by the time any compensatory strategy kicks in during this second stage, the geographical location of the options has been set through the elimination strategy in the first stage. In support of this idea, the sociologist Annette Lareau finds in her in-depth interview study of how people ended up living where they did that when discussing their housing options, people rarely compared across neighborhoods—almost all of the detailed comparisons and evaluations were focused on different housing units within a given neighborhood.[21] At this stage, the evaluation criteria may look more like a system of trade-offs that involves multiple evaluation criteria and may be compensatory, so an apartment that scores low on one characteristic (not quite the right layout) might end up the first choice because of several high scores on other features (very convenient to shopping and spouse's work).[22]

Thus, as Bruch and Swait argue, this first stage relies on *heuristics*—or shortcuts—that help people winnow down their choices. The psychologists Gerd Gigerenzer and Wolfgang Gaissmaier describe heuristics as "a strategy that ignores part of the information, with the goal of making decisions more quickly, frugally, or accurately than more complex models."[23] This reliance on heuristics stands in sharp contrast to the assumption that the selection of the neighborhood choice set involves a careful vetting of all the information on the neighborhood attributes that are important to the individual.

Gerd Gigerenzer and his colleagues' ideas underlying "fast and frugal heuristics" are helpful in directing our attention to dimensions and concepts of neighborhood selection processes that, because of our adherence to traditional theories, have heretofore flown mainly under the radar of students of segregation.[24] Instead of considering each alternative in turn, evaluating its features and weighing the various options, people quickly determine which places to eliminate from consideration. Bruch and Swait propose that of the many heuristics, a useful one is "take-the-best"—making a decision based on one reason and relying on the cue that is perceived as providing the best information. Although we have neither the data nor the methods that would allow us to definitively test—or make the case for—the specific contours of the heuristics used by housing searchers, we find the concept valuable as a tool for understanding—and ultimately breaking down—the patterns of segregation. Our ultimate hope is that scholars will take up the task of collecting the needed data and conducting the analyses that will pinpoint which heuristics are at play in this set of decisions. Our intermediate goal in this book is to provide qualitative data that reveal how race and racialized perceptions play out in a neighborhood selection process in which the outcomes are driven by heuristics—rather than by complete information and rational choice.

Picturing the Housing Search Under the Social Structural Sorting Perspective

At its core, the social structural sorting perspective argues that (1) residential segregation is maintained by dramatic racial differences in residential mobility processes; (2) these mobility differences are rooted in a multistage search process that is much more complex than is typically recognized in research on residential stratification; and (3) each of the stages of this process is informed by social dynamics that remain largely unrecognized in popular explanations of segregation. These dynamics are summarized, stylistically, in figure 3.1 and developed in greater detail in subsequent chapters.

While racially differentiated mobility processes are key to understanding the perpetuation of segregation, the core of our argument is that this racial stratification originates long before mobility decisions are made. What we refer to as the pre-search stage can be reasonably thought of as all those experiences throughout the life course that shape levels of knowledge about, and perceptions of, neighborhoods in the metropolitan area. These include residential histories and daily activities (work, school, shopping, and so on) that provide individuals with direct exposure to specific neighborhoods and allow for the development of familiarity with these spaces and the formation of opinions about their characteristics. But as we argue later in the book, these perceptions and knowledge may also emerge out of indirect exposures through media depictions of places or the experiences of those in the social network. Individuals are likely to have little knowledge about places that they never access, either directly or indirectly, or they may develop opinions of these areas that differ markedly from the opinions of those who have experiences in these places. As depicted in figure 3.1, the result is that individuals may largely disregard significant swaths of metropolitan space during the pre-search process, even before the search begins, because they know little about these places or do not perceive them as relevant to their daily lives. Thus, whereas traditional explanations of residential segregation implicitly assume that residential decision-makers objectively weigh the attributes of all neighborhoods in the metropolitan-based housing market, the social structural sorting perspective recognizes that residential decisions are likely to be restricted to the subset of metropolitan neighborhoods making up the individual's perceived system of neighborhoods and seeks to elaborate the segregation implications of this imperfect knowledge by focusing on racial differences in that system.

Figure 3.1   The Housing Search Process Under the Social Structural
Sorting Perspective

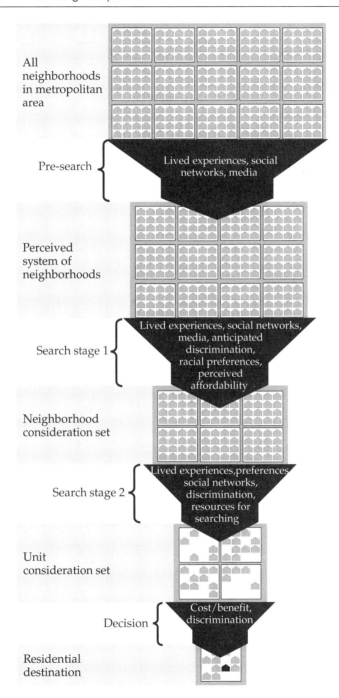

All
neighborhoods
in metropolitan
area

Pre-search
Lived experiences, social
networks, media

Perceived
system of
neighborhoods

Search stage 1
Lived experiences, social networks,
media, anticipated
discrimination,
racial preferences,
perceived
affordability

Neighborhood
consideration set

Search stage 2
Lived experiences, preferences
social networks,
discrimination,
resources for
searching

Unit
consideration set

Decision
Cost/benefit,
discrimination

Residential
destination

Source: Refinement and adaptation by the authors of a figure developed in collaboration with Michael D.M. Bader and Elizabeth Bruch.

This pre-search bounding of residential decision-making has important implications for segregation. As we argue later in the book, sharp racial differences in residential experiences and daily activities, racially bounded social networks, and racially differentiated engagement with sometimes racialized media depictions are likely to produce perceived neighborhood systems that also vary sharply by race. Although much research is based on the notion that racially differentiated mobility processes reflect differential selection across a common set of neighborhoods—that is, the sorting of individuals across all neighborhoods in the metropolitan area as a function of some combination of economics, preferences, and discrimination—the reality is that members of different races are likely to be sorted among separate sets of neighborhoods that may overlap only minimally. This separation of social worlds, made up of racially distinct sets of neighborhoods, represents an important context in which housing searches take place.

These distinct sets of neighborhoods are likely to become distinguished along racial lines to an even greater degree when the search for housing takes place. In stage 1 of the housing search process, individuals weigh their residential options and select from their perceived system of neighborhoods the set of areas they consider viable residential destinations. We argue that, for most people, this neighborhood selection process probably does not reflect a concerted search for the optimal neighborhood. Instead, this definition of the residential consideration set is also a function of a variety of more subtle, and racially differentiated, social processes that shape what ends up in the consideration set. Once again, lived experiences, indirect exposures through social networks, and media depictions all help to shape perceptions of specific neighborhoods as potential destinations, but factors from traditional theories of segregation are likely to play a role as well. For example, the residential consideration set may be shaped by individuals' perceptions of the affordability of a particular location, their assumptions about the racial composition of the neighborhood, or their assessment of the likelihood that they will experience discrimination in the neighborhood. Thus, the social structural sorting perspective does not contradict the notion that factors like discrimination, residential preferences, and economics play important roles in processes of residential stratification, but it does articulate effects of these forces that are much more subtle than is often recognized in traditional theories.

In stage 2 of the search process, the consideration set is further funneled down into the subset of neighborhoods in which the individual actually assesses specific housing units.[25] Again, subtle and highly racialized social dynamics of lived experiences, daily activities, and networks play a role in this narrowing process by shaping the quality and quantity of information about specific housing opportunities within various neighborhoods in the consideration set. And as with the first stage, these factors are likely to complement factors implicated in more traditional theoretical arguments—factors such as racial steering and other forms of discrimination, but also economic forces that shape the time, money, and tools available to facilitate the search. For some, the unit consideration set is highly restricted by these forces in ways that produce racially stratified residential outcomes.

Finally, the search culminates with a residential decision. Consistent with traditional depictions of this process, we view this stage as involving an analysis of the potential benefits of specific units relative to their drawbacks and affordability. But the social structural sorting perspective draws attention to the constraints on this rational decision-making process, including those related to the urgency of the mobility decision and the perception of viable alternatives. Similarly, we recognize that discrimination may play an important role in blocking some searchers from gaining access to a desirable location, but we also argue that this is just one of the many ways in which discrimination—and the anticipation of discrimination—may play out in the mobility process. In other words, even the final stage of the residential search process is fraught with complexities rarely recognized in the residential mobility literature. Most importantly, these decision complexities, described effectively by Bruch and Swait, involve the considerable narrowing from all possible neighborhoods in the metropolitan area to a limited number of units in a select set of neighborhoods. Our social structural sorting perspective highlights the effects on this winnowing process of a complex set of social processes. As we argue in subsequent chapters, these social dynamics are highly racialized—and therefore crucial for understanding the perpetuation of segregation.

DATA AND METHODS

Reflecting the fact that no single existing data source provides information sufficient for understanding the complex processes of the neighborhood selection and housing search and of residential stratification, we draw on a wide range of qualitative and quantitative data to assess the basic tenets of the social structural sorting perspective. Throughout the book, we also rely on published research (which itself uses a range of methods, from census data to survey data analysis, in-depth interviews, and administrative records). In many cases, we cast the results and implications of this published research in a different light, showing how they can be viewed through the lens of the social structural sorting perspective.

Our goal is not to provide definitive tests of the perspective, but to piece together available data to create a basic empirical foundation for our core arguments. The empirical foundation is built around original analyses of both in-depth interviews and focus groups in Chicago and large-scale national survey data sets. By drawing on multiple methods, we are able to offset the weaknesses of one method with the strengths of another. For example, the large-scale survey data analysis provides evidence to support the generalizability and prevalence of key dynamics and provides hints that we are on the right track in our linkages between the processes we unpack and the outcome of interest. The in-depth interviews and focus groups, by contrast, are limited to a single metropolitan area and so cannot be understood as representative or as permitting us to gauge prevalence. Instead, they allow us to dig deeper into the processes and meanings that people draw on when they think about neighborhood and residential choices. These interviews also allow us to start to unpack the logics and linkages that people make between communities, racial dynamics, and housing search processes. Where the survey data analysis can tell us, for example, how many people (and what kinds of people) use "word of mouth" to find a place to live, our in-depth interviews can point us toward why they do this, and what it looks like when they do.

More specifically, we draw particularly on our qualitative data to provide insights about the processes of residential decision-making, including respondents' perceptions of specific neighborhoods, descriptions of the approaches used to differentiate between these areas, and the major motivations for specific residential decisions. The complementary quantitative analyses allow us to describe general patterns of residential stratification, as well as specify racial and ethnic differences in specific aspects of the residential search and mobility processes. More generally, they also help us develop a stronger case for the external validity of our arguments. Before proceeding with our argument, then, we review the methods used to collect and analyze the diverse sources of data that we rely on to provide clues about the efficacy of our new theoretical frame.

In-Depth Interview and Focus Group Data

The original qualitative data reported in this book are based on three separate studies conducted in the Chicago metropolitan area, hereafter referred to as the Search for Housing Study (2003), the Housing Study Focus Groups (2003), and the Perceptions and Experiences with Communities and Neighborhoods in the Chicago Metropolitan Area Study (2012). In all three cases, Maria Krysan was the principal investigator and oversaw the details of the data collection, while Kyle Crowder and Michael Bader were co-PIs for the summer 2012 study. The 2003 studies (in-depth interviews and focus groups) were conducted in collaboration with Reynolds Farley and Mick Couper at the University of Michigan, and Tyrone Forman at the University of Illinois at Chicago. In all three cases, the primary purpose was to examine different aspects of the residential search process and community perceptions, but only the 2012 study was directly focused on the core issues that form the basis of this book. The earlier studies were conducted in order to develop the survey instruments for the 2004–2005 Chicago Area Study (CAS) and the 2004 Detroit Area Study (DAS).[26]

That our qualitative data come from a single metropolitan area must be kept in mind when evaluating and interpreting their contributions to the evidence we are assembling. As noted elsewhere, Chicago is a valuable context because it represents a type of metropolitan area where segregation is high, long-lasting, and consequential. Not all cities have these features, but Chicago is also not the only one in its class (see chapter 2). It is also worth noting that our qualitative data are used, not to test hypotheses, but to do what qualitative data do best: to illustrate processes and logics and unpack what these experiences are like for people. Throughout the book, where possible, we also bring in evidence from other methods (original analyses of national survey data and published studies) that complements and goes some way toward overcoming the shortcomings of our reliance on interviews in a single city with a small and nonrepresentative sample of residents.

"The Search for Housing" In-Depth Interviews (May to October 2003)   In 2003, we conducted twenty-five one-on-one in-depth interviews with residents of the Chicago metropolitan area who were at least twenty-five years old and who had changed residence within the prior five years. Participants were recruited via newspaper ads (the *Chicago Defender*, the *Chicago Tribune*, and *La Raza*) and fliers posted in libraries, community centers, and other public places. The interviews were conducted in person in a variety of places convenient to the respondent, including public library study rooms, an office in the Survey Research Laboratory of the University of Illinois at Chicago (UIC), and occasionally in a respondent's home.

The interviewers were the principal investigator (Krysan) and two trained graduate students. Interviewer and participant racial-ethnic background were matched. The Latina interviewer was bilingual, and two of the nine interviews with Latinos were conducted in Spanish. Interview length ranged from 60 to 210 minutes, with an average of 97 minutes, and respondents were compensated $50 for their participation. Interviews were recorded and transcribed for analysis.[27]

Interviewers used a semistructured interview protocol, though they were also encouraged to spontaneously probe for additional detail or information. Card sort techniques (for example, cards with names of different neighborhoods to consider, or cards with a range of neighborhood characteristics) were used to encourage participants to consider different aspects of housing searches as well as to prompt discussion of what neighborhood and unit features they considered important. In addition, perceptions of a range of Chicago neighborhoods as well as suburbs were gauged. Broad interview topics included: (1) current neighborhood experiences and evaluations; (2) characteristics of an ideal neighborhood; (3) perceptions of Chicago-area neighborhoods and communities; (4) the search for housing, including questions on the length of the search, its intensity, strategies used, sources of information, and areas searched; (5) racial residential preferences; and (6) experiences with discrimination.

"The Housing Study Focus Groups" (October to November 2003)   In the fall of 2003, we conducted six focus groups (ranging in size from four to twelve participants) at the University of Illinois at Chicago. Participants were recruited through newspaper ads in the *Chicago Tribune,* the *Chicago Defender,* and *La Raza.* Individuals were paid $50 for their participation in a two-hour focus group discussion. The groups were divided into the following six categories: white owners, white renters, black owners, black renters, Latino renters, and Latino owners. The race-ethnicity of the moderators matched that of the participants. The moderator guide covered a range of issues related to housing, including a segment in which participants watched short (twenty-five- to thirty-second) unnarrated neighborhood videos with actors of different races and ethnicities posing as residents. These videos were being tested for their possible use in a survey-based experiment looking at the effect of neighborhood racial composition on the evaluation of neighborhoods by Chicago-area residents.[28] Participants were also asked to discuss: (1) their experiences searching for housing, including what resources and information they drew on; (2) their experiences and perceptions of discrimination in the housing market; and (3) their perceptions of the causes of racial residential segregation. The analyses for this book focused on items 1 and 2.

"Perceptions and Experiences with Communities and Neighborhoods in the Chicago Metropolitan Area" In-Depth Interviews (June to August 2012)   In 2012, we conducted twenty-four in-person, in-depth interviews with residents of the Chicago metropolitan area who were at least twenty-five years old. Participants were recruited via Craigslist ads. The interviews were conducted in either the focus group facility or a standard office at UIC's Survey Research Laboratory. The Survey Research Laboratory staff were responsible for fielding email inquiries from volunteers, of which there were several hundred, and filling the quotas to maximize racial-

ethnic diversity, suburban/city residence, homeownership status, and to some extent age and gender.

Three trained graduate students were the interviewers, and the principal investigator (Krysan) observed the majority of the interviews through the one-way mirror of the focus group facility. Interviewer and participant racial-ethnic background were matched. Although the Latina interviewer was bilingual, all interviews were conducted in English. Interview length ranged from 48 to 150 minutes, with an average of 88 minutes. Respondents were compensated $75 for their participation. Interviews were recorded and transcribed for analysis.[29]

Interviewers followed a semistructured interview protocol, though they were encouraged to spontaneously probe for additional detail and information. The majority of the interview was focused on the use of a series of large colorful maps that, when pieced together, represented the totality of the Chicago metropolitan area (Cook County and its surrounding counties, also known as the "Collar Counties"). A separate "zoomed-in" map showed just the city of Chicago and was labeled with the seventy-seven Community Areas. Throughout the interviews, participants were asked to use colored markers to circle, check, or otherwise demarcate the communities that applied to the question being asked. Specifically, participants were asked to identify the communities where they: (1) currently lived; (2) had ever lived; (3) had ever searched for housing even if they had not lived there; (4) had ever spent time in, either currently or in the past (for example, for work, school, visiting friends, shopping, doctor or other health care appointments, social activities, having fun, or attending church); (5) would seriously consider living; and (6) would never consider living.

Using this map, the interviewers then asked an array of questions about participants' perceptions of the places they spent time in or had ever spent time in, as well as their impressions of places where they had never spent time. For the latter category, interviewers were instructed to ask questions to find out where participants got their information about these places. Finally, interviewers selected a subset of specific communities in participants' sets of places where they had "spent time" and had "never spent time" and asked them to give their best guesses about the community characteristics, including the cost of housing, the crime level, the quality of the public schools, the racial composition, and how welcoming it would be to the participant's racial-ethnic group.

A Note on Sampling   Although our sampling approach differed across the three studies, all three relied on convenience samples of adults who were recruited through various media.[30] Our results therefore cannot be construed as representative. That having been said, we used quotas to ensure variation in racial-ethnic background, as well as city/suburban residence and renter/owner tenure. The tenure status helped ensure some variation along social class, as homeowners tend to be relatively better off financially than many renters. To be sure, our respondents were individuals looking for opportunities in newspapers or on Craigslist to make a little extra money, and some subset of them were people who regularly scanned ads for research studies for which they could be paid. The ads generated many more volunteers than we needed—in some case hundreds of them—so we were able to obtain our desired quotas along racial-ethnic and homeowner-ship lines and be somewhat selective to ensure gender and age variation. However, it is certainly the case that our participants as a group probably had below-average incomes and perhaps less stable employment.

In general, however, we were impressed at the diversity of life experiences of our respondents, who ranged from recent arrivals to Chicago to lifelong residents; from a single mother with six young children to an empty-nester living in the western suburbs and others with no children; from those with a high school diploma to those with a master's degree. It is hard to tell how our sampling strategy affected our results, but one possibility is that our participants (especially for the 2012 interview study and the focus groups held at UIC) were more highly mobile around the city than a representative sample would have been. To participate, individuals had to be willing to come to UIC's downtown campus, and be comfortable doing so. From the standpoint of the topic of our study, it is therefore possible that our sample was more familiar with a broader expanse of communities throughout the metropolitan area than would have been the case with people who were unable or unwilling to travel into the city of Chicago to participate in the study.

Analysis Approach   Krysan conducted all analyses of the qualitative data. Because the interviews included topics that were not directly relevant to this research project (as they had been conducted for different initial purposes), she first read all of the transcripts, coding them for relevance to the substantive and theoretical focus of this analysis. Transcripts were coded to identify sections that were of broad relevance to housing searches and perceptions and experiences of communities. Memos were written that summarized the emergent themes in the interviews. Based on these memos, a core set of themes for more systematic coding was constructed. These themes included: (1) the variety of ways in which social networks impact and inform people's housing searches and perceptions of communities; (2) the structure (stages) of housing searches, including both the construction of a choice set and the nuts and bolts of a search; (3) the content and structure of community perceptions; (4) the sources of information upon which community perceptions are based; and (5) discussion of racial discrimination or racial dynamics. All transcripts were coded in multiple ways. For example, each transcript was read and analyzed in its entirety in order to get a picture of the individual respondent's overall housing "story." Transcripts were then read again in order to code segments of the text into the core themes. Finally, the transcripts were read and coded in groups for each racial-ethnic group to understand how the processes were similar or different across racial-ethnic groups. Krysan moved back and forth between close and thematic coding as she made sense of the patterns and core insights that emerged within each theme.

Why Chicago?   As discussed earlier, our qualitative data are drawn exclusively from interviews and focus groups with residents of the Chicago metropolitan area. This focus on a single metropolitan area was necessitated by the significant logistical undertaking of qualitative research, while the specific focus on Chicago is consistent with our central goal of understanding the persistence of segregation. Chicago has been a focus of research on residential segregation dating back nearly one hundred years, to the earliest days of urban ecological research.[31] As such, it provides the perfect location for the development of our new perspective on segregation in that studying the dynamics of residential selection in this context allows for direct comparisons to more traditional arguments developed in the same location.

More generally, Chicago provides an ideal setting for understanding the processes that have perpetuated segregation for decades. To understand the factors perpetuating segregation, we need to focus on a place where segregation has remained high, despite broader forces that should theoretically have led to integration. This is certainly true of Chicago. Despite considerable economic change, population growth, and demographic diversification, segregation in the Chicago metropolitan area has remained remarkably stable. Studying Chicago provides the opportunity to gain insight into the stratified residential mobility processes that continually cycle members of different races through separate sets of neighborhoods. In addition, as argued in the preceding chapter, Chicago fits squarely in the relatively large group of metropolitan areas that have remained segregated (so-called legacy metros) and that contain a very large share of the country's black population. Thus, understanding the forces operating in places like Chicago is an important endeavor.

As we explore and report on the Chicago-based data throughout the book, a few features of Chicago—and other hypersegregated places—and their possible impact on residential processes are worth keeping in mind by way of qualifying and contextualizing the results. First, Chicago has a substantial black population; in areas with smaller black populations, racial isolation and social closure are less likely—that is, social networks may be more diverse, and lived experiences may be less isolated. Also, Chicago is defined by large agglomerations of black neighborhoods; to the extent that this feature results in greater definition of separate geographic spaces, there may be an impact on the extent to which the daily activities and lived experiences of blacks and whites are separate. Chicago is also a slow-growing metropolitan area, and relatively few new neighborhoods have been added in recent decades. Consequently, fewer new neighborhoods have been added in the context of antidiscrimination legislation and metropolitan population diversity, and those areas that have been added tend to be predominantly white.[32] In addition, Chicago is noteworthy for having well-established and well-known neighborhoods; thus, the content and durability of its residents' perceptions about the city's communities and neighborhoods will almost certainly look different from the perceptions of residents of newer and faster-growing metropolitan areas about their communities.

Nevertheless, in spite of the considerable value in studying processes of residential stratification in Chicago, we remain focused on uncovering more general residential dynamics and how they may vary across different types of metropolitan areas. Thus, we analyze national-level data from secondary sources for clues about the residential processes that reinforce segregation. Throughout these analyses of quantitative data, we conduct supplemental analyses to assess the extent to which the residential processes under examination differ between the three segregation regimes introduced in chapter 2. In general, these analyses indicate that the mobility and housing search processes that tend to reinforce segregation operate fairly similarly across different types of metropolitan areas, but we highlight exceptions to this general rule in the text.

Secondary Analysis of Survey Data

Our book draws heavily on original analyses of two large-scale, nationally representative data sets: the American Housing Survey (AHS) and the Panel Study of Income Dynamics (PSID). Neither source of data provides complete information on processes of residential stratification, but taken together, they provide important insights into broad patterns of residential mobility and key aspects of the housing search process. Because both surveys rely on national samples, they also allow us to develop a stronger case for the external validity of conclusions drawn from our qualitative data from Chicago. Because we utilize the data from the PSID and AHS in a variety of ways throughout the subsequent chapters, we provide a brief overview of these surveys here; additional details of specific analyses are provided as they are introduced.

The American Housing Survey   Begun in 1973 and conducted by the U.S. Census Bureau, the AHS microdata provide information on a representative sample of about 167,000 housing units in U.S. areas. The data provide information about the quality of housing in the United States, and the longitudinal nature of the AHS affords the opportunity to assess housing and household changes over long periods of time. Each year, Census Bureau interviewers visit each unit in person or telephone the household occupying the housing unit. For unoccupied units, they obtain information from landlords, rental agents, or neighbors. The sample of housing units included in the AHS represents a cross-section of all housing in the nation. Data on these units and their occupants are collected every two years until a new sample is selected. The Census Bureau updates the sample by adding newly constructed housing units and units discovered through coverage-improvement efforts.

Because we utilize the data to assess contemporary housing patterns, we rely on the 2011 and 2013 AHS—the two most recent releases of the data available at the time of our analysis. For these years, we include housing units located within one of our core metropolitan areas and focus primarily on the AHS "Recent Mover" module, which asks householders who moved into an AHS unit within the twenty-four months preceding the survey a series of questions about their recent housing search. The AHS provides the opportunity to assess racial and ethnic differences in the housing search process, including the reasons for moving, the tools used to search for housing, and the conditions of the new place of residence.

The main weaknesses of the AHS for our purposes are that it does not allow for detailed analysis of the types of units and neighborhoods that movers visited and it does not show how they adapted their search process and expectations over time. Also, because the AHS is a sample of housing units, recent movers are included in the data set only by virtue of having moved into a sampled unit. Thus, it is not possible to analyze the data longitudinally to compare respondents' housing conditions or individual circumstances before and after their moves.

The Panel Study of Income Dynamics   The PSID is a longitudinal survey of almost 9,000 families distributed across hundreds of metropolitan areas. Begun in 1968, members of the initial panel of approximately 5,000 families (about 18,000 individuals) were interviewed annually until

1997 and biennially thereafter. New families have been added to the panel as children and other members of original panel families form their own households.

Two valuable features of the PSID are its national scope and the inclusion of data for a wide range of individual- and family-level characteristics that have been shown to affect residential location.[33] An equally valuable feature of the PSID is found in the supplemental "Geospatial Match Files," which record each household's census tract at each survey wave. We use the Geospatial Match Files to link the addresses of individual PSID respondents at each annual (or biennial) interview to corresponding codes for geographic areas. This allows us to attach data on the neighborhoods and metropolitan areas occupied by PSID respondents at each year of interview from 1968 to 2013. We utilize data from the 1970, 1980, 1990, 2000, and 2010 censuses to characterize the composition of tracts and metropolitan areas at each interview, using linear interpolation/extrapolation to estimate values for areal characteristics in noncensus years. Potential problems associated with changes in tract boundaries across decennial censuses are overcome by our use of the Neighborhood Change Database (NCDB), which normalizes census tract data between 1970 and 2010 to 2010 boundaries.

The PSID lacks questions about the housing search process, but it does allow us to track households' mobility patterns over time and to distinguish between different types of moves—including those between neighborhoods and those between housing units within the same neighborhood— and to examine several moves carried out by the same householder at different points in time. We utilize the PSID data and linked census data for several types of analyses. To take advantage of the longitudinal structure of the PSID, for most analyses we structure the data as a series of person-periods, with each observation referring to the period between successive PSID interviews. To focus our attention on the observations in which the individual has a central role in making residential decisions, we include only those observation periods in which the individual was reported as either a householder or a partner of the householder at the time of the interview. We restrict the analyses to observations with nonmissing values on mobility and related variables and, unless otherwise noted, focus on respondents living in a core metropolitan area at the time of the interview.

For most of our analyses, we focus only on data from the most recent survey years in order to capture contemporary patterns of residential stratification. For some analyses, however, we take advantage of the greater temporal reach and multigenerational structure of the PSID to assess the role of residential histories in the processes of contemporary stratification. For example, in analyses involving the link between kin location and residential attainment, we identify kin networks using the 1968 "Family ID" variable, which is the same over time for all members of an extended family. We also use the PSID's supplemental "Parent Identification File" to identify the nature of each kin relationship. Starting with the initial parent-child relationship defined in the Parent Identification File, we infer additional relationships, including siblings, grandparents, grandchildren, aunts and uncles, cousins, and current stepparents, stepchildren, and stepsiblings.

For analyses involving the link between adolescent and adult residential context, we utilize data from the 1970 to 2013 waves of the PSID. We limit this part of the analysis to those individuals observed in a PSID family during adolescence (between the ages of thirteen and eighteen) in interview years after and including 1970, the first year for which continuous PSID geocodes are available, and track the residential location of these individuals from the time they established their own household (after age eighteen) and through a maximum age of fifty-six. This focus on residential context in early to mid-adulthood allows us to assess the effects of residential experiences throughout adolescence using the data available in the PSID; respondents older than fifty-six in the latest data collection year (2013) entered adolescence before 1970.

Again, these secondary data, combined with insights gleaned from extensive interviewing and focus groups, allow us to shed considerable light on the complexities of the housing search process, characterize some underappreciated drivers of residential stratification, and outline the basic tenets of the social structural sorting perspective.

Chapter 4 | Social Networks: The Social Part of the Theory

ONE OF THE key claims of the social structural sorting perspective is that the residential mobility decisions that constantly shape residential segregation are the result of social processes. Traditional theoretical arguments tend to treat residential decision-makers as isolated individuals who choose to move to, or remain in, neighborhoods that best match their own individual residential preferences, within the constraints defined by economic resources and discrimination. In reality, individuals make these mobility decisions within the context of the needs and desires of other actors in their social network, and they often make decisions that are motivated largely by the need to maintain social connections. Moreover, social networks represent an important source of information about residential options. Thus, if we are to better understand how segregation is maintained and propagated through constant population churning, we must pay attention to the ways in which social networks shape individual mobility decisions. Although the data necessary to fully examine these social processes do not exist, significant clues are provided by both national studies and our interviews with Chicago-area residents.

When we focus our attention on how people end up living where they do, it is quickly apparent that social networks—family, friends, relatives, and coworkers—play a significant role. Research on the neighborhood selection and housing search process identifies two central ways in which this can unfold. First, social networks are an important source of information about neighborhoods and housing units, and they function both directly and indirectly in that they can provide advice about communities as places to live while also providing leads about specific apartments or homes available to rent or buy. Second, social networks influence individuals' decisions about which neighborhood or housing unit they should choose simply by virtue of the fact that many people want to live near their friends and family—that is, their social networks.

66

To shed light on both of these ways in which social networks operate, we draw on published research and original analyses of secondary data to establish that searchers frequently use social networks as a source of information, and that these networks are a motivation to select one location over another. Drawing on in-depth interview data to give texture to the survey data insights, our analysis becomes attuned to the many and complex ways in which social networks inform our perceptions of communities and neighborhoods (the pre-search stage). The qualitative data are especially well suited to this analysis because the impact of social networks can be quite amorphous and would be difficult to capture in survey-based studies. By asking in-depth interview participants to tell us their impressions of places—what they thought of them, not what they could necessarily verify—we gain understanding of the assumptions about communities that people bring with them when they begin a housing search. The search may, of course, ultimately upend some of these assumptions, but our point is that people enter a search with information that has been built up throughout their lives. And our in-depth interviews provide a window into the logic and extrapolations that shape community perceptions—often of places that people have never set foot in, or have only passed through. As with all of our in-depth interview data, caution must be exercised: these are convenience samples of individuals, and they are not representative or generalizable to a larger population. In less segregated cities, the content of the information obtained from networks—especially the extent to which it is racialized— may differ, but the larger point remains: namely, that social networks feed community and housing information to people in complex ways.

SOCIAL NETWORKS AS INFORMATION SOURCES

There are three ways in which social networks serve as information sources during the three stages of the housing search process: in shaping searchers' perceptions of communities; as an influence on searchers' consideration sets; and in providing searchers with specific information on housing units available.

The Pre-search Stage: Social Networks Shape Our Perceptions of Communities

We argue that people come to a housing search having accumulated information about places and their features. But as the term implies, this "pre-search" happens before people actually begin to search and is an accumulation of information acquired in part through social networks. Our in-depth interviews convey the many strong, weak, and very weak network ties that function in this way, as well as the varied ways, both direct and indirect, in which they do so.

For example, Destiny, an African American renter, knew the locations of the good and bad places in Chicago because of information from her social networks:

> I mean, it's just known. It's the word on the street. . . . Just to be honest, I had a lot of family that sold drugs and was involved in a lot of crime in the city. I know just growing up around it and being around them . . . I knew the word of where to go and where not to go and what was happening here, what was happening there.

The world of social media also provides network-related impressions—or just "the feel"—of a place, even if one has never visited the family members who live there: "I see all the stuff my cousin is talking about on Facebook," Destiny said. "You kind of get a feel of what's there. . . . My cousin is my friend on Facebook. All her messages is connected to her Facebook page, so I kinda see all the trouble she has out there [*laughs*]."

Coworkers are another source of information about where the good and bad places are to live. For example, one participant noted: "From what I hear from my coworkers [who lived in the area], it's pretty peaceful and clean." And another participant, Dorothy, had this to say when she explained why Naperville was one of the places she would seriously consider living:

> When I worked downtown, the last boss that I had in my department was from Naperville. Very nice gentleman. Very very very very nice gentleman. Had two little girls, and he always talked about living in Naperville. He loved it and always talked highly about it. That's about the only thing I've heard about those—that area.

Dorothy also drew indirectly on her social networks to form an impression of Calumet City as a welcoming place, even though she had never been there either. She had friends who talk about Calumet City, "so there's probably some happening stuff for African Americans in Calumet City. I've never been there, so I don't really know."

Our in-depth interviews also suggest another possible (indirect) impact of social networks: people often make inferences about a place—often one they have never visited—based on the race, age, family status, or occupation of the person or people they know (or knew) who live (or lived) there. These connections can be strong, weak, and even very weak, and the inferences often come from knowing "someone who knew someone" who lived in the place or grew up there. This indirect impact of social networks highlights the idea that many people's perception of a community can come from fleeting knowledge of who lives there and that this perception can shape—perhaps subconsciously—where they decide to look for a place to live. It is these impressions and inferences that help constitute the backdrop against which housing searches happen—what we call the "pre-search" stage—and that inform which communities and neighborhoods end up in a consideration set.

Belinda is a good example. She knew something about a person who lived in Elgin and used that knowledge to paint a picture of a place she had never been. Indeed, she was not even sure where Elgin was located:

> BELINDA: I know some people that I've worked with that live in Elgin. I had no idea it was in Kane County. Carpentersville, I've heard of that suburb, but that's really about it. St. Charles and—actually all these suburbs—I know people that live in these suburbs. I had no idea they were in Kane County.
>
> INTERVIEWER: Have you—do you have any impressions about the actual cities or anything that you've even, stuff that you've heard or anything like that?
>
> BELINDA: Basically, they're just a general suburban—suburbs primarily, I would say, Caucasian—not a lot of African American presence from my understanding. I could be wrong. I haven't really looked at the stats on these suburbs. People that I work with that I mentioned, they're all—they're not African American, and they're family people who live in these suburbs.

Joann drove home this same point:

> JOANN: Well, if you extrapolate information from who you know, and if Paul lived there, it must be comfortable, semi-affluent and fairly white.

Later JoAnn had this to say about Elgin:

> JOANN: I don't know anything about it at all. My old boss's dad lived out there. She was white, middle-class, Catholic. I assume if that's where she grew up and that's where her dad lived—yeah, I think she grew up there. I assume that's at least part of what comprises Elgin. I don't know anything about it. I have no reason to know anything about it. Not like I'd ever move there.

Presumably, if Joann had reason to move to Elgin, she would look into it in more detail. But it is not clear whether this information about Elgin was enough to put Elgin in or out of her consideration set, and the possibility remained that she would consider it—for example, if she had a job there, perhaps she would take the time to learn about it. The point is that such indirectly acquired information from social networks probably factors into what goes into people's "noggins" and is part of what they use in constructing their consideration set.

Apart from family and coworkers, other people in social networks provide information about communities and neighborhoods. Russell explained how he knew about Cicero:

> I think probably most of that experience came from—or my feelings for that probably came from—the people in my church, when I was going to the church over in the South Lawndale community. So my experience—just hearing things like, "Be careful when you go into Cicero," and things like that may have shaped it a little bit.

Luisa had a particularly creative way of putting together information that was informed by both her social networks and her regular routine to figure out what kind of people lived in Logan Square:

> I go to my hairdresser a lot in Lincoln Park and Lakeview. . . . Most of the hairdressers, which are American mainly ladies, and all of them live in Logan Square, which makes me think it's changing. So it's a mix, or it's maybe more bohemian becoming like that.

Luisa's comment illustrates how experiences can help people paint pictures of places—pictures that may be mediated through social networks, either because their network exposes individuals to communities or because they make inferences about a community based on the people they know who live there. But social networks and daily routines also shape what people know about places. Jerome lived in Evanston (a racially diverse inner-ring suburb to the north of Chicago), but his young son lived on the South Side of Chicago. After naming several South Side neighborhoods where he would not live, Jerome explained why:

> South Side, I think like 90 percent of the killings that's been goin' on in Chicago since this year started has been on the South Side of Chicago. I don't even take my son to the park. When I'm over at his mom's house, I don't take him to the park. Me, personally, I don't even like to be out, especially not at night or when the sun starts goin' down or even those real hot days because that seems that's when the knuckleheads come out.

Thus, Jerome's social network ties brought him to a South Side neighborhood on a regular basis, and these visits gave him experiences that made him dislike the place. We also heard stories from our interview participants about the places where their family, friends, and coworkers lived becoming the places where they went to shop, run errands, provide rides to work, attend celebrations, and the like; all of these activities increased their direct exposure to various communities. Thus, social networks beget lived experiences that shape community knowledge.

The theme that emerges from our interviews is that individuals derive important information about neighborhood options from interactions with family and friends, and this information may shape their residential decision-making in profound ways. Thus, social networks provide direct and indirect exposure to various neighborhoods in a metropolitan area, shaping people's perceptions of their character.

Stage 1: Social Networks Influence Our Consideration Set

Jerome's comment illustrates how social networks can shape perceptions of a place at a time when one is not actively searching for a place to live. But if Jerome *were* searching, he said, he would not include these South Side neighborhoods in his consideration set. We now turn specifically to the idea that social networks can play a role in stage 1, when an active search is undertaken and a consideration set is being constructed. Donald Hempel, in his study of the information that people use when buying a home, highlights the varied impact of social forces:

> The buyer can . . . refer to more informal channels of communication to supplement the information he obtains from commercial sources. . . . This information is usually a by-product of normal interpersonal relations with friends, coworkers, and relatives. It often takes the form of word-of-mouth communications which were motivated by active information-seeking on the part of the buyer, or a chance comment by an acquaintance. In some cases, the buyer engages in social interactions specifically to solve a problem by steering the conversation in such a way as to obtain the desired information. Other buyers may be influenced by the information which was derived from the spontaneous comment of a friend who learns of the buyer's search, or an overheard comment made by a person the buyer wishes to emulate.[1]

Our in-depth interviews provide an example of this kind of influence. Cesar, a Latino homeowner, reflected on his recent housing search and reported that his social networks did not help. When we pressed him, however, we learned that his networks had shaped his past consideration sets:

> INTERVIEWER: Can you name people that helped you during your search? Maybe someone suggested something about a neighborhood or house?
>
> CESAR: No, I don't think so. Not this time.
>
> INTERVIEWER: Nobody helped you?
>
> CESAR: No.
>
> INTERVIEWER: In the past, have people helped you, like giving you advice?
>
> CESAR: Yeah, they tell me where are the areas that are nice to live, you know. . . . I don't recall any of the places right now. But I remember them telling me about getting an apartment in the Park Ridge area.

Survey data on housing searches suggest that Cesar's experiences are not unusual. When Hempel asked recent home-buyers in two housing markets in Connecticut what sources of information they used to identify their preferred neighborhood, friends, coworkers, and family were the most frequently cited source of information, and about one-third identified social networks as the most influential source for this information.[2] Duncan Maclennan and Gavin Wood report a similar pattern for searchers in Glasgow—about one-third of searchers cited "friends or relatives" as influential in their selection of the area in which to search, and about one in four said that their networks suggested new areas in which to search.[3] More recently, Detroit residents who had searched for housing in the ten years prior to the survey were asked in 2004 and 2005 whether, in general, they had used their social networks (specifically, friends and relatives) in their most recent search: 35 percent said that they used friends, and 28 percent indicated that relatives had contributed information.[4]

Bianca, another Latino owner, illustrated how social networks can both identify places to look for housing and also paint pictures of the neighborhoods recommended (or not recommended):

> I talked to friends and relatives, coworkers . . . to tell me more about the areas, what they would suggest. Where would they recommend, things like that. . . . And friends, they were helpful in the sense that they would tell you more about the area, how much the property cost, what kind of people live around the area. That was good.

In a study of home-searchers in Syracuse, New York, Gary Talarchek affirms the prevalence of Bianca's experience.[5] One the one hand, searchers learn about housing unit features from personal inspection or real estate agents, but information about "environmental and locational attributes" comes from several different sources, with friends and relatives an important and common one.[6] Fifty-two percent of the searchers Talarchek studied relied on information from a friend or relative (in general) in their search. In terms of specific kinds of information, one in three searchers relied on friends or relatives to give them information on the quality of the schools in the neighborhoods they were considering and the type of people who lived there.[7]

Stage 2: Social Networks Provide Information on Specific Housing Units

In addition to using social network influences in the construction of their neighborhood consideration set in stage 1, searchers tap their networks to find specific units to buy or rent during stage 2.

The word-of-mouth strategy is often successful for identifying units, as demonstrated by national-level survey data. For example, the most recent data from the American Housing Survey show that 32 percent of recent movers found their new house or apartment through word of mouth, and the number is close to 40 percent for Latino and black movers.[8] This figure dwarfs the proportion of recent movers using any other single method and aligns well with what we know about decision-making in closely related school choice processes. Specifically, several recent studies of housing and school choice have revealed that parents seldom use formal information sources, such as online reports of average test scores, when selecting schools. If they are used, it is generally to confirm the recommendations they have received through social networks.[9] We also know that reliance on information from social contacts can alter the dynamics of a housing search. For example, people who use social networks and other nonmarket information during their housing search are more likely to be aware of places near where they currently live.[10] And Kevin McCarthy has reported that housing outcomes appear to be more contingent on "who you know" than "how hard you search."[11]

Our in-depth interviews bring life to such uses of social networks and in some cases explain why it is useful. One Latino owner in our focus group referred to the value of word of mouth in terms of getting a better deal:

> I would talk to friends. I probably would choose a neighborhood that somebody I know already lives there and I would talk to them, say, "I'm looking

for something. If you hear anything, this is what I'm looking for, this is the range that I can afford. You know, let me know, spread the word." . . . A lot of folks nowadays are selling their homes on their own, so you have to put that word out.

Renters also used their networks as extra pairs of eyes, as Paula, a Latina, explained: "It was useful in a way because that's also like how people tell you, 'Oh, there's an apartment for rent over here and over there.'"

Survey data also show that searchers use social networks to find real estate agents, and therefore networks indirectly influence the units that they end up considering. In Connecticut in the 1970s and Detroit in the early 2000s, the majority (more than 50 percent) of searchers reported that they found their real estate agent through a referral from a friend or relative. Social networks were also used to find mortgages: about one in four of the Detroit residents we interviewed said that they found their mortgage broker through a referral from a friend or relative.[12] This participant in our Latino owners focus group offered one reason why she had to shop around and suggested that her social networks were responsible for her eventual success at getting a mortgage:

> I finally found one [a mortgage] through my sister . . . from a friend [of hers] at work. That, you know, referred her to him, and he helped her out and he helped me out. But I tried like three other times to refinance, and it was always, "No, you don't make enough," "You're a single parent."

All of these examples illustrate how social networks can help searchers navigate the "nuts and bolts" of the search process.

THE LEASH OF SOCIAL NETWORKS

In addition to providing information, knowledge, and leads on possible housing units, social networks help define consideration sets because people often want to live in close proximity to family and friends. Karen, a middle-aged white suburban homeowner, related the many factors that shaped her housing decision:

> We [she and her husband] wanted to stay close to home [where she grew up]; we're a very, very close family, but we also looked. Let's see what's out west. Let's see what else we can find. We found an awesome house in Lisle. Of course, budget constraints were our biggest thing. We had enough money to do—to look in certain places. We found a house in Lisle that we loved, but it had a foundation issue. And it was too far from my parents. So all of these

areas we really, really liked and we looked. But it was almost like the leash pulling me back toward home . . . we were used to everything there. We knew where everything was. I also worked in [the town we ended up moving to]. I worked a mile from home. So I could either go home to my house, or home to Mom, to have lunch every day. It was very familiar, so that was one of the reasons. And because it was so quiet and the taxes were ridiculously low.

For many people we talked to, like Karen, being close to family and friends was among the most important criteria for choosing a neighborhood and remaining in it. This is consistent with national-level data from the American Housing Survey and the Panel Study of Income Dynamics. Recent research by Amy Spring and her colleagues indicates that, all else being equal, mobile PSID householders tend to choose neighborhoods that are in close proximity to members of their kin network.[13] And among recent movers in the 2011 and 2013 AHS, just under 14 percent reported that convenience to family and friends was the *most* important reason for choosing their new neighborhood. Only proximity to work was more often listed by recent movers (20 percent) as the primary destination-selection criterion. Because the AHS asks respondents to report only the most important reason for selecting their neighborhood, these data probably provide a very conservative estimate of the extent to which social networks influence mobility decisions. In fact, another 15.5 percent of recent movers reported that all of the potential criteria, including proximity to family and friends, were equally important in choosing their new neighborhood.

Moreover, these data say nothing about how likely it is that proximity to social contacts plays an important role in the decision *not* to move. In fact, recent research indicates that having family nearby significantly decreases the likelihood of moving.[14] Once people live in a neighborhood, that place and the people living there become familiar, and this can become a justification to stay close or stay put. Russell and his wife had recently discussed the idea of moving, so the question was at the front of his mind at the time of the interview. He explained why he and his family were likely to stay put in the predominantly African American southern suburb where he had lived for the last six years, even though he found a number of other—whiter—suburbs attractive:

INTERVIEWER: I know you've talked a little bit about these, but Naperville [a mostly white, middle-class suburb northwest of the city]? What about there [is it] that you like?

RUSSELL: Good place to raise my kids. The schools are good like I said—plenty of activities, things like that. It's a great place to raise my kids.

INTERVIEWER: Okay, and why don't you currently live there?

RUSSELL: Just haven't—we haven't decided to make that move yet. . . . We're just kinda settled here. Yeah, I don't know. We've recently talked about moving, in the last couple of weeks—not really discussing it seriously, but what if, or I wonder . . . what type of house we could get for X amount of dollars, but Richton Park—oh, you know what? Olympia Fields too—this whole area here are the areas that we've talked about, and I think what it is, is that we've grown accustomed to the South Side, the south suburbs, so that's probably why we haven't considered Naperville because . . . we now have a new church out here, friends out here, so to uproot and start all over here—it would be—I don't think we'd be willing to do that at this point.

INTERVIEWER: I understand. Okay, and just Winnetka and Wilmette [two very expensive, white, North Side suburbs]—just why—what about those things that—

RUSSELL: It's beautiful. It's million-dollar homes. Obviously, I can't afford that stuff [*laughs*] so that's why we're not there. If we could afford to live here [Wilmette], I would have no problem uprooting my family [*laughs*] to go here. This—Naperville is similar to where we are. They may have a little more here, but it's very similar, so I don't see it being necessary to move from this area to way out west to start over, but for this jump [to Wilmette], if—yeah. I would do it.

Russell's explanation reveals that, all else being equal, he was not willing to uproot his family for a "lateral move"—that is, to a community with largely the same amenities and qualities as his current neighborhood—because his friends and networks were now firmly planted where he was. But if he had had the money or ability to make a "jump" in neighborhood quality, he would have moved outside his comfort zone. This example highlights how social bonds with people make it hard to consider moves to new areas.

Russell's overall residential history provides another glimpse at how social networks shape residential outcomes. If we look back to when Russell first came to the Chicago area, he seemed destined—almost by accident—to always live in an integrated neighborhood. When he first moved to the Chicago area, Russell lived in a North Side neighborhood with a significant white population because "I'm originally from Iowa, and I ended up [there] simply because the direction that I came in Chicago— that was the first apartment I saw for rent, and that's the apartment I took." His subsequent moves were all oriented toward getting where he decided he really wanted to live: Lincoln Park (a predominantly white, upper-middle-class neighborhood also on the North Side of Chicago). But he never got to where he was striving to get in large part because of his social networks—specifically, his eventual wife and her family. Instead, he initially ended up in an all-black neighborhood on the West Side of Chicago. When the interviewer asked, "Why there?" Russell explained:

> I got married. [*laughs*] My wife was from the West Side of Chicago, and I moved to—we bought a house [there]. That is how we ended up—how I ended up there. It was not really my first—wouldn't have been my first choice, but it was close to her family.

Despite a racially atypical introduction to Chicago residential choices, the social network that Russell built up after arriving in Chicago had a very specific and direct effect on his housing outcome—he ended up in a predominantly black neighborhood [on the West Side] entirely because his social network, his wife, chose the neighborhood. She, in turn, chose it because it was close to *her* social network—her family.

Latinos in our study frequently explained that they lived where they did because of their family ties. Teresa is an example of the phenomenon of chain migration: "Because when I came from Mexico, my brother already lived in Little Village, so I lived there." Diana, a Latino renter, reflected at length about this kind of migration. Although her trajectory led her to a different place, she realized that the process was the same: "I know that if my sister-in-law lived on Twenty-Sixth Street, I would have lived there too. I would have stayed there. It's a Mexican neighborhood; Mexicans come here, and they settle in these neighborhoods."

The account of Simon, a white homeowner, illustrates how social networks can influence the process directly and indirectly by "gearing" someone in a particular direction—in his case, the northwest suburbs:

> My parents prefer them more than I do. Um, they're nice areas, Arlington Heights, Schaumburg, Libertyville, I guess if I was living there I wouldn't be unhappy. But I kind of got used to the southwest suburbs now. I didn't know anything about them until I met my fiancé. She geared everything there. She helped me find a job. Then she helped me find an apartment over there. Then she helped me buy a house over there, so she kind of geared me that way.

Finally, Melissa, a young Latina college graduate, drew a link between her social networks and where she ended up living. Specifically, she suggested that her move to the North Side did not reflect a bias toward or against the South Side but was simply a function of her friends' choices: "I never had anything against the South Side neighborhoods, but I think that most of the people I knew ended up moving there [the North Side], and I think [that] was a big influence."

Social networks play an important role in shaping both the information that people acquire about places and their desire to be in a particular place. To this point, our goal has been to portray the salience of this social networks role, which has been overlooked by the neighborhood selection and housing search processes implicit in the traditional theories of segregation. Race has come up somewhat, but the point is that this is a general process with racial implications because of our stratified society. We now explore how social networks may specifically impact mobility in a way that perpetuates segregation.

On the face of it, individuals' reliance on social networks for information is race-neutral, as are the processes of neighborhood selection that are influenced by their desire to remain near their social networks. But of course, since the social networks comprising this information source and rationale are racially circumscribed, their neutrality is clearly superficial by virtue of segregation itself. Both the survey and in-depth interview data point to the varied ways in which social networks can shape residential outcomes. Once we overlay this observation with the observation that these networks are typically racially homogenous, the racial implications of this "neutral" force become apparent.

In the account given by Karen, the white woman whose family was the "leash pulling [her] back," we see how a "race-neutral" force can profoundly shape an outcome. When we return to her story in chapter 8, we will learn that where she lives is now predominantly African American. In some ways, then, Karen is the "exception that proves the rule": as a result of the pull to remain close to family, she ended up living in a neighborhood where she eventually (because of changes in the neighborhood racial composition) was in the racial minority. But typically when a residential decision is based on proximity to family, the outcome—at least in a residentially segregated metropolitan area like Chicago—is a move that perpetuates segregation. Thus, social networks are implicated in perpetuating segregation to the extent that these social networks are racially homogenous and their residential experiences are circumscribed.

Two recurrent themes of research on social networks are important here.[15] First, largely because of asymmetrical opportunities for interpersonal interaction, social networks tend to be made up of individuals who are similar in terms of race, ethnicity, and a variety of other sociodemographic characteristics. Second, because of this homophily principle and the importance of social networks in the flow of information, members of different sociodemographic groups tend to have access to very different bases of information about social and economic opportunities.[16]

In the context of residential decision-making, racial homophily within social networks often leads members of different races to rely on racially distinct social networks—and the disparate sets of residential experiences encompassed in these networks—in accumulating knowledge about residential options. As a result, people who initiate a search for a new place to live are likely to have substantially more information about the types of neighborhoods occupied by people with racial and ethnic backgrounds similar to their own. This information asymmetry can lead to racially circumscribed residential searches, with residential destinations defined to a large degree by the residential experiences of racially homogenous social networks. Given sharp racial differences in residential experiences, then, these network dynamics can reinforce racially disparate mobility outcomes. For example, black and white home-seekers may move into different types of neighborhoods simply because they are relying on different sets of social contacts, who have distinct patterns of residential experiences, to form their knowledge about, and impressions of, specific neighborhood options and housing units. The "leash" of social ties can also perpetuate segregation as individuals choose to move to, or remain in, neighborhoods occupied by members of their social network. Thus, segregation may be maintained, at least in part, by the operation of social network dynamics that directly and indirectly funnel members of each race toward neighborhoods occupied by their own group.

Hints of the possible role of social networks in residential outcomes and in the maintenance of segregation are available in data from the PSID. First, figure 4.1 summarizes the types of neighborhoods occupied by the kin networks of PSID householders. Specifically, we select those householders appearing in the PSID in the years between 1997 and 2013, and then, taking advantage of the multigenerational nature of the PSID, we calculate the average composition in a given year of census tracts occupied by parents, siblings, aunts, uncles, cousins, and grandparents in the same core family, as well as other PSID respondents who were connected to that family.[17] Because we take the average of these kin neighborhood characteristics across multiple annual observations for PSID householders, the results can be interpreted as the average racial composition of neighborhoods occupied by individual PSID householders between the years 1997 and 2013.

These data show that individuals from different racial and ethnic groups had extended family networks that occupied very different types of

Figure 4.1   Average Composition of Neighborhoods Occupied by
PSID Householders Who Are Members of Kin Networks,
by Race-Ethnicity, 1997–2013

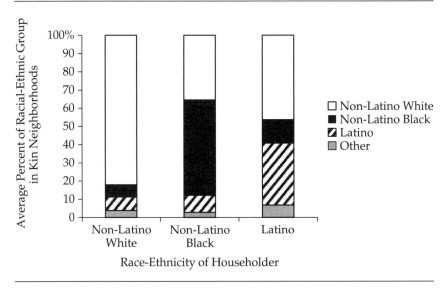

Source: Authors' calculations from the Panel Study of Income Dynamics (PSID 2016).

neighborhoods. For example, among white PSID householders, the average member of the extended kinship group lived in a neighborhood that was 82 percent white, 7 percent Latino, and just over 6 percent black. In contrast, the average kin neighborhood for black householders was only 35 percent white, 9 percent Latino, and 53 percent black. Put simply, these data reveal the completely unsurprising fact that members of different racial and ethnic groups have family networks that are heavily concentrated in neighborhoods with large proportions of the family's racial-ethnic group. By focusing only on family connections and not on the broader set of social connections (friends, coworkers, and so on), these data provide an incomplete picture of the potential role of social networks in shaping residential outcomes. Nevertheless, they suggest that members of different racial groups are tied into social networks that are defined by racially circumscribed residential experiences and that probably offer distinct bases of knowledge about neighborhood options.

 These differences in network experiences, of course, simply reflect the broader impact of residential segregation; racial and ethnic groups tend to be distributed across separate neighborhoods, and this creates, given

racial homogeneity within families, drastic racial and ethnic differences
in the geographic distribution of kin. Nevertheless, these figures highlight
the fact that members of different races are exposed, indirectly, to dramatically different kinds of neighborhoods through their kin networks. When
they visit parents and siblings, they are gathering information about those
neighborhoods that they may eventually draw on when constructing their
consideration sets.

In fact, data from the PSID provide at least circumstantial evidence that
individual mobility outcomes are significantly shaped by the racial composition of neighborhoods occupied by kin. For example, there is a close
association between the racial composition of neighborhoods selected
during a residential move and the composition of neighborhoods occupied by kin. Among those householders who moved to a different census
tract in the two-year period between PSID interviews, the bivariate correlation between the concentration of whites in the destination tract and
the average concentration of whites in tracts occupied by members of the
kin network is 0.61.[18] Similarly, the correlation between the concentration
of blacks in the destination tract and the average concentration of blacks
in neighborhoods occupied by kin members is 0.64, and the correlation
between the concentration of Latinos in the destination tract and the average concentration of Latinos in neighborhoods occupied by kin members
is 0.56. Thus, mobile households tend to move to neighborhoods that are
quite similar to those occupied by their kin.[19]

Moreover, as shown in figure 4.2, group differences in the location of
kin explain a sizable share of racial and ethnic differences in neighborhood
destinations. Again, this figure is based on an examination of residential
destinations for mobile householders living in one of our core metropolitan
areas and appearing in the PSID between 1997 and 2013. We use ordinary
least squares (OLS) regression to examine the links between mobility destinations, kin location, individual race, and a set of basic sociodemographic
controls implicated in past research as important destination determinants.
For illustration purposes, we focus on the concentration of white neighbors
in the tract of destination for these mobile householders, although similar
results are derived from models examining other measures of neighborhood racial composition.

The first set of bars, "no controls," shows the concentration of white
residents in destination tracts entered by white, black, and Latino PSID
householders who moved to a new neighborhood between sequential
biennial interviews. These bars show that, when they move, average white
householders move to a tract in which about 77 percent of the population is non-Latino white. In contrast, mobile Latino householders move to
neighborhoods that are, on average, about 45 percent non-Latino white,

Figure 4.2   Racial Composition of Destination Tracts for Mobile PSID
Householders, 1997–2013

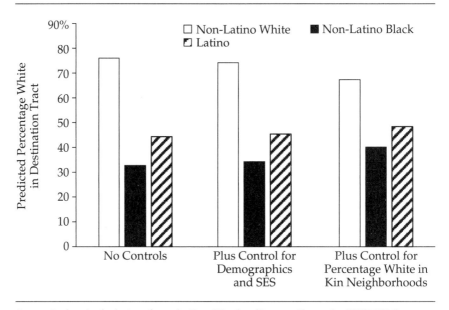

Source: Authors' calculations from the Panel Study of Income Dynamics (PSID 2016).

and mobile African Americans move to neighborhoods in which only
33 percent of the population is non-Latino white. As demonstrated in past
research, these racial differences in mobility destinations represent a key
mechanism in the maintenance of residential segregation by race. That is,
segregation persists largely because, when they move, members of different racial and ethnic groups tend to move to drastically different types of
neighborhoods.

Also consistent with past research, the second set of bars in figure 4.2
shows that this racial difference in destinations largely persists even when
we take into consideration group differences in household economic characteristics and other individual- and family-level predictors of mobility
outcomes.[20] After we control for education, income, family composition,
age, and a wide range of sociodemographic conditions known to affect
residential destinations, racial differences in destination characteristics
barely change from the "no controls" set of bars. Specifically, the gap
between the percentage white in the destinations of white movers and
the percentage white of the destinations of black movers declines from 44
to 40 percentage points when sociodemographic controls are introduced,

while the gap between white and Latino destinations drops from 32 to 29 points.

The substantial racial difference in destination outcomes that persists even after controlling for economic resources and other family and individual characteristics has typically been interpreted as reflecting the effects of unobserved group preferences or discrimination. That is, proponents of popular theoretical perspectives assume that black, white, and Latino householders with similar characteristics end up in different types of neighborhoods either because African Americans and Latinos have weaker preferences for neighborhoods with large concentrations of whites or are blocked from gaining access to such neighborhoods by the force of discriminatory treatment.

But these traditional arguments ignore a potentially important driver of segregation by overlooking the impact of kin location and other network dynamics. As shown in the third set of bars in figure 4.2, controlling for group differences in the average racial composition of kin explains a substantial share of the remaining group differences in the composition of neighborhood destinations. In fact, about one-third of both the black-white difference and the Latino-white difference in the concentration of whites in destination neighborhoods can be explained by group differences in the location of kin. Specifically, controlling for the concentration of whites in the average neighborhood occupied by members of the kinship network reduces the black-white difference in the concentration of white neighbors in destination tracts from 40 to 27 percentage points, and the Latino-white difference from 29 to 19 percentage points.

The bottom line is that the racial composition of neighborhoods occupied by kin appears to have a large impact on the racial composition of individuals' mobility destinations, above and beyond the effects of economic resources and other characteristics that affect residential outcomes. And a large part of the racial difference in mobility outcomes—a difference that is central to the maintenance of racial residential segregation—is reflective of the large group differences in the residential location of kin. Although the relative shortage of data prevents us from fully testing the mechanisms involved in the link between kin residential experiences and the mobility outcomes of individual PSID householders, these results are highly consistent with the general notion that residential decision-making is influenced by information that flows through family ties or by the "leash" of social networks. At the very least, we are able to conclude that a significant part of the racial disparities in residential outcomes that continuously reinforce residential segregation by race may reflect the influence of social network dynamics that are completely ignored in popular debates on the topic.

These kin ties and information may pull movers to specific neighbor-hoods occupied by members of their family. As our interviewee Karen put it, kin ties are the "leash pulling on people." But the mechanisms behind these kin effects are likely to be more subtle as well, affecting mobility outcomes by shaping the construction of the consideration set and provid-ing a disproportionate level of knowledge about neighborhoods occupied by coethnics. That is, white movers probably end up moving to predomi-nantly white neighborhoods in part because they gain knowledge about conditions and housing opportunities in such areas through their social networks. In contrast, Latino and black movers end up in destinations with relatively few whites because the location of their kin and social networks affords them information about neighborhoods where white populations are relatively small. Although data do not exist to fully test the argument, it is reasonable to expect that residential outcomes, as well as broader pat-terns of segregation, are similarly shaped by the experiences of the broader network of friends, coworkers, and acquaintances.

In sum, this chapter has highlighted the social dynamics of housing searches and neighborhood selection processes about which popular theo-ries of segregation are completely silent. Social networks appear to shape information about, and evaluations of, possible residential outcomes in ways that produce racially distinct residential processes that continu-ally reinforce segregation. Even if seemingly race-neutral in origin, these social-network forces are far from racially neutral in their consequences. The traditional theories of segregation are inadequate in that they over-look this engine of segregation. In the next chapter, we draw attention to another such engine.

Chapter 5 | "From What I See": The Structural Part of the Theory

AARON, OUR SUBURBAN homeowner introduced in chapter 3, told us that he knows about communities "from what I see." This pithy phrase masks the fact that these lived experiences are many and varied: they can be past experiences or current ones, and they can come about through regular occurrences, such as a commute to get to a job, or because one's job itself requires traversing through many different places, such as work as a delivery person or a home health care aide. Experiences that go beyond the daily and the routine can also generate impressions and perceptions. Our lived experiences, above and beyond the information they impart to us, also shape our priorities—we can be tethered to the place we have lived in and experienced in ways that are a function not just of wanting to be near family and friends but of simply wanting to be in a familiar place.

THE PRE-SEARCH STAGE: LIVED EXPERIENCES SHAPE OUR PERCEPTIONS

The wide-ranging information and priorities that flow from our lived experiences shape our residential outcomes in ways that are independent of economics, racial residential preferences, and discrimination. Although some aspects of our lived experiences are racialized, these experiences need to be viewed as additional drivers of segregation beyond the drivers emphasized in the traditional "big three" theories. Our in-depth interview data can be used to capture the many ways in which people pick up perceptions and impressions of a neighborhood or community simply through living there. People sometimes get their information about places "just from driving through," which can be an uneventful

85

experience. For example, Anna explained how she knew what she did about Aurora:

> Driven by there but never actually stopped in Aurora anywhere. . . . There's an area I think—where is it? I think when you first come here, south Aurora, I guess it would be, not that nice. I think it's nicer as you go north. The housing gets nice. The streets are nicer and cleaner.

This impression contrasts sharply with her impression of communities south of Chicago—including Hammond, Dalton, and Calumet City—which she also learned about by just passing through:

> I've driven by there, and it looks like a very crime-ridden neighborhood, especially Calumet City. . . . It's not very well kept. There's people hanging outside. You know when the intentions are good and when they're not. People just hanging out there by the street corner doesn't make me feel very safe.

People are also minimally exposed to places when they search for jobs or deal with other employment-related issues. For example, Claudia went to Hinsdale "for a drug test for a job" and to Melrose Park for "unemployment." During her interview, Destiny pulled out her phone and used the GPS app to tell her interviewer the places she had driven through in her recent job search; all of them were white suburbs or upper-income Chicago neighborhoods where her potential home health care clients lived. Despite being a very fleeting experience, such exposure can leave a lasting impression, as Destiny explained when asked about Jefferson Park; according to her phone, that was a place she had been passing through the day before the interview:

> I really just kinda was focused on where I was going and getting there. I think that the neighborhood is . . . you don't see what you would see on the West Side of Chicago, people standing out selling drugs. . . . It seemed to be a lot different and safer than the areas I've lived in.

People are also exposed to places when they go to cultural events or attend their children's sporting events. Volunteer work often brings people from the suburbs into the city of Chicago itself, and city and suburban people visit different suburbs for summer festivals, county fairs, Christmas walks, and the like. People also learn about places because their job takes them to different neighborhoods, such as HVAC installers, truck drivers with widespread daily routes, people who work for companies that visit public schools, or home health care workers who visit their patients. In other words, the pre-search stage involves a huge variety of experiences that feed into the information and impressions that people have of potential places to live.

Another interesting pattern that emerges from our in-depth interviews is that moving to a different metropolitan area does not completely dissolve the influence of lived experiences on community perceptions. In our interviews, newcomers to Chicago sometimes recalled their experiences in *other* cities, or even what they knew about cities in general, to draw conclusions about Chicago-area communities. Tom, who moved to Chicago a few months before he was interviewed, illustrated this when he was asked for his impression of Juliet, where he had never been: "I mean, I don't really have any ideas about what it's like out there. Just sort of a general idea about how things would be if Chicago were like most cities."

David was another relative newcomer to Chicago who grew up in New York City but also spent time in a moderately sized city in the South. He frequently referred to his experiences in these cities and described how they were similar to—or different from—what he had experienced and perceived in Chicago-area communities. For example, when asked to talk about Hyde Park, he had this to say:

Hyde Park [is] viewed as being its own little enclave or kind of . . . separated. . . . It's viewed as being very different . . . from the rest of the South Side. Very similar to like Striver's Row in Harlem . . . or Englewood Cliffs in California. I think it's Englewood Heights, or whatever it is, or the Hills. Baldwin Hills, for example.

At another point in the interview, David said:

When I got to Chicago—although I initially remember saying to myself, *Oh, wow, it's gonna be like a wild city out there, you don't wanna mess with the wrong person, blah blah blah, etcetera, etcetera.* It's like every other urban American large city, to an extent.

The point here is that lived experiences that accumulate through living in a metro area—or in some cases other areas—have an impact on the information and perceptions that people have about places. Taken together, this information and set of perceptions form the backdrop against which any future housing searches unfold—that is, they help constitute the pre-search stage of a search.

STAGE 1: LIVED EXPERIENCES INFLUENCE OUR CONSIDERATION SET

Turning to the point when an active search is undertaken, lived experiences clearly help shape the construction of a consideration set, since these experiences shape our impressions of the quality of life in particular communities, as well as their composition and opportunity structures.

Survey data of housing searchers reveal the profound influence of lived experiences on the process that unfolds. In a survey in Syracuse, New York, in the late 1970s, Gary Talarchek found that 69 percent of recent movers relied on their "own prior knowledge of the Syracuse area" in their housing search. Moreover, a follow-up question revealed that more than one in three searchers turned *first* to their "prior knowledge of the area" when they undertook a search. Finally, when asked about their source of information specifically about neighborhood features like distance to work, school quality, and the people in the neighborhood, "prior knowledge" was the source most frequently cited.[1]

While these survey data give us a sense of the prevalence of relying on prior knowledge, our in-depth interviews affirm its importance and suggest what kinds of experiences contribute to prior knowledge. Prompted to reflect on which places would be possibilities for their consideration set, our in-depth interview participants talked about a range of lived experiences that informed their assessments. Sometimes these lived experiences stemmed from routines: for example, Luisa, who lives in the Chicago neighborhood of Little Village, drives through South Side neighborhoods to get to her school. She was asked why she would eliminate Archer Heights—a neighborhood just south of hers—from her consideration set:

> LUISA: I don't want to live in an area that is too much African American. . . . I mean, I don't have a problem with them. I know a lot of African Americans, but I don't feel that I will feel comfortable around [them].
>
> INTERVIEWER: Is that how you feel about this area in general? [*pointing to the South Side*]
>
> LUISA: Yeah, I mean, all the South Side is very mainly African Americans, and now that I drive around there and I go to school around there, I see that it is.

Other impressions come from not-so-routine experiences, such as accidentally ending up in a place. That is how Joann came to rule out Englewood:

> JOANN: I've driven through there once by accident. [*laughs*] I just never felt more conspicuous in my life.

INTERVIEWER: Okay, conspicuous because of . . .

JOANN: I was white and no one else was. Driving a white German car where no one else does. [*laughs*] I was just glad it's daylight. How do I get outta here? Where's the closest— how do I get back to where I need to be, cuz I was trying to get over here to get outta town, and I was in this neighborhood and trying to take a shortcut and that was not very—I don't have a GPS.

Luisa's and Joann's lived experiences resulted in their elimination of certain communities from their consideration sets, but the opposite happened with Beth:

I'm a North Sider. I was born and raised on the North Side. Generally south of the 00 line wasn't really a consideration.[2] Not so much because I would absolutely not live there, just because that's what I was familiar with. Once I started working farther south and started exploring more neighborhoods south, that's when I started opening up my search south.

Beth was the unusual white participant who had lived in many different neighborhoods where she was a minority, probably in part because her boyfriend was African American. But as her story illustrates, it was the "daily routines" that her job required that pushed her outside of her "comfort zone" on a regular basis. Also revealing is that Beth described these job-related experiences as having served to overcome the influence of her early life experiences and expand her consideration set.

Frank, a working-class Latino, is a particularly vivid example of how job-related experiences—he installed HVAC and cable/satellite systems— can inform one's community perceptions. Belying the expectation that, as a working-class Latino, he would have had relatively little direct experience in upper-class white communities, his job had led him to develop a highly disaggregated picture of several far-flung white suburbs that he otherwise would have been likely to lump together and presume to be equally unwelcoming to people of color. Frank initially said that he spent little time in the northern suburbs, but upon probing by the interviewer, he related that his job had taken him to several of these suburbs and he had in fact formed quite strong impressions of them:

FRANK: Okay, Barrington Hills. You wanna know a place [that is] our version of a truly secluded, reclusive neighborhood? Barrington Hills.

INTERVIEWER: Really? Why do you say that?

FRANK: Them fuckers, they got money. But everybody who lives—well, in a certain part of it, like the northwest part of, the northwest corner of Barrington Hills—they got money. They [his employer] used to send me out there. It was—I mean these people are like ritzy. They really think their shit doesn't stink. . . . That's based on how much money they make. That's not—. . . I don't know how they were raised or whatnot. This all stems from having money.

Crystal Lake, they're not that bad out there. Zion, in Zion a lot of people built their own homes so they designed it. So I've been in people's houses that have their own basketball courts, that have pools on the first floor, and on the second floor are the rooms. It's— I mean, it's sorta cool, but that's not the way I would have my house. Anyway, Zion tripped out houses. Barrington Hills, them people, man. There's not one person I ever actually slightly liked in Barrington Hills.

INTERVIEWER: Why is that?

FRANK: Cuz they honestly think their shit doesn't stink. They— I'm like, I'm Mexican, so I'm like the gardener to them. I don't know. I don't accept—if they tell—in the slightest if they speak to me in that manner . . . mmmm . . . fuck you. Well, not at that time, no. That's the bottom line. Now I am . . . but at that time, I bit my tongue and I, fine, whatever, blah blah blah, we'll send someone else out here then. We'll send the white guys out here cuz that's the way it is. I'm telling you that they are—they're racist to a point. . . . It's just the way it is.

INTERVIEWER: Okay, so you said Crystal Lake wasn't that bad?

FRANK: No. Crystal Lake was cool. Everybody I met in Crystal Lake at that—I never had a problem in Crystal Lake, and we did a lot of work out there.

Thus, Frank brought his work experiences to bear on his impressions and knowledge of communities. Explaining that not all "rich" (white) communities were the same, he noted that some were distinctively racist as well. Clearly, if Frank won the lottery, he would consider living in Crystal Lake—but never Barrington Hills.

The Tether of Lived Experiences

Lived experiences result in the accumulation of a substantial knowledge base about different communities. We argue that this information informs and shapes the neighborhood selection and housing search processes. But the realities of "living life" also shape preferences about which communities to live in through the familiarity and practicalities of everyday life, which build up ties and connections to institutions and also, as described in chapter 4, to people. All of this works together to tether people to the community they are in, thus geographically defining their consideration set—and not always because of the people.

Art is a middle-aged white man who lives in a neighborhood in Chicago, and he exemplifies the idea that lived experiences—even absent social network ties—can tether people to a place. When asked how he ended up living where he does, he explained:

> Well, I grew up in Lakeview. And I ended up with the family house, in the end. My siblings moved away, and married of course. My parents died. I ended up with the family house. And it was . . . well, I grew up there, I went to school around there, I worked around there. It was just too big for me. A nine-room family home. I'm not married. It was just too expensive. The taxes were really high because it's—whatever the term is—gentrified or whatever now, in that area. So I wanted to stay in Lakeview when I was selling. But taxes are too expensive. I tried to stay in close proximity. This area is like ten to fifteen minutes away, if I want to go back for restaurants, or friends, or whatever. And that's how—that's basically how I ended up over there. I'm just west of where I used to live.

Later, when Art was asked why he didn't live in some of the other places he had identified as places where he would consider living, he reiterated the role of lived experiences in shaping his preferences:

> Well, I've lived here all my life, in Lakeview. I was born at [street names]. Then my parents moved a quarter-block west. So I lived all my life here, until about six years ago. So this is really—from here to here, that's the only time I really remember moving. Because I was eleven months old when they moved from wherever they lived, to the house [I grew up in]. So this is the first time that I ever remember moving. Selling the home and moving. So, I mean, I'm not a person that, actually I don't like change a lot. Who's to say that if you move here to here, that you're going to be any happier or more content, or like the neighborhood more? Perception is, maybe you will. But perception and actually doing are two separate things. I don't like a lot of change. I like stability in my life. I like familiar things.

Denise, an in-depth interview participant, explained that she and her husband had recently moved to a new home not far from their prior one because of "the conveniences, and things with our home-based business, and friends, and things like we had built up over the years." Although the leash of networks and the tether of lived experiences often get tangled up, it is clearly the case that mere familiarity and convenience, the results of daily living, are also influential.

The importance of daily activities in shaping housing preferences is probably one reason why individuals tend to relocate in neighborhoods close to their previous dwelling. In fact, among PSID respondents who remained in the same metropolitan area when they moved, the average distance between the origin and destination neighborhoods was only about two miles, and about 39 percent remained in the same neighborhood when they changed dwellings.[3] To be sure, the residential neighborhood of origin defines just a small part of the overall daily round for many individuals, yet it clearly helps to shape residential decision-making.[4] Put simply, the geographic locations that define our daily activities are likely to become important centers of gravity (or tethers) in our housing searches and residential decisions. In these different ways, lived experiences shape the set of communities that people will and will not consider as desirable destinations.

STAGE 2: LIVED EXPERIENCES PROVIDE INFORMATION ON SPECIFIC HOUSING UNITS

In addition to lived experiences giving us opportunities to form impressions of communities and creating preferences—impressions and preferences that we use to filter out some places—lived experiences can also influence the second stage of a housing search: when we are identifying and evaluating potential housing units within the neighborhoods in our consideration set. We are more likely to learn—either directly or through our contacts—about housing opportunities in the neighborhoods in which we live, work, go to school, shop, worship, and play. Data from the 2011 and 2013 American Housing Survey are suggestive of the role of lived experiences. Specifically, about 10 percent of recent movers found their new home after seeing a "For Sale" or "For Rent" sign; about the same percentage reported that they used a real estate agent or rental agency. Identifying housing options through conversations with neighbors and coworkers is another form of direct exposure to local housing opportunities. All of these highly localized search methods are likely to be mainly relevant to finding housing in the neighborhoods in which the mover spends time. Our in-depth interviews with Chicago residents point to the different ways in which the "daily round" can identify an available housing unit. Alexia, a Latina renter, explained:

ALEXIA: If I'm walking by and I see a "FOR RENT" sign, you never know. Because they didn't advertise in the paper doesn't mean that it might not be good, so I've found an apartment like that before. . . . It was in Cicero. It was, uh, near my mom's, and it was $550, three bedrooms, living room, dining room, kitchen, back porch, full attic, complete use of backyard, the garage, all utilities included, a balcony. I would have been a fool not to take it.

INTERVIEWER: And you found it just by walking.

ALEXIA: I happened to be walking by and I asked, and no deposit. And, um, it was a young couple. I could throw a party on the weekend and it didn't bother them. So . . . they kept to themselves, I kept to myself. Their daughter played with my daughter. It was really convenient. You know, it was really good.

Alexia's account highlights the role of lived experiences *and* social networks in shaping housing outcomes, since she found the unit because it was in a neighborhood where she often spent time visiting her mother. Presumably, if her mother had not lived there, she never would have "happened to be walking by" this available unit.

Maria, another Latina renter, told a similar story when she was asked, "What stood out about your search?"

What stood out was that it was right across the street from my mom's. The rent wasn't that bad. It was $550. . . . And the house outside, itself, looked nice, you know. . . . The landlord had been taking care of it. What caught my eye right away was that it was right across from my mom's. And it took me three months. At the third month of my searching around the area, I happen to get this one. He had finally put the sign up, and I grabbed it.

Although Maria had a lengthy housing search, she got this unit because she was regularly at her mother's home, not because she just "happened" to get it. Finding this unit was clearly no accident. Her daily round exposed her to it, it was advertised through a sign in a window, and it was exactly where she needed her next home to be—near her mother.

Quite independent of *racial* residential preferences, these kinds of lived experiences shape people's residential preferences for certain kinds of

. The mere fact of these patterns, however, though seemingly
ral, has deeply racial consequences in segregated places—a point
to which we now turn.

RACIALIZED CONSEQUENCES
OF LIVED EXPERIENCES

The fact that our experiences in a geographic area help to shape our knowledge and preferences for particular neighborhoods, our perceptions of residential options, and our residential decisions has important implications for
the maintenance of segregation because race has an impact on all of these
experiences. Although research on the topic is still developing, there is growing evidence of sharp racial differences in the geographic location and scope
of daily activities.[5] For example, in their research on common daily destinations for a large sample of individuals that included where they went for
work, school, recreation, and other activities, Malia Jones and Anne Pebley
found that members of different racial and ethnic groups not only live in
separate areas but also tend to conduct their daily lives in separate spaces.[6]
And importantly, these daily activity spaces are almost as circumscribed by
race as are residential neighborhoods: people carry out their daily rounds
in geographic areas in which their own racial or ethnic group is overrepre-
sented. These patterns persist even after accounting for racial and ethnic differences in education, income, and other individual characteristics. Whites,
for example, tend to live, work, go to school, and shop near other whites,
while African Americans, Latinos, and Asians tend to carry out these daily
activities among large shares of members of their own groups.

These racial differences in activity space are of little surprise to most
observers of metropolitan life, but the implications for the maintenance
of residential segregation by race remain underappreciated by traditional
theories of segregation, which have focused on discrimination, preferences, and economics. This segregation of daily activity space means that
members of different racial groups come into contact with drastically
different neighborhoods and residential options as a function of the fact
that they live, work, and conduct their daily lives in somewhat separate
geographic spaces. Thus, African Americans would develop the greatest
quantity and quality of information about neighborhood conditions and
housing options in black areas, while whites would develop direct knowledge about the predominantly white areas in which they live out their
daily lives.

Viewed another way, drastic racial and ethnic differences in the neighborhood location and mobility outcomes that continually reinforce residential segregation by race should be seen partly as a function of group

differences in activity spaces. Importantly, these are likely to operate independently of the effects of economic affordability, experiences of discrimination, and what we typically think of as racial residential preferences.

While currently available data do not allow for a complete test of these ideas, there are data that provide strong hints about them. For example, the link between the types of neighborhoods that individuals enter when they move and the characteristics of the neighborhoods they leave may reveal the consequences of racial differences in neighborhood experiences. Existing research shows that the composition of the daily activity space is strongly correlated with the composition of the neighborhood of residence.[7] Thus, partly because neighborhoods with similar racial compositions tend to be highly clustered in metropolitan space, individuals living in neighborhoods with high concentrations of a particular group are likely to have activity spaces that, to a certain extent, are defined by relatively large shares of that group as well. This consistent exposure to neighborhoods of a particular composition is likely to produce disproportionate knowledge of conditions and housing options in those areas, thereby increasing the likelihood that the individual will end up in such an area when they move. In short, lived experiences in a segregated city beget housing processes that beget more segregation.

This dynamic is certainly consistent with basic patterns of residential mobility among householders in the PSID. As the solid line in figure 5.1 indicates, there is a strong association between the racial composition of the neighborhoods that people leave when they move and the racial composition of the neighborhoods they enter. In fact, the correlation between the concentration of own-group populations in the origin and destination neighborhoods is 0.69. This is a common finding: individuals not only tend to originate in neighborhoods that are dominated by residents from their own group, but when they move they tend to move to areas that are similarly racially homogenous.[8]

Although we are unable to directly account for other possible reasons for this link (such as discrimination or preferences), the dotted line in figure 5.1 shows that this strong connection between racial composition in origin and destination neighborhoods persists after controlling for socioeconomic resources, family characteristics, and other important factors. This simple link is basically consistent with the potential influence of the daily round in shaping the patterns of residential knowledge that, in turn, inform housing decisions. To the extent that the composition of people's residential neighborhoods reflects the types of neighborhoods that are part of their daily activities, they may end up moving between similar neighborhoods simply because these are the types of neighborhoods that they have the most information about. Moreover, the neighborhoods encompassed by

Figure 5.1   Association Between Racial Composition of Origin and
Destination Neighborhoods for Mobile PSID Householders,
1997–2013

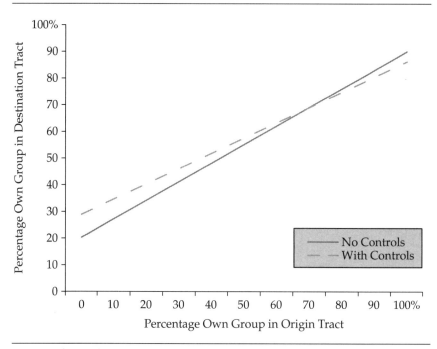

Source: Authors' calculations from the Panel Study of Income Dynamics (PSID 2016).

their daily activity space become comfortable and preferred destinations because ties and familiarity are built up there.

Interestingly, this basic relationship between origin-neighborhood and destination-neighborhood racial composition differs depending on the distance of the move. Among those moving less than five miles, the correlation between the racial own-group concentration in the origin and destination tracts is 0.71. Among those moving more than fifty miles away, the correspondence is still pronounced, at 0.63, but less so. For those moving over longer distances—either because their activity space put them in contact with more distant residential options or because they moved to a new neighborhood outside of their original activity space—the connection between origins and destinations is considerably weaker. Such moves are, of course, the exception more than the rule; individuals more often move over short distances and tend to move to neighborhoods with racial and ethnic compositions similar to the neighborhood they left.

Although the geographically defined daily round is likely to be important in determining exposure to specific housing options and therefore defining the geographic location of housing searches, the lived experiences that affect residential outcomes are likely to develop over the entire life course. For example, people's residential experiences as children, adolescents, and young adults form an important source of knowledge of the various neighborhoods in the metropolitan area. Individuals are likely to have more information about residential options in neighborhoods with which they have had direct experience and to want to stay near the familiar. Our lived experiences also shape our residential decision-making by allowing us to continually develop neighborhood perceptions and gather information about the characteristics of neighborhoods and their suitability as potential destinations.

The importance of early life experiences for residential outcomes is reflected in several recent studies linking the continuity of residential advantage and disadvantage across generations, as well as in patterns of neighborhood location in the PSID.[9] The long temporal sweep of the PSID allows us to examine how residential experiences in adolescence shape residential location during the first three decades of adulthood—after people leave their parental home and establish their own household. To highlight how these early life experiences maintain residential segregation, which is often measured in terms of residential parity with whites, we examine the link between the concentration of non-Hispanic whites in the neighborhood of residence in adolescence and the parallel white concentration in the neighborhoods occupied during adulthood. Specifically, table 5.1 displays select coefficients from a set of multilevel regression models predicting the racial composition—here measured as percentage white[10]—in the neighborhood occupied during adulthood as a function of the average racial composition of neighborhoods experienced during the adolescent years (thirteen to seventeen years old).[11]

We start with a model (model 1 in table 5.1) in which the only predictor of neighborhood racial composition in adulthood is individual race. The story is familiar: in comparison to white householders, the average black householder in the average year of adulthood lives in a neighborhood in which the percentage of the population that is white is over 53 points lower ($b = -53.523$).[12] In model 2 of table 5.1, we add a predictor for the average concentration of white respondents across the tracts occupied by respondents when they were adolescents. The coefficient for this variable ($b = 0.693$) points to a strong connection between the neighborhoods in adolescence and adulthood: each additional percentage point in the

Table 5.1   Selected Coefficients from Multilevel Regression Model Predicting Neighborhood Percentage Non-Latino White in Adulthood for Black and White PSID Householders

Predictors	Racially Pooled Models			Black Heads Only	White Heads Only
	Individual Race Only (Model 1)	Plus Adolescent Neighborhoods (Model 2)	Plus All Controls (Model 3)	All Controls Plus Interactions (Model 4)	All Controls Plus Interactions (Model 5)
Black (1 = yes)	−53.523***	−12.638***	−11.277***		
	(0.393)	(0.461)	(0.460)		
Average tract percentage white, age thirteen to seventeen		0.693***	0.594***	0.551***	0.556***
		(0.006)	(0.006)	(0.011)	(0.014)
Interactions: tract percentage white age thirteen to seventeen					
By age				−0.017***	−0.011***
				(0.001)	(0.001)
By high school graduate				−0.025*	−0.018
				(0.010)	(0.014)
By college graduate				−0.045*	−0.053**
				(0.018)	(0.018)
By black-white segregation				0.151***	0.100*
				(0.045)	(0.045)
By moved to a different metro				−0.433***	−0.327***
				(0.014)	(0.014)

Source: Authors' calculations from the Panel Study of Income Dynamics (PSID 2016).
Notes: Slope coefficients with standard errors are in parentheses. N = 87,264. Models 3, 4, and 5 also control for parental education and income during adolescence, age at adult observation, gender, year of observation, marital status, presence of children, family income in adulthood, educational attainment, homeownership, metropolitan racial composition, and metropolitan segregation. Multilevel models account for clustering of observations at individual and metropolitan levels.
*$p < .05$; **$p < .01$; ***$p < .001$ (two-tailed tests)

concentration of white neighbors during adolescence is associated with an increase of about seven-tenths of a percentage point in the concentration of white residents during adulthood. Thus, even after they move away and start their own households, individuals tend to end up in neighborhoods that are remarkably similar, at least in terms of their racial composition, to the types of places they experienced during adolescence.

Perhaps most important is that this continuity explains a very large share of the overall racial difference in the composition of neighborhoods in adulthood. This can be seen by comparing the coefficients for individual race in models 1 and 2 of table 5.1: controlling for the composition of neighborhoods during adolescence explains over three-fourths of the racial difference in adult racial composition ($(53.523 - 12.638)/53.523) = 0.764$). Among black and white adults growing up in similar types of neighborhoods, white respondents live in neighborhoods with concentrations of white neighbors that are, on average, about 12 percentage points higher than the average among black respondents. Important racial stratification remains, but adolescent residential experiences clearly play an important role in determining where people live in adulthood.

Of course, the strong link between adolescent context and adult residential outcomes could be attributable to many different factors. For example, given the effects of neighborhood context on educational attainment, employment, and income, it could be that individuals growing up in predominantly white neighborhoods are better able to accumulate the socioeconomic resources necessary to gain access as adults to neighborhoods containing larger shares of whites. Similarly, those spending their adolescence in mostly white areas may develop other sociodemographic characteristics associated with the choice of residence in a white neighborhood in adulthood. Along these lines, it could be that residential experiences early in life influence adult residential outcomes by shaping racial residential preferences. However, it is also likely that residential experiences during the adolescent years shape subsequent residential decision-making by shaping individuals' knowledge about different types of residential options.

The absence of data combining information on residential preferences, economic characteristics, perceptions and knowledge of neighborhood options, and actual residential location throughout the life course prevents us from fully adjudicating between the potential mechanisms linking adolescent and adult residential context. At the same time, the results presented in model 3 of table 5.1 provide evidence that this continuity of residential context cannot be fully explained by the mechanisms implicated in traditional theoretical arguments or by a wide range of other factors affecting residential sorting. For example, to account for the possibility that the adolescent and adult contexts are jointly influenced by the socioeconomic status of the family of origin, we control for the average education of the individual's parents and their average family income during adolescence. Similarly, in order to test the possibility—drawn from a basic economic model—that the adolescent context affects adult neighborhood location by shaping the individual's own socioeconomic trajectory, we control for the individual's educational attainment and household income at the adult observation. At the individual level, we also control for the age of the respondent at the adult observation, the period in which he or she was born (to control for temporal trends in the composition of neighborhoods generally), gender, marital status, presence of children, employment and student status, homeownership, and whether the respondent moved to a different metropolitan area from adolescence to adulthood. To account for potential influences of broader opportunity structures, we also control for the racial composition and level of black-white segregation in the broader metropolitan area of residence during adulthood.

Even with this full range of controls, the link between adolescent and adult residential context changes little, from 0.693 in model 2 to 0.594 in model 3. Thus, among those who come from families with similar resources and who have similar individual-, family-, and metropolitan-level characteristics in adulthood, the connection between adolescent neighborhood composition and adult neighborhood composition remains pronounced. So even though we know that adolescent neighborhood experiences help to shape neighborhood location later in life by affecting educational attainment, income, and other adult characteristics, there is clearly more going on.

The PSID data also provide strong hints that the profound link between adolescent and adult neighborhood outcomes may partly reflect the accumulation of uneven knowledge of neighborhood options over the life course. That is, there are clues that individuals end up, as adults, in neighborhoods that are similar in terms of racial composition to the types of places in which they lived as kids because these early life experiences create greater familiarity with these types of neighborhoods and the housing opportunities they contain. Again, in the absence of direct measures of what individuals know about various types of neighborhoods, never mind specific areas, these clues, coming mainly from observed variation in the effects of adolescent neighborhoods, are largely indirect. Nevertheless, they are quite consistent, in several ways.

First, the relationship between adolescent and adult contexts diminishes with age during adulthood. The significant negative interaction between the racial composition of adolescent neighborhoods and age for both black and white householders (table 5.1, models 4 and 5, respectively) indicates that the link between adolescent and adult residential experiences is strongest in early adulthood, when residential experiences beyond those in adolescence are limited. As individuals age and accumulate experiences in a wider range of neighborhoods through their own mobility and daily routine, the grip of adolescent residential experiences on residential context in adulthood may be loosened. Recall that Beth, for instance, was raised a "North Sider" but was exposed, as she became an adult and entered the workforce, to neighborhoods on the South Side, which "opened up her search south."

Second, education significantly moderates the link between adolescent and adult residential experiences. Earlier research by Gary Becker and Theodore Schultz and more recent work by Catherine Ross and John Mirowsky support the argument that education increases problem-solving and information-gathering skills, which are useful beyond just the accumulation of economic resources.[13] This benefit is probably reflected in the fact that education leads individuals to utilize a larger set of information sources, including in their assessments of residential options. This wider set of sources would lessen the impact of residential knowledge derived simply from residential experiences accumulated during early childhood and adolescence, thus reducing the effect of adolescent context on adult residential location. The significant interactions between educational attainment and adolescent context shown in models 4 and 5 of table 5.1 are consistent with this idea. Among both black and white householders with at least a college education, the association between adolescent and adult neighborhood contexts is substantially weaker than among those with lower levels of education.

Our in-depth interview with Destiny, an African American single mother who has lived her entire life in segregated black neighborhoods on the South and West Sides of Chicago, brings life to one way in which education can change community knowledge and perceptions. From her classroom experiences at a community college, Destiny has white informants who have told her what it would be like to live in predominantly white places—in her example, Lincoln Park, an overwhelmingly white and wealthy neighborhood in Chicago. She described the reception she would probably get there:

> DESTINY: I think it would—they would be wary. They would just kind of watch. They probably wouldn't verbally say it, and you probably would get some people with some smiles that welcome you or whatever, but a lot of people would be kind of wary seeing you there, because they wanna—they have to see you and know you and kinda get your background. It's always the nosy ones that'll come over and then tell everybody else in the neighborhood watch what's going on. There's always

the investigator that'll come and see what you're like. Okay, we got a new neighbor. Okay, let's have a party and invite the new neighbor over so we can see what they're like. [laughs] There'll always be that one to be able to tell you, "Hey, they're a really good person. They seem to be nice. The family's upkept" and stuff like that. Then they would kinda blend in with you, but until then people would kind of watch you real close.

INTERVIEWER: What informs that belief?

DESTINY: I think just because I got a lot of—I have some Caucasian friends, and so being in school has helped me out a lot. At first I only knew people that grew up in my neighborhoods and stuff like that, because I didn't leave my neighborhood. When I went back to school and went to college, and got to meeting different people and socializing with different people, you kind of find out.

Destiny's insights are interesting because she has never lived in a predominantly white neighborhood, but through her higher education experience she has social networks that cross racial boundaries. These networks have made her more knowledgeable about the nuances of how she would be treated in white neighborhoods.

A third clue about the role of knowledge in shaping the link between adolescent and adult residential contexts is in the effect of metropolitan area segregation on that link. As indicated by the interactions between adolescent residential context and metropolitan segregation in models 4 and 5 of table 5.1, the link between neighborhood percentage white in adolescence and neighborhood percentage white in adulthood is stronger for those individuals living in cities like Detroit and Cleveland that, as reflected in their high scores on the index of dissimilarity, are more residentially segregated; this link is substantially weaker for individuals living in places like Phoenix and Seattle, where black-white segregation is lower. Although the stronger continuity of residential context across the life course for those living in highly segregated metropolitan areas may reflect any number of structural forces, including high levels of discrimination, it is also consistent with arguments that highlight the importance of neighborhood knowledge. In the most segregated areas, adolescent residential and daily experiences are likely to be especially circumscribed by race, such that individuals develop highly restrictive neighborhood knowledge and thus become less likely to move outside of racially defined neighborhoods in adulthood. In contrast, in metropolitan areas that are less racially stratified, adolescents are likely to be exposed to more neighborhood diversity, regardless of the composition of their neighborhood of residence, and this exposure allows them to develop knowledge about, and move into, neighborhoods that are racially distinct from those in which they grew up.

Destiny's analysis of her own residential trajectory provides a poignant example, illustrating that what people are exposed to with respect to their neighborhoods and communities—particularly early in life—not only shapes the mundane aspects of a housing search but can also constitute the very essence of what a person aspires to be or do in life, especially in a deeply segregated city like Chicago. Her story highlights the effect of extremely geographically circumscribed exposures and routines on what is imagined as possible—not simply *where* one might live, but also *what* one could do in life. Destiny lives in a very disadvantaged South Side neighborhood but likes to spend time in the Loop, a preference she explained this way:

> DESTINY: I think being in the Loop is just lovely. There's plenty of window-shopping you can do. [*laughs*] Which women love. You get to fantasize a little bit, especially when you don't have the money. [*laughs*] You get to see all this nice stuff, and sometimes you might even be able to go in a store and try it on and picture yourself being able to do more with your life. So that you can obtain some of those things. I think going to the Loop is always a getaway from being on the West Side or the South Side. It was a place where you can really think about bettering yourself and obtaining some of the things that you see. . . .
>
> INTERVIEWER: Anything else about the Loop?
>
> DESTINY: No, it's just, for me, it's just a place to get away. It's my getaway, and my mind can travel a little bit, because by me being in school, sometimes stuff get real tough, and I wanna go a lot farther than what I am right now. Going to the Loop just kinda lets me see what I can obtain and what the future holds for me if I just stick and stay and continue with my education.

Indeed, Destiny pointed out how her lived experiences and exposure to places outside of the poor neighborhood she grew up in shaped who she is today:

> If my family wouldn't have been out south [South Side of Chicago], I think I never would have been anywhere but right here on the West Side. [The West

Side] is my comfort zone, and I had never been taken out of that. For a very long time, I wouldn't even go to the Loop. I knew nothing about how to get downtown or what to do downtown. People's mind-set get stuck right there in their comfort zone. You don't go outside of that. Since I've been grown, I've been trying to stray out and do some stuff by myself. . . . But normally you just stay right there where you know. That's not a good thing, though. . . . I was afraid to expand my mind, meet new people, and try new things because I was stuck right there in my neighborhood. Those were my comfort zones. Going out beyond any of that was scary for me. . . . I would never go back to the heart of the West Side . . . because my mind has expanded so much more since I was there. I could see something so much better, so why would I subject myself, as well as my children, to that environment if I didn't have to? When I was there, I dropped out of school and had all these kids and stuff. Now that I've had a chance to go back to school and see something different in life, it's like, "Why go backwards?" . . . It took me a long time to get that, believe me. Seriously, because once you get stuck in these neighborhoods, your mind-set is so just—you get to become hopeless if you don't continue right away. I got caught up, and then I had a baby at fifteen. I had my first daughter when I was fifteen, and then I had another one at sixteen. I had another one at seventeen, so I got stuck. I dropped out of school my freshman year of high school. I dropped out of school because I started having all these kids. I got into other stuff, and it took me a long time to get up out of there before I figured, "Oh, wait a minute, your kids are getting older and how can you show them to do anything better if you're still stuck?" That's what motivated me two years ago to go back to school.

David, a young middle-class African American, had a similar perspective on how a lack of exposure shapes one's outlook, though his observations are less personal. David had lived in Chicago for only a few months, and much of his discussion throughout the interview revealed that his impressions of different neighborhoods in Chicago were often based on his experiences in other cities and on representations of Chicago neighborhoods in popular culture:

I think that's displayed by the lyrics in music by guys like this new guy Chief Keef, or whatever. The things in his songs, and you look at his music videos, it kind of confirms that you got this huge skyline—if you stand on the South Side, you got this huge skyline of downtown Chicago which you always see. You stand on your side. If I grew up on the South Side of Chicago, I would never venture downtown. It would just seem too far and too difficult to get to. . . . You see that skyline, because it's all flat land, and you see it so far out, it's kind of like Emerald City in a way.

The upshot is that lived experiences—whether daily or not so daily, whether current or in the distant past, whether in Chicago or any other city—can importantly shape the content of our knowledge, impressions, and perceptions of communities. And as these examples illustrate, communities can also shape our view of the future and our own hopes and ambitions. At a less profound level, these experiences also no doubt shape what places go in and out of our consideration sets as we contemplate a residential move.

The examples of Destiny and David are consistent with Jennifer Darrah and Stefanie DeLuca's analysis of low-income participants in a Baltimore program designed to assist voucher holders in moving to "opportunity areas" (for more discussion of this program, see chapter 10).[14] Confirming the impact on residential decisions of lived experiences and, in turn, the impact of neighborhood experiences on what people think they can become, they explain that 60 percent of these suburban movers fell into one of the following groups, which they described as changing their "residential decision framework":

> Participants who talked very *explicitly* about making decisions differently after their participation in the program; those who reported (often despite pressure from family and transportation woes) *staying* in their neighborhood to which they moved with BMP [the Baltimore Housing Mobility Program] because they appreciated the amenities of the area, such as shopping centers, or the schools; and cases where parents remarked strongly that the neighborhood they experienced through the program made them *think differently* about what kinds of places they wanted to live, who they could be, and what their kids deserved.[15]

Our fourth clue about the linkage between adolescent and adult contexts focuses on the fact that moving to a new metropolitan area diminishes the impact of adolescent neighborhood context on later-life neighborhood racial composition (as indicated by the significant negative interactions in models 4 and 5 of table 5.1). Although it remains possible that this diminishing impact is explained by unobserved factors that affect intermetropolitan migration, this interaction involving long-distance migration is *inconsistent* with the argument that preferences for particular neighborhood racial compositions explain the association, since these preferences would presumably guide residential decisions in the new metropolitan area as well. Instead, the negative interaction between adolescent residential context and intermetropolitan migration appears to be more consistent with an interpretation based on knowledge of neighborhoods. In comparison to those remaining in the same metropolitan area, people who move to a new metropolitan area may end up in neighborhoods that look less similar to their adolescent context because they are unable to rely on their "prior knowledge" as they make their adult residential choices.

Together, chapters 4 and 5 illustrate the complexity of where community information and perceptions come from and highlight the social factors—the daily (and nondaily) routines and social networks—that profoundly shape them. The important point is that the information that individuals gather through their life course experiences, their interactions with members of their social networks, and their daily observations circumscribes the housing search process, leading them to focus their consideration set on a handful of neighborhoods or communities. This circumscription of the consideration set stands in sharp contrast to the common assumption that individuals hold solid information about a wide range of neighborhoods in their metropolitan area and are sorted in their residential choices across these areas as a function of simple racial residential preferences, economic resources, or experiences of discrimination. The analysis here points to housing search and residential location processes that are highly contingent on social interactions and lived experiences. And it points to ways in which race and ethnicity can order these processes so as to perpetuate rather than dismantle segregation. In the next chapter, we provide the third key ingredient of our social structural sorting perspective: how decisions are made about housing.

Chapter 6 | Residential Stratification and the Decision-Making Process

IN ADDITION TO their inattention to the role of social networks and lived experiences, traditional theories on the causes of segregation are largely silent on _how_ decisions are made. As we have noted, the explanations of segregation that have dominated segregation research for decades rely on two dominant assumptions about this process that are rarely, if at all, explicitly acknowledged: (1) residential decisions are made based on complete and accurate knowledge of all the available options; and (2) the decision-making process itself—how people actually decide which selection to make—can be described as rational. Drawing on insights from psychology, decision sciences, geography, and economics, we suggest several ways in which these assumptions are incorrect.

First, people do not proceed with complete and accurate information about all options. Second, housing searches are multistaged: searchers first winnow down all possible neighborhoods to a manageable set based on certain criteria, and then, within the smaller set, they identify and evaluate specific units before settling on a final selection. Third, especially at the first stage, the process does not involve a careful cost-benefit analysis but instead uses heuristics—or simplifying decision rules—that allow the elimination of large numbers of options. We draw on these principles and observations, which were first identified by housing search scholars and decision scientists in some cases decades ago and have been recently introduced to segregation scholars by Elizabeth Bruch and her colleagues. Our core argument is that we can use this more robust and realistic picture of the process as a scaffold that directs our attention to the importance of having a careful consideration of the content and source of the information that feeds into the process and how that information is used in order to understand the causes of segregation. We reviewed the general principles in chapter 3; here we dig deeper into the features of neighborhood selection and housing search processes, relying on the ingredients outlined in the earlier chapter to unpack this process and the implications for the perpetuation of segregation.

PEOPLE DO NOT HAVE KNOWLEDGE OF ALL RESIDENTIAL OPTIONS

In metropolitan areas, it is unlikely that people are aware of every possible option, and since it is difficult to move into a neighborhood or community if you have never heard of it, understanding community familiarity is an important foundation to understanding residential choices. Thus, one way in which the searcher winnows down all possible options is to filter out unfamiliar places. Of course, which places are filtered out can shift over time during any given search, since people may come to learn about places they were not familiar with at the outset—for example, when a real estate agent gives a searcher suggestions, or when a searcher notices a new place during the information-gathering process. But the principle is the same: there will always be some places that a searcher is unfamiliar with, and moving into any of them will be impossible.

From the vantage point of the perpetuation of segregation, what is of great interest is whether there are racial differences in which communities get filtered out in this way. As Maria Krysan and Michael Bader have demonstrated, whether a person has ever heard about a community is shaped by both its racial-ethnic composition and the person's own racial-ethnic background.[1] Specifically, people know more about places where their racial group dominates. This is more often the case for whites, however, than it is for blacks and Latinos. That is, black and Latino respondents tend to claim some knowledge of much larger sets of neighborhoods than do whites, who tend to claim to know nothing about neighborhoods outside of the predominantly white communities in a metropolitan area. In addition, whites more often filter out from their consideration sets those places where other groups dominate, as well as racially diverse places (even if whites are the majority group). The places that a person filters out because they are unfamiliar cannot, by definition, be where the person moves.

There are at least two important implications of unfamiliarity with a community being systematically related to the racial-ethnic background of the searcher and of the community. First, the fact that individuals have considerable blind spots calls into question the basic decision-making model assumed in most segregation research. If individuals are simply unaware of some neighborhoods and the residential opportunities they offer, then it makes little sense to conceive of the residential sorting process as reflective of a rational choice of outcomes that best matches some set of residential preferences or economic constraints.

The second implication of the connection between unfamiliarity with a community and the racial-ethnic backgrounds of searchers and communities is more important to attempts to understand racial residential segregation—namely, that members of different racial-ethnic groups can be choosing from disparate sets of neighborhoods. And these neighborhoods are racially defined, perhaps especially in a place like Chicago where space and race are so tightly—and historically—bound up together. Given this, to a certain extent, we may be asking the wrong questions when we seek to understand whether black or white or Latino householders are more likely to choose a particular neighborhood, or how racial differences in the likelihood of ending up in that neighborhood reflect group differences in economic resources, preferences, or experiences of discrimination. Given racial differences in neighborhood familiarity, such factors may simply never come into play as members of one group or another filter out particular neighborhoods that are unfamiliar to them. With members of different racial and ethnic groups eliminating disjoint sets of neighborhoods from their consideration set, residential segregation may be driven, to an underappreciated extent, by racial differences in the unfamiliarity of particular neighborhoods.

A more subtle way in which community unfamiliarity operates is that people differ in the scale of their knowledge. Although we may think of unfamiliarity functioning at the level of specific neighborhoods and communities, our research has shown that people also lump together different sections of a metropolitan area into a larger unit and make inferences about what that larger unit is like—and therefore about what all of the communities located within it are like. As a consequence, people can claim familiarity with a large area of the metropolis even if they "know nothing" about any individual neighborhoods or communities. In other words, people can infer the characteristics of places based on their relative locations within an urban context and eliminate certain individual communities embedded within it—even if they are unfamiliar with those individual communities. For example, someone may have never heard of the North Side community of Edgewater, but "knowing" about the North Side of Chicago, they may extrapolate what Edgewater is like. Or they may not have heard of Schaumburg but they "know" about the western suburbs.

Our in-depth interviews called our attention to this possibility. We found that people varied—sometimes substantially—in their ability to disaggregate certain parts of the Chicago metropolitan area. And there was a racial pattern to this dynamic. When describing certain parts of the city of Chicago, most of our African American participants—longtime residents of Chicago and relative newcomers alike—referred to drastic differences ("like night and day") from one block to the next. Wilson, a longtime resident, talked about the South Side:

> If you go three blocks west, two blocks north, you might still be in Washington Park, but it's gonna be different from the area I'm thinking and talking about. See, I'm talking about Fifty-Seventh and King—I mean Cottage Grove. Whatever. Maybe go on down to Sixty-Third and Cottage Grove and see how different and changed. You see, just those few blocks. The difference is night and day.

A similar ability to make street-by-street distinctions came through in Destiny's interview:

> Even in the West Side and the South Side, you know it's some streets that are worse than others. On my cousin's, that block where they used to live on Seventy-Third and Wolcott, it was like all the houses there, it was nice houses. The houses were upkept. The lawns were mowed. No trash all over the floor, and the drug dealers weren't standing on the corner and stuff. Then you can go two blocks over and it looks like night and day. Where you got an abandoned building here and you got the drug dealer sitting on the porch hollering out. With these suburbs, you can really tell that it's—the people have a different mind-set of—and a different goal than they do in these areas.

Here Destiny revealed a street-by-street knowledge of Chicago, but then she characterized the suburbs in one sweeping statement: "I mean, just stuff, all the little suburbs, and stuff that you don't really hear too much about, but you know that they have the upkeep of the neighborhoods and things like that." For Destiny, *all* suburbs are quiet, but the South and West Sides of Chicago only have *pockets* of quiet. In our interviews, it was the rare African American—even among newcomers—who did not have detailed knowledge of the city of Chicago due in part, perhaps, to our sampling strategy, which tended to attract people who lived or frequented the city more often; there was much more variation, however, in their knowledge of the suburbs, with some offering many details and others very few.

Researchers studying the residential processes of low-income participants in the HUD voucher program have found that this street-by-street knowledge—what they refer to as "telescoping"—helps explain residential decisions to prioritize the features of units over the features of a neighborhood.[2] Telescoping, in their view, explains why some voucher holders end up in neighborhoods that are not very different from those they were living in prior to receiving a voucher. Specifically, "telescoping to define their living space by the block face meant that families rated their neighborhoods that might on the whole seem unsafe as manageable because of their assessment of the space right outside the front door."[3] In other words, this block-by-block knowledge is useful for those needing to make decisions within severe constraints—the overall neighborhood might be unsafe, but they know the specific area is safe enough.

Belinda, an African American, directly articulated the idea that although she herself saw the South Side as a differentiated place, many others do not:

> I would say Hyde Park, Kenwood, and South Shore would be the areas that stand out more on the South Side. The South Side has the perception of—has a really bad reputation in my opinion, and a lot of people, when you say South Side, they think of—what's the neighborhood that Jennifer Hudson used to live in? . . . Englewood. People think of Englewood, which is really probably one of the worst neighborhoods in the city. Yeah, a place that I really would not want to spend a lot of time there, even passing through. . . . But as you can hear every day on the news, there's the South Side killings and shooting, and it has an overall bad reputation, but they just lump everything into the South Side. . . . But I would say Hyde Park, the ones I mentioned, Kenwood, are more of an upscale South Side neighborhood where you have predominantly black—most of the black population live on the South Side, but in Hyde Park and Kenwood and South Chicago you have more of an upper-income black people in those neighborhoods.

In contrast, and similar to the aggregate patterns in Maria Krysan and Michael Bader's work, the white residents we interviewed tended to paint city spaces with a very broad brush, making general assumptions about their characteristics.[4] Mark and Art, both middle-aged white men who lived in Chicago (North Center) and the inner-ring suburb of Forest Park, respectively, illustrate this tendency. Speaking about the North Side of Chicago, Mark had this to say: "The North Side of Chicago? I think it's one of the more safer parts, than the West and South Side." And Art, when asked where in the metropolitan area he would never live, said, "Where never live? Well, the West Side, because crime. I mean, that's the big issue. South Side too. That's the big issue. Crime." These Chicago residents were not making detailed decisions about specific neighborhoods or communities, but lumping them together and dismissing them as options based on a larger geographical lens. Although "familiar" with the general location (the West Side), Mark and Art were quite unfamiliar with the specific neighborhoods, but what they did know of the neighborhoods was sufficient to convince them not to consider them. In this way, and to foreshadow the argument to come, they were using location as the "one best cue" to infer what a neighborhood was like. Mark and Art were just familiar enough with the West and South Sides to rule them out as residential choices.

As discussed in chapters 4 and 5, people become familiar with and develop perceptions of communities through social networks and lived experiences. And because networks and lived experiences are racially circumscribed, it is little surprise that there are racial differences in what we can refer to as "familiarity sets." But there is another source that feeds community perceptions that we have not yet touched upon: the media.

In an interesting study of heuristics, the psychologists Daniel Goldstein and Gerd Gigerenzer affirm the media's influence on which places people *recognize*.[5] They calculated the number of times various German cities were mentioned in the *Chicago Tribune* and compared the totals with the extent to which a sample of University of Chicago students recognized these cities. The correlation was 0.79. In a similar study examining the relationship between German students' recognition of U.S. cities and the mentions of U.S. cities in a German-language newspaper, they again found a robust relationship (correlation of 0.86). Thus, media depictions of communities are an important way in which people come to be familiar with them.

In addition to recognition, the media also provide information about places that may affect whether searchers filter those places out of their consideration set. In this sense, the line between familiarity sets and consideration sets is blurry: once a place moves from unfamiliar to familiar, information has been gained about it. And that information shapes decisions about whether to consider it or not. As we argue later, decisions can be based on just a small bit of information.

Our in-depth interviews illustrate the many direct and indirect ways in which the media provide information about a place and make it recognizable. In Aaron's "noggin" quote—and indeed, in virtually every one of our in-depth interviews—the media figured prominently in how people described their source of information about places they had never visited. Most often, they referred to local news stories about crime, but they also mentioned media "puff pieces"—for instance, newscasters visiting a diner in the suburbs and having breakfast with the locals, or promoting events such as an upcoming strawberry festival or pancake breakfast. Many people—especially, but by no means exclusively, those new to an area—also got impressions of places from popular culture: in the Chicago area, some communities had been made famous by movies, such as Aurora (featured in *Wayne's World*) and Plainville (where *Superman* was filmed), or had become well known from rap music (the South Side).

People also glean information from the kinds of jobs and stores that are advertised in the media. David, a new resident of Chicago, observed that DuPage County must be blue-collar because "when I've looked for ads and things like that, for jobs and stuff like that, it's all factory jobs that I've seen out there. That's the only assumption I can make; it's an area that has a lot of, maybe kind of like industrial." People also form impressions based on the retail stores in an area; for instance, Stacy explained that much of what she knew about Orland Park was "probably just from the commercials I've seen on stores there." Other participants described how retail presence is a signifier of the characteristics and desirability of a community; if a neighborhood has check-cashing stores and Popeye's Chicken restaurants, they explained, it is probably not as good as a neighborhood with a Chipotle.

In an interesting twist, the *absence* of media coverage can also affect people's inferences about community features. Returning to the experiment by Daniel Goldstein and Gerd Gigerenzer, recall that their purpose was to see if people who used recognition heuristics—whether or not they recognized a city—were accurate in their predictions about the population size of the city; the researchers proposed that people would reason that if they have heard of a community it was because it was large.[6] Our in-depth interviews pointed out that with respect to community desirability, newspaper coverage may be a signal that it is a *bad* place to live. Consistent with a finding of the sociologist Elliot Weininger, we found that people inferred something from the "nonstory."[7] Destiny, who grew up in the West and South Sides of Chicago, had this observation:

> Best thing is when you *don't* hear stuff about neighborhoods, and that lets you know that when you're not hearing about them on the news and somebody's body was found. Every now and then you may hear something about one of the suburbs, but other than that, it's always Englewood and the West Side of Chicago that you hear it, "A dead body was found in a lot," or something like that. I think that with most of the suburbs it's kept—everything is kept kinda quiet. Every now and then you hear something big might happen [in the suburbs], but nothing that would make you fearful to live in the neighborhood or something of the sort.

Jerome echoed this sentiment when his interviewer asked him what he was basing his assumptions that a place was low in crime on: "Like the fact that I've never heard anything." And when asked about the public schools, he said: "You don't really hear too much negative about suburban public schools." Finally, as Aaron pointed out, "I don't see a lot of stuff on the news, you know, somebody got shot in Skokie [a well-off predominantly Jewish suburb on the North Side]. I don't ever hear that."

It is worth elaborating on the *kind* of coverage of communities that the media provide, since this coverage is not only an important source of information but also, it turns out, a source that is not race-neutral. Geographers and communication scholars in particular have focused on describing the content of media portrayals of communities and how those portrayals relate to communities' actual features and the prospects for their future.[8] How race is implicated in this process is well documented, particularly in terms of media coverage of crime.[9] A few patterns are worth noting. First, local news is dominated by stories about crime. For example, a study of local news coverage in fifty-six cities found that 75 percent of the stories focused on crime.[10] Second, in a study of media coverage of disadvantaged neighborhoods in Toronto, the journalism professor April Lindgren found that news about thirteen disadvantaged areas was dominated by negative subject matter, particularly in comparison to the coverage of the downtown area, which focused on arts, entertainment, and sports.[11] Other studies replicate this pattern in other cities and neighborhoods.[12] These media images provide the only information that some residents will ever have about some communities.[13] Negative stereotypes of, and fear about, urban places can be fueled by these portrayals.[14] In an innovative analysis, the communications professors Sorin Matei, Sandra Ball-Rokeach, and Jack Linchuan Qiu investigated this possibility when they studied fear of urban space in Los Angeles. Their results show that "mental images of fear in urban spaces are more influenced by communication processes and ethnicity-based stereotyping than more intuitive causes, such as crime victimization likelihood."[15] Interestingly, they highlight a specifically social component of the effects of media:

> A holistic model, which emphasizes the interactive effects of two communication channels, gives a better account for feelings of fear toward other ethnicities. The augmented effect of television on fear—but only in the presence of interpersonal communication—suggests that it is not simple exposure to the medium that constructs the mental images, but their elaboration through face-to-face conversation.[16]

Thus, media coverage of communities in connection with social processes plays a role in shaping whether a community is in a person's consideration set. What our interview examples and this body of research highlight is that for many residents who have never been to a particular place, media exposure is likely to persuade them to filter certain neighborhoods out of their consideration set.

RESIDENTIAL PROCESSES HAPPEN IN STAGES

In chapter 3, we summarized what existing research tells us about the basic features of housing searches and decision-making. We return now to explore these features in more detail, focusing on how they may shape racial residential outcomes in particular. One feature is critical to our argument: People do not simultaneously consider all possible options in a metropolitan area and then select the option that best fits their preferences and resources in one stage. Instead, as observed decades ago by housing search scholars, and as reiterated by Bruch and Swait, searches happen in stages as searchers winnow all possible housing options down to only those they will consider.[17] It is within the communities in this consideration set that people then search for available units to evaluate and eventually select. Given this framework, two questions become relevant to the question of how people end up living where they do and how these features of the process contribute to segregation:

1. What factors are responsible for people filtering places out of their consideration set?
2. How do people accomplish this winnowing process? How do they decide whether or not to consider a particular neighborhood or unit?

   In the remainder of this chapter, we review the answers to these questions suggested by existing research and frameworks, and then consider the racial consequences of the answers in light of the racialized context of information sources and experiences.

Constructing the Consideration Set

How do people take all of the places they recognize and are familiar with and decide which ones will be in or out of their consideration set? A key observation from decision sciences is that when faced with a complex decision with many alternatives, people use a sequential screening process to winnow down their options from far too many to a manageable number. This simple point is supported by the results of Maria Krysan and Michael Bader's studies in Detroit and Chicago—among the first to systematically measure the areas where people would "seriously consider" or "never consider" searching for a place to live.[18] In Detroit, out of 33 possible communities presented on a map, the average respondent identified 3.5 places they would seriously consider and, on average, 15 places they would never consider. In a similar study in Chicago, which gave 41 communities as options, respondents also eliminated many more options than they retained: on average, they would seriously consider 3.4 of these communities, while 19.2 communities were places they would "never consider."
   Many housing search models and analyses are based on theoretical models; less often are they accompanied by empirical data on the process itself. One exception is the work of Gary Talarchek.[19] In a survey study of residents of Syracuse, New York, Talarchek provides a relatively rare

instance of detailed inquiry into the search process. The results provide support for the idea that searches proceed in multiple stages and, importantly, that different criteria function at the different stages:

> First, decision makers obtain information on environmental and locational variables, such as distance to work, people in neighborhood, location of friends and relatives, location of schools, quality of schools, property taxes, profit-making potential, and distance to a supermarket, a shopping center, and a bus stop. As the residential search progresses, decision makers eliminate portions of the metropolitan housing market and cease gathering information on locational and environmental variables. Then, they begin to obtain information on housing unit variables, such as number of rooms, utilities cost, lot size, floor plan, architectural style, and landscaping. Acquisition of information on housing unit variables dominates the middle and end portion of the search process. Housing cost seems to be monitored throughout the decision process.[20]

In a more recent study, Elizabeth Bruch and Joffre Swait apply insights from decision sciences to the question of housing choices to develop a "cognitively plausible" model of neighborhood choice. Like Talarchek and others, they advance the idea that searches are multistaged and that people use different criteria at different stages. As they explain:

> A large body of work shows that, when choosing from among more than a tiny handful of options, people engage in a multi-stage decision process in which the first stage involves eliminating all but a small subset of alternatives—the choice set—which are given closer consideration. . . . Decision rules guiding what to include in the choice set are fundamentally different from the rules guiding the final choice. . . . When identifying the choice set, people use less cognitively taxing *screening rules* that rely on only a small number of choice attributes. Later on, people may use more complex compensatory valuations, which involve offsetting a less desirable value on one attribute with a more desirable value on another.[21]

In an innovative analysis using data from the Los Angeles Family and Neighborhood Survey (LA FANS), Bruch and Swait demonstrate that a model specifying that searchers use screening rules (related to cost of housing and distance of the move) provides a better fit to the observed neighborhood sorting than the traditional model in which all neighborhoods receive equal consideration. Importantly, however, and unlike the Talarchek study, Bruch and Swait base their models on presumed screening criteria rather than on information from the searchers themselves.[22]

Although the criteria they use are perfectly reasonable and supported by the research literature on housing processes—cost and distance from current home—the question remains open as to what the individuals they studied were actually using to guide their process. Talarchek's study affirms their choices, to be sure. But considering the goal of our argument, an important neighborhood feature is missing, and it is one that Talarchek's data showed was important: the people in the neighborhood. He characterized this feature as "a surrogate measure of decision makers' evaluation of the social character of an area."[23] The decision-making framework assembled by Bruch and Swait, alongside Talarchek's empirical data on what people consider important when searching, both point in the same direction: searches happen in stages, and people use different decision criteria at different stages.

Winnowing Down Involves the Use of Heuristics

How do people approach the first task—reducing all possible options down to a manageable number? Research suggests that people use screening rules to quickly eliminate large numbers of alternatives. But how do they decide whether a particular location does or does not have the desired value on a given attribute? As Bruch and her colleagues point out, decision science tells us that people seek a simple way to make complex decisions—and it is very different from a classic model of rational choice.[24] As Gerd Gigerenzer and Daniel Goldstein explain:

> The classical view of rational judgment under certainty is . . . to search for all reasons, positive or negative, weigh each carefully, and add them up to see where the balance lies. This linear combination of reasons carries the moral sentiment of rational behavior: carefully look up every bit of information, weigh each bit in your hand, and combine them into a judgment. . . . But in real-world situations with sufficient complexity, the knowledge, time, and computation necessary to realize the classical ideal of unbounded rationality can be prohibitive—too much for humble humans, and often also too much for the most powerful computers.[25]

Instead, "people . . . often look up only one or two relevant cues, avoid searching for conflicting evidence, and use noncompensatory strategies."[26] In other words, they use heuristics.

We agree with Bruch and others who argue that we need to embrace the idea that theories about the causes of segregation should be grounded in more realistic models of decision-making. Indeed, Bruch and Feinberg make this point when they observe that sociology as a discipline has largely ignored the substantial body of research in judgment and decision making (JDM).[27] Specifically, they note that JDM debunks the notion of unbounded rationality in which people make decisions with complete information and use complex computations to select the alternative that maximizes their utility; JDM also draws attention to the need to understand how people actually make decisions. What is true of sociology in general is certainly true of residential segregation research: our traditional models assume antiquated notions of how people make decisions. In defense of sociology, Bruch and Feinberg observe that there are good reasons why sociology has been slow to adopt JDM theories and perspectives: JDM research typically ignores social context altogether; the rational-choice framework, though influential, was never as fully embraced by sociology as it was by other disciplines (notably economics); and data are difficult to come by. But perhaps most importantly, the decisions that are the focus of JDM have a "right" answer, while many decisions that sociologists care about do not have a clear and obvious right answer, including decisions about neighborhood selection and housing.[28] The social structural sorting perspective incorporates these valuable insights and couples them with the insights of other disciplines to construct a scaffolding that draws attention to the social processes that sort people into residentially segregated neighborhoods.

We are not equipped to offer a detailed neighborhood selection and housing choice decision-making model; nor do we make claims about *which* heuristics best describe the process. Rather, our purpose is to illustrate how heuristics may help us understand the racialized outcomes of this process. We lack the data necessary to make definitive claims about which heuristics in particular are at play, but we use the "take the best" heuristic as one that holds promise.[29] The heuristic, as applied to the neighborhood selection process, would work something like this: People use a specific criterion or cue (for example, distance to work) and eliminate all options that fail to meet that criterion. If there are still too many possibilities, the next good cue is applied (for example, housing cost), and so on until the consideration set is more manageable. A "good" cue is one that people believe will most effectively distinguish between places. Importantly, for this heuristic to "work" there needs to be the sense that certain features of the environment are correlated and that one cue can stand in for other aspects. If racial composition is one of those cues, then places will be filtered out or in based on that one cue regardless of whether the correlation holds for a given community. The implications of this are important for the perpetuation of segregation: a self-fulfilling prophecy can be set in motion whereby perceptions translate into behaviors that further perpetuate disinvestment in a neighborhood. This disinvestment then further feeds the perception that impacts the behavior. This process further solidifies the correlation of these characteristics in reality. And so the cycle continues.

In addition to the more general support for the framework about how decisions are made, reviewed earlier, there is evidence in both survey data and our in-depth interviews on three specific points related to how race becomes implicated in this process: (1) people perceive that various features of neighborhoods are correlated; (2) they appear to use a single cue to make inferences about a range of other neighborhood features; and (3) race figures importantly in this process.

Let's start with the simple observation that in the contemporary United States, certain kinds of neighborhood features "hang together" and that people recognize this. Our in-depth interviews revealed this logic, suggesting that people can, with a fair amount of confidence, paint a picture of what a community is probably like, based on a single piece of information. Tom, a young white renter who is relatively new to Chicago, had opinions about many places he had never been. We found that if he knew the "value" of a place on a particular "cue" or "aspect," he could paint a complete picture:

INTERVIEWER: Waukegan and Gurnee?

TOM: They seem like . . . very settled places. Very suburban, very calm. Subdued. I don't know. I don't really know if they're really upscale, but there's tons of shopping out there . . .

INTERVIEWER: What's your impression of who lives out there?

TOM: . . . I think it's mostly like people in their thirties, forties, fifties, who have families and want to live somewhere that's a bit more quiet. I don't get the impression that's a very diverse neighborhood. So it's mostly white. I mean, it's a nice place to visit for Six Flags and for shopping. . . . I get the impression that schools there are nice. The crime is probably pretty low. It's not as densely populated.

INTERVIEWER: Will County?

TOM: Um, I mean, it's a very suburban [place]. I get the impression. It's gonna be very spread out, lots of houses, not a lot of apartment buildings. Everybody drives to get everywhere. You know, less diverse, people are primarily white. Families with kids.

INTERVIEWER: Okay, the crime and schools?

> Tom: I think crime is probably low and the schools very good. It'd be a good place to go to raise a family if you have kids in school.

Later, when asked about Berwyn and Cicero (two inner-ring suburbs that are now predominantly Latino), Tom revealed how he saw a less well-off place:

> Interviewer: You've been to Berwyn and Cicero?
>
> Tom: Um, no, I haven't been to either of those neighborhoods.
>
> Interviewer: Oh, okay. So you read about these neighborhoods. Is there anywhere else you get your impressions from?
>
> Tom: I can't think of anywhere outside of that where I get . . .
>
> Interviewer: Okay. What's your impression of some other qualities of the neighborhoods, like the restaurants, stores, general environment?
>
> Tom: I mean, there hasn't been any restaurants or stores that have drawn me out there, so I imagine probably not as good. And the stores and the shopping probably not as good.
>
> Interviewer: Okay. You mentioned crime. And you said not as nice, which previously has sort of meant what the houses look like . . .
>
> Tom: Yeah, and the income level of the people living there. More like lower-middle-class to poor.
>
> Interviewer: Okay. And what's your impression of who lives there? What are the people like who live there?
>
> Tom: Just poor, probably very diverse, you know, a range of ethnicities.

In this discussion, the thread that makes it all unravel—or come together—is the fact that there were no restaurants or shops that attracted Tom to Berwyn or Cicero. That thread led him to make a number of assumptions about other features of these neighborhoods, culminating in guesses about the racial-ethnic background of the poor residents who live there.

For Joann, a middle-aged white woman living in an upscale northern suburb, retail offers hints about who probably lives in a neighborhood. Here she is describing the Chicago neighborhood of Lincoln Square:

JOANN: My experience is, I haven't been in the more residential areas, but as I drive through, and I've been down there to eat and socialize and what have you, it's pretty white. I would say at least 75 percent white, if not more.

INTERVIEWER: What's the 25 percent who's not white?

JOANN: Probably more Asian and Hispanic, maybe not quite as much African American. Just cuz, that's not, generally speaking, their kinda neighborhood. I mean, I know that sounds really racist, but honestly, how many black people do you know go to the bistro? Seriously? I mean, it's a more trendy kind of neighborhood than I like, but I like the feel of it.

Thus, the racial makeup of a neighborhood is one of those features that people freely infer, especially in cities like Detroit, Chicago, and other legacy metros. That the cue of race figures centrally in inferences about other neighborhood features is reinforced by the results of a video experiment that manipulated the racial composition of the people appearing in a neighborhood.[30] Maria Krysan, Reynolds Farley, and Mick Couper asked respondents to evaluate the neighborhood's level of crime, property upkeep, future property values, and school quality. If there were black people walking down the sidewalks as opposed to white people, white respondents negatively evaluated the neighborhood.[31] Their evaluations were not a function of observable characteristics; in other words, if a neighborhood was shown to have black residents, then whites, on average, presumed that it was of lower quality than the exact same neighborhood shown with white residents.

Social psychologist Courtney Bonam and her colleagues' series of innovative experiments also provide quantitative evidence of the patterns suggested in our in-depth interviews. Their general argument is that just as people can be stereotyped, so too can places. And, their work finds, stereotypes of black spaces are widespread, consensual, and have consequences. In one study they sought to identify the content and extent of agreement of the perceptions of black space. Using a diverse national sample recruited using Amazon's Mechanical Turk, they found that people hold "a negative and prevalent picture of Black space as failing: physically degraded, unpleasant, unsafe, and lacking resources. . . . We have identified not just one stereotypical characteristic of black areas, but a host of characteristics that cohere, forming a full, nuanced image of stereotypical black space."[32] Additional experiments further demonstrated, like the video experiment conducted by Krysan and her colleagues, that people downgrade and devalue uality of the home (and the neighborhood in which it is located) if the purported homeowner is black as compared to white. In other words, these negative black space-focused stereotypes have consequences. In an actual housing search, we can imagine that when whites visit prospective neighborhoods that are racially mixed or all-black, their very perception of its qualities—regardless of what they actually see—will be colored by the race of the residents.

Relatedly, the sociologists Lincoln Quillian and Devah Pager find that the racial composition of a community more accurately predicts respondents' perceptions of how likely they are to be victimized in their own neighborhood than actual crime rates:

> Respondents notice and utilize relevant contextual information in forming their estimates of risk, but do so in a way that amplifies the relevance of certain factors (e.g., racial composition) while downplaying the relevance of others (economic conditions). Resulting estimates exaggerate the level of risk in black neighborhoods, particularly those in working class or middle class neighborhoods, where levels of risk are substantially lower relative to those at the bottom end of the income distribution. Strong associations between race and crime appear to lead to a privileging of this noisy proxy for risk while true culprits (economic conditions) receive far less emphasis.[33]

That race may be, for many whites, the "best cue" they rely on when deciding whether or not to include a community in their consideration set suggests that even though in theory we could conduct an experiment to isolate the effect of neighborhood racial composition (as opposed to social class), these factors may be virtually impossible to disentangle when it comes to people's real-world decisions and choices. That is, as Quillian and Pager note, "even if neighborhood evaluations and decisions to move are largely determined by nonracial considerations, such as perceptions of neighborhood crime, if these perceptions are themselves influenced by racial context, then they can no longer be thought of as race-neutral."[34]

In one sense, then, whether people use race or something other than race as their "best cue," their perception is not necessarily race-neutral. As such, neighborhood social class characteristics can become the vehicle through which racial stereotypes and perceptions shape overall perceptions of communities. Quillian and Pager speculate about how this can play out in residential decisions:

> If basic ideas about the operation of stereotypes are correct, then neighborhood racial composition would probably have an even larger influence on the perceptions of persons who know the neighborhood less well [than its

residents], such as prospective residents considering a neighborhood as a possible place to live.[35]

The intractability of race as a cue for neighborhood perceptions is also apparent in studies of whites' (in particular) and blacks' (to some extent) neighborhood consideration sets in Chicago and Detroit.[36] These studies examined the impact of a community's racial composition—above and beyond other community characteristics—on whether it would be seriously considered or never considered. Maria Krysan and Michael Bader found that the communities that whites would "seriously consider" were those where the strong majority of residents were white; in a multilevel model, even after controlling for an array of other individual and community characteristics, the percentage white in a community was statistically significant.[37] For African Americans, racial composition also mattered, but differently. First, many African Americans would "seriously consider" heavily African American communities, but they would also seriously consider communities with just a handful of African Americans. Second, in multilevel models, the percentage white in a community was not a significant predictor of whether African Americans would consider a community. In addition, the finding that African Americans were less likely than whites to "never consider" places suggests that racial composition is a more fluid cue for blacks. The lived experiences of African Americans may result in the heuristic operating somewhat differently in the sense that they may perceive race as a less valid cue.

Bader and Krysan conducted a similar study in Chicago and found that social class characteristics mattered but that, by and large, racial-ethnic composition still influenced the evaluations of whites.[38] Racial-ethnic composition was less influential in the evaluations of African Americans and Latinos. In the context of the "take the best" heuristic, these studies suggest that racial composition is a cue that is perceived as one of the "best" (most valid) for helping whites (and less so for other groups) quickly determine the other features of a community and decide whether to include or exclude it from their consideration set. We explore this more fully in chapter 8.

Of significance is that people often "take the best" cue and use "one good reason" to make the decision to eliminate places from consideration. That is, in using heuristics, they do not take the time to learn everything about a place during the first stage of the process and rely instead on one good reason, or on the best one. Joann's description provides an exception that "proves" the general tendency:

I know about Beverly [a neighborhood in the city of Chicago] because I know there's a Montessori school down there. I was surprised to find out that it's a pretty wealthy white community, cuz it's on the South Side of Chicago, and when you don't grow up here and you don't know these things, you just make assumptions about neighborhoods, cuz it's just easier to make decisions that way.

This excerpt highlights several key points. First, as was often true of whites in our study, for Joann, the South Side of Chicago (which has a substantial African American population) is a large aggregated swath of sameness, and she assumes that a neighborhood on the South Side could be neither white nor wealthy; as she noted, "It's just easier to make decisions that way." This sentiment is entirely consistent with the idea that at the early stage of a housing search, people rely on shortcuts to draw conclusions about the desirability of places.[39] The consequences for racial segregation are significant if people eliminate communities from consideration based on a heuristic and then never do further research. Because race is correlated in reality (as a structure of the environment) with a host of other features that matter to people in deciding where to live, they may rarely search to find the exception. For whites, that would be a black neighborhood with good schools. For blacks, it would be a white neighborhood that is welcoming to people of color. We explore this more fully in chapter 8.

The dominant existing theories of the causes of segregation generally ignore three things. First, they fail to appreciate the role of information in shaping where people live. Second, and relatedly, they generally do not acknowledge the social contextual factors that feed that information. And third, as Bruch and her colleagues' pioneering work has argued, traditional segregation scholars ignore the reality of how people decide which neighborhoods to search and which units they will consider. Our core argument is that although these are superficially race-neutral processes, race factors into the process in profound ways. We now turn the question on its head and ask: how does the social structural sorting perspective help us understand how the *traditional* drivers of segregation operate? The next three chapters take on that question.

Chapter 7 | The Social Structural Sorting Perspective on the Role of Economic Factors

ONE OF THE most widely accepted explanations for residential segregation by race focuses on the role of socioeconomic resources. Here the key argument is that group differences in the ability to reside in, and move to, advantaged neighborhoods reflect group differences in the resources necessary to afford housing in these areas. The fact that blacks and whites, for example, occupy separate and qualitatively different neighborhoods reflects the fact that blacks, on average, have less of the income, wealth, and other resources necessary to gain access to the neighborhoods typically occupied by whites.

In this chapter, we revisit these economic arguments through the lens of the neighborhood selection and housing search process and the context of residential choice. In doing so, we offer two main insights. First, in addition to reviewing basic evidence for the impact of economic forces on racially disparate patterns of residential mobility and the broader patterns of segregation, we link these effects to the search process in order to highlight some underappreciated mechanisms through which economic forces play out. Second, we show that viewing economic resources through the lens of the neighborhood selection and housing search highlights some more subtle ways in which economic resources may shape the process. We argue that these subtle mechanisms are not currently well appreciated and in fact contradict some of the basic assumptions informing existing research. Thus, attention to these more subtle mechanisms highlights new ways of thinking about how economic forces shape segregation.

THE STANDARD ECONOMIC MODEL

Economic models of segregation trace their roots to the classic human ecology perspective.[1] Key components of this perspective hold that metropolitan neighborhoods differ significantly in their proximity to resources, in the style and value of housing, and in overall quality. Individuals and groups are sorted into these various neighborhoods based on whether or not they have the resources necessary to access the most desirable places. This general argument suggests that residential outcomes—the residential location of individuals and the aggregate patterns of segregation these individual patterns define—are primarily determined by access to *economic* resources. According to the spatial assimilation model, members of the white majority typically occupy the most desirable residential locations—characterized by valuable housing, low poverty and economic distress, stable institutions, and low exposure to crime, pollution, and other disamenities—largely because they tend to have the highest average levels of education, income, and wealth.[2] Members of many immigrant and racial minority groups, in contrast, lack the resources needed to buy their way into these highly desirable neighborhoods and are therefore relegated, at least temporarily, to separate and often less desirable neighborhoods. Thus, group differences in residential location are assumed to reflect group differences in education, income, access to wealth, and other socioeconomic resources.[3] Blacks and whites, for example, occupy separate and qualitatively different residential locations simply because, on average, blacks have fewer economic resources with which to buy their way into neighborhoods similar to those occupied by whites.

Research from several lines of inquiry provides support for the basic tenets of the assimilation perspective. First, at the aggregate level, variation in overall levels of residential segregation in metropolitan areas is clearly linked to differences in average levels of income and education between racial and ethnic groups in the area, with lower levels of segregation prevailing in metropolitan areas with greater economic parity between racial and ethnic groups.[4] This link between local economic disparities and segregation is illustrated in figure 7.1, which utilizes data from the 2010 U.S. census and the 2008–2013 American Community Survey to assess the association between black-white segregation and the relative economic standing of black and white residents of our 331 core metropolitan areas. Along the vertical axis of this figure is the level of black-white segregation (as measured by the index of dissimilarity) in the metropolitan area. Along the horizontal axis is the median income of the black population in the metropolitan area relative to the median white income in the area. A value of 1 on this variable indicates that the median income for blacks in the area

Figure 7.1   Black-White Segregation as a Function of Income
Stratification in Core Metropolitan Areas, 2010

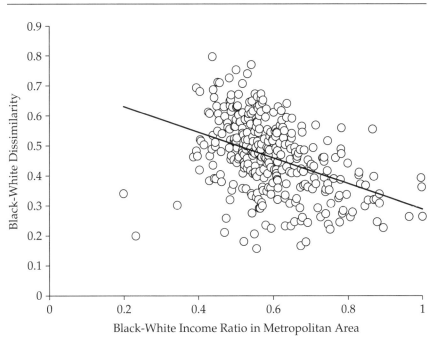

Source: Authors' calculations from the 2010 decennial census and the 2009–2013 American Community Survey.

matches that of whites. Pronounced economic inequality by race is indicated by the fact that in the average metropolitan area the median black income is about 60 percent of the median for whites.

Consistent with past research on the topic, the link between segregation and relative group income is fairly clear in this figure. The level of residential separation of African Americans from whites tends to be lower in metropolitan areas in which the minority group has a higher average level of income relative to that of whites in the metro. Specifically, basic regression analyses indicate that a 10 percent difference in the black-white income ratio is associated with a reduction in black-white segregation of about four points ($b = -0.387$). Moreover, this basic association between group income levels and segregation holds even after controlling for many other features of the metropolitan area shown in past research to be associated with patterns of segregation.[5] Economic resources are also an important factor in explaining the residential attainment of subgroups and within racial groups. Past research has shown that the highest-income subpopulations of most minority groups tend to be less segregated from whites than lower-income segments of these groups.[6] This fact is especially apparent when the focus is restricted to experiential measures of segregation rather than simple unevenness.[7]

A large body of research on patterns of neighborhood attainment and residential mobility among individuals and families also supports the basic tenets of the economic explanation of segregation. This type of evidence is exemplified in figure 7.2, which summarizes the results of several regression models predicting the characteristics of neighborhood destinations of PSID households that moved to a different housing unit during the two-year period between successive interviews.[8] Here we utilize data from the most recent years of the PSID (1997 to 2013) and focus on families residing in one of our core metropolitan areas. To highlight the role of economic factors in shaping neighborhood racial composition and, by extension, residential segregation by race, panel A of figure 7.2 shows the link between family income and the concentration of non-Latino white residents in the destination neighborhood. Panel B predicts the poverty rate in the neighborhood of destination, a measure often used as a general indicator of neighborhood quality because of its connection to other local socioeconomic features and a multitude of other neighborhood conditions, including crime and environmental hazards. We use race-specific regression models to predict each of these outcomes and display destination values for households between the fifth and ninety-fifth percentiles in the race-specific distributions of total family income in the year prior to the residential move. Neighborhood conditions are operationalized using tract-level data from the U.S. census.

As a whole, the results in figure 7.2 provide solid support for economic explanations of the residential processes that shape residential stratification. For householders in each of the broad racial groups, higher income tends to translate into mobility into neighborhoods with higher concentrations of white residents and lower levels of poverty, although the effect for whites is quite weak. For black and Latino households, a $10,000 difference in income predicts an increase of just over one percentage point in the concentration of whites in the neighborhood of destination and a reduction of just under one percentage point in the poverty rate of the destination neighborhood. For householders from each group, and for both destination outcomes, the effects of family income on destinations are statistically significant and remain so even after controlling for age, gender, family composition, regional location, and other factors shown in past research

Figure 7.2   Association Between Family Income and Residential
Destinations for Mobile PSID Householders in
Core Metropolitan Areas, 1997–2013

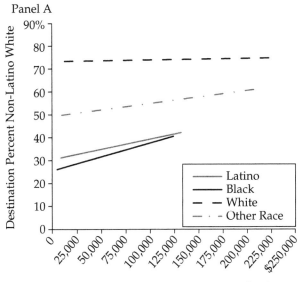

Panel A

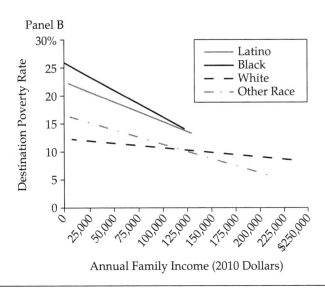

Panel B

Source: Authors' calculations from the Panel Study of Income Dynamics (PSID 2016).

to affect residential outcomes. Moreover, these basic effects of income are mirrored by similar effects of education and family wealth. Thus, the general conclusion is that economic resources do provide access to more economically stable neighborhoods and those occupied by the white majority, supporting the notion that group differences in economic resources help to explain the racially disparate mobility patterns that continually reinforce segregation.[9]

However, these findings—which are completely consistent with the vast bulk of work on microlevel mobility dynamics—also highlight some of the shortcomings of a simple economic argument. Apparent in figure 7.2 are substantial racial and ethnic differences in neighborhood destinations even among those with similar economic resources. When they move, white householders enter, or remain in, neighborhoods in which, on average, about 77 percent of their new neighbors are white. In contrast, the average concentration of white residents in neighborhood destinations is just over 32 percent for black movers and just over 36 percent for Latino movers. Because the effect of income is more pronounced for black and Latino householders than for white householders, this difference is least pronounced among the highest income strata. However, even among mobile householders with annual incomes of $125,000 (just above the ninety-fifth percentile for blacks, the ninety-third percentile for Latinos, and the seventy-eighth percentile for whites), black householders still enter neighborhoods with an average concentration of white residents (41.96 percent) just over half that found in the average destination of their mobile white counterparts (76.93 percent), and Latino movers end up in neighborhoods with average white concentrations (44.85 percent) that are more than 30 percentage points below those of whites with the same income.

In fact, past research indicates that racial differences in income, education, and family wealth—the three most common markers of socioeconomic resources used in studies of neighborhood attainment—explain only a tiny percentage of the overall racial differences in the composition of residential neighborhoods or the residential destinations of movers.[10] Similarly, metropolitan-level variations in the level of economic inequality between racial groups appear to explain only a small portion of the overall variation in segregation in metropolitan areas.[11] For example, at most only about 15 percent of the metropolitan-level variation in black-white segregation in 2010 (see figure 7.1) can be attributed to variation in the black-white income ratio and all of the structural features to which income stratification by race is related.[12]

Thus, overall, while economic arguments provide a partial explanation for the persistence of residential segregation, there is also ample evidence that this assimilation perspective falls well short of explaining patterns of residential stratification. This failure of basic economic resources to explain contemporary residential patterns has been interpreted as a general short-coming of the classic assimilation model and, by extension, confirmation of the strong roles of group differences in residential preferences and housing market discrimination in shaping segregation.

Such conclusions are valid, of course, only to the extent that we can be certain that our common strategies for testing the assimilation perspective fully capture the effects of economic conditions on residential sorting pro-cesses. In reality, the version of economic explanations tested with our stan-dard approaches is highly simplistic. Individuals are assumed to enter the housing market with nearly complete knowledge of their neighborhood options and rationally sort themselves into the best, most advantageous neighborhood they can afford. Under this common conceptualization, economics enters the residential search process simply by determining what individuals can afford to pay at the time they search for housing. By extension, the role of economic factors in driving residential segregation is assumed to be captured with a focus on group differences in the ability to pay for valued residential locations.

REAL AND PERCEIVED ECONOMIC CONCERNS IN THE NEIGHBORHOOD SELECTION AND HOUSING SEARCH

Absent from the simple application of traditional economic explanations for segregation is recognition of the ways in which economic factors shape the neighborhood selection and housing search process itself, includ-ing perceptions of residential options and the strategies used to investi-gate these options. In short, standard tests of the economic models fail to account for the on-the-ground mechanisms through which economic considerations shape the residential selection process. Assessing these mechanisms through the lens of the neighborhood selection and housing search process reveals a more nuanced picture of how economics affects residential sorting and segregation. This reexamination also suggests that subjective features of economics and social class—extending well beyond an individual's ability to pay for particular housing options—are crucial for understanding who ends up where. Importantly, these more complex economic forces can be deeply racialized, thus complicating the traditional endeavor to disentangle the roles of race and economics in shaping resi-dential outcomes.

Reexamining the role of economic forces in the neighborhood selection and housing search process does reveal a good bit of support for the com-monsense notion that affordability and housing costs are primary criteria shaping residential selection. Data from the American Housing Survey show, for example, that about 55 percent of recent movers listed financial considerations as an important factor in choosing their new place of residence, and 47 percent said that affordability was the main reason they chose a particular unit. In fact, the affordability factor appears to be important early in the search process as well—not just in determining which unit to move into but, more basically, which neighborhoods to focus on in the search process. Our interview data point to housing costs as an important elimination criterion in stage 1. For example, one of our focus group participants explained that he used newspaper ads to figure out "where the areas are, the price ranges, which I think is *numero uno*."

Another in-depth interview participant, Russell, a forty-something African American homeowner in the suburbs, relied on prior knowledge to eliminate two North Side suburbs that he thought were out of his price range:

> INTERVIEWER: Okay, and just Winnetka and Wilmette, just why—what about those things that—
>
> RUSSELL: It's beautiful. It's million-dollar homes. Obviously, I can't afford that stuff [*laughs*], so that's why we're not there.

These examples point to the salience of affordability as a screening criterion, suggesting that individuals eliminate from their consideration set those communities where housing costs exceed their ability to pay. But these examples also highlight the complexity of the effects of this economic consideration in shaping search processes. Especially important here is the distinction between actual and *perceived* affordability. Whether searchers have the money to pay the rent or mortgage necessary to gain access to a particular neighborhood is obviously an important determinant of where they search for housing, but as Donald Hempel argued several decades ago, their perceptions of the housing market, more than the objective characteristics of the market, are crucial for understanding their residential decision-making.[13] Presumptions about the affordability of particular neighborhoods may lead some searchers to eliminate entire areas of a city at the earliest stages of the search process, long before they assess specific units for their affordability.

In this way, the kind of residential processes imagined under traditional applications of the economic model—in which individuals are sorted into neighborhoods based on their ability to pay—are highly contingent on the accuracy of assessments of the affordability of the housing options in different neighborhoods. If individuals systematically eliminate neighborhoods from the search process because they over- or underestimate the cost or value of housing in these areas, then the correspondence between individual resources and residential outcomes assumed under basic models is severely weakened. Individuals may eliminate from consideration certain communities they think are out of their price range while not realizing, for example, that affordable options may exist in some of the areas they assume are unattainable. Others may deem whole neighborhoods to be too poor or economically unattractive and remove them from consideration without realizing that these areas contain high-value housing options.

On several levels, this distinction between actual and perceived affordability is highly relevant in considering the role of economic factors in explaining patterns of residential segregation by race. Again, traditional applications of economic arguments focus on racial differences in the financial resources necessary to afford housing in particular neighborhoods, suggesting that members of different racial and ethnic groups tend to end up in separate and qualitatively different spaces because they tend to have different economic resources. In reality, at least part of this racial residential stratification may reflect group differences in *assumptions* about which places are affordable and which are not. These racial differences in perceptions of neighborhood affordability may reinforce residential stratification by leading members of different groups to search for housing in separate areas of the metropolitan area. The tendency of black and white Americans, for example, to be sorted across largely separate sets of neighborhoods may reflect, in part, the tendency of black and white Americans to disregard distinct sets of neighborhoods as unaffordable or economically unattractive.

In this more nuanced way of looking at the role of economic factors in residential stratification, group differences in neighborhood knowledge, as well as the sources of this knowledge, become crucial. In his study of the information-gathering process in Syracuse, New York, Talarchek argues that people draw on multiple sources of information to assess housing costs in an area.[14] These sources often include real estate agents, advertisements, and personal inspections, but prior knowledge of specific neighborhoods and impressions from friends or relatives also play crucial roles. In fact, our interviews with Chicago residents indicate that individuals develop fairly strong assumptions about the cost or value of housing, as well as other characteristics, in specific neighborhoods without much direct exposure to or concrete information about them. For example, Anna, a thirty-something Latina, in reflecting on a large area of the metropolitan area in which she had never lived or worked and which she knew only through what her friends and family had told her, revealed strong assumptions about its potential costs: "That county, se suburbs are really nice to live in. I would think it'd be expensive. I'm not really even sure how the housing is, but I think it would be expensive to live there."

Whether these assumptions about housing costs are accurate or not, the fact that they are based on informal sources of information has important implications for racial differences in residential outcomes. Given the racially homogenous nature of social networks and racially distinct residential experiences, the amount and content of information received by members of different races about specific neighborhoods is likely to be quite distinct. This may result in very different levels of knowledge about housing costs in various neighborhoods. Thus, when members of different racial groups assess their housing options, they come armed with different sets of direct and indirect exposures to specific neighborhoods and may have developed sharply different perceptions about affordability in these areas. As a result, members of these groups may eliminate different sets of neighborhoods in the initial stages of their housing decision-making. Members of different races may thus come to live in separate neighborhoods not simply because they hold different levels of resources to dedicate to desirable residential outcomes, but also because they hold different assumptions about which neighborhoods are affordable and therefore choose from separate sets of options.

Exacerbating this dynamic is the fact that perceptions of the affordability and value of specific neighborhoods are themselves highly racialized. That is, the racial composition of neighborhoods is likely to impact assumptions about housing costs in an area, and to do so differently for members of different racial groups. This dynamic is apparent in experimental research by Maria Krysan, Reynolds Farley, and Mick Couper in which respondents were asked to share their perceptions of the characteristics of neighborhoods viewed in video vignettes.[15] These vignettes showed neighborhoods that had identical physical characteristics, housing, and cues about social class composition but differed in their apparent racial composition. The results demonstrated that white participants in the study consistently rated neighborhoods occupied by black residents as having lower-cost housing and poorer future property values than otherwise identical neighborhoods with visible white residents. Thus, racial composition seems to be an important driver of assumptions about the affordability and value of neighborhoods.

This effect was also apparent in many of our interviews with residents of Chicago. For example, in offering her assessment of a particular neighborhood to which she had had little direct exposure, Luisa guessed that housing there would be relatively expensive "cuz they are big areas and good schools and mainly white American." When an interviewer asked

Jerome, a black man from Chicago, to talk about his impressions of one
specific neighborhood, his response was similar to Luisa's:

INTERVIEWER: Let's go to, let's pick Wheaton.

JEROME: Never heard nothin' about Wheaton.

INTERVIEWER: Really?

JEROME: Never been there, never heard nothin' about it.

INTERVIEWER: Okay, so let's cross that one out. I mean, well, let me just
ask you the question anyway. What would be your best
guess? Would you say it would be expensive or inexpen-
sive to live in there?

JEROME: I would probably say expensive. It's the suburbs . . . I
mean, I've never been up there and I don't know anybody who stays there, so it's hard to say, whereas like
I know how Schaumberg and Hoffman Estates is just—
it's predominantly white.

With limited exposure to predominantly white neighborhoods—either
directly as a result of residential history or daily activities or indirectly
through the experiences of friends and family—some African Americans
like Jerome may eliminate neighborhoods from the search process based
on dubious assumptions about the cost of living in these areas. Similarly,
even in the absence of direct or vicarious exposure, white searchers may
eliminate minority-populated areas without firm knowledge of the extent
to which these areas match their economic criteria. Because members of different races rely on different social networks, different residential experiences, and different neighborhood exposures, even with similar resources,
they may develop very different ideas about which neighborhoods match
their economic resources. In this sense, segregation is driven not only by
racial differences in what individuals can afford—although this clearly
matters—but also by racial differences in perceptions of which neighborhoods are valuable and affordable.

These dynamics may help to explain why in many cities even high-
income members of racial and ethnic minority groups often end up in
neighborhoods that put them in or near relatively poor neighborhoods.[16]
Middle-class African American families, for example, may end up in neighborhoods in close proximity to poorer black areas as a function of racial
affinity, but also because their sources of information about neighborhoods effectively eliminate from their decision-making some more affluent

and racially heterogeneous areas that they could actually afford. Similarly, even white families with modest means may be able to gain access to more economically stable neighborhoods in part because their residential experiences, daily activities, and social networks provide sources of information about such areas. These dynamics also reinforce Massey and Denton's arguments about the structural linchpin of neighborhood inequality: even poor whites are somewhat protected from the worst neighborhood poverty by the fact that, because of their residential experiences and social networks, they operate within the set of neighborhoods dominated by the group with the lowest level of poverty.[17] On the other hand, even high-income blacks are exposed to relatively high levels of poverty and related social dislocations because their distinct residential experiences, social networks, and other racially circumscribed sources of information have led them to the most advantageous of the largely black parts of the city.

Again, this sorting based on racially disparate perceptions of the affordability and value of neighborhood options is at odds with the basic assumptions of simple economic arguments that individuals and groups are sorted efficiently across the neighborhoods of the city based on their objective ability to afford housing in these areas. These economic models have typically seen the city as a giant sorting machine, funneling individuals into the neighborhoods that match their ability to pay, but it is very likely the case that, given racial differences in neighborhood exposures, residential experiences, social networks, and sources of information, members of different racial and ethnic groups are sorted through different parts of the machine, among distinct sets of neighborhoods.

ECONOMICS AND THE CONTEXT OF THE SEARCH

The sociologist Matthew Desmond's seminal work on eviction processes and repercussions in Milwaukee clearly illuminated the role of extreme economic hardship in residential outcomes.[18] Locating and maintaining stable housing is a constant struggle for poor families, the vast majority of whom receive no housing assistance from public sources. In the most extreme cases, economic hardship is punctuated by formal eviction, though it is likely that far more low-income families decide to move in the face of an economic crisis, realizing that allowing the process to end in a formal eviction will dramatically undermine their ability to find stable housing in the future. Under such circumstances, simply finding a roof in the context of little opportunity to plan and fewer resources is a desperate, all-encompassing endeavor that leaves the tasks of assessing all residential options and carefully weighing the full slate of the costs and benefits of various residential locations clearly beyond the realm of possibility. For the people Desmond studied, extreme poverty undermined their hopes for residential stability and prevented the kind of logical, rational decision-making assumed under the classic economic arguments of residential sorting.

Desmond's depictions of eviction and extreme poverty may appear to apply to only the most desperate circumstances, but they offer important insights into additional complexities of the role of economic resources in the housing search process. Most importantly, his observations suggest that economic conditions affect not only the housing and neighborhood options a family can afford but also the very context of the residential move. Economic conditions affect the motivations for moving, the extent to which a move is fully planned, and, by extension, the extent to which the rational, exhaustive searches imagined under traditional economic models are actually realized. In addition, economic conditions help to shape the tools and strategies utilized in the search for housing. Because all of these dynamics are highly racialized, and because of substantial racial differences in economic resources, this observation has important implications—beyond those typically offered in traditional economic explanations—for group disparities in neighborhood outcomes and segregation.

The role of economic factors in establishing the basic context of residential decision-making is partially reflected in the link between income and the reasons for undertaking a move. Figure 7.3 offers basic descriptive statistics of AHS data for householders who had moved into their housing unit within the two-year period preceding their interview. These respondents were asked to report their reasons for undertaking the recent move. Although the categories of reasons are neither completely unambiguous nor mutually exclusive, they do allow us to roughly distinguish between purposive moves motivated by the desire to upgrade housing conditions or improve economic prospects and moves necessitated by external events or circumstances that might have been beyond the volition of the householder. Specifically, we distinguish between four broad categories of moves. What we refer to as *involuntary reasons* include evictions, foreclosures, fire or other disaster causing damage to the previous housing unit, and forced moves as a result of one's property being condemned or the government or a private party wanting to use it for another reason. The second category encompasses reasons for moving that are related to *family change*—for example, the formation of an independent household or a change in marital status. It is important to note that this category is likely to reflect a combination of voluntary decisions and events beyond the control of the householder. *Voluntary economic reasons* for moving include moves undertaken to be closer to the current or prospective places of work or school. Finally, *voluntary housing reasons* are related to the desire to upgrade

Figure 7.3   Reasons for Moving Reported by Recent Movers, by Family Income Quintile, 2011–2013

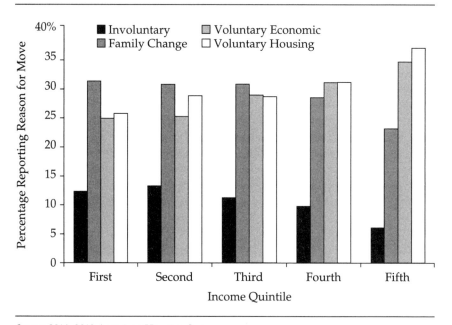

Source: 2011–2013 American Housing Survey.

housing conditions—for example, by moving to a larger or higher-quality unit or making the transition from renting to buying.

Again, it is important to note that individuals typically report multiple motivations for a single residential move and that the line between voluntary and involuntary reasons can be blurry. Nevertheless, even this rough distinction highlights some important differences in the reasons for moving for households in different economic strata.[19] Moves for those with relatively high incomes are often motivated by the effort to upgrade housing conditions; 36 percent of recent movers in the top fifth of the AHS distribution of family income reported moving in order to upgrade the quality or size of their unit or to make a housing-tenure transition. While fairly apparent across all economic strata, this housing-upgrade rationale increases as income rises; among those in the lowest quintile of family income, 25 percent reported moving for voluntary housing reasons. A similar pattern is apparent in voluntary economic reasons for mobility: 24 percent of those in the lowest income quintile reported moving to be closer to a job, to school, or to employment opportunities, whereas 34 percent of those in the highest income category reported this type of economic rationale.

In contrast, the likelihood of reporting that a move was precipitated by a change in marital status, the formation of a separate household, or another family change declines with income, from 30.6 percent in the lowest income quintile to 22.6 percent in the highest. And even though individuals from all income strata experience involuntary moves, this reason for moving is much more common for those at the bottom of the economic distribution. About 12 percent of those in the bottom two quintiles of income reported moving because of an eviction, a foreclosure, damage to the previous unit, or loss of the unit to another purpose, whereas fewer than 6 percent of those in the top quintile reported this type of involuntary move.[20] Given racial differences in economic standing, this link between income and mobility rationales has important implications for racial and ethnic differences in reasons for moving. Just 9.4 percent of white householders in the AHS reported involuntary reasons for undertaking a recent move, compared to 11.6 percent of Latino householders and 12.5 percent of black household-ers. This is consistent with past research showing that black households are especially likely to experience an unanticipated, unplanned, or forced move.[21]

Although typically ignored in traditional arguments, acknowledging the variations in reasons for undertaking a move are crucial for understanding the full role of economics in maintaining residential stratification. These reasons for undertaking a move determine the context of the move and are likely to shape both the process of searching for housing and the resi-dential outcome. Hints of this dynamic are revealed in figure 7.4, which displays income variations in the basic tools that households use to find housing, based on the American Housing Survey's series of items asking recent movers to report how they first learned about the unit into which they recently moved. As before, the AHS data do not provide the basis for definitive conclusions, especially since householders may have used other tools to search besides the one that proved successful.

Nevertheless, figure 7.4 is at least suggestive of income differences in the basic search process. Within each income stratum, a substantial number of recent movers identified their new unit through word of mouth, a fact that highlights the important role played by social networks in the housing search process. But this tendency to rely on interpersonal sources of infor-mation appears to be particularly strong among those with the fewest eco-nomic resources: 42 percent of recent movers in the lowest income quintile and 41 percent of those in the second quintile reported finding their new unit through word of mouth, versus only 18 percent among those in the highest income group. Lower-income movers are also more likely than

Figure 7.4   How Recent Movers First Heard About the Current Unit, by Family Income Quintile, 2011–2013

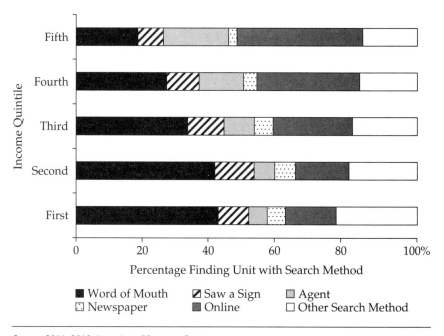

Source: 2011–2013 American Housing Survey.

those with more resources to have found their current unit by seeing a sign during their search or daily round. In contrast, higher-income movers are much more likely to have used formal search processes. Specifically, the percentage of recent movers who found their unit through online sources is more than twice as high among those in the highest income category (36.7 percent) than among those in the first or second quintile (14.8 and 15.6 percent, respectively).[22] To the extent that different methods for finding housing provide access to information on housing options that differs in both quality and quantity, these income variations have important implications for broader patterns of residential stratification. And the effects of relying on informal sources of information about housing options may be exacerbated by the tendency of lower-income movers to view far fewer potential destinations before making a move. Specifically, whereas recent movers from the top income quintile view almost a dozen housing units, on average, before deciding on a new place to live, the numbers are 5.0 and 5.4 for those in the first and second quintiles, respectively.

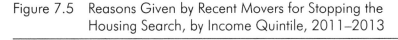

Figure 7.5   Reasons Given by Recent Movers for Stopping the
Housing Search, by Income Quintile, 2011–2013

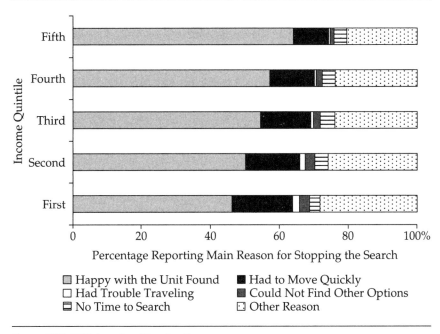

Percentage Reporting Main Reason for Stopping the Search

☐ Happy with the Unit Found   ■ Had to Move Quickly
☐ Had Trouble Traveling   ■ Could Not Find Other Options
⊟ No Time to Search   ▣ Other Reason

Source: 2011–2013 American Housing Survey.

The central point here is that economic resources shape residential processes not only by determining which housing options a family can afford but also by shaping the very context of the search and determining the resources available to dedicate to the search. The housing searches of those with relatively few economic resources, whose access to at least some search tools is likely to be restricted, may be substantially more constrained than is typically imagined in classic depictions of residential attainment models. Moreover, time is often of the essence for these families, many of whom move out of necessity rather than by choice; their search for new housing may not end when an optimal outcome is reached, but when any minimally adequate residential option is identified.

This dynamic is reflected in figure 7.5, which displays responses by recent movers in the AHS to items related to why they stopped their most recent housing search. For all five income groups, the most commonly reported reason for stopping a search was being happy with the unit that was found, but the frequency of this outcome varies by income. Among those in the lowest income category, just under half (46.2 percent) reported stopping the search because they were satisfied with the unit, while 64 percent in the highest income quintile stopped the search because they found what they were looking for. By itself, this points to the importance of economic resources in determining satisfactory residential outcomes.

More telling of the subtle role of economics in driving residential search processes are observed variations in the likelihood of ending a search because of time constraints or restricted options. About 18 percent of those in the lowest income category, but just 10.3 percent of the highest-income movers, reported stopping the search because they had to move quickly. Similarly, the proportion of respondents reporting that they stopped the search because they could not find better options was about one and a half times larger in the lowest two income strata than in the highest three strata. Although the overall proportion of recent movers who reported stopping the search because they had trouble traveling is small, the likelihood of reporting such transportation restrictions was more than five times higher among the lowest-income respondents than among those in the highest economic category.[23]

RESIDENTIAL CHOICE UNDER CONSTRAINT

Among the repercussions of these search constraints are pronounced income differentials in the extent to which the housing search leads to improved residential environs. When asked to compare their new housing unit to the unit they lived in before their most recent move, almost 60 percent of recent AHS movers in the highest income category reported that the new unit was better than the old one. The corresponding numbers for those in the first and second income quintiles were, respectively, 48 and 49 percent. Similar contrasts emerge when movers were asked to compare the relative quality of their new and old neighborhoods: in comparison to high-income movers, lower-income movers were more likely to report that their housing unit and neighborhood quality were lower after the move. Clearly, and not surprisingly, economic resources have an impact on the ability to achieve residential upgrades.

Innovative research by the sociologist Stefanie DeLuca and her colleagues on housing choice voucher holders offers a compelling example of the impact of social class on the very calculus used in the residential selection process. She argues that the traditional models of housing decision-making are not very relevant for those with few resources because these models fail to acknowledge how low-income searchers' "experiences and survival strategies shape their view of the costs and benefits of various residential and school options."[24] Under such circumstances of extreme economic deprivation, and especially in the context of constrained residential history, a housing unit's characteristics appear to take priority in the search process over the characteristics of the neighborhood in which it is located. This is not to say that low-income households disregard neighborhood conditions in the housing search process. Rather, their relative lack of economic resources and associated constraints are likely to severely alter their construction of a consideration set of neighborhoods—the first stage of the search process—in ways that further diminish their opportunities to gain access to better neighborhoods. In essence, low-income householders may not have the luxury of filtering out the neighborhoods at the very low end of the housing cost scale, and this constraint would make it difficult to apply any other filters, such as those related to school quality, crime levels, or access to economic opportunities. Whereas searchers with more resources can eliminate neighborhoods with certain undesirable qualities, low-income searchers cannot afford to do so. In part, this dynamic is consistent with traditional depictions of the role of economic resources: low-income people end up in poor neighborhoods because they cannot afford to live elsewhere and therefore do not bother to look in more expensive environs. Those with higher incomes can filter out many neighborhoods with poor schools, high crime, or environmental hazards, but these criteria may play a relatively minor role in the residential decision-making of some low-income households because their residential experiences have led them to believe that avoiding these types of neighborhoods is not possible.

It is not the case that lower-income householders find these kinds of neighborhoods desirable. Rather, as Peter Rosenblatt and Stefanie Deluca suggest, their very choice framework is profoundly shaped by their lived experiences. In constrained contexts, there is a trade-off between unit and neighborhood.[25] The decision is often to go with a better unit in a worse neighborhood—a choice driven by lived experiences that enable these searchers to feel confident that they can live in the "worse neighborhoods." As Rosenblatt and DeLuca explain:

> It was these skills, honed over years of surviving in dangerous places, rather than discomfort in low-poverty communities, preferences for same-race neighbors, or desire to be close to kin, which seemed to be more important for shaping where families moved after their initial MTO unit. When combined with difficulties of obtaining affordable housing in low poverty areas, these skills and world views explain how families adjusted their expectations about what constitutes suitable neighborhoods and drew them back into poorer neighborhoods over time. . . . The existence of these strategies does not imply that families prefer to live in unsafe neighborhoods, but suggests a willingness and an ability to cope with such places should the need arise.[26]

Our interview with Paula, a thirty-eight-year-old Latina living in a heavily Latino inner-ring suburb, brought this dynamic to life, though Paula did aspire to choose differently next time:

> PAULA: My housing experiences have just been moving and moving and moving because I've never had the money to live in a place, the right place. And it's just been, I've lived in a lot of bad neighborhoods and in a lot of places that I don't want to live, because of money.
>
> INTERVIEWER: And those bad neighborhoods, what about the apartments compared to the apartment you have now?
>
> PAULA: Well, I've had really nice apartments in a bad neighborhood, really nice apartments for cheaper money. The only thing is that the neighborhood is not good, gangbangers, shootings, and everything. But I have had better apartments before when I was living on the North Side of Berwyn. In the really bad part where there were shootings, I had a really nice apartment there. And I remember, I think I was paying only, I think, $400 a month for a two-bedroom apartment, $350 or $400 or something like that.
>
> INTERVIEWER: But the neighborhood?
>
> PAULA: Ugh, the neighborhood was horrible. [laughs]
>
> INTERVIEWER: So then you moved over here?
>
> PAULA: Then I moved to a different part of Cicero. I stayed in Cicero for most of my years in Chicago. But I'm always trying to look for better neighborhoods than Cicero.

When asked what lessons she had learned from her many moves, she said:

Well, [laughs] I learned that the next time I move it's gotta be for the best, for the better, you know. I don't want to move to a worse neighborhood like I used to do before. I used to move to a worse neighborhood just because the rent was cheaper, and what I've learned now is that I got to look for the best place and school for my kids to be in and an affordable rent.

In this case, we see that in the past Paula seldom eliminated neighborhoods and instead prioritized unit characteristics. She seldom eliminated bad neighborhoods from her consideration set because her options were severely constrained by financial resources. Clearly her resource constraints constructed the situation she was in—if she had had more money, she would not have had to sacrifice one for the other. She would have been able not only to get a unit suitable for her family and its size and needs but also to have it located in a neighborhood with schools of high quality. But she had determined that the next time she searched she would be more selective in her neighborhood consideration set, even if that meant living in a worse unit, so that she could be in a better neighborhood. Paula's example also hints at a key finding of research on poor women who have successfully moved to opportunity areas: their preferences are mutable, and their priorities (such as prioritizing unit features over neighborhood features) can shift over time based on lived experiences.[27]

In general, Paula exemplifies the challenges faced by lower-income householders as they try to remain housed; the residential options of many households are so constrained that gaining access to an affordable unit that has desirable features and is also in a good location is unrealistic. In essence, if searchers apply other kinds of neighborhood criteria besides the affordability of units, the consideration set might end up empty. The recognition of this challenge is likely to influence how householders go about searching for housing and evaluating options and neighborhoods. This example turns on its head the idea that searchers simply sort themselves into neighborhoods that match their preferences, or even their ability to pay. Because lower-income householders have restricted resources and the sense, in some cases, that neighborhoods do not differ that much on a range of qualities, they make decisions in stage 1 that result in search sets with options that searchers with fewer economic constraints would have eliminated at the outset. Examining residential stratification through the lens of the housing search reveals that economic factors can alter the relative weight given to housing and neighborhood conditions in the search process. Under extreme economic hardship, and especially in the context of extremely circumscribed residential experiences, unit characteristics can become more important, often leading low-income households to choose the best unit among those available in a relatively poor set of neighborhoods.

In general, then, the process of winnowing down neighborhoods and identifying and investigating residential options may be severely constrained by a shortage of economic resources. On top of this, time and access to transportation and the other resources necessary for a full search tend to vary by income. People with substantial financial resources do have real choices: they can afford to live virtually anywhere they like, and they have the resources necessary to investigate these options. These higher-status individuals are likely to have a successful housing search, resulting in a residential outcome that matches their preferences and economic means, simply because they have greater resources—the time and the money—to dedicate to the search.

For those at the other end of the economic spectrum, a particular housing outcome may not represent a choice per se because resource limitations and related circumstances constrained their options; that is, economic necessity filtered most options out of their consideration set. In fact, Rhodes and DeLuca's study of low-income African Americans problematizes the idea that residential outcomes represent actual housing *choices* at all.[28] Under pressure—from problems with paying housing costs, for example, or the threat of being evicted—households with limited resources may have few "choices" for their housing. These families "select" the first housing opportunity that they can reasonably afford even if it is less than ideal. The residential outcomes of households with economic resources that fall between these two extremes of great abundance and tremendous scarcity reflect a combination of constraints and opportunities. In light of this, understanding the full effect of economic resources on patterns of residential stratification requires not just attention to the links between socioeconomic status and residential outcomes but also attention to the context and process of the search.

IMPLICATIONS FOR RACIAL SEGREGATION

In many ways, the available evidence is consistent with the traditional story of the role of economics in residential sorting—that individuals seek to maximize their residential utility by buying their way into the best possible neighborhood they can afford. Accordingly, higher-income households are simply better able than those with fewer resources to afford the best housing and are therefore more likely to end up in high-quality neighborhoods, a dynamic reflected in observed associations between economic resources and neighborhood context. Following this logic, the tendency of members of different racial and ethnic groups to end up in separate and qualitatively distinct residential areas is clearly affected by group differences in average levels of income and other financial resources. As a result, residential segregation is most pronounced in those areas with the greatest racial disparities in economic resources.

Yet, through the lens of the housing search—the on-the-ground processes through which individuals and families sort themselves into neighborhoods—a much more complex role of economic resources is revealed. Most obviously, sharp racial and ethnic differences in economic resources suggest stratification in the context of the search—especially the level of volition and urgency attached to a residential move—and the resources available to carry out a comprehensive search. In fact, available data suggest that people of color, especially Latino and African American householders, are more likely than whites to experience an unplanned or involuntary move and more likely to end their search because they had to move quickly or could not find better options.[29] Largely because of group differences in economic resources, black and Latino householders are also more likely than white householders to rely on social networks and other informal sources of information in searching for housing.[30] In short, group differences in economic resources not only affect stratification in the set of housing units that can reasonably be afforded but also lead to sharp racial differences in the process through which members of different groups search for, and select, housing and neighborhoods.

These dynamics are likely to be magnified by substantial racial variations in neighborhood perceptions—especially assumptions about which neighborhoods are affordable. People do not usually know the full price range of all the housing options in a community, much less the full slate of communities making up the places they can afford. To the extent that information about communities in general and affordability in particular is shaped by social networks and lived experiences, we can readily imagine that the quality and accuracy of that information depend on what are racially different lived experiences and racially homogenous networks. As we suggested in chapters 4 and 5, both of these shape community perceptions and probably have an impact on outcomes. Thus, if members of different racial and ethnic groups hold different levels of knowledge about specific neighborhoods, they are likely to approach the housing market with very different lists of places they think they can afford. As discussed in chapter 6, there is ample evidence to suggest that patterns of residential knowledge are highly ordered by race in ways that are likely to produce sharp differences in housing search parameters even between members of different races with similar economic resources. These variations, of course, call into question the efficacy of the process of residential sorting assumed under the traditional economic model.

These more subtle effects of economic conditions shed new light on a persistent question related to the drivers of racial residential stratification: why do the constraints of low resources seem to have relatively little impact on residential outcomes for whites? Even white families with few economic resources manage to live in, and move to, neighborhoods with relatively low levels of poverty and related dislocations. For example, as shown in figure 7.2, the ability to gain access to neighborhoods with large white concentrations is similar across the entire income distribution for whites, and the ability to avoid a poor neighborhood destination is only slightly lower for the lowest-income white movers than for the highest-income white movers. This finding stands in contrast to the dynamics for Latinos and African Americans, among whom the effects of socioeconomic resources on residential destinations tend to be more pronounced.

As discussed elsewhere, part of this differential effect of income may reflect complex variations in residential preferences, and part may be due to the differential effects of discrimination. But not to be discounted are important racial differences in how economics shapes the search process. Especially salient here are the roles of personal residential histories and social networks in magnifying or ameliorating the effects of economic hardship. Because of the long history of residential stratification and the intergenerational nature of neighborhood disadvantage, low-income black and Latino householders are relatively unlikely to have any personal experience with life outside of relatively poor neighborhoods and in fact may have relatively few friends or families with such experiences. In contrast, a relatively greater proportion of even low-income whites have had either direct exposure to more affluent neighborhoods or indirect exposure through the experiences of family and friends. As a result, even poor whites may be less likely than similarly positioned blacks and Latinos to exclude better neighborhoods from their consideration set. Moreover, when economic hardship and related resource constraints necessitate a reliance on word of mouth and other informal means of searching, whites are more likely than blacks and Latinos with similar resources to learn about options in relatively better neighborhoods. In this sense, understanding the role of economic conditions in the residential stratification process requires attention to not only racial differences in the economic resources available to pay for housing in particular neighborhoods but also differences in the effects of these resources on residential search processes.

In sum, racial and ethnic differences in the context of the search, resources available to dedicate to the search process, and sources of information about residential options are likely to produce important stratification in residential outcomes that cannot be attributed simply to affordability. Although existing data sources do not allow a test of this argument, it is reasonable to assume that the context of the search has a direct impact on the outcome of the search; an urgent or unplanned housing search conducted with limited access to transportation and the other tools necessary for a full search is presumably more likely to end with the selection of the most readily available housing outcome rather than an outcome that is most advantageous or matches residential priorities. In this way, the economic constraints experienced by some groups may drive stratification in residential outcomes not just by determining what different groups can afford but by shaping the parameters of the search and assessment of residential options. In comparison to whites, blacks and Latinos may be more constrained during the housing search process and thus more likely to settle for a new location for less-than-ideal reasons. The extent to which this racial-ethnic stratification reflects, and emerges out of, differences in more nuanced features of the search process deserves considerably more attention.

Chapter 8 | The Social Structural Sorting Perspective on the Role of Preferences

ACCORDING TO ONE of the traditional explanations for segregation, racial differences in residential location and broader patterns of segregation reflect group differences in racial residential preferences. As such, segregation is driven by a desire among people to live near neighbors of their own racial-ethnic group. Driving much of the traditional research about the relationship between preferences and segregation is a simplistic and often implicit model: people hold preferences for a particular racial composition, and those preferences translate into residential outcomes that, in the aggregate, perpetuate segregation.

This simple model is deceptive, and existing studies leave unanswered a number of questions about how preferences play out in the real world. What drives preferences? What obstacles are there to achieving one's preferences? How does a neighborhood's racial composition compare to other neighborhood features in terms of driving choices? At what stage do preferences function? Because of how preferences have been measured and theorized, traditional studies of segregation and the role of preferences in it are generally ill equipped to answer these questions because (1) they assume that preferences are independent of other drivers of segregation, and (2) they lack a model of the neighborhood selection and housing search process that specifies how preferences function. After providing an overview of the general pattern of preferences as revealed in traditional studies, we review efforts to connect preferences to residential segregation at the individual and aggregate levels. With this review in mind, we draw out the assumptions that guide these studies and illustrate how the lens of the social structural sorting perspective can help overcome the shortcomings of existing approaches.

151

MEASURES AND PATTERNS OF
RACIAL RESIDENTIAL PREFERENCES

Beginning in 1976, Reynolds Farley and his colleagues developed a tool that provided the first comprehensive, survey-based picture of racial residential preferences. White and black Detroit-area residents were presented with small cards, each showing a simple drawing of a neighborhood with fourteen houses (with a blank in the middle for the respondent's house) that were shaded to represent white or black families living in them. White respondents were shown cards with one, three, five, or eight black families and asked (1) how comfortable they would be living in such a neighborhood and, if they would not be comfortable, (2) would they try to leave if their neighborhood came to look like the one on the card. Black respondents were asked to rank-order cards with zero, four, seven, twelve, and fourteen white families from their top to bottom choice and then to identify neighborhoods in which they were *willing* to live. The measurement was repeated in 1992 and 2004.[1]

The results of these studies support several conclusions. First, the willingness of Detroit-area whites to live in neighborhoods with a single black resident grew substantially between 1976 and 2004, from 76 to 93 percent. There were reduced levels of comfort with neighborhoods that had a 20 percent black population compared to a single black neighbor, but there was still increasing openness, from 58 percent in 1976 to 83 percent in 2004. In the most recent survey, white Detroiters continued to express limited tolerance for living in majority-black neighborhoods, with 51 percent reporting that they would be uncomfortable living in a neighborhood where just over one-half of the residents were African American. Overall, whites' stated willingness to live in a given neighborhood clearly declines as the percentage of blacks increases.[2]

Whites' residential preferences stand in sharp contrast with those of African Americans. In all three time periods, between 50 and 63 percent of Detroit-area African Americans selected as their first choice the neighborhood that was about 50 percent black and 50 percent white.[3] Importantly, when asked where they were *willing* to live, African Americans indicated that a range of different neighborhood compositions were acceptable: between 85 and 99 percent of blacks were willing to live in 20 percent, 53 percent, and 73 percent black neighborhoods across all three time periods, with little clear trend one way or another. Moreover, it is the all-white and all-black options that are least popular: between 65 and 75 percent (depending on the survey year) of Detroit-area blacks were willing to move into an all-black neighborhood; and between 31 and 43 percent were willing to move into an all-white one.[4] A key finding of these studies is that African

American Detroiters preferred neighborhoods that were more integrated than those in which the typical African American Detroiter lived.

National-level data are more limited in both temporal breadth and substantive depth. Between 1990 and 2010, white General Social Survey (GSS) respondents were asked about living in a neighborhood in which half of their neighbors were black, while black GSS respondents were asked about the prospect of living in a neighborhood in which half of their neighbors were white. The national trends are consistent with the Detroit patterns in that there has been increasing openness among white survey respondents to living in a neighborhood that is one-half black: between 1990 and 2010, the percentage of whites who said that they would oppose or strongly oppose living in a half-white, half-black neighborhood dropped from 48 to 20 percent. Conversely, the percentage who said that they would favor such a neighborhood grew from 10 percent in 1990 to 24 percent in 2010. As with the Detroit data, the national data show that blacks are more interested in living in half-white, half-black neighborhoods than whites: fewer than 10 percent of African Americans across all time points said that they would oppose or strongly oppose a neighborhood that was half-white. Conversely, the majority of blacks across all years would somewhat or strongly *favor* living in a half-white neighborhood (the remainder said that they were neither in favor nor opposed). In other words, both the Detroit and national GSS data suggest that blacks maintain a strong preference for integration with whites. In contrast, despite some liberalization, whites still have a very limited preference for the types of neighborhoods that African Americans find most desirable.

With the growing diversity of metropolitan areas, the focus on attitudes about black-white neighborhoods has become a specious strategy for understanding residential preferences. Studies of Los Angeles in the 1990s provided the first insights into racial residential preferences among groups besides blacks and whites. In one approach, the Detroit showcard technique was adapted by experimentally varying the racial-ethnic background of the "other" group in the neighborhood.[5] With respect to comfort, the vast majority of whites living in Los Angeles (92 percent or more) said that they would be comfortable living with a single black, Latino, or Asian neighbor. Importantly, at this level of integration, there is no distinction based on which "other" group (blacks, whites, or Asians) is involved. But when asked about larger representations of the "other" group, the response depended on which specific group was being considered. Although white comfort dropped to 88 percent with three black neighbors, there was no reduction when the other group comprised either three Latino or three Asian neighbors. As the percentage of the "other" group got larger, the responses became even more distinctive based on the identity of the out-group. For the most diverse neighborhood presented to respondents, 57 percent of whites said that they would be comfortable if the nonwhite neighbors were black; 72 percent of whites, however, said that they would be comfortable if those neighbors were Latino, and fully 80 percent said that they would be comfortable if the neighbors were Asian.

The pattern for black respondents suggests that neighborhoods with whites were more attractive than neighborhoods with Latinos; Asians appeared to be the least attractive neighbors for blacks.[6] That Latinos are also influenced—but differently—by the race of non-Latino neighbors is revealed strikingly in the percentage of Latinos selecting the all-Latino neighborhood depending on whether the alternative was a black-Latino neighborhood or a white-Latino neighborhood. Specifically, nearly 80 percent of Latinos picked the all-Latino neighborhood as their first or second choice when the other residents in the neighborhood were black, but when the other residents were white, the percentage selecting an all-Latino neighborhood as their first or second choice plummeted to just 21 percent. In the middle are those Latinos who were asked about living with Asians— here 55 percent of Latinos picked the all-Latino neighborhood as their first or second choice.

Asians had similar patterns to Latinos in that all-own-race neighborhoods were least attractive to them when the "other" neighbors were white (just 18 percent picked this neighborhood) and most attractive when the other neighbors were Latino (53 percent), but especially when they were black (77 percent). Looked at another way, almost three-quarters of Asians were not willing to move into an all-black neighborhood, but only about one-quarter objected to an all-white neighborhood.[7]

Overall, this analysis reveals that all groups prefer to live in neighborhoods with substantial numbers of their coethnics. But at the same time, the substantial differences based on which groups are integrating with whom reveals that neutral ethnocentrism—where the motivation behind the preferences is a desire to be around one's own group rather than a desire to avoid another group—is not responsible for this pattern.

A second measure of preferences in a multiethnic context recrafts the show-card technique and permits people to design their own ideal racial composition. The same stylized "neighborhood card" was presented to respondents, but this time all of the houses were blank and people were asked to fill in the houses so that the neighborhood showed their ideal racial-ethnic combination. Though the 1992–1994 results are now rather dated, the general patterns are informative and provide a rare glimpse into white, black, Asian, and Latino attitudes about living with whites, blacks,

Asians, and Latinos. The sociologist Camille Charles reports that, on average, all four racial-ethnic groups in the Los Angeles sample created ideal neighborhoods that included substantial integration.[8]

But at the same time, each of the groups—but especially whites— preferred neighborhoods where their own racial-ethnic group was the largest. For whites, the average ideal neighborhood was 50 percent white; for Latinos and Asians the same-race preference, on average, was 41 percent. The same-race percentage for blacks was the lowest of all four groups: the average black Los Angeles respondent created a neighborhood that was 37 percent black. Additionally, whites were the most likely to create an all–own group neighborhood as their ideal. The racial hierarchy—which was evident in the traditional show-card results reported earlier—is also evident in this ideal neighborhood: blacks were always the least preferred out-group neighbors, and whites were always the most preferred out-group neighbors.[9] The technique was replicated in the 2000 GSS, and the pattern of the national results was not too different from what was reported for Los Angeles whites and blacks in the late 1990s.[10]

The "draw your ideal neighborhood" study was also replicated in the 2004–2005 CAS, whose results were consistent with the national data in that whites, blacks, and Latinos were interested in neighborhoods that were quite diverse.[11] Additionally, all three groups preferred diverse neighborhoods where their own group was numerically largest—though it was only whites who created a majority-white (more than 50 percent) ideal neighborhood. Whites were again the most desirable other-race neighbor for blacks and Latinos. For whites, there was little sign of the racial hierarchy beyond the size of the white population—the sizes of the black, Latino, and Asian populations were about the same (13 to 14 percent), with the population of Arab Americans smaller in size than the other groups.[12]

The CAS respondents were also asked to create their *least* desired neighborhood racial composition. The comparison in the results between the most and least desired neighborhoods revealed the racial hierarchy that was missing in the "most desired" neighborhood results. For whites, there was a dramatic increase in the size of the black population (from 14 percent on average to 38 percent on average) and the Arab American population (from 7 percent to 24 percent) between the least desirable neighborhood as compared to the most desired neighborhood. Conversely, the Latino population increased only minimally (8 percentage point difference), and the Asian population declined by 7 percentage points. Similarly, Latinos' least desired neighborhood had substantially fewer Latinos and strikingly more Arab Americans (from 7 percent to 17 percent) and, especially, African americans (from 14 to 46 percent) compared to the most desired neighborhood. Interestingly, African Americans' most and least desired neighborhood racial compositions were quite similar, with the changes generally involving a reduction in the size of their own group and increases in the sizes of the Arab American population and, to a lesser extent, the white population.[13] Juxtaposing the most and least desirable neighborhoods for all groups, the authors show that commitment to diversity is fragile and depends on the relative size of the population and, importantly, the specific out-groups being considered.

RESEARCH ON THE IMPACT OF PREFERENCES ON SEGREGATION

Research attempting to pinpoint the effect of these kinds of preferences on segregation has taken one of two approaches. The one with the longest history uses aggregate patterns of preferences and neighborhood racial composition to create simulation models designed to assess processes of neighborhood change under varying assumptions. For the most part, the simulations suggest that the general pattern of preferences (blacks prefer more blacks in their neighborhoods than whites are willing to consider) are incompatible with integration. The economist Thomas Schelling famously observed that even small differences in racial residential preferences between aggregate groups can translate into "tipping points" that become the engine of perpetual segregation.[14] Under this model, given whites' limited tolerance for black neighbors, the introduction of any black population into a neighborhood is likely to spawn the out-mobility of at least some white residents. And given their stronger preference for integrated neighborhoods, blacks are more likely than whites to fill the resulting vacancies in the now racially mixed neighborhood, thereby increasing the black concentration of the neighborhood and violating the residential preferences of more of the white residents. In essence, Schelling's model provided an early depiction of the process through which differences in racial residential preferences can precipitate neighborhood transitions from all-white to all-black—thereby reinforcing segregation.

A number of other simulation studies have applied the preferences identified in survey research (generally assuming that whites will object if more than 20 percent of their neighborhood is black and that blacks prefer a fifty-fifty split) to support the notion that preferences are an important engine of segregation.[15] One more recent and promising turn in this type of analysis is the exploration of models with more dynamic assumptions about preferences.[16] But even with these more sophisticated models, the assumptions about how the neighborhood selection and housing search process unfolds and how these preferences factor into it—which is ultimately at the core of the process—are rudimentary.

A second approach to studying the role of preferences in segregation has used individual-level survey data to determine the statistical association between hypothetical racial residential preferences and the racial composition of a person's current neighborhood. Using data from the Multi-City Study of Urban Inequality (MCSUI), this research has found that racial residential preferences *are* related to outcomes, though the relationship is far from deterministic.[17] For example, the economists Keith Ihlanfeldt and Benjamin Scafidi have found that in Atlanta, Detroit, and Los Angeles, blacks who preferred to live with higher percentages of blacks lived in neighborhoods with higher percentages of blacks.[18] But they reject the conclusion that their study supports the hypothesis that segregation comes about because of black preferences to self-segregate, because all three cities are more segregated than blacks prefer. For example, African Americans living in Atlanta prefer a 71 percent black neighborhood, while on average blacks' block groups are 81 percent black. These differences are starker in Detroit, where the preferred percentage black is 62 percent and blacks live in blocks with, on average, 92 percent black residents. These studies also show that regardless of preferences—whether for an all-white, all-black, or racially mixed neighborhood—the size of the actual black population at the block level lies between a very narrow range (80 to 95 percent). In short, although individual blacks with stronger preferences for black neighbors do reside in neighborhoods with a higher percentage of blacks, this cannot explain persistent patterns of segregation in these cities.[19] The urban planning professor Lance Freeman examined a similar question using these data and drew the same general conclusion.[20]

Also using the MCSUI data, but focusing on the middle class—the group in the best position, arguably, to fulfill their preferences—the sociologist Robert Adelman found that black middle-class residents were unable to achieve their preferred racial composition, while white middle-class residents were closer in correspondence between their preferences and their current neighborhood. Adelman concluded that

> the residential preferences of middle class blacks and whites play significant roles in their neighborhood outcomes. Nevertheless, the analyses also show that even when middle-class blacks prefer to live in integrated neighborhoods they remain in neighborhoods largely composed of other African Americans. This supports the idea that residential preferences are less determinative factors for middle-class blacks in their neighborhood outcomes compared to middle class whites.[21]

THE ASSUMPTIONS ABOUT
HOW PREFERENCES OPERATE
TO SHAPE SEGREGATION

At the core of our argument is that both the traditional measurement approach and the assumptions underlying efforts to draw and test connections between racial residential preferences and segregation fail to appreciate the complexity of preferences and the realities of the neighborhood selection and housing search process. Specifically, those assumptions are: (1) that racial residential preferences are separable from other explanatory factors such as discrimination and economics; and (2) that there is a simple relationship between a person's racial residential preferences and the racial composition of the neighborhood into which he or she moves. In the next section, we challenge both of these assumptions by exploring *how* racial residential preferences operate—both alone and in conjunction with other drivers—in ways that may perpetuate segregation. We draw attention to three features of preferences that are generally overlooked: (1) racial residential preferences are driven by complex factors and are in some cases inseparable from other drivers of segregation; (2) in a realistic model of neighborhood selection and housing search, it is untenable to imagine a simple correspondence between preferences and segregation; and (3) given that neighborhood selection and housing search processes are multistaged, racial residential preferences can operate and shape outcomes differently at different stages.

THE COMPLEXITY OF WHITES' PREFERENCES:
SEPARATING RACE AND CLASS?

One of the core debates in traditional studies of whites' racial residential preferences centers on the question of whether race per se drives preferences, or whether a community's racial composition is a proxy for social class considerations.[22] That is, do racial prejudice and stereotypes underpin whites' preference to avoid living in neighborhoods with more than a few African Americans, or are these attitudes based on perceptions of the social class characteristics of such neighborhoods?

It is apparent from the preceding review of studies on racial residential preferences that there are limits to whites' tolerance for living near neighbors of other races. While many have interpreted these preferences as indicative of underlying racial attitudes, some have argued that whites avoid minority neighborhoods because they are perceived as having higher levels of poverty, less stable housing prices, higher crime rates, and other characteristics that make them generally undesirable.[23] In short, *racial* residential preferences have a *social class* component to them.

This debate is a classic example of the tendency to view the forces implicated in the traditional models of the drivers of segregation as mutually exclusive. In fact, this either-or perspective has motivated a substantial amount of the research on racial residential preferences. On one side are those who argue that neighborhood racial composition is a proxy for social class characteristics, so that when people (especially but not exclusively whites) state an objection to a neighborhood with black residents, their preference is driven by the social class features that they presume are present in a black neighborhood (poor schools, high crime, high poverty), not by anything to do with the black residents.[24] To support this argument, the sociologist David Harris showed that individuals' satisfaction with their current neighborhood was significantly influenced by the perceived social class characteristics of the area, and that once these class characteristics were controlled, racial composition had no independent effect on satisfaction.[25]

Other research looking at either neighborhood satisfaction or actual mobility instead uses objective measures of social class characteristics (school test scores, crime rates, poverty rates) to show that neighborhood racial composition maintains an independent effect above and beyond social class.[26] Similarly, using vignette and video experiments, several researchers have shown that although a community's social class features impact evaluations of hypothetical neighborhoods—everybody wants to live in a neighborhood that has nicer homes, lower crime, better schools, and so on—its racial composition also matters.[27] The preponderance of evidence, then, confirms that the racial composition of a community impacts preferences—even when its social class characteristics are held constant either experimentally or statistically.

Above and beyond the question of which direction the evidence leans in, our point is that past research has treated the debate about the relative roles of neighborhood racial composition and neighborhood socioeconomic characteristics in a traditional either-or framework. But a closer look at white racial residential preferences points to the fundamental difficulties of disentangling economic dynamics and racial attitudes. As described in chapter 6, racial composition and neighborhood social class features are tightly correlated in whites' minds. This was revealed in video experiments and statistical models in which whites especially appeared to use neighborhood racial composition to infer neighborhood social class characteristics.[28] In one way, these results are consistent with a "race as proxy" interpretation. But digging deeper reveals this answer to be too simplistic. To take the video experiment as an example, not only were the

tions not a function of observable (nonracial) neighborhood char-acteristics, but they were related to the extent to which the observer held negative stereotypes about African Americans. Neighborhoods with black residents present were, on average, presumed by whites to be of lower quality than the exact same neighborhood with white residents present. Race may be a proxy, but it is a "proxy constructed in respondents' minds and shaped by their racial stereotypes."[29] Lincoln Quillian and Devah Pager's survey-based data analysis comes to a similar conclusion (see chapter 6).

In the quotes from our in-depth interviews provided in chapter 6, the tight bundling of neighborhood features was also evident. Often, almost without thinking, our interviewees figured out one feature of a place (social class, racial composition, location relative to the city itself) and could then rattle off a long list of what else was likely to be true about it. And what is generally true is that most people (especially but not exclusively whites) associate white neighborhoods with comfortable, peaceful, and quiet suburban lives and perceive African American neighborhoods as run-down, crime-ridden, and undesirable.[30] If we think about how these perceptions impact housing decisions, we can imagine that if a white person knows that an area has an African American population, he or she may rule it out, even in the absence of a desire to avoid living in a black neighborhood per se, based on the assumption that it is also high in crime, has poor schools, and provides bad city services. As Quillian and Pager demonstrated, these sometimes erroneous assumptions make racial composition a "noisy proxy" with racialized implications. And because they rely on heuristics in constructing their consideration set, people often do not realize those instances when racial composition is especially "noisy."[31]

Our point is that the line between race and social class as drivers of preferences—two interpretations often pitted against each other in traditional research on the drivers of segregation—is blurry. The strong tendency to view them as mutually exclusive is deceptive, and future research on the causes of segregation should loosen the field's grip on the need to identify the singular and untainted role of any particular driver and instead seek to understand the complex and interweaving ways in which drivers may actually function. Our purpose should be to identify ways to disentangle these drivers in the real world rather than simply in our statistical models and experimental designs.

Beyond the overemphasis on an either-or interpretation of preferences, studies have also adopted an unrealistic model of how preferences are likely to function during a neighborhood selection and housing search process. With the more complicated model spelled out in chapter 6 in mind, we now consider how this perspective helps us rethink the possible role of racial residential preferences in perpetuating segregation.

PREFERENCES THROUGH THE LENS OF THE
SOCIAL STRUCTURAL SORTING PERSPECTIVE

Traditional studies of racial residential preferences rely on measures that gauge preferences in hypothetical neighborhoods rather than considering the lived experiences of people as they make decisions about housing in real communities. One consequence is that there is very little research that can answer this question: in neighborhood selection and housing search processes, what effect do racial residential preferences have on outcomes as compared to the effect of preferences about other neighborhood features, like location, size, price, school quality, or safety? Once we ask the question in this way, given what we know about how searches unfold in stages and how people invoke different decision processes at different stages of a search, it becomes evident that our assumptions of a one-to-one correspondence between racial residential preferences and the racial composition of a neighborhood are untenable. As argued in chapter 6, it is also implausible that the process resembles a rational-choice framework in which the racial residential composition of a neighborhood is just one of many factors at the foundation of a detailed calculation of the trade-offs of various choices and associated characteristics. Rather, preferences are shaped by social factors, play out in a particular context, and ultimately flow through a multistage process guided by decision-making processes and heuristics.

The need to be mindful of this has been noted by Stefanie DeLuca and her colleagues in a number of studies of the residential outcomes of low-income households participating in voucher programs. She has observed that researchers and policymakers often attribute outcomes (such as the failure to move to opportunity areas) to preferences. But she calls this conclusion into question, noting that it fails to unpack which preferences drive decisions, where they come from, and how they intersect with the constrained environment faced by low-income searchers in particular. Indeed, she concludes in her analysis with Rosenbaum, "preferences, rather than being inherent attributes of people, are affected by the kinds of neighborhoods people have experienced."[32]

Our failure to adequately theorize the social processes underlying neighborhood selection and housing searches in general and the role of racial residential preferences in particular is suggested by a recent study comparing Chicago-area residents' preferences (as measured using traditional hypothetical neighborhood questions) to the racial composition of the places they *actually searched* for housing, and then to the racial composition of their current neighborhood.[33] Table 8.1 shows the results of this analysis. Looking at panel A, across all three groups, a minority (27 percent of whites and 31 percent of blacks and Latinos) reside in communities with the same

Table 8.1   (Mis)Match Between Percentage Own-Racial-Ethnic Group in Ideal Neighborhood, in Search Locations, and in Current Neighborhood, by Race-Ethnicity, 2004–2005

	Whites (n = 123)	Blacks (n = 114)	Latinos (n = 145)
A. Percentage own group in current neighborhood is			
Similar to percentage in ideal neighborhood (plus or minus 15 percent)	27.2%	31.1%	30.5%
Larger than in ideal neighborhood (more than 15 percent greater)	67.6	63.9	56.0
Smaller than in ideal neighborhood (more than 15 percent fewer)	5.3	5.0	13.6
B. Average percentage own group in search locations is:			
Similar to percentage in ideal neighborhood (plus or minus 15 percent)	40.3	61.7	47.1
Larger than in ideal neighborhood (more than 15 percent greater)	52.1	20.5	28.8
Smaller than in ideal neighborhood (more than 15 percent fewer)	7.6	17.8	24.1
C. Percentage own group in current neighborhood is			
Similar to percentage in search locations (plus or minus 15 percent)	63.8	35.6	35.5
Larger than in search locations (more than 15 percent greater)	24.4	59.8	56.3
Smaller than in search locations (more than 15 percent fewer)	11.8	4.7	8.2

Source: Havekes, Bader, and Krysan 2016, citing Chicago Area Study (CAS) data.[34]

percentage own-racial-ethnic group as the percentage in their ideal neighborhood and instead live with higher percentages of their own group than they say they desire.

But the step where the mismatch occurs differs for each group. For whites, the mismatch is between their ideal racial composition and the racial composition of the places where they search: the majority of whites (52 percent) search in locations with a higher percentage of whites than they say they prefer. And they end up living in the less diverse neighborhoods they search in, as reflected by the fact that 63 percent of whites live in neighborhoods that match the racial composition of their search locations.

African Americans and Latinos show a mismatch, but at a different stage. African Americans live in communities with not only more African American residents than they prefer but also more African Americans than reside in the communities in which they search: about 60 percent of blacks and 56 percent of Latinos live in neighborhoods with a higher percentage of their own group than the percentage own group in the neighborhoods where they searched. In other words, African Americans and Latinos tend to search in the communities that match their hypothetical preferences, but they fail to move into these more diverse communities.

There are a number of possible explanations for these mismatches across the three racial-ethnic groups, but all of them require a more explicit conceptualization of what shapes where people end up living and how racial residential preferences function in that process. Because preferences are so often measured using hypothetical neighborhoods, in a way unmoored from the realities of a housing search, we are seldom able to illuminate their role in the search process. This leaves us uncertain about how exactly a neighborhood's racial composition factors into neighborhood selection, particularly in comparison to other neighborhood features (location, cost, proximity to family, school quality, and so on) and unit attributes. We also often assume that preferences are immutable, a conclusion not supported by recent research—both observations made in recent studies by Stefanie DeLuca.[35]

How Preferences for Racial Composition Play Out in the First Stage

Recalling from chapter 3 and figure 3.1 that housing searches are multi-staged processes whereby all possible options are winnowed down across the stages, using heuristics and other decision-making processes informed by perceptions and knowledge, we now ask: how are preferences about a community's racial composition deployed—or not deployed? How does racial composition actually function in people's decisions to eliminate communities? Is it a question of explicit preferences about racial composition? Or is it more indirect or complex? Is neighborhood racial composition a "preference" or is it a "cue" that is invoked in the heuristic used to eliminate neighborhoods from consideration?

Traditional theories of segregation are largely silent on these questions, although as noted earlier, recent research examining the residential decision-making processes and outcomes of low-income voucher holders has turned attention to this question.[36] As a result, what the residential decision process looks like and the *way* in which racial residential preferences operate are almost entirely unspecified. Two key observations described in chapter 6 are suggestive. First, a search is sequential, with different criteria used to evaluate options at different stages.[37] One set of criteria is used to screen out neighborhoods in the first stage, and another set to evaluate specific units in the second stage.[38] Second, especially in the first stage, people rely on heuristics to guide their decision-making.[39] So how might a community's racial composition—and one's preferences related to it—operate within this framework? We turn to Donald Hempel's study as one of the few that provide survey data on this question.

In his survey of home-buyers in two housing markets in Connecticut, Hempel explains the challenges in gauging people's decision criteria. When people are asked, in an open-ended survey question, "Why did you pick this unit?" the focus tends to be on the very specific criteria related to minor differences across particular units (for example, a larger garage or a finished basement). But as he points out, this does not mean that neighborhood criteria are irrelevant. Rather, he explains, evaluative criteria are a "nested hierarchy" that operates and looks different at different stages of the housing decision process.[40]

To support his contention that neighborhood criteria are crucially important even if not explicitly mentioned by people when asked why they made the selection they did, Hempel compares two slightly different survey questions. First, when recent home-buyers are asked "Why was your present home chosen over all the other housing units which you considered?" the most common responses, he notes, were related to financial considerations and the convenience of the location. Features of the house (size and attributes) were next most frequently mentioned. The neighborhood itself and a range of features associated with it were the least common.[41]

But when recent buyers were asked to compare their actual choice to the alternatives they considered, Hempel was able to see where compromises were and were not made. First, home-buyers often compromised on attributes like price, number of rooms, and garage size, as reflected in the fact that about one in five buyers rated the unit they ended up in as "worse" than the alternatives they considered on these features.[42] Conversely, essentially no respondents (0 to 1 percent) said that their final choice was "worse" than their alternatives on the criteria of "neighborhood reputation," "quality of schools," and "people in neighborhood." These results can be reconciled if we recall the multistage housing search process and distinguish between crucial features and salient decision determinants. Hempel explains:

> Some factors, such as neighborhood reputation and type of people who live in the neighborhood, are likely to be represented in specifications which were applied in the earlier stages of the search process to screen available alternatives. They represent the initial criteria by which the choice process is narrowed down to a smaller number of acceptable housing alternatives. In deciding among these alternatives, other factors—such as price and quality of construction—may become paramount. In other words, the buyer's final choice criteria may be applied to a set of alternatives that have already been sorted through another set of screening criteria.[43]

A final piece of the puzzle requires that we recall the propo
people use heuristics in sorting through all possible options in tnis first
stage. If the construction of a consideration set is driven by heuristics, and
if race is regularly used as the cue that is "best" for helping white searchers
(in particular) efficiently decide whether a place should be in or out of the
set, then racial composition can play a profound role even if white searchers
would seldom identify racial composition as an important criterion when
asked how they selected the unit they did.[44]

Racial residential composition, then, may not merely be one of many
neighborhood features that are weighed to help determine which option
is the best. Rather, racial composition may be a fundamental organizing
principle—the feature used for elimination. Or it may just be perceived as
correlated with it. Whether explicit or implicit, whether salient to a person's
consciousness or not, racial composition's impact may be no less profound.

Thus, preferences may affect segregation not—as the standard depiction suggests—because units in neighborhoods that are most in line with a
person's racial residential preferences are affirmatively selected, but rather
because a person's consideration set, by virtue of elimination and through
the use of their screening criteria, may include communities that all have
the same racial composition. We lack the data to rigorously test this set
of ideas, but there is circumstantial evidence in several corners. First,
Hempel's study bolsters the basic argument about how different criteria
operate at different stages and how infrequently people compromise on
neighborhood features of this sort. Second, there is research showing that
the consideration sets of white searchers tend to be racially homogenous
in general and are also more racially homogenous than those of African
Americans.[45] The latter point suggests that race as a cue that helps determine consideration sets may be more influential for whites than for African
Americans and Latinos.

Third, our in-depth interviews illustrate logics that point in this direction.
For example, the profound—but initially unstated—role of racial composition is eventually revealed in this interview with Joann, the middle-aged
white woman living in a predominantly white suburb. In discussing how
she eliminated places from consideration, Joann repeatedly insisted that
"nothing is off the table" and that job opportunities drove her assessment.
But over the course of her interview, something else emerged that was even
more fundamental:

INTERVIEWER: What about . . . places that you would not consider living
even if they were this close to your job and they gave you
a free house—but you would be like, "I would never live
there."

JOANN: [*points to Englewood*] . . . It's only because I know that is a very dangerous place to be, even if you belong there. Where would I live? Where would I not live? It isn't that I don't know about these neighborhoods cuz I'm not interested. I've just never had any reason to know about them, so if somebody offered me a job that was in Jeff Park—or, it doesn't matter to me. As long as it's a place that I feel like I have a place. . . . Not ever consider living? I don't know enough to know, except what I have heard. I probably wouldn't live in Cicero. I probably wouldn't live in Berwyn. I probably wouldn't live in South Lawndale or . . . I don't know anything about these places.

INTERVIEWER: What's the deal-breaker for those? Berwyn, Cicero, South Lawndale, Oak Lawn?

JOANN: . . . Anything's on the table. I mean, honestly, except for places that I know are high-crime areas, anything is on the table.

INTERVIEWER: Englewood and where else would you consider high crime enough that you wouldn't—

JOANN: Well, I don't know of anyplace else that's that violent off the top of my head. I think Austin. I don't watch the news. I don't wanna know. There's something to be said for ignorance. [*laughs*] There isn't anything that is off the table, except for places that I clearly don't belong, like in an all-black neighborhood. Seriously? Yeah, just put me right there. That'd be really brilliant. Or an all-Hispanic neighborhood, or an all-Indian neighborhood or whatever.

INTERVIEWER: What's the reason for that?

JOANN: I don't fit in culturally. "Hi. What do we have in common? Nothing." I mean, not that I wouldn't—I mean, I have black friends. I have Hispanic friends. I have Indian friends. I have friends from every walk of life. It isn't a problem for me. It's, "What are you doing here? Why would you live here?" Seriously, why would you live here? This is why there are so many neighborhoods in Chicago. People tend to gravitate. That's why there's a Chinatown. That's why Devon Street exists. People gravitate towards things that are comfortable and familiar to them, or they feel like they have something in common with the people that are around them so that they can make friends and socialize and have a barbecue, whatever that means to them. This is dangerous. Living in a predominantly black neighborhood would be fine if I thought I had somebody to talk to and somebody to hang out with, but why would they welcome me into their homes? Unless you found some really random pocket where everybody's really friendly to everyone else and skin color doesn't really make any difference, show me that neighborhood and I would happily live there. I can't live in a place where I would feel more isolated than I feel right now living amongst my own. I actually, theoretically, belong in the North Shore, given how I was raised and what my religious and political beliefs are and how I was educated and the whole shootin' match about my professional history. I am completely isolated up there.

For Joann, a community's racial composition was fundamental to the construction of her consideration set, and it was so obvious (to her) that she almost deemed it not worthy of explicit mention. Indeed, she repeatedly insisted that "nothing is off the table," and only after being probed did she explain what she meant by "fitting in" and how a community's racial composition would absolutely put a place "off the table." Race permeated Joann's thinking about where she would fit in, and therefore where she would consider living. For Joann—and, we suggest, for others as well—racial residential preferences may swamp the decision-making process. But because they function at the elimination stage (stage 1), where they are profoundly influential in terms of geography but can also be so mundane and obvious, they may seem not worth mentioning. Notably, racial composition, if it functions like this, does not emerge as a detailed and involved assessment and evaluation, but is a "natural" and "obvious" deployment of a community characteristic.

How Preferences for Racial Composition Play Out in the Second Stage

The second key observation we make about how preferences about racial composition can operate begins from the premise that even though searchers' consideration sets may often hold places with similar racial compositions, that is not always the case. That is, not all searchers' consideration sets have been screened to result in a set of communities that all have the same racial composition. There are several reasons why the places in a searcher's consideration set might vary in terms of their racial composition. The places in a consideration set may vary in racial composition because a different criterion was more important to the searcher, or because lived experiences, social networks, or information-gathering strategies lent themselves to a more diverse set of options. Regardless of how the consideration set may come to have communities with a range of different racial compositions, we suggest that a searcher's preferred racial composition may not match the racial composition of the residential outcome for a number of different reasons. But importantly, the existing research on preferences suggests that Latinos and African Americans are the most likely to have variety in the racial composition of the places in their consideration sets and the least likely to achieve their desired racial composition.[46]

Two examples from our in-depth interviews remind us that racial residential preferences do not operate in a vacuum and so preferences related to neighborhood racial composition can take a backseat to other factors that shape the process and impact the final outcome. We begin with Karen, who illustrates how other factors such as lived experiences (as described in chapter 5) shape a person's consideration set and may ultimately be prioritized over racial composition. Karen's case is unusual. On the one hand, her racial residential attitudes are typical of many whites: she reported that she would feel uncomfortable in many predominantly black neighborhoods because she would feel "out of place" and, she assumed, because such neighborhoods would have many other undesirable features. Indeed, when asked about the possibility of living in a predominantly black neighborhood in the future, Karen said that she would rule it out from her future consideration set because of her strong reservations about not fitting in and about the safety of the neighborhood. On the other hand, we learned in the interview that when Karen moved eighteen years earlier to her present home, it was to a majority-black neighborhood (54 percent in 1990). This part of her story is described in chapter 5 where we explored the important role of social networks: Karen's family was the "leash" that pulled her and her husband to a particular neighborhood that was close to her family. We are not privy to her racial residential preferences at that time (she may have been more or less open to racially diverse neighborhoods then), but it seems clear that being close to her family was her dominant reason for selecting the neighborhood she did. By 2010, the black population in her inner-ring suburb had grown to 76 percent. Despite her statements throughout the interview that she did not want to live someplace where she "stood out," she made no mention of a desire to leave her current neighborhood because of its racial composition. The interviewer asked

her about the apparent contradiction between her racial residential preferences and where she currently lived:

INTERVIEWER: So a little bit ago you mentioned that you would not feel
               comfortable in some neighborhoods over here that were
               like 95 percent black. For example, that you would stick
               out. So, what is it about your community that makes you
               feel welcome?

KAREN: Very longtime residents. We know each other. Um,
               just the sense of community. You don't see boarded-up
               houses. Longtime people live there. There's a history
               there.

INTERVIEWER: Okay, so even across racial groups, people have just
               known each other for years?

KAREN: Oh, definitely. Definitely. Whether it's through voting,
               just walking down the street. I mean, there's some peo-
               ple that I've met just through the bus. Walking down
               the block and I'll introduce myself. All of a sudden I'll
               know . . . actually, I *didn't know* somebody's wife. She
               pulled out with a school bus and was like, "Hey, do you
               want a ride to the bus? You don't even know me, but you
               know my husband." So, you know, it's more of a . . . you
               talk more.
                  I've got one story about our neighborhood which, you
               know, feeds into this. There was a kid that sat at my bus
               stop. He and I just started talking . . . introducing each
               other—ourselves—to each other. And he said he moved
               from the West Side. He said, "Yeah, and I moved here
               to the 'hood from the West Side." I said, "This isn't the
               'hood. This is a neighborhood." A couple weeks later,
               he said, "Yeah, some of my friends from the West Side
               came over to the neighborhood." And I started laughing
               to myself. Ha ha. I got to him. Well, he and I got excep-
               tionally close. He's black. Obviously I'm white. One of
               my bus friends, she was talking to me, she was like, "Do
               you know Tyrone?" And I said, "Yeah." He's [Tyrone]
               one of her son's best friends. Well, Tyrone was at their
               house and she's like, "Do you know this girl Karen? She
               lives on the next block?" And he's like, "Yeah, that's
               my sister." She's like, "No . . ." My friend Tara, who's
               black, didn't want to say anything. "That's my sister."
               "No, she's a Caucasian girl, she can't . . ." "That's my

sister!" It gave me such a good feeling, thinking that this is a sophomore in high school who came from the West Side and he's developing that same kind of community, slowly. And this is just from talking at the bus stop. He knows my husband. He knows some of my friends. You know, you just share. He's introduced me to his family. This is the way the neighborhood is. To me, it's just comfortable. Very, very homey.

INTERVIEWER: So do you feel like some of these other neighborhoods wouldn't be that way? You know, some of these neighborhoods—like I think some of these neighborhoods we've talked about are not necessarily places you've been or places you've had occasion to hang out.

KAREN: Right, I think this area would be more guarded. . . . They're more used to certain . . . they're used to the crime. There's certain things. They're used to hearing fire engines and everything else. You get an influx of white people, they'd be wondering, "What are you doing here?" Suspicious. Whether or not you had a motive, or you just wanted to live there because it's a nice place to live. Maybe, you know, you've got a best friend that lives there. I think they'd be more on guard. Not as—just like. What are you doing here? Cautious. With good reason.

INTERVIEWER: And that's not the case . . .

KAREN: We've just been so integrated for so long. Those that want to live there are there for a reason. It's an affordable place to live, it's a good place to live. Our taxes are low, and the people are friendly. We do have a huge sense of community. And there's a lot of pride of ownership.

As noted, other parts of Karen's interview make it apparent that neighborhood racial composition would shape her *future* consideration set; she would avoid minority-populated areas where she would "stick out like a sore thumb" and where the racial composition, to her mind, would be indicative of undesirable features. In describing her residential choices, she sees *her* neighborhood as the exception to the general rules she applies to black neighborhoods. In fact, in discussing the desirability of other neighborhoods in the area, it became apparent that there are no black neighborhoods into which Karen would consider moving.

The important point is that individuals can retain a strong set of racial residential preferences and yet, because of the competing factors that come into play in *actual* residential decision-making, end up in neighborhoods that contradict these preferences. In Karen's case, despite holding preferences typical of whites, other factors (lived experiences, social networks) trumped racial preferences, leading her to make a residential choice that contradicts, almost diametrically, her racial residential attitudes. In this case, the other factors were living near her family, fitting in, affordability, and knowing the neighborhood well. Karen's example highlights that, in comparison to the strong role of racial residential preferences often depicted in debates about the drivers of residential segregation, preferences can play a more subtle and malleable role in the concrete decisions made during the housing search. Her story is particularly illuminating because she highlights the social factors described in chapters 4 and 5—social networks, daily routines, early life experiences—that play such an important role in shaping residential outcomes.

Karen's complicated story is a compelling illustration of how racial residential preferences can be subverted. Other social factors (lived experience, social networks) have "tethered and leashed" Karen, a white woman, to living (atypically) in a majority-black neighborhood. The point of the social structural sorting perspective is that these social processes, generally speaking, serve to continually perpetuate *segregation,* not *integration.* In other words, if we turn the tables and imagine Karen as a white woman who had lived her entire life in a white neighborhood, the tethering and leashing forces in her residential decisions would have perpetuated segregation. And if she were ever motivated to move to a new neighborhood, her racial residential preferences would probably filter out places with substantial numbers of African Americans. Or imagine if her racial residential preferences had led her to be open to an integrated neighborhood. The "tethers" of her lived experiences and social networks might still create an overall decision-making process that perpetuates segregation.

As noted, the limited survey-based data we have on the makeup of African Americans' consideration sets confirm that there is more variety in the racial composition of search locations among African Americans than among whites; in other words, racial composition may not always be the cue that African Americans use to screen out places in the first stage. This next in-depth interview example is just such a case: an African American searcher's consideration set did include communities with different racial compositions, some predominantly white and others predominantly black. Here we see how racial residential preferences can "lose out" during the second stage of a housing search—that is, racial composition can be a feature that is weighed and considered explicitly in the evaluation process but that ultimately takes a backseat to other factors or forces.

Alicia, an African American homeowner, described how she ended up moving into a predominantly black inner-ring suburb, despite her preference for a more diverse neighborhood:

> ALICIA: The price range and the time frame. I had to buy a house pretty quickly. Yeah, I was pregnant, like eight months, and I didn't, I lived in a townhouse in Chicago. . . . So I had to buy a three-bedroom, and I looked since October and I bought my house in February and I had them [the twins] in March. . . . I think the rushing made me not research like I would have ordinarily done.
>
> INTERVIEWER: So time and money.
>
> ALICIA: But it's a first home, so I figured we'll get out. [*laughs*]

Later in the interview, when Alicia gave more details of the search, we see that her consideration set was very expansive:

> INTERVIEWER: How many different towns or neighborhoods did you look in?
>
> ALICIA: We looked everywhere, the city and the west suburbs, because I worked in the city and my husband works in the west suburbs. So whatever was in our price range and were the bedrooms we required and the garage we required, cuz we didn't want to park in the street in winter. . . . We didn't mind looking in any area.
>
> INTERVIEWER: . . . So how many different homes did you look at? Can you remember how many?
>
> ALICIA: Oh, it was a lot. [*laughs*] It was a lot.
>
> INTERVIEWER: Like a ballpark number?
>
> ALICIA: I would say like fifty or more. . . . Because some days, you know, we tried to look at least three times a week, or less, maybe two or three times a week, and we would look sometimes at three homes cuz she [the real estate agent] had a lot of lock boxes. . . .
>
> INTERVIEWER: So the current house you have, why did you end up deciding on this particular house?
>
> ALICIA: It was the bedrooms we required, garage, the bathrooms, the price was exactly what we wanted, um. It just seemed to be the best fit. It was not the very best. Okay, "this is the best fit we have for the time we have."

The "west suburbs" include a wide variety of neighborhood racial compositions—from all-white to all-black—and there are also some racially and ethnically diverse neighborhoods in these suburbs. When the conversation turned to a discussion of the performance of Alicia's real estate agent, we become privy to why the outcome was "not the very best." Alicia was generally happy with her real estate agent, who showed them many homes, had lots of details about them, and would prescreen units to steer them away from ones she thought needed too much repair work. However, the truncated nature of the search because of her impending due date forced Alicia and her husband to rely heavily on the real estate agent to identify potential properties, and as it turned out, their agent zeroed in on locations that differed fairly substantially from the racial residential preferences of Alicia and her family.

> INTERVIEWER: Did she [the real estate agent] suggest areas where you should look at all?
>
> ALICIA: Sometimes she would go where, "I know there are a lot of houses in this area. Let's go look in that area, you know." In Maywood [a predominantly black, lower- to middle-income inner-ring suburb], she would—knew a lot was coming up, so we would look at a lot of homes in that area.
>
> INTERVIEWER: Okay, so she suggested Maywood. Did she suggest any other areas?
>
> ALICIA: Maywood, Bellwood, Hinsdale, the areas she knew were in our price range most of the time.[47]

Later in the interview, it became clear that Alicia had reservations about the geographic concentration of the units their agent was showing them. When asked if her agent ever "only showed her homes/apartments in certain neighborhoods," Alicia agreed with this characterization, then went on to explain:

> ALICIA: I just felt like we could have a broader search. Knew we were looking for things like that, but she only kept showing us Maywood, Bellwood. Kinda pushing us to those areas. It was already a black mix. We didn't like that. But it shows she didn't know us, cuz we don't like that, you know. [laughs] And my daughter feels very, you know, she's like, "Why are there no white people here?" She's born and raised in [city in southern Illinois], where it's a mix in her schools down there. So, she was just like, it's a big cultural change. [laughs]

RVIEWER: Right, so when your agent is showing you these places, how do you respond to that happening?

ALICIA: Most of it is fine, but we let her know that we would like . . . a little bit broader base, but . . . we did need to find something. And I know it takes time to close and all those things, so we were basically pushing the clock. And I'm not afraid to live in just one black area, so I knew, okay, I'll live there. We'll be fine, you know. This is fine. It's just not ideal.

Even though Alicia held a particular racial residential preference (for a racially diverse neighborhood), constraints related to how much time she had to search, as well as the behavior of her real estate agent, conspired against achieving a residential outcome that matched this preference. Alicia's story illustrates the trade-offs that can be made during real-life housing searches, particularly when undertaken in less-than-ideal circumstances. For example, Alicia did not end up in an area that matched her racial residential preferences, but she did get the number of bedrooms and the attached garage she was seeking.

Interestingly, Alicia settled for a less-than-ideal racial composition in a way that none of the whites we interviewed reported experiencing, perhaps because community racial composition operates most significantly for whites at the *first* stage of a housing search, when they are determining the consideration set. At this stage, racial composition may operate less as an attitude or an attribute and more as a guiding principle. In other words, whereas Alicia talked about the trade-offs she made during stage 2 of her search between racial composition, number of bedrooms, and yard size, we suspect that whites rarely engage in this kind of trade-off in the second stage. Instead, it is likely that whites' consideration sets are generally quite homogenous (in terms of racial composition), and so, during stage 2 of their search, racial composition is not a feature on which compromise is necessary or even possible, as Hempel found was true more generally.[48]

Whites might choose a house with a second bathroom over one with an attached garage, or one that is close to work over one with a backyard. But they will rarely need to choose (or have an opportunity to choose) a house that has any of these features over one with a sizable presence of nonwhite neighbors, because they probably eliminated any such option at the first stage. Except when whites value racially diverse communities and include them in their consideration set, racial residential preferences are unlikely to be a primary feature in the evaluation process at the second stage. This stands in contrast to the experiences of black searchers, for whom the consideration set might include a more heterogeneous group of neighborhoods; in this case, neighborhood racial composition may remain an important feature in the comparison of specific units during stage 2. The mismatches between hypothetical neighborhood racial composition preferences and search locations described by Esther Havekes and her colleagues supports this general observation.[49] By contrast, black and Latino residents include in their consideration set communities with a variety of racial compositions but may end up not choosing whiter neighborhoods in the second stage because other features or contexts push those more diverse options to the side.

Our point, then, is not that racial residential preferences are unimportant. They are certainly important in determining what comes out of the meat grinder of the neighborhood selection and housing search process. But their contribution is likely to be highly variable, subtle, and complex. Moving beyond hypothetical neighborhood racial composition preferences to approaches that examine the ways in which racial composition can play out during a residential process points to how "preferences" shape segregation in far more subtle and complex ways than suggested by the simple model and implied by previous studies examining the statistical link between preferences and segregation. Instead, we argue that other neighborhood factors, social processes, contexts, and constraints are at play besides racial composition, and that for some—especially whites— racial composition may be a guiding principle more than an attitude or attribute as generally construed.

One critical feature of Alicia's search, and the reason she ended up in a predominantly black neighborhood, is that her real estate agent steered her family toward such a neighborhood, though Alicia implied that this happened because the agent simply knew about more available units in these communities. In Alicia's case, the impact of steering was subtle—and the steering was ultimately successful—because of another factor: the time pressure on finding a place made it easier to take the agent's suggestions. In addition to the general point that, in a diverse consideration set, racial composition can lose out to other factors in the search, this example of steering illustrates the complex way in which discrimination can occur. In the next chapter, we explore in more detail what the social structural sorting perspective can offer to our understanding of how discrimination plays out in the neighborhood selection and housing search process and how it can complicate our understanding of this driver of segregation.

Chapter 9 | The Social Structural Sorting Perspective on the Role of Discrimination

As the traditional debate goes, if economics and preferences cannot explain persistent residential segregation, then discrimination must be at play. For example, if even higher-income African Americans remain strongly segregated from whites, and this segregation cannot be attributed to a strong preference among blacks to live in racially isolated neighborhoods, then any desire among middle-class African Americans for access to more integrated areas must be inhibited by discriminatory treatment at the hands of landlords, real estate agents, and other gatekeepers in the system. Although this deduction makes logical sense, evidence is elusive, given that discrimination in the housing market often takes subtle forms and has been illegal for nearly half a century.

As we reviewed in chapter 1, discriminatory policies and practices at the local, state, and federal levels helped establish, perpetuate, and cement racial segregation in the United States. In this chapter, we begin with a summary of what we know about the current existence, shape, and prevalence of housing-related discrimination. We then consider the underlying—and we argue overly simplistic—model that guides research on the role of discrimination in perpetuating segregation. Finally, using the insights of the social structural sorting perspective, we draw attention to three features of discrimination as a driver of segregation: (1) how discrimination can operate at the first stage of a housing search; (2) the complexity of the outcomes of discriminatory treatment; and (3) the inseparability of discrimination from the other traditional drivers of segregation—economics and preferences.

THE PATTERNS AND PREVALENCE OF
HOUSING DISCRIMINATION

There is a long history of research focused on identifying and measuring the prevalence of racial discrimination in the housing market. Audit studies in which pairs of testers pose as potential tenants or home-buyers to inquire about housing with landlords or real estate agents are our best source of evidence about whether people of different races or ethnicities are treated differently when they attempt to secure housing. This experimental design is considered the gold standard because it controls for other factors (the potential client's age, gender, income, family status, and so on), and so any differences in treatment can be attributed to the one observable difference: racial or ethnic background. The approach, though not without its critics, has been used to detect housing discrimination in person, over the phone, and on the Internet.[1]

On four separate occasions spanning thirty-three years (1977 to 2010), HUD has used national housing audits to measure discrimination faced by people who inquire about housing advertised in newspapers of major U.S. metropolitan areas. Although the initial contact by the tester with the landlord or real estate agent may have been by telephone or Internet, these audits focus on what happens during an in-person visit to secure housing. The most recent audit, conducted in 2010, found declines (to the point of being quite rare) in certain kinds of discrimination. For example, white and minority renters were equally likely to be given an appointment to see an available unit and, upon arriving, to be shown at least one available unit (although Hispanic renters were slightly more likely to be told there were none available). But differences emerge in more subtle practices: Whites were told about, and shown, more units than minorities and were quoted lower rents. In addition, black and Latino testers were treated less favorably on indicators like whether credit requirements were mentioned, whether the landlord offered to negotiate on security deposits, and whether rent incentives were promised. Notwithstanding these three factors, the results of most of the other measures of general helpfulness suggested equal treatment.[2]

The results for home-buyers were similar: minorities were rarely denied an appointment—though blacks were slightly less likely to be given an in-person appointment—and almost always were told about at least one available unit. But whites were favored over blacks and Asians (but not Latinos) in that they were shown more homes, they were given more information and assistance, and more homes were recommended to them. Although many indicators show few racial-ethnic differences, black home-buyers were more likely to be shown homes with problems, to be asked whether they were prequalified, and to be asked to provide more information about their credit. Audit studies also revealed that although, compared to African American buyers, white buyers saw homes in neighborhoods with slightly larger percentages of white residents (a difference of less than two percentage points), whites were more likely than minorities to get positive comments about white neighborhoods and negative comments about minority neighborhoods.[3]

A growing number of audit studies provide windows into discrimination at stages other than an initial in-person visit—specifically, during initial telephone or Internet inquiries. For example, relying on the finding that people, with a reasonably high degree of accuracy, can identify a caller's racial background based on speech patterns and other cues, Douglas Massey and Garvey Lundy conducted an audit study of Philadelphia landlords to determine whether they discriminated over the telephone when people inquired about rental units advertised in newspapers.[4] They found that blacks were significantly less likely than whites to have their phone calls returned and less likely, if their calls were returned, to be told that a unit was available. Another phone audit study found evidence of discrimination against minority buyers seeking home insurance for their potential new home.[5]

Another fertile area of recent research is Internet-based audit tests. In addition to tapping into an increasingly important mode of communication for the rental housing search process, these studies address the criticism that subtle differences between testers cannot be "controlled" in an in-person visit. An audit of 14,000 rental units advertised on Craigslist found that email inquiries from names more common among African Americans were significantly less likely to be invited to have additional contact with the landlord.[6] A second Internet field experiment reported a similar pattern.[7]

Another body of research has explored discrimination in the mortgage industry. Historically, mortgage discrimination was explicit and institutional. The Home Owners' Loan Corporation, the federal agency responsible for shaping the credit market, practiced "redlining": HOLC would not write loans for applicants from predominantly minority communities, or neighborhoods adjacent to them, and marked these communities in red on maps it created. These maps were also adopted by private mortgage underwriters.[8] More recently, audit studies and analyses of administrative data point to the persistence of mortgage discrimination, though it looks different in contemporary periods.[9] A recent review of mortgage discrimination studies concludes that both types of data draw the same conclusion: minorities experience higher denial rates, receive less coaching, and are provided with less information about how to secure a loan.[10]

Notably, the increase in mortgage discrimination is not in loan denials, but in the *kinds* of loans that are approved, with racial disparities emerging in their terms and conditions.[11] For example, redlining has now been replaced by reverse redlining: loans are granted, but they come through predatory lenders who urge minority and low-income customers to buy expensive and risky loan products. Even more problematic is that these products are marketed to minority customers who would meet the credit and income requirements of traditional—and therefore less costly and less risky—loan products.[12] One consequence has been that the neighborhoods targeted for these loans were at greater risk of foreclosure when the housing crisis hit in 2007.[13]

In short, although homeownership rates among racial-ethnic minorities have increased, they have come at a price, as anticipated by the sociologist Richard Williams and his colleagues, who observed (prior to the housing crisis):

> Many of the recent homeownership gains [among racial minorities] represent real progress, and if they continue, inequalities will diminish further. But as the old inequality has declined, a new inequality has also emerged. The new inequality is characterized by less-favorable loan terms, sometimes problematic forms of housing, and a lack of adequate consumer protection from predatory and abusive practices. . . . The new inequality in home mortgage lending is part of a greater phenomenon in which apparent gains made by minorities and low income groups have come at far higher costs than have gains made by other segments of society.[14]

This was a prescient observation: just a few years later, the housing bubble burst, and the consequences of these risky loans began playing out in neighborhoods—primarily low-income and minority neighborhoods—throughout the nation as people lost their homes and life savings.

Given the role of predatory lending in the housing crisis, and the resultant explosion of foreclosures, researchers have studied who was hit the worst by the crisis, whether banks and other actors in the industry behaved in discriminatory ways, and whether the costs of this crisis have been differentially felt by different racial-ethnic groups.[15] Most of the evidence finds that mortgage quality, predatory lending, and the foreclosure crisis all disproportionately impact communities of color.

That discriminatory denial of access to a mortgage may not be as important as the discrimination occurring because the loan products offered are by predatory lenders is a reminder that having access to a rental property or being able to buy a home in a preferred neighborhood is just one way in which discrimination can unfold. An important question arises: What happens next? How are people treated once they have moved in? If individuals are treated negatively after securing housing, then that negative treatment may have important implications for segregation if it influences whether they stay in the neighborhood. Or whether, upon deciding to move, that experience affects their decision to seek residence in a similar neighborhood in the future or to eliminate such neighborhoods from consideration.

From an analysis by Vincent Roscigno, Diane Karafin, and Griff Tester of case materials filed in verified claims of housing discrimination in Ohio between 1998 and 2003, we gain a window into this kind of non-exclusionary discrimination, which they describe as "actions and practices that occur within an already established housing arrangement most often entailing racial harassment, differential treatment of tenants, or disparate application of contractual terms and conditions of residency."[16] As the authors argue, prior research on the prevalence of housing discrimination has tended to document a narrow view of what they refer to as "exclusionary discrimination." As a result, we now have a great deal of information about whether minorities are denied access to particular housing units by specific landlords or real estate agents, but little insight into other institutional actors, and even less into what happens once a person occupies a new housing unit. For example, do landlords or homeowners' associations differentially enforce rules and regulations or unequally levy fines? Do neighbors or other residents make life difficult through harassment or intimidation?

The importance of assessing non-exclusionary discrimination is reinforced by the finding that by 2003 non-exclusionary cases had surpassed exclusionary cases in number.[17] Further, the bulk (84 percent) of non-exclusionary discrimination cases involved differences in the terms and conditions of the lease or purchase—such as the financing, loan, or appraisal; unfavorable services and facilities; and, most frequently, the rental terms, conditions, or privileges. The remaining 16 percent of non-exclusionary cases involved harassment, intimidation, or coercion.[18] This study by Roscigno and his colleagues reminds us that being able to view a unit is only the first step in a housing search process. Subsequently, applications must be completed, terms of the arrangement settled upon, and promises in the leases upheld. Each of these areas is susceptible to discrimination. Because traditional audit studies miss these types of discrimination, its implications for the perpetuation of segregation are largely ignored.

DISCRIMINATION'S IMPACT ON SEGREGATION

The direct effect of instances of discrimination on the perpetuation of segregation—vis-à-vis the success of discriminatory actions at keeping certain people out of certain neighborhoods—is unknowable from housing audits like those described here because these audits are experimental in nature and test only a single in-person visit, not, for example, what happens when an application is submitted, an offer for a house is tendered, or a lease is negotiated. The presumption is that segregation persists in part because blacks and other racial-ethnic minorities are prevented from buying or renting in particular neighborhoods by gatekeepers such as loan officers, landlords, and real estate agents. We can use housing audit study data to provide circumstantial evidence of discrimination's effects on segregation by testing the relationship between audit results and the racial composition of the community in which discrimination occurred. The simple model is that discrimination effectively bars a person from a unit or neighborhood in a community where their move would be integrative and therefore results in a move that perpetuates segregation. One approach uses audit data to determine whether discriminatory treatment is affected by the racial composition of the neighborhood in which the unit is located. Using HUD's 1989 and 2000 Housing Discrimination Studies (HDS) reveals somewhat inconsistent results, but generally points to the idea that neighborhood racial composition does impact whether a landlord discriminates. One study using the 1989 HDS shows that as the "tipping point" was reached (in their study, 20 percent minority), instances of discrimination against minority clients increased.[19] An Internet audit study has also found that discrimination was more likely to occur in neighborhoods that were closer to the tipping point (in their study, between 80 and 95 percent white).[20] In both cases, then, minorities were discouraged from moving into neighborhoods where their presence might ultimately have prompted racial turnover to an all-black neighborhood. Conversely, this means that they were discouraged from making integrative moves.

Another study using the 1989 HDS found redlining against suburban integrated neighborhoods: specifically, agents were more likely to discourage black searchers from moving to white neighborhoods that were near integrated ones.[21] By discouraging moves into integrated areas—or into white areas near integrated neighborhoods—real estate agents may have been reducing demand and decreasing stability in these communities, both of which can perpetuate segregation. Interestingly, however, when a client's initial inquiry was about a unit in an integrated neighborhood, steering appeared to happen less often.

A study of the Philadelphia rental market provides similar evidence on the relationship between discrimination and segregation. It shows that levels of discrimination were predicted by three ecological variables: the percentage minority residents, whether the unit was inside or outside Philadelphia, and the distance between the advertised unit and the nearest minority census tract. The authors summarize their results and the implications for segregation:

> [The] pattern of access to rental housing suggests the systematic channeling of white middle class housing demand *away from* areas that have some but not yet a preponderance of black residents (5%–31%), combined with a simultaneous channeling of middle class black demand *toward such areas.* Racially mixed areas are precisely those where the risk of racial turnover has been greatest and over time racial disparities in housing access appear to fuel a process of residential succession. In contrast to being channeled *toward* the very whitest areas (those under 5 percent black) and with the exception of middle class black females, black demand (whether middle class or not) is deflected *away* from these neighborhoods. This pattern of ecological variation in relative access to rental housing would clearly operate over time to perpetuate segregation and promote re-segregation across neighborhoods in the Philadelphia metropolitan area.[22]

Another form of discrimination is encouraging clients to move to neighborhoods where their own racial-ethnic group predominates—so-called racial steering. The HDS 2000 data set was used to detect racial differences in which homes agents took their clients to inspect, which homes they suggested that their client consider, and which neighborhoods agents made comments about ("editorializing").[23] This study found evidence of racial steering, and it mostly involved the agent making gratuitous comments about the neighborhood. Twelve to 15 percent of the time, whites were given more information than blacks, and the information was in the form of encouraging white clients to buy in areas with more whites and fewer poor people. (There were no significant differences in the treatment of white and Latino testers.)

As in the audit studies reported earlier, the racial-ethnic differences in treatment detected in this study were not about gaining access to neighborhoods, but about the messages that agents conveyed to clients about the quality of the neighborhoods they visited and the subtle steering that resulted from it. Seventy percent of the editorializing focused on the neighborhood's racial-ethnic composition. The majority of these comments (two-thirds) were neutral on the face of it, but they must be taken in context: "Many of the comments we labeled neutral carried an implicit message that whites who might consider living amid minority neighbors were unusual, as revealed in the following agent [quote], 'There are a lot of blacks there, but that's up to you.'"[24]

The idea illustrated by these audit study data is that landlords and real estate agents editorialize about neighborhoods in a way that steers people to certain neighborhoods (in this case, whites to segregated white neighborhoods). Our in-depth interviews vividly illustrate the idea that such comments are not race-neutral, that they are deliberate, and that they can emerge in both stage 1 and stage 2 of a housing search.

In our first example, the editorializing provided by the real estate agent was very confusing for the searcher. When asked whether her real estate agent commented on the neighborhoods she was searching in, Emily, a white suburbanite, had this to say:

> EMILY: I think she could have been a little bit more educated on the neighborhoods than she was.
>
> INTERVIEWER: In what way? What makes you say that?
>
> EMILY: Well, because she would take us into—we told her, "... we don't want to be in a dumpy neighborhood or . . . rundown neighborhood, or whatever," and sometimes the houses we were going to look [at] were. And it's like . . . if you're more educated on the neighborhoods you would know . . . if they're nice or not and that would help a little bit more, instead of wasting our time going there. . . . There were certain areas she knew for sure. We'd say, "There's a town house in Hoffman Estates." She'd say, "Well, what area? No, you don't want to live there."
>
> INTERVIEWER: Why was she . . . what was wrong with [the area]?
>
> EMILY: I'd have to ask my husband. . . . I'm like, "Why [does] she keep saying this?" And she'd just say, "You don't want to live there." And that's all. She really didn't say why. She just kept saying, "You don't want to live there."

Emily's experience exemplified a subtle (or perhaps not so subtle) steering on the part of her agent. It may be this kind of steering that whites experience when they consider neighborhoods that are not predominantly white. By not explaining why the client would not want to live in certain neighborhoods, the agent was following the "letter of the law" to avoid what would have been *racial* steering, but she was successfully eliminating neighborhood options using vague generalities. We cannot be sure that Emily's agent thought it was their racial composition that made certain areas undesirable, but we can be sure that whatever the reason was, the agent was not willing to explain it.

In her study of landlords in Baltimore who specialize in voucher holder rentals, the sociologist Eva Rosen uncovered not only evidence of steering but a process so landlord-driven that instead of people choosing places, landlords were choosing people, "recruiting, selecting, and then sorting tenants into the units and neighborhoods where the greatest profit can be made."[25] She describes how the role of race played out in this unusual context where 90 percent of the voucher holders were black and landlords, though not denying anyone access (which would have been exclusionary discrimination), absolutely steered based on race:

> Whether or not landlords make explicit distinctions according to race as opposed to socioeconomic background is a question for further empirical research. Results from this study do not show race to be a salient trait on the basis of which landlords *select* a tenant, but race is relevant in the *matching* of tenant to property. In other words, while there is no evidence here that Baltimore landlords turn away black voucher holders, there is evidence that the interplay between the race of the voucher holder and the characteristics of the neighborhood inform landlords' actions. Landlords place black voucher holders in particular types of neighborhoods, that is, those where whites do not want to live.[26]

Lisa, an in-depth interview participant who was a licensed but not practicing broker, broke it down for the interviewer and revealed that this practice is a very well-developed strategy with a vocabulary designed specifically to avoid the appearance of racial steering. Lisa is a middle-aged white woman who spent much of her life pioneering in racially diverse Chicago-area neighborhoods, purchasing properties and then "flipping" them for profit. When the interviewer asked Lisa whether real estate agents "do a lot of advising" on which neighborhoods are "good and bad," she had this to say about agents' impact on searchers' consideration sets:

LISA: They're ethically not supposed to, okay, but there's code words, you know.

INTERVIEWER: Okay, and what are the code words?

LISA: You know, like "urban." It's a very "urban" neighborhood. Meaning that it's all black people.

INTERVIEWER: What are the other words?

LISA: "Diverse."

INTERVIEWER: Okay, what does that mean?

LISA: It means that there's a lot of people who aren't white.

INTERVIEWER: Okay, is that different than "urban"?

LISA: Um, "diverse" means it includes Hispanics but "urban" doesn't always. "Urban" has a more negative connotation than "diverse." Um, "urban" often means there's crime. "Diverse" just means there's potential for crime. Um, let's see, what are some of the other code words? . . . Another code word is "interesting." . . . That's an "interesting" neighborhood.

INTERVIEWER: Okay, and what's that code for?

LISA: It just means "I really can't say anything, but you can infer from what I'm saying or I'm not saying that you really don't want to go there." See all these rules, you can't do this. You can't do that. People always find ways around them, okay. Only the most egregious violators of these laws are caught. Like "Oh, you wouldn't want to live there. That's, you know, black people on that block." . . . and they have to protect against discrimination, which is a noble goal, but people always find ways around it, so it's like, you know, you're almost spitting at the wind, because it's going to happen.

This example brings to life the quantitative findings of the housing audit studies on steering and highlights the contemporary version of steering: using code words that mask the intent but effectively steer people away from neighborhoods with specific racial compositions.

Clients with less knowledge and lived experiences are probably more susceptible to this kind of steering, and so this may be a powerful method through which newcomers to a metropolitan area are sorted into neighborhoods according to prevailing systems of segregation. Although overall levels of discrimination generally declined between 1989 and 2000, studies suggest that steering has actually increased among blacks (but not Latinos).

Researchers have also examined the relationship between the levels of discrimination detected by audit studies and the level of segregation in an area. The traditional discrimination explanation for segregation would lead us to expect segregation to be higher in metropolitan areas where discrimination is most virulent. Yet there is surprisingly little support for this expectation. For example, one study found only modest associations between measured levels of discrimination in the housing market and levels of residential segregation between blacks and whites at the metropolitan level.[27] And another more direct study found that metropolitan-area levels of discrimination as measured by housing audits are not strong predictors of racial differences in mobility patterns within metropolitan areas, independent of other factors that affect residential attainment.[28]

Of course, the weak associations revealed in these studies do not necessarily mean that discrimination is inconsequential for the maintenance of segregation. Indeed, it could reflect the relative lack of variation in both variables; both segregation and discrimination might be too ubiquitous to pick up an association at the metro level. Alternatively, such weak associations may reflect the use of fairly blunt measures of discrimination. That is, audit studies are designed to detect discrimination at a single point in the residential attainment process and may miss subtle differences in patterns of discrimination across metropolitan areas that may impact levels of segregation. Moreover, these studies presume that home-seekers of different races identify and respond to the same housing ads, and that they approach the same agents and landlords.

All of these possibilities remind us that, as was true of models of preferences and economics as drivers of segregation, an overly simple premise dominates the traditional model of discrimination: racial-ethnic minorities show up to rent or buy a home, but the landlord or real estate agent does something to deny them access to it. In a more subtle version, real estate agents and management companies steer potential renters or buyers to particular neighborhoods, such that when a searcher makes an inquiry about a unit in a neighborhood not dominated by their own racial-ethnic group, the agent encourages them to consider units in other neighborhoods that have more of their "own kind." In both cases, the assumption is that agent discrimination denies or discourages people from making the moves they are attempting—moves that would have the result of reducing segregation. By applying the social structural sorting perspective and the lens of the neighborhood selection and housing search process, we reveal both a more realistic and more complicated story about how discriminatory processes operate—at multiple stages of the housing search, not always directly and successfully, and not always in a way that is separable from other drivers of segregation. We consider each of these ideas in turn.

DISCRIMINATION AND THE CONSIDERATION SET

Scholars and policymakers have focused on assessing racial differences when a person shows up to rent or buy a particular home. One shortcoming is that this approach fails to consider what goes into whether that person shows up on that doorstep in that neighborhood in the first place. Viewed through the social structural sorting perspective, it becomes apparent that discrimination—the expectation or anticipation of it—critically shapes the construction of the consideration set. Therefore, to understand how discrimination can drive segregation, we need to view its role in all stages of the residential selection process.

The idea that the anticipation or expectation of discrimination can shape a search long before the possibility of experiencing discrimination when attempting to actually rent a unit in a particular neighborhood is not new. In his comprehensive study of housing processes in the late 1970s, Robert Lake recognized this possibility when he argued that people adapt to discriminatory institutions, meaning that searchers respond to prior experiences of discrimination when undertaking subsequent searches.[29] The result is that blacks (and probably other minorities) approach a neighborhood selection and housing search process using different information sources, searching in different places, and prioritizing different unit or neighborhood features in order to avoid discrimination. Our in-depth interview data, collected more than thirty years after Lake's survey—and well after housing discrimination was made illegal—also reveal that the anticipation of discrimination is a powerful force. Thus, when thinking about the present-day impact of discrimination, we cannot overlook that discriminatory practices and policies in the rental and sale of housing throughout our nation's history have shaped how people of color view communities as viable places to live. In short, discrimination impacts a searcher's consideration set. The implication is that even if all landlords, homeowners, and real estate agents stopped discriminating today, people of color, having experienced decades of discrimination individually and collectively, would still select neighborhoods and undertake searches in ways shaped by that experience.

The significance of this is clear when we consider the role of discrimination in shaping the general racial residential preferences of blacks. In the 1990s, researchers suggested that persistent segregation in the face of societal changes was due to black preferences.[30] Thus, researchers turned their attention to understanding what drives blacks' racial residential preferences and concluded that there was a fundamental role for concerns about discrimination.[31] In short, it is difficult to talk about black racial residential preferences without understanding that they are part and parcel of the discriminatory system in which racial-ethnic minorities have had to operate, both before and after the Fair Housing Act of 1968. Our point is that perceptions of likely discrimination in certain kinds of communities has an influence on the consideration sets of African Americans and Latinos. Thus, discrimination is implicated in the formation of the preferences that feed into the system of segregation. Discrimination certainly has operated, and still operates, to bar people—or steer people away from—certain kinds of neighborhoods, but it has also played a role in shaping preferences and eliminating from serious consideration certain neighborhoods because of a desire to avoid hostile, unpleasant, and potentially dangerous encounters.

In addition to these studies showing the impact of perceptions of discrimination on African Americans' racial residential preferences, our in-depth interviews provide more concrete examples of how perceptions of discrimination in specific communities can manifest themselves in the construction of consideration sets. Four patterns reveal the varied ways in which discrimination can influence the process through its role in shaping perceptions of communities: (1) perceptions of a community's reputation for or history of housing discrimination; (2) assumptions about a community's racial climate; (3) the possibility of experiencing both exclusionary and non-exclusionary discrimination in a community; and (4) perceptions of discrimination, not in a housing market per se, but in the community where it is located. Future studies focused specifically on connecting these perceptions to actual mobility decisions are needed to test these ideas. Our in-depth interview data are suggestive, but require the caveat that some of these features may look quite different in metropolitan areas with lower levels of segregation and those without lengthy histories of racialized community processes.

Knowledge of a Community Reputation for Racial Discrimination

Consistent with survey-based analyses of community perceptions in Detroit, Los Angeles, Boston, and Atlanta, our Chicago in-depth interviews revealed that certain communities have salient racist histories or reputations, particularly among African American participants. For example, Jerome, a thirty-something African American renter in Chicago, has had relatively limited direct experience outside of the predominantly black communities where he has lived and spends time. We asked him to explain why the upper-income, overwhelmingly white suburbs of Wilmette, Glenview, and Winnetka were not on the list of places he would consider:

> JEROME: I never had no problems out there, but just, I don't know, something about Wilmette, it's just—I don't know—not really my cup of tea.
>
> INTERVIEWER: . . . So are any of these places—would you decide not to live in a particular area because of race or class or things like that?
>
> JEROME: Wilmette.

INTERVIEWER: Okay.

JEROME: Yeah, it's just Wilmette, going further north.

INTERVIEWER: Going further north this way?

JEROME: Yeah, like Wilmette, Kenilworth, Winnetka. Maybe Highland Park is okay. That's really it. Mainly these three.

INTERVIEWER: Okay. What about those three in particular?

JEROME: Yeah, the race thing kinda. That's really it.

INTERVIEWER: Just so I can be clear . . . have you heard particular things?

JEROME: Yeah, I'm going off what I heard mainly. I guess I can't say based on that experience cuz I'm not out there like that . . . I've been to Wilmette—the few times I've been there, I didn't have any problems.

INTERVIEWER: Okay. These are—even if you haven't personally experienced something, we really just want general impressions, so even things that you've heard about a particular town.

JEROME: Yeah, I've heard many of those three are like racist towns or whatever. You see a black person or Latino, think it's trouble coming or something. Like I said, that's hearsay.

INTERVIEWER: No, I understand. Is it particularly, so you said black and Latino. If you're one of those, then there would be trouble for you?

JEROME: Yeah.

INTERVIEWER: Is this a particularly white area?

JEROME: Yeah, predominantly white people, yes.

A second example of specific community reputations comes from Denise, whose past residential decisions were shaped by communities' reputations for both exclusionary and non-exclusionary discrimination. During her interview, Denise reflected on why she and her husband ended up in Naperville over Oak Park when they first moved in the 1980s:

You had the Frank Lloyd Wright [in Oak Park], a lot of quaint little stores, real cool restaurants, and things, ethnic diversity, pretty good schools and things too. That was back in the '80s too. . . . We looked. I don't know if [my husband] had a deal with like—something with redlining. Something he had heard about redlining or something else that really ticked him off. . . . He didn't like that.

Two communities that border Oak Park (also inner-ring suburbs that at the time were overwhelmingly white) were also never on their radar screen:

> Always heard that Cicero and Berwyn can be kind of racist. . . . In the past I always heard you really couldn't cross over. If you were a minority that tried to cross over into those areas and things, either you'd have a . . . like a cross burnt in your lawn. But this was probably more in the '60s and '70s. I don't know so much anymore, but I always heard people—it wasn't really hospitable to people of color coming into those areas. That's my knowledge in the past, so yeah, we never really looked at anything over there in those areas.

This retrospective account of why Denise and her husband did not consider Berwyn, Cicero, or Oak Park during their first search several decades ago illustrates how communities are dropped from the consideration set because of their reputations for the threat of violence or housing discrimination by lenders. The assumptions held by Denise and her husband were not based on direct experiences of these communities; nevertheless, their reputations led the couple to eliminate all of them from their consideration set.

Assumptions of Likely Discrimination

In the prior examples, a community's reputation is rooted in its history—stubborn remnants of past racial violence and discrimination that often become common knowledge among African Americans and perhaps also Latinos. But places are eliminated even in the absence of obviously racist histories and specific experiences. People can assume, even without knowledge of a community's specific reputation or history, that it is "not for people like me"—by which they often mean people of their own racial-ethnic group.

Thus, people of color *assume* that some places would discriminate against them and thus eliminate them from consideration. For example, Anna, a Latina, explained why she would not bother trying to live in the predominantly white suburb of LaGrange:

> ANNA: That is even more upper-class than Brookfield, because those houses are gorgeous. They're really old; they're almost like Victorian. They're really nice houses, especially in [the downtown area]. And I know cuz I used to look there for somewhere to live, but I was like, "No, it's not gonna happen."
>
> INTERVIEWER: Why is that?

ANNA: Oh, the properties—they're huge, but they're gorgeous, but the area, it's very—it's very nice, but it also feels like it's very segregated. There are Hispanics there, but it doesn't feel like—like they're almost welcome. There's an area that's very upper-class white people. They would not even rent to me if I had even asked. That's what it feels like, yeah.

Although nothing specific had happened to exclude her from the neighborhood, Anna realized that there was little point in seriously considering it.

Interestingly, though, the perception of *likely* exclusionary discrimination is not *always* enough to eliminate a place from the consideration set, though clearly it was on our next searcher's mind. In her candid self-reflection, we learn that Belinda, almost in spite of herself, ended up buying into a predominantly white (75 percent) neighborhood in the city of Chicago. She described the reality as compared to her assumptions:

INTERVIEWER: How welcoming do you think the neighborhood is to African Americans?

BELINDA: In terms of people being welcome there, that's really why I like it. . . . I think African Americans are welcome [with] open arms in my community. I'm just speaking from my experience and what—I've been there seven years and I've—I really love it. I get along very well with my neighbors. Some of them are African Americans, and a lot of them are not. But I've never had any issues in that community, which is interesting cuz I thought I would.

INTERVIEWER: Really?

BELINDA: The perception of going—moving into an area like that, I'm thinking, "Do I really want to do this?" It's really been a good experience.

INTERVIEWER: What was the perception you had going in?

BELINDA: The perception is that I didn't feel that—maybe I wasn't ready to move to that type of community yet. Maybe it was all just in my crazy thinking, but the thing—you have to have a certain income level—I'm an African American woman, single. I don't know. . . . So when I went and saw something I liked and went through the process of getting my loan and everything, I didn't have any problems at all—cuz you hear about housing discrimination.

A lot of that stuff goes on because people don't want African Americans or Hispanics or any minority in their community, but I've never experienced anything like that. My perception was a lot different than reality, and I see couples coming in all the time now, moving in, renting out units, and it's a great building where I live in, a great community. We have parties every quarter and summer parties and all that stuff, so it's good. [*laughs*]

INTERVIEWER: Yeah, when you heard about—you said kind of your perceptions going in, were there things specifically that you heard about that particular community?

BELINDA: . . . It was just my perception of it, thinking I don't see a lot of African American people . . . that live in that area. Don't know a lot that live in that area that are in my income bracket, so I just felt like, okay, maybe this is not the place that I want to be. But I went through the process, and it happened for me. It was—again, it was just me. I hadn't really—I probably should've dismantled all those negative thoughts and just went in without that perception of, "This is not where I should be." I don't know. It's good. It turned out fine.

Belinda did not expect to be "welcomed with open arms" into her new neighborhood, and in fact she thought she would be denied the opportunity to live there. These assumptions were not based on specific reports of discrimination in the neighborhood or a particularly racist history, but simply on her assumption that it was not a place for "people like her." She reported with some surprise that she succeeded in buying into the neighborhood and was perhaps even more surprised at how much she liked it.

Russell was even more explicit about his perception and assumptions that certain places were simply not for people of his racial group in his discussion of a number of predominantly white (he assumed) communities where he had never spent any time:

RUSSELL: Okay, so Crete, Monee, Mokena, Frankfort, New Lenox— I know these are all upcoming neighborhoods . . . at some point there was a lot of development, a lot of new houses being built there. . . . I think it started out being a very upscale neighborhood. I think the economy has had its impact on that, and I don't think the houses are as much— as expensive as they'd started out to be, but I know the taxes, the property taxes are very high in this area here.

Richton Park is a nice area. It's more of [an] African American community, but really nice homes, really nice large homes—same with Olympia Fields and this way, Flossmoor and Homewood, very nice homes. The thing that sticks out with me for Flossmoor and Homewood is that they have one of the best school districts in Illinois, so that's one of the things that stands out for me.

INTERVIEWER: Are there any other perceptions that you have about these areas, or about the area?

RUSSELL: No. I think that some of the areas like New Lenox, Mokena, Frankfort—it seems like a community that was built for a specific type of family. A specific type of people. I don't foresee many African Americans living here. I don't—I think that it's going to cater towards wealthier white families in this area.

INTERVIEWER: Why do you think that?

RUSSELL: I think just because of the—with the property taxes being so high with it—it just—economically, it doesn't seem feasible for your average African American family, where Richton Park would be more for—more of an African American community, which is really weird because the property taxes are similar—maybe not as high, but similar to these. The houses are not as new, but are, in some cases, bigger in Richton Park. Yeah, that's a good question. I never really thought about why I feel like that. I just got the impression like, "Ugh, that's not a neighborhood that would welcome me," kind of thing. Not saying that they would do anything to dissuade me or redline me or anything, but I don't see that being—it's nowhere I ever considered living.

Russell wrestles with the role of economics and affordability, but interestingly, he maintains a perception that even beyond economics, these communities are simply not for people like him. Importantly, these "new developments" have no concrete racial history, but they still carry impressions and assumptions for some searchers.

Wilson, another African American who lives in the city of Chicago, echoed these impressions of relatively new housing developments. Throughout the interview Wilson was asked about a range of different suburbs, and his answers were almost always the same. Although he had eliminated many from his consideration set because they were too far away or lacked public transportation options, it was very clear that Wilson also felt that he would stick out and not be allowed to stay in these places. Here is the exchange with the interviewer when Wilson was asked about Monee, an outlying, predominantly white suburb:

> INTERVIEWER: How welcoming do you think this neighborhood would be towards your racial or ethnic group? To African Americans?
>
> WILSON: My opinion, I don't think so, cuz it probably used to being to theyselves. Be with they own kind. If I walked in there, everybody . . . [laughs] especially me. Oh man, they look at me like, "Oh crap."
>
> INTERVIEWER: Now you said especially you. Why especially you?
>
> WILSON: I just—big, black, six feet, 280 pound. They just think I'm lost when I walk in. What are you—can we help you? They try to follow me in that town. Out of that town.

Wilson elaborated on how he felt he would be treated if he moved into a predominantly white suburb like Monee: "You might get one or two people that come and shake your hand and welcome you to the block, but the other ones, they ain't gonna have nothing to do with you." Russell echoed this sentiment when talking about North Riverside, Cicero, and Berwyn (all communities with very few African Americans): "Yeah, I wouldn't wanna live here just simply because of the whole aspect of not feeling wanted in this situation or in this area. That's why I wouldn't wanna live here."

Importantly, these examples paint a picture of an unwelcoming community, but it derives not from specific instances or events, but from assumptions. Racial composition may be viewed as a cue that is used to eliminate a place because of the assumption that it is likely to be unwelcoming to people of color, and this cue might be used as a heuristic to eliminate such a community from the consideration set.

Perceptions of Non-exclusionary Discrimination

Wilson's observation that he would "not feel wanted in this situation" highlights the idea that discrimination is not simply a question of whether or not one can access a neighborhood, whether one is seeking to avoid exclusionary discrimination; also important are perceptions of non-exclusionary discrimination. As Vincent Roscigno and his colleagues note, standard efforts to measure and understand discrimination in the housing market rarely address the non-exclusionary forms it takes—that is, the kinds of discrimination that would make life difficult, unpleasant, or uncomfortable.[32] The possible impact of the *anticipation* of non-exclusionary discrimination has been almost completely ignored in research that attempts to gauge the impact of discrimination on segregation, although it has figured prominently in studies of the factors shaping blacks' racial residential preferences.[33] In our in-depth interviews, it was common for African Americans to report the expectation of non-exclusionary discrimination if they were to seek residence in white neighborhoods, and that expectation also sometimes shaped their consideration sets.

Belinda has had considerable direct experience in diverse and predominantly white neighborhoods. Although she does not think that the door would be slammed in her face, that crosses would be burned on her front lawn, or that discrimination would be likely, her concern is that such places would just not be very welcoming. We see this in her description of Schaumburg, a majority-white, upper-middle-class suburb:

> I think it'll be open. You can't really discriminate against—the housing discrimination laws, you really can't discriminate against anybody in terms of race, but I think as far as welcoming, I think it'll be okay. So-so. I don't think that they would—that people would greet you with open arms—but I think it'll be all right.

Dorothy, who is African American, provided an additional twist on this when she talked about how welcoming her own predominantly white neighborhood has been: "There's been no eggs on my porch, none of that type of stuff. My landlord has not come to me and said of any complaints anybody has said about us or anything like that. Me, in general? I feel welcomed because nobody's harassing me about anything." Dorothy's standard of expected treatment by her neighbors is both revealing and sobering. She does not expect to be "greeted with open arms," and she views the absence of harassment and overt hostility as evidence that she is welcome.

What this highlights about the forces that maintain segregation is the importance of *expectations* about the likely reception in certain types of neighborhoods. Relatively few of the African Americans and Latinos we interviewed expressed concerns about exclusionary discrimination in predominantly white areas. They rarely expected to be told explicitly that they were unwelcome, to be denied the opportunity to purchase or rent a specific unit, or to be steered toward another neighborhood. More common were concerns about whether neighbors would treat them coldly or otherwise make them feel unwelcome. To be sure, some of them had ended up in predominantly white neighborhoods despite their expectation of non-exclusionary discrimination. But our interviews highlight the possibility that these expectations can for some be an important criterion used to eliminate neighborhoods from consideration—and sometimes the cue is a community's racial composition.

Non-exclusionary Discrimination Outside the Housing Market

Relatedly, concerns about discrimination can extend beyond the housing market so that options are eliminated because of perceived discrimination by other institutions in a community, such as police or retail establishments. This adds a twist to the impact of perceived non-exclusionary discrimination on housing processes. For example, in explaining why she would rule out Bellwood, Claudia, a forty-something Latina, explained:

> CLAUDIA: I haven't seen nothing. Nothing has happened around me, but that's not my area. I feel like I've—I don't feel comfortable with it. I don't know. It's just a feeling. It's just a feeling, yeah.
>
> INTERVIEWER: Okay. Is it safety? Do you feel safe there?
>
> CLAUDIA: Maybe for other people, but I wouldn't feel safe there.
>
> INTERVIEWER: Why?
>
> CLAUDIA: I mean, I haven't seen anything. I haven't seen anything, but to start with, I know one thing. [laughs] . . . The police there in Stone Park, they say, when you get off the expressway onto Mannheim, that those policemen, they see you're Hispanic, they stop you right away.
>
> INTERVIEWER: Really?
>
> CLAUDIA: Yeah, cuz they think that you don't have no insurance. Especially like me. I drive an old car, and so you have to be very careful. They're very careful with the speed. If you go over the speed. If you're Hispanic, I know . . . that they will stop you.

Claudia's friend once asked her for a ride to work, she said, and she responded:

> I'm "Damn, I gotta go to your house?" She's, "Yeah, well, just get off Mannheim. Don't be lazy. You live right off 290. It's only five minutes.

Come on, Claudia." I'm "Oh, man." I'm scared them police are gonna give
me—they gave my sister a ticket. . . . The cops are really, really strict, but
I know that if you are Hispanic, they'll stop you . . . the police. Well, that's
their job, right?

Extending community reputations for discrimination beyond home
sales and rental agents to include neighbors and other actors (police, sales
clerks, employers, and so on) is important in order to capture the full
impact of perceived discrimination on shaping consideration sets. It is
important to bear in mind, however, that African Americans' and Latinos'
consideration sets, to the limited extent that we have data on them, are
more varied in terms of their racial composition than are whites' consideration sets. Therefore, particularly—though not exclusively—for people of
color, it is important to consider the possible impact of discrimination and
perceived discrimination in stage 2 of a housing search—the stage when
available units are being researched and options are evaluated. We turn
now to a discussion of how discrimination might operate at this stage of
the process.

THE (ATTEMPTED) STEERING OF A PLACE
OUT OF THE CONSIDERATION SET

One of the more persistent and contemporary forms of housing discrimination is real estate agents and landlords or management companies attempting to steer housing searchers toward particular neighborhoods where
their group predominates. The traditional model of how steering works
to perpetuate segregation is uncomplicated: searchers approach an agent
with a specific neighborhood or unit in their preferred set, and the agent
works to get them to stop considering it. Our in-depth interviews highlight
that when steering happens, it is not always clear that searches unfold as
presumed by this model. That is, the model typically assumes that steering, when it happens, is successful. To be sure, it sometimes is. But our
models need to acknowledge how searches work in real life and capture
the heterogeneity of likely exposure to steering attempts and whether such
attempts will be successful.

For this more complicated picture of steering, we turn to insights
from our in-depth interviews. A dominant theme in these interviews is
that while some searchers sought advice about neighborhoods to consider from their real estate agents, many approached an agent with a
clear idea of the places they wanted to search and seldom experienced
steering. Even if they did, it often did not change their consideration set.

Teresa is an example of someone who knew exactly where she wanted to live:

> INTERVIEWER: Did the agent give you opinions about the different neighborhoods?
>
> TERESA: She asked me where I wanted to buy a house. I told her that I wanted to live here. She also wanted to know the streets I had in mind within Berwyn.
>
> INTERVIEWER: Oh, she asked?
>
> TERESA: And I told her between Roosevelt and Cermak and not any further.
>
> INTERVIEWER: Why? What's further down those streets?
>
> TERESA: Well, it was because I was caring for the children, and I didn't want to be too far from the parents' home. So I didn't want my home to be too far out.
>
> INTERVIEWER: Did she suggest looking in a different neighborhood?
>
> TERESA: No, because I told her I wanted my home here.
>
> INTERVIEWER: And she never insisted you look elsewhere?
>
> TERESA: No, because I wanted to live here.

Another Latino renter, Oscar, was asked if the rental agent he used offered any opinions about the neighborhoods he was considering, and he replied: "Not at all. No, he didn't." The interviewer then asked whether the agent said much about the kind of houses they might look at. "No, he didn't say. He asked us what we were looking for and what neighborhoods we were looking for. And then searched under what we were looking for." An African American homeowner had a similar response:

> INTERVIEWER: Did the agent suggest a neighborhood that you hadn't thought of searching in?
>
> SHAUN: Um, no. I don't think so.
>
> INTERVIEWER: So he pretty much stuck to neighborhoods . . .
>
> SHAUN: He pretty much knew what I wanted. I mean, if he saw a great place in Harvey, he wouldn't recommend it because he knew I didn't want to live in Harvey, so . . .

INTERVIEWER: Okay, that's good. He knew exactly what you wanted, stuck to that list, you know, instead of pulling you around somewhere.

SHAUN: I mean, you know, I mean they could have been the greatest place in the world that was in Uptown. I wouldn't move to it, so why waste my time telling me about it?

All of these examples illustrate that searchers do not search as testers in audit studies do—picking agents and landlords at random. Rather, many searchers enter into the process with fixed consideration sets that are difficult to alter. Such searchers seldom reported efforts by agents to change them. In many cases, in fact, real estate agents were explicitly selected for their expertise in a particular geographical area and so had no motivation to steer a client elsewhere. The impact of attempted steering may be minimal in such cases.

Those most susceptible to steering are those who choose agents without a geographic specialization, those who enter the search process without a strong sense of their consideration set, and, of course, those who search in racially atypical locations. To be sure, some of these groups are of primary importance to the question of steering's impact on segregation. But the point is that audits may be unrealistic measures of the kind of discrimination that matters, because they assume that searchers choose agents without regard to agents' geographic specialties and without strong attitudes toward their consideration sets. This is not to deny the impact of steering, but to complicate it and to clarify its consequences when it does happen. For instance, here is what happened with Sheila, one of our African American renter interview participants who reported being steered:

He [the agent] come showing me like Englewood [a disadvantaged overwhelmingly African American neighborhood in Chicago]. . . . And I'm like, "Could we go a little bit farther?" And he said, "No, that's as far as." I said, "You cannot sit here and tell me this is all the houses you have because I saw your map." And I told him, "You know what, I don't even want." I just got up and left. And my husband said, "That's $50 you blew," and I told him, "That's okay. I learned something with that $50." . . . They did give me a refund because I ended up calling and letting them know I didn't like the way I was treated. And for you to think that because I was black, I couldn't move to this neighborhood. Crap.

Although this is a textbook case of steering, Sheila's experience is a reminder that steering is not always successful. When her white rental agent refused to "go further" (by showing a black client houses in a whiter neighborhood), steering no doubt had the consequence of making her search more frustrating and time-consuming. But instead of being a victim of steering, Sheila simply walked away from the agent and sought assistance elsewhere.

RESPONSES TO STAGE 2 DISCRIMINATION

We know from audit studies that when individuals investigate specific housing units, they can face varied forms of discrimination, including blatant and outright denial of access, slow responses to inquiries or no response at all, cold treatment by real estate agents or landlords, excessive scrutiny, and harassment and intimidation.[34] But audit studies cannot speak to what happens next—that is, how do people react when they experience, or perceive they have experienced, discrimination? The experiences described in our in-depth interviews remind us that discrimination can have varied effects on the outcome, and not always the ones intended by the perpetrator.

We begin with a Latino homeowner, Cesar, who describes his experience trying to buy a house in the same neighborhood where he eventually moved:

> I wanted to buy the house because it's right on the corner and right across the street to where I'm at. And it's a nice house and . . . my wife and I, we called and called. And we leave our names, and they never returned our calls. And the house was for sale for almost a year, and they never even bothered to return our calls because I'm thinking that maybe because they could tell it was a Spanish name. And these people, they were Polish people, so. . . . They refused because they never answered me back. They wouldn't give me no information whatsoever.

When asked how they responded, Cesar replied: "I just gave up. After I make so many attempts, I never get no answer back, I just said, 'Well, forget them.'" Although Cesar regrets that he didn't "report them" or try to work around the Polish agent, the discrimination he believes he experienced affected only his unit outcome and had little effect on his neighborhood outcome.[35] Cesar was unable to get the specific property he wanted, but it did not dissuade him from seeking other options in the same neighborhood, and in fact, he was ultimately successful in purchasing a home across the street from the property he was denied. His experience with likely discrimination, while demoralizing and frustrating, did not have the intended outcome of eliminating the neighborhood from his search set.

But sometimes discrimination does have that outcome. In this next example, a Latino focus group participant described a similar experience:

> I actually looked at a house, and it was, you know, within reach, and I called the guy, and I guess the guy didn't know who I was and he said, "Yeah, the house it, it's going really cheap. It's going for X amount of money. You can come look at it tomorrow." So I called the next day, and they told me the house is sold: "We sold it a week ago." [*laughs*] And the house was sitting there like for, the sign was sitting outside the house like for maybe a month. . . . But you think of it this way. If they don't want to sell me the house, why would I want to move into a place where I'm not wanted? Right, because then who knows what the rest of the neighborhood's like too. You know?

An experience with apparent discrimination during the second stage of the housing search sent a message to this searcher about what the neighborhood would be like for him. So in this case discrimination not only denied him access to a specific house but also drove him away from the neighborhood altogether. This example illustrates the dynamic nature of housing searches, with consideration sets being revised based on new information gained in the course of a search.

In another example of discrimination from our in-depth interviews, our respondent, after feeling like he was being mistreated, conducted his own "experiment" by comparing and contrasting the quality of service he received from Hispanic and non-Hispanic real estate companies:

> I've been going to these Hispanic realty companies. Well, these couple of houses that I went to, they weren't Hispanic real estate companies, you know. They were white agents . . . and when I went to go look at the houses . . . it seemed to me like they were jacking up the price even more and it took . . . like five days to see the house. You know, every time, "Oh, you can see it tomorrow." "No, well, call me back tomorrow. I'll be there Saturday." And they were just, like, they were playing with me. . . . When I would go to the Hispanic companies, they were calling me at my job. "Hurry up and get here." . . . I know these [other] people were jerking me around. I just know it.

We asked whether he thought it was the agent who was mistreating him, or perhaps the sellers as well.

> I think it was more the agent. I think some of these people are a little bitter about selling to Hispanics for, I don't know what the problem is really. They kind of look at the, they kind of look at a Hispanic person (coming) through their neighborhood, and I'm not really sure what's going through their mind you know. That's what I think.

This searcher's response to bad treatment was to switch his information-gathering approach and rely on Hispanic real estate agents. Survey data from Detroit and Chicago suggest that the use of same-race-ethnicity real estate agents is common, and the story told by this in-depth interview participant reveals one possible explanation for doing so.

What is unclear is the impact of using same-race-ethnicity real estate agents on residential segregation. It is conceivable that Latino agents, for example, are more likely to market neighborhoods with larger Latino populations compared to the neighborhoods that white agents market. The consequence for this searcher may have been buying in a less diverse neighborhood than he would have if the white agents had not given him the runaround. Recent studies of real estate brokers lend credence to the possibility that the race of the agent has consequences for the racial composition of the properties the agent markets. In one study of New York City brokers, it was found that black and white brokers marketed racially distinct segments of the housing market, with brokers offering properties in neighborhoods that matched their own racial background.[36] And in a national survey of black real estate agents, it was found that black agents worked in offices with mostly other black professionals, that their clients were predominantly minority, and that they largely marketed homes in black neighborhoods.[37]

As was true of the steering example, our models of how discrimination impacts segregation generally fail to allow for the variability in responses to instances of discrimination that all of these examples provide.

VARIABLE RESPONSES TO NON-EXCLUSIONARY DISCRIMINATION IN STAGE 2

Audit studies show that African Americans and Latinos experience more hassles when inquiring about possible housing units, and our in-depth interviews provide some examples of what this can look like. These discriminatory behaviors may not technically be exclusionary, but they can nevertheless have the same consequence, as described by a Latino focus group participant:

> Well, I was looking for an apartment, but I had the guy constantly telling me how much it was, reminding me how much it was, like I wasn't going to be able to afford it, and then when I showed him that I had money, he wanted to come to my house. He said he had to come to my house and check out my house first to see what kind of person I was and how I lived and I was like "Whoa." That's okay. Keep your apartment. . . . I'll just, I'll go somewhere else.

This humiliating treatment affected the searcher so much that he stopped his pursuit of this option. We don't know whether he went to another unit in the same neighborhood or gave up on the neighborhood altogether (that is, whether he removed it from his consideration set), but we do know that he did not move into a place in which he was interested and for which he was qualified.

It doesn't always play out this way, however, as Marcus's story about a recent search reveals:

> MARCUS: [The landlord is asking me,] "Where do you work at? Are you going to school? What are you majoring in?" "I work, I work at the hospital, I've been there for X amount of years. I went to school here, and um, my goals in life are . . ." They throwing these questions at me. . . . Had I not been a black guy in the area that I was looking [a majority-white neighborhood] . . . it wouldn't have been a factor. Had I been a white guy, no problem in that area.

> INTERVIEWER: So being [black] and being male at the same time?

> MARCUS: Right. So that went hand in hand there. Uh, as far as some areas was a lot easier for me because of the fact that I was familiar with these areas. . . . I was a little bit closer to Wrigley Field, but it was like, "Where you work?" I said, "Okay, I work for the Chicago Tribune Tower." "Oh really? What else do you do?" See, I'm like, "Wait a minute, I ain't got to listen to this. Why you asking me these questions? I just told you where I'm currently living . . . so why are you asking me these questions?" And the guy, flat out, he told me, "One of the reasons being is not a racial thing. None of that." He says, "You could see the building system mixes Indians, China, you know, whatever." He said, "It's not that. I had a couple of people, tenants in the building that was drug sellers, distributors." That's what he said. So, he said, "And guess what?" I said, "You don't have to tell me. It was black guys, right?" He said, "Yeah."

> INTERVIEWER: So it *was* race then?

> MARCUS: Right. So I said . . . "So now you said it's not race, but then again it is, because those guys you had a problem with was black guys. I'm a black guy, a single guy. So, you think that, you know. But I'm telling you, I work.

I don't sell drugs for a living, you know what I mean? I don't sell drugs at all." . . . [he gave in] cuz he told me, "See, that's not fair." You know, he said, "I'm not the only person. This is management." He said, "I'm not the only person that deals with this. I'm just a small piece of this puzzle, you know." He said, "But it's not right." And he said, "I don't see any problems with you getting apartment 260, Mr. Wilson. You qualify."

This example has a happy ending because Marcus pushed back against what the agent agreed was discriminatory treatment and Marcus ended up with the place he sought. The point is that discrimination is real, but it is not always effective and it can happen at different stages of the search process.

THE BLURRING OF DISCRIMINATION, SOCIAL CLASS, AND PREFERENCES

To this point, our discussion of discrimination as a driver of segregation has focused on what it looks like in the first and second stages of a housing search and its different impacts on outcomes when viewed through this lens. But stepping back, we need to consider that there is an underlying premise in traditional debates about the causes of segregation that is also problematic. Specifically, much of the traditional research asks: how does discrimination shape the housing outcomes of racial minorities, particularly *as compared to* social class and preferences? One of the weaknesses of existing approaches, as suggested here, is that we can neither disentangle discrimination from social class nor separate both of these from preferences. That is, discrimination is not independent of other causes of segregation.

Three examples from existing research and from our in-depth interviews illustrate this point. First, African Americans of different social class standing are exposed to different kinds and levels of housing discrimination.[38] Second, perceived social class—that is, the social class characteristics that people involved in the housing market attribute to African American and Latino home-seekers—can influence the discrimination process and its effects. And third, all three elements—discrimination, preferences, and economics—can blur together to shape residential outcomes.

Social Class and Discrimination

Existing theoretical frameworks assume that landlords, real estate agents, mortgage brokers, and other housing market institutions discriminate against

African Americans of all social class levels equally, but there is evidence that this is not the case. First, relying on the fact that audit studies vary the reported income of their testers (in order to present an applicant who meets the financial requirements of the housing unit being tested), researchers found that blacks with higher reported income encountered less discrimination in face-to-face interactions with landlords and real estate agents than those with lower reported income.[39] More recent online and phone-based audit studies of the rental market show a similar pattern. For example, one telephone-based audit study reported that prospective tenants who spoke black-accented English (a signal for middle-class status) gained more access to rental units than did black prospective tenants who spoke black English vernacular (a signal for lower/working-class status).[40] In an online audit, different social class levels were signaled by altering the grammar and mentioning credit ratings and references in the email inquiry. This study showed that discrimination was greater when the inquiry sent a lower-class cue. In fact, there was little sign of unequal treatment among blacks and whites who signaled higher social class.[41]

Studies of home-buyers also point to possible differences in discrimination based on social class, particularly in the mortgage market that preceded and coincided with the buildup to the housing crisis.[42] For example, one analysis showed that foreclosures disproportionately hit black residents and black neighborhoods because these were the targets of predatory lending.[43] Among white borrowers, subprime lending rates declined as incomes increased, but among borrowers of color the opposite occurred.[44] Jacob Rugh and his colleagues argue that this pattern may explain why black-white differences in foreclosures were greatest at higher income levels.[45] Thus, the social class differences in the patterns of discrimination experienced by home-buyers appear to be opposite to those of renters: among aspiring homeowners, higher-income blacks experienced more disadvantaging treatment.

In addition, even where rates of foreclosure were similar across all income groups, blacks with different incomes experienced different consequences. Specifically, higher-income blacks paid a greater penalty than lower-income blacks: "Based on our analysis, compared with $14,904 for all African Americans, the projected cumulative cost of discrimination for blacks earning over $50,000/year was $19,026."[46] Higher-income blacks were also more likely to be foreclosed upon and more likely to have been subject to predatory lending than their lower-income counterparts.

Although the data preclude a direct test, these examples suggest the possibility that allowing discrimination to operate differently based on the home-seeker's social class can provide clues about why white and black homeowners of the same social class do not live in the same neighborhoods.

...erintuitively, African Americans with higher income suffer the greater consequences of discrimination in the home-buying market. Among renters, those who are most discriminated against are at the lower end of the social class ladder. Thus, although in both cases discrimination influences housing outcomes, those most impacted may be quite different in the two markets, an idea that existing models seldom take into consideration.

Perceived Social Class and Discrimination

Discrimination and social class are also inseparable because of the impact of *perceived* social class on how minority searchers are treated. Specifically, individuals and institutions in the housing market may discriminate based on *assumptions* about the social class characteristics of their minority clients or potential tenants. Social class and discrimination are therefore linked because some agents and landlords rationalize discrimination based on their assumptions about the financial capabilities of their clients. This observation is not novel—it is among the theories offered by economists and sociologists to explain why actors discriminate in the housing market. Our point is that because there are *social* processes related to social class that can underpin how discrimination operates, we cannot readily declare that segregation flows from *either* discrimination *or* economics.[47]

When landlords and real estate agents make assumptions about the financial status of potential tenants or home-buyers based on their understanding of the average characteristics of people in that group (their racial-ethnic group in this case), they are practicing statistical discrimination.[48] In the housing market, statistical discrimination functions as follows: Agents and landlords may know that African Americans and Latinos, on average, have lower incomes and less wealth than whites. If they apply this perception to any individual African American or Latino client who approaches them to buy or rent a home and then treat that black or Latino client differently than they would a white client—for example, by directing the black or Latino client to lower-priced homes and neighborhoods, or discouraging this client from considering certain higher-priced options—then they are engaging in statistical discrimination. Even if the perception is, on average, accurate, it is discriminatory and illegal under the Fair Housing Act to treat any particular individual from a group differently. And such treatment may also serve to perpetuate segregation.

Analyses of audit studies find evidence of this type of statistical discrimination. For example, one study reported that discrimination against black testers increased as the price of the unit about which the tester was inquiring increased.[49] Real estate agents also spent less time showing higher-priced units to blacks—a pattern that could have been due either to the expectation that these clients would not qualify for more expensive homes or that they would be discriminated against by lenders or home insurance companies. Marketing efforts are also impacted by the race of the client: when whites inquired about more expensive units, agents' marketing efforts increased, but with black clients, asking price had no effect on agents' marketing efforts. Finally, agents appear to take the initial unit about which whites inquire as a signal of their financial abilities, but the same is not the case for black clients: agents were more likely to show homes of a lower value than that of the unit in which a black client initially expressed interest. These findings led the economist Jan Ondrich and his colleagues to conclude that "agents practice statistical discrimination on the basis of the perception that blacks, but not whites, request more expensive units than they can afford."[50] In essence, agents appear to rely on preconceptions (based on "average" group characteristics) as a more valid indicator of their black clients' economic resources than the information presented to them in the inquiry. By contrast, agents take their white clients at face value.

Our interview data bring life to these audit study numbers and further illustrate how African Americans and Latinos may modify their behavior in anticipation of, or response to, statistical discrimination. Brandon, a black homeowner, shared his perception that agents practice statistical discrimination:

BRANDON: A lot of times, people will judge, a lot of people judge books by their cover. I mean, if somebody shows up to meet wearing jeans and a T-shirt doesn't mean that they're broke. [The agent says:] "Oh, let me show you something in your price range." How do you know what my price range is? I mean, I might be looking for a $3 million penthouse on Lake Shore Drive. And have the means to pay for it. But you think I can't afford it. So you get a lot of that kind of steering. "Oh, let me show you something more in your price range." So, yeah, you get a lot of that.

INTERVIEWER: Do you think that's something you just accept as happening as part of the process of looking, particularly being a black male, or do you try, you know, have you ever tried to do something about it?

BRANDON: I think if the realtor would prequalify every buyer that calls in his or her office, that could be avoided. So you know what, you already know what their price range is; you're not making that kind of assumption.

INTERVIEWER: Based on?

BRANDON: Based on their color.

This example and those described earlier about the excessive scrutiny experienced by racial-ethnic minorities hint at how race-based perceptions of socioeconomic status can powerfully influence the neighborhood selection and housing search process, potentially steering black and Latino searchers toward neighborhoods with less expensive housing—but also, in all likelihood, higher poverty, greater structural disadvantage, and racial isolation—regardless of their ability to pay for housing elsewhere. This steering may be done by agents directing searchers elsewhere explicitly or by home-seekers giving up on certain options based on the excessive scrutiny they have to endure.

Preferences, Discrimination, and Social Class

Although traditional studies of the causes of segregation tend to retain separate forces for each of the three primary drivers, we close this chapter by highlighting the intersection of the three drivers, insofar as preferences are shaped by perceptions of discrimination that are themselves shaped by social class. Our in-depth interview data draw attention to this possible complexity. African Americans, when asked to discuss communities that they might or might not include in their consideration set, revealed the sometimes tight link between social class and discrimination in defining those preferences. Specifically, communities are perceived as having both racial *and* social class features that come together to create a particular kind of concern about potential discrimination. This shapes, in turn, whether they would include those communities in their consideration set. When Wilson answered the question of how welcoming Lake County would be to black people, he said that Lake County residents would use skin color to decide whether a person belonged there. But then he qualified his conclusion:

WILSON: I believe they could almost look to see if you belong around there or not.

INTERVIEWER: Why? I'm interested as to why you think that—

WILSON: I just—I don't know. That's just my way of thinking. I think that—now, if I was well-to-do off or whatever. Driving my Mercedes or whatever. My Guccis or whatever they wear up there. Then I probably wouldn't get too many stares. If I drive my little old '90 Chevy with my music up, something like that, they gonna say I lost.

The need to have the trappings of the middle class to overcome assumptions by residents and thwart discriminatory treatment has been reported in numerous studies of the black middle class.[51] In this example, the perceived need to adapt in this way is a result of an attribute of a community and may even lead to its elimination from the consideration set. Thus, discrimination and social class become conflated in a way that shapes preferences. Quite apart from whether or not a person *could* afford to live in a neighborhood, what that person presumes about how he or she would be treated may be sufficient cause for elimination.

This three-way intersection also came out in David's interview when he talked about living in his racially mixed (but predominantly white) upper-income apartment building in Chicago's Loop area. He revealed how his choices were influenced by his earlier residential experiences and his perspectives on race, class, and discrimination:

DAVID: Originally, when I lived in [a medium-sized city in the South], I lived in a . . . prestigious zip code. . . . I got that same feel whereas people wouldn't initiate conversation with you unless you initiated it with them. You'd get like a glance, and someone would look away really, really quickly, as opposed to when I moved to a [different] zip code that was just on the outskirts of the city. It was a neighborhood in which it was predominantly black, probably on a medium to low socioeconomic level. The kids in the neighborhood—I'd let them set up their basketball hoop in front of my house. My neighbor across the street would let me know what was going on in the neighborhood or if he saw someone coming around my house and . . . he'd invite me over for dinner with his wife sometimes . . . which . . . is something that you kind of forgo . . . when you live—and just to be frank—in urban neighborhoods that are, I guess, kind of like high socioeconomic levels. To an extent, when you live in suburban neighborhoods that are those high socioeconomic levels, if you don't fit the mold—those that typically live in those neighborhoods—you kind of forgo that community feeling, to an extent.

INTERVIEWER: Is the mold just socioeconomic? I know you had also talked about race.

DAVID: I think it's a mixture of both. From what I've seen, race is becoming less and less of an issue in some neighborhoods and in some, I guess, states and cities that I've lived in. I think, initially, it's still there. I mean, it's the first thing that you really see on a person's face when you meet them. If you move into a new building or if you move into a new neighborhood, I think, initially, people—I would assume—or I should say maybe predict that some do initially base their perceptions of individuals on their race or the way they look. An example is if a couple sees me coming onto an elevator in a new building in one of those more affluent neighborhoods, for example, urban neighborhoods—they see me getting onto an elevator, and I'm going out for a social event with friends, I may have on like a fitted baseball hat or may have on a pair of Jordans. I don't look as if I fit the mold of the average person who lives there and I fit the mold more of a typical, I guess, kind of young, black male in a way that's portrayed in the media.

Initially I think sometimes, more often than not, people are kind of hesitant to say anything or they're quiet. Even if they've had a few drinks, they kind of crowd in the corner of the elevator. I've had situations in which people have actually been quite friendly in situations like that, maybe to break the ice or whatever else it may be. Coupling that with one situation—the exact next morning I saw that exact same couple. I had on my work clothes and I was headed to work. We got off the elevator into the parking lot. Before he got off, he was like, "Have a good day." And looked at me and smiled. That makes me believe that it's more of kind of like a socioeconomic than it is race at this point now. . . . You can argue that race and socioeconomic status kind of play into each other hand in hand.

David has a complicated perspective on how race and class have combined to shape his expectations about how he will be treated living in certain neighborhoods. These expectations have informed how he approaches residential decision-making. If people believe that in some types of neighborhoods their daily experiences with discriminatory treatment will be determined by a complex interaction of their race and apparent socioeconomic status, they may avoid such areas when constructing their consideration set. If race and class go "hand in hand" in shaping interactions between neighbors, this may be at least as important as affordability in steering people of color away from predominantly white neighborhoods.

SUMMARY

This discussion of discrimination's impact on residential location processes— viewed through the lens of how people pick places to include in their consideration set, as well as what happens throughout a search process—reveals a much more complicated picture of the influence, both direct and indirect, of housing discrimination. Although direct discrimination might prevent home-seekers from gaining access to specific units they have selected during the search, the anticipation or expectation of discrimination is likely to shape where they decide to search for housing in the first place. We argue that consideration sets constructed in the first stage can be affected by concerns about discrimination and that racial composition is sometimes used as the cue to eliminate them. Minority home-seekers may thus limit their consideration set based on their expectation of discrimination—an expectation that could be a general sense that they will be denied housing, or treated poorly, in a community, whether because of its particular racial composition or because of what they know about its racial history. Of course, the extent to which community racial composition is linked to perceived discrimination is probably itself a function of the particular metropolitan area—that is, this may describe legacy metros like Chicago, Detroit, and Milwaukee more than other cities with less extreme segregation or smaller black populations.

Thus, we need to keep in mind the social factors that shape knowledge and perceptions of places and understand that discrimination is not just the kind of simple driver of segregation that can be detected by conventional housing audit studies. Testing the magnitude of racial differences in the treatment of individuals responding to ads for the same unit is likely to dramatically underestimate the overall effect of discriminatory forces on segregation, particularly in places with long histories of segregation and discrimination. Additionally, discrimination must be understood as substantively intertwined with economics and preferences.

In short, the social structural sorting perspective reveals a much more complicated story about how discrimination operates than is traditionally told. It is not a foregone conclusion that instances of discrimination always result in segregative moves, nor can discrimination be considered separate from either economics or preferences. Finally, discrimination can function even more substantially through its impact on a home-seeker's construction of a consideration set—especially when the anticipation of discrimination results in the elimination of certain kinds of communities where people of color expect either to be denied housing or to be treated poorly if they manage to move in.

Part IV | The Implications of the Social
Structural Sorting Perspective
for Segregation

Chapter 10 | Policies That Could Help Break the Cycle of Segregation

On August 9, 2014, we received another high-profile reminder of the racial divisions that still affect this country with the shooting of an unarmed black man, Michael Brown, by a white police officer in Ferguson, Missouri, a predominantly black inner-ring suburb of St. Louis. This shooting was not unlike many other videotaped incidents of police violence against people of color, dating back at least to the beating of Rodney King by several Los Angeles police officers in 1991. Like many of those earlier incidents— and like similar incidents since—the shooting of Michael Brown touched off public protests and strident debates about the police use of force, racial profiling, biases in the criminal justice system, and, in particular, young black men's interactions with police.

Also reemerging, although at a lower volume, were discussions about the broader structural forces that set the stage for Brown's shooting. At least some community leaders, public officials, and social scientists traced the roots of the shooting to the fact that Ferguson is a nearly all-black community in which residents not only face poor housing choices, dilapidated and underfunded schools, and few high-quality job opportunities but are aggressively policed by a local force made up almost completely of white officers from outside of the community.[1] Echoing the Kerner Commission's depiction of the roots of the urban riots of the 1960s, these reports highlighted the extreme disparities between the opportunities available to residents of racially isolated black neighborhoods and those available in white neighborhoods.[2] They suggested that the extreme acrimony that had emerged between the nearly all-black population of Ferguson and the nearly all-white police force was just a symptom of broader systems of racial

215

inequality upheld by the extreme residential stratification of St. Louis and similar metropolitan areas.

On the one-year anniversary of that shooting, the *New York Times* published an article whose title and content made a direct link between the tragic event and residential segregation: "A Year After Ferguson, Housing Segregation Defies Tools to Erase It."[3] It is rather remarkable that the media—and some measure of public discourse—have come to understand that issues of police violence have at their core the problem of racial residential segregation. Also noteworthy is that the *New York Times* chose on this one-year anniversary to frame its discussion of issues of segregation with a profile of one young black woman's experience with a federal housing assistance program and the housing search that it precipitated.

The article opened with the following words: "When she tore open the manila envelope on a sweltering morning in early June, Crystal Wade thought she had unlocked her ticket to freedom. 'The St. Louis Housing Authority is pleased to inform you,' the letter read, 'that you have been determined eligible to participate in our Housing Choice Voucher Program.'"[4] The Housing Choice Voucher (HCV) program provides assistance to individuals, in the form of housing subsidies, so that they can rent a unit on the private market. This individual-based approach contrasts sharply with earlier policies, which involved building large public housing projects into which poor people were funneled. As HUD's fact sheet explains:

> Since housing assistance is provided on behalf of the family or individual, participants are able to *find their own housing,* including single-family homes, townhouses and apartments. The participant is *free to choose* any housing that meets the requirements of the program and is not limited to units located in subsidized housing projects. . . . A family that is issued a housing voucher is *responsible for finding* a suitable housing unit of the family's choice where the owner agrees to rent under the program.[5]

In her first attempt to find a place to rent, Crystal did an Internet search using a tool on which many landlords who accepted housing choice vouchers advertised:

> When the hits came back, not a single property was in one of the more affluent towns where the schools are better and crime lower. The few that were near promising areas had months-long wait lists. Some landlords told her that they would rent to her and the children but not to her boyfriend. And so Ms. Wade, who grew up in all-black projects and went to predominantly black schools, recalibrated her expectations. She began to confine her search

to the communities where most of the region's black people live, where the majority of the region's Section 8 holders—95% of whom are black—are able to find obliging landlords, on the city's north side and in north St. Louis County, which includes Ferguson. Segregation was laying its trap.[6]

Despite starting her search with the clear goal to move away from the kinds of neighborhoods where she grew up and lived at the time she received the voucher, Ms. Wade ended up using the voucher to move to a segregated neighborhood not too different from the one she was living in when she was accepted into the program. In short, although her consideration set was more expansive as a result of her increased resources, other factors conspired against an outcome consistent with her dream. Her experience shows how the theory of the program—that low-income families can be provided with assistance in meeting their housing needs to enable them to move outside of disadvantaged and segregated neighborhoods—collides with the reality of the neighborhood selection and housing search processes through which it must be applied. Large-scale studies examining the residential locations of voucher holders reveal that Ms. Wade's experience was not unusual.[7] The assumption of the policy is that the only impediment to housing that is safe, sanitary and decent, is having the monthly rent to pay for it. This assumption is called into question by scholars who have examined both the voucher program in general, as well as Mobility Programs that seek to help voucher holders move to opportunity areas. As some have concluded: the voucher program cannot assume that people will make moves into opportunity areas without assistance.[8] In other words, the neighborhood selection and housing choice process must be understood.

The challenges faced by HCV participants trying to "find their own housing" were summarized in a 2015 *Washington Post* article:

"There are so many barriers," says executive director [of a mobility program in Chicago] Christine Klepper. "Sometimes I wonder how we get any moves." The units are too expensive. Or voucher holders have to compete with market-rate tenants who don't entail the same paperwork load. Or landlords reject them because of their vouchers, even though that's illegal in Chicago. Or families can't find the right-sized home in the 90-day window the housing authority gives them, or the right-sized home turns out to be in a place where you need a car. Or, more often, there just isn't much affordable housing in good neighborhoods, because the nicest places to live are the most effective at keeping out new development, whether in the city or the suburbs.[9]

These barriers include financial considerations, but they also extend beyond this concern. And the executive director's list highlights a core argument of this book: we need to understand the complex and nuanced factors that shape how people end up living where they do in order to understand how segregation is perpetuated—and how to break its cycle.

Discouragement—even paralysis—about how to tackle the problem of segregation in the face of the complexity implied by the social structural sorting perspective would be understandable. If, to date, we have failed to undermine even the most obvious pillars of segregation, the chances of developing policies that address the more subtle, self-perpetuating, and insidious forces seem remote. In their most simplified form, the traditional theories would suggest that to eliminate segregation we need to increase the incomes of racial minorities, increase the tolerance of whites, or eliminate racial discrimination. Any one of these policy goals is daunting, politically unlikely, and overly simplistic—and therefore unlikely to be successful. A positive consequence of the more complex story we lay out in this book is the realization that there are many more possible policy levers to pull in order to erode, rather than build up, segregation. Because segregation is perpetuated through many mechanisms, there need not be a single cure to eradicate it. Instead, we can chip away at different aspects of the self-perpetuating segregation machine in order to rein in galloping segregation. No one lever alone will eliminate segregation when pulled, but pulling many levers could help reduce it.

Acknowledging this complexity also opens up the possibility that actors at different levels—advocates, nonprofits, community organizations, local, state, and federal governments—can undertake efforts tailored to particular individuals or communities to influence this complex and self-perpetuating process. In the remainder of this chapter, we organize our discussion of potential policy solutions around the different stages of a search. The goal is to ask two questions: How can we return to consideration or contention those residential options that have been filtered out through the residential selection process? And if adopted, would these options break down segregation rather than build it up?

As with other claims in this book, we must be cautionary in our assertions about policy proscriptions, given the circumstantial evidence underpinning our framework. However, our discussion of policies leans heavily on evaluation research of voucher-based programs and other housing programs that have been in operation for decades. Our intention is not to argue that any particular program is the magic bullet, but rather to extend our overall argument to draw out the policy areas that we might explore based on the proposed framework.

POLICIES TARGETING THE PRE-SEARCH STAGE

The social structural sorting perspective suggests that residential segregation is perpetuated in part because the kind of information people have at their disposal prior to a search comes from social networks and lived experiences that are themselves racially segregated. Thus, the obvious—though challenging—implication is that residential segregation could be reduced through policies that integrate social networks and expand lived experiences in a way that would impact the information that flows from them. This could have positive effects on people's prior knowledge and the social networks they consult when they form impressions of communities as places to live. But direct policy interventions targeting this pre-search stage—apart from efforts that focus on increasing integration in other social institutions such as workplaces and educational settings—are hard to conceive.

Studies suggest—and our in-depth interviews illustrate—that in addition to lived experiences and social networks, the media, broadly construed, also play an important role in shaping community perceptions. And studies demonstrate that the content of that information is not always race-neutral. It is here where there are more obvious possible interventions. Community leaders and policymakers interested in supporting integration should consider education, public relations, and media campaigns that push back against the images people have or are receiving through other information sources. Communities that are diverse or diversifying—either by design or by circumstance—are one source of ideas for such campaigns.[10] One example is Oak Park, Illinois.[11] Particularly in the early years of its intentional integration efforts, Oak Park expended resources to advertise the community's charms outside of its borders, with the goal of putting Oak Park into people's consideration sets. These ads were placed both in metrowide outlets, such as *Chicago* magazine, and national publications, such as *The New Yorker*. Similarly, the sociologist Michael Maly describes how three communities (Uptown in Chicago; Jackson Heights in New York; and San Antonio–Fruitvale in Oakland, California) sought to affirmatively market their integrated communities by embracing diversity as an asset and "attempt[ing] to brand the area as diverse," the goal being "to sell the diversity and integration as community strengths rather than as risks."[12] The intention of these concerted marketing and media campaigns is to raise awareness so that searchers will include these communities in their consideration sets when they are searching for a new place to live.

Another kind of marketing campaign could be undertaken in predominantly white communities. Given that such communities can suffer from a reputation among people of color as being unwelcoming, education and marketing campaigns to not only put their community on the radar screens of people of all races and ethnicities but also overcome perceptions of anticipated discrimination may be productive. Since integration can only be stable if there is demand from all races and ethnicities, efforts to influence the kind of information disseminated about communities and to add (or perhaps undo) what is learned through lived experiences and social networks would position these places in people's consideration sets when they start a search.

We now turn to a discussion of efforts that explicitly target the first stage of a housing search—the point when searchers winnow down all possible places to those that they will consider.

WAYS TO INTERVENE IN STAGE 1: CONSTRUCTING A CONSIDERATION SET

People enter the first stage of a housing search armed with all of the experiences, perceptions, knowledge, and information they have accumulated up to that point (during what we refer to as the pre-search stage). Once they decide to undertake a search, the first stage involves winnowing down all possible communities so as to create a more manageable subset of places that they are familiar with and where they would consider living. Given the social factors that feed into this process, as well as the shortcuts used by decision-makers, the question becomes: What might be done to disrupt the ways in which this process unfolds that lead to the perpetuation of segregation? Where in the process might programs be targeted so as to interrupt the cycle?

Expand the Sources of Information That Contribute to Knowledge and Perceptions of Communities

The social structural sorting perspective draws attention to the sources of information that feed a neighborhood selection and housing search process and suggests that these sources are socially constructed and constrained. For instance, the information sources people rely upon in neighborhood selection and housing search processes—specifically, social networks, lived experiences, and the media—are often racialized. As such, one way to break out of this pattern is to expand the sources of information that people use in their search. The goal is to create new sources that overcome the blind spots and misinformation that may otherwise guide a search.

For example, racially integrated suburbs can provide guided tours of their communities to people who otherwise would be either unfamiliar with or misinformed about the features of their community. Such tours are offered to prospective home-buyers by South Orange–Maplewood, New Jersey, through the South Orange–Maplewood Community Coalition on Race, and by Shaker Heights, Ohio, through its website.[13] The goal here is clearly to get these racially diverse communities into the consideration sets of searchers who might otherwise be reluctant to think about them. The challenge in this type of intervention is attracting people who are not already aware of and interested in the community to sign up for a tour. It is people who are unfamiliar with these communities or have misperceptions about them who are most in need of these information interventions; they may be the least likely, however, to stumble across a tour advertised on a website or community bulletin board.

Another way to reach prospective renters and buyers more proactively may be through general online housing and rental search engines. In theory, these could be designed with the goal of providing searchers with information about places that fit their search criteria and that they might otherwise not have considered owing to inaccurate or nonexistent knowledge or perceptions. This style of intervention has been implemented in the mobility programs that assist HCV holders in moving to opportunity areas.[14] These programs clearly understand the importance of expanding information sources and content during a housing search in order to influence the construction of the consideration set. Mobility programs such as the Inclusive Communities Project, Housing Choice Partners (HCP), the Baltimore Mobility Program (BMP), and the King County Housing Authority (KCHA) have done this by providing information about neighborhoods or communities with high opportunity through online search tools, brochures, and colorful maps. This information is disseminated online, in group presentations (some of which are required of new voucher recipients), or in one-on-one counseling.

Mobility program organizers clearly recognize the importance of supplementing existing and traditional influences (social networks and personal experiences) on consideration sets, since these influences are often racially circumscribed and frequently lead to segregative moves. As the Baltimore Mobility Program staff explained:

> For many inner city families, the suburban counties and towns exist beyond the realm of consciousness. There is a good chance they've never visited suburban neighborhoods and don't know firsthand that these areas have plenty of shops and other amenities. When applicants entering the program come to MBQ's [Metropolitan Baltimore Quadel, the private contractor that

administers the BMP] office in downtown Baltimore for their orientation, one of the first things they do is board a charter bus for a tour of some of these communities. On these tours, MBQ housing counselors ask riders to notice how the streets with closely packed homes and small yards and corner grocers and liquor stores give way to strip malls with an array of stores and townhouses with bigger yards and driveways not alleys. Guides also point out schools, doctor's offices, businesses, bus and metro stops, and other notable amenities.[15]

Mobility programs take clients on bus tours of opportunity areas, giving them direct experience of communities they might have never heard of or visited before and dispelling some of their concerns. Thus, in addition to providing information through maps, brochures, and online programs, mobility programs also recognize the power of lived experiences in elevating a community from a familiar one to one where people would consider living. The effectiveness of this approach is attributed to both the information and the lived experiences. As the sociologists Jennifer Darrah and Stefanie DeLuca explain, "While counseling provided respondents with information to evaluate county neighborhoods, direct experience allowed families to see the benefits for themselves."[16]

The goal of these efforts is to encourage opportunity moves by expanding the information sources used by HCV participants. There is ample evidence from evaluation studies and from assessments of the outcomes of voucher programs that do not provide search assistance of this sort that, without some kind of intervention, and in the face of substantial efforts by landlords, voucher holders tend to use their vouchers to move to places that are not very different from where they started.[17] Indeed, as one study puts it, "if creating more racially integrated neighborhoods is a goal for our society, available evidence suggests that merely giving out housing vouchers will not be sufficient; this approach often leads families to choose neighborhoods like the ones in which they already reside."[18]

In a study of participants in the Baltimore Mobility Program, Darrah and DeLuca provide compelling evidence that this program was successful at increasing knowledge of communities. This greater knowledge was probably useful when the participants undertook their next search and may partly explain why their next moves tended to be into the same kinds of opportunity areas as their initial move. As Darrah and DeLuca explain:

The program also appears to have helped erase some of the blind spots (Krysan and Bader 2009) held by respondents when it came to mixed race or predominately white suburban locations—an important step toward the broader goal of expanding access to safe and resource-rich neighborhoods for low income African American families. When asked to evaluate lists of neighborhoods in the greater Baltimore region (something we also did with prop lists during interviews), BMP participants indicated that they had increased the number of places about which they were familiar and in which they were willing to live as a result of their program participation. In doing so, the program provided families with more options for where they could live.[19]

In essence, the Baltimore Mobility Program was successful in part because it intervened in the process, providing information and removing all kinds of structural barriers. What made the moves "stick," however, were the lived experiences and supports, which fundamentally changed how the recipients thought about housing decisions.[20]

The lessons learned by mobility programs could be adapted and applied to people outside of the narrow reach of the HCV population. That is, an approach worth considering is finding creative ways to encourage people to consider places they would not otherwise consider or even know about from relying on traditional sources of information.

The sociologist Eva Rosen provides a cautionary reminder that there are actors who seek to intervene in the neighborhood selection and housing search processes in ways that undermine the goals of some policymakers and programs.[21] Specifically, her study of landlords who specialize in voucher rentals uncovered a number of strategies used to funnel voucher holders toward exactly the kinds of neighborhoods that policymakers do not want them to move into. Landlords do this because they recognize the challenges faced by voucher holders in their search process, especially the constraints under which they operate and the ways in which they assess unit versus neighborhood characteristics. As Rosen explains, these landlords take advantage of voucher holders' limited knowledge about other kinds of neighborhoods and attract tenants by upgrading the unit features to compensate for the quality of the neighborhood. As Rosen puts it, "Landlords capitalize on these vulnerabilities by 'building a better mousetrap.'"[22]

Expand the Radius of the Places People Are Willing to Consider

As noted in chapter 6, studies of housing searches have found that a common initial elimination criterion is the location of a place. People often want to live near work, family, or friends, and so they eliminate places that are too distant from the people and places in their lives. This is a clear example of how segregation can be self-perpetuating. The policy prescription, of course, would be to reduce segregation itself. But in addition, increasing the availability of affordable, fast, and efficient transportation around the city and suburbs could reduce the *effective* distance between places and increase the radius perceived as an acceptable distance from one's family, work, school, and the like.

Specific to the Housing Choice Voucher program, staff and advocates have pointed to the challenges inherent in the program's location constraints. That is, the rules make it challenging for voucher holders to move outside the public housing authority (PHA) that granted the voucher. It is possible to "port" their voucher from one PHA to another, but it is a complex and constrained process. For example, the voucher holder must port to a PHA that has a voucher program, meet the eligibility requirements of having been a voucher holder for at least a year, and not be in the middle of a lease. Given these challenges, a voucher holder has a proscribed and constrained consideration set (only those in the PHA's jurisdiction). One feature of the Baltimore Mobility Program that researchers have identified as contributing to its significant success in achieving opportunity moves is that it is regionally administered and thus eliminates these kinds of portability issues.[23]

Another example is a HUD-funded demonstration project that created a regional partnership in the Chicago metropolitan area to identify ways to help voucher holders more easily move into communities outside of their voucher-granting PHA's jurisdiction.[24] Interestingly, one of the findings from this pilot study not only highlights the value of a regional approach but also makes the case that location is an important factor driving housing decisions. Specifically, of their 297 pilot study participants (who had to be recruited to participate from among voucher recipients), 151 were families porting from outside of the Chicago area. As Housing Choice Partners explains:

> These families . . . were more interested in working with HCP than families who were from within the region. One possible explanation is that these families had fewest ties in the area and were less familiar with the Chicago area housing market and thus really needed the assistance of a counselor. They may have been more open to an opportunity move because they did not have social networks in the region, nor come with a firm picture of the racial complexion of different communities and housing markets, compared to families who had already lived in the region.[25]

Of course, all searchers—voucher holders or not—face constraints in the location of their search options. Some need to live near an aging parent for whom they are the primary caretaker; others must live in a particular city as a condition of their job; and still others need to live near relatives who care

for their young children. No policy or program can eliminate a
barriers, but any attempts to intervene in the cycle of segregatic
be mindful of the fact that housing decisions are complex and constrained
by an array of individual considerations that can ultimately funnel people
toward segregation or toward integration. To the extent that regions and
communities can recognize large-scale locational barriers that affect many
people, policies could be targeted to address them.

Disrupt the Assumption of Correlated Characteristics and the Use of Heuristics

The social structural sorting perspective relies on a model whose emphasis is that people use heuristics when constructing consideration sets—
especially in the first stage—so as to guide their quick elimination of
many options; as a result, they often make decisions based on "one good
reason."[26] To the extent that the one good reason people use to eliminate
places is racial composition, then the implications for segregation are clear.
For whites, negative associations with a community's racial composition
(higher crime, poor school quality, lower property values) often lead them
to eliminate diverse or predominantly black communities from the very
start. African Americans, for their part, may presume that a predominantly
white community will be hostile to African Americans and eliminate it
from consideration for this reason. The challenge is to disrupt these bundled
perceptions. Again, there are examples from diverse communities that
have attempted to do this.

As mentioned earlier, South Orange–Maplewood, New Jersey, took
proactive steps to counteract people's assumptions about their community. The law professor Myron Orfield recounts what happened: "In the
mid-1990s, a drop in property values combined with increased racial
diversity in the local housing market, led some community leaders to
consider that White homebuyers avoided South Orange and Maplewood in
the fear that the communities would re-segregate."[27] With funding from the
municipal government, the nonprofit group South Orange–Maplewood
Community Coalition on Race undertook pro-integration programs focused
on marketing itself to whites—who were the underrepresented group in
this market:

> The coalition ran advertisements in local newspapers "positioning South
> Orange and Maplewood as attractive communities for families seeking a
> suburban lifestyle and strong public schools, but wishing to live in a cosmo-
> politan neighborhood." The coalition also offers potential homebuyers tours
> designed to "subvert potential steering by real estate agents." Moreover, the

Coalition communicates with real estate agents to make them "aware of all the positive aspects of the communities."[28]

In their study of successful racially integrated communities, Philip Nyden, Michael Maly, and John Lukehart describe the importance of community leadership and intentional efforts to combat the messages, both implicit and explicit, about the assumed correlation between a community's racial composition and its other social and economic characteristics.[29] Their recommended policies include: "expect government leaders and agencies proactively to promote diverse neighborhoods; encourage local chambers of commerce and other business associations to view diverse communities as 'potentially strong markets'[; and] encourage the media to tell 'the positive stories of diverse community successes.'"[30]

The Oak Park Regional Housing Center (OPRHC) has a similar goal of breaking apart these presumed correlations, but its target is potential renters.[31] The OPRHC offers a free apartment referral service for individuals looking to rent in the village of Oak Park, Illinois. In addition to providing listings of available units, the staff also counsels its clients, and often this involves disrupting their use of heuristics. Although Oak Park is already in the consideration set of all who come to the center, its clients routinely arrive with preconceptions about where *within* Oak Park they want to move: white apartment seekers have been advised by friends, family, and sometimes personal observation to avoid the east side of Oak Park (where a higher percentage of African Americans live). Black apartment seekers have been told that they should avoid the west and north sides of Oak Park (where a higher percentage of whites live). Clients have eliminated these parts of Oak Park because of what they believe goes along with a community's racial composition. Whites eliminate areas with a larger African American population because they perceive these areas as having bad schools and high crime rates, and blacks eliminate the whiter parts of Oak Park because they perceive these areas as unwelcoming to African Americans. The purpose of the one-on-one counseling is to interrupt the heuristics that would otherwise funnel black clients to the "blacker" parts of Oak Park and white clients to the "whiter" parts. This intensive counseling effort has been quite successful: out of approximately 3,500 clients each year, about 1,000 end up moving to Oak Park. Of those, about 70 percent move into an area or apartment building where their own racial group does not predominate.

With respect to the bundling of racial composition and concerns about discrimination, the survey data and in-depth interviews reported earlier suggest that concerns about discrimination are sometimes based on a community's specific racial history. But other times it comes from a more general impression that white (and especially middle- and upper-class) communities are just "not for people like me." Just as diversifying communities need to dispel stereotypes about the characteristics of integrated neighborhoods, so too do predominantly white communities need to dispel the impression of being unwelcoming to racial-ethnic minority residents. In addition to the obvious need to ensure the enforcement of fair housing laws within their housing market, a commitment and openness to people of all races and ethnicities could be publicized through public statements, public relations campaigns, and visual images conveying a diverse community. In addition, mobility counseling and any other efforts to expand the consideration sets of African Americans and Latinos to include such places need to give explicit attention to this issue. The goal of these efforts is to intervene in how people make decisions about their consideration set, encouraging them to use a different "cue" to eliminate options. Left to their own devices, people in segregated metropolitan areas may use the cue of racial composition and justify their decision based on its presumed correlation with an array of other quality-of-life features. People make these assumptions and often fail to do any further research to see if they are correct.

Efforts to disrupt the use of heuristics that filter out communities will differ depending on the type of community in question. Those that are already diverse and want to stay that way need to market themselves (particularly to whites, since it is this group that holds more strongly to these tightly correlated beliefs) as diverse and safe places with high-quality schools where people from their group will fit in. For their part, predominantly white communities need to recognize that their current racial composition may be correlated in the minds of African Americans and Latinos with a community that is not welcoming to people of their racial-ethnic background. White segregated communities need to attend to these perceptions and figure out ways to disrupt them, perhaps through media and marketing campaigns and intensive counseling that assures potential residents that their community is welcoming and inclusive of people of all races and ethnicities.

In other words, communities need to recognize that people often use their perception of the racial characteristics of a place as a basis for drawing conclusions about a range of other characteristics. Communicating the reality of their community to potential and current residents through direct counseling or broader messaging is a promising step forward. Of course, any efforts to encourage one group to consider new kinds of places must be countered with assurances that people already living in a community are not being pushed out of it in any way.

rupt the Reality of Correlated Characteristics

Many of the policy recommendations discussed thus far involve marketing: counselors and communities are advised to change the kind of information that is circulating about their communities and to make efforts to overcome the assumption of correlated characteristics that people rely upon in their heuristic-driven housing search process. But all of the marketing in the world cannot be effective if the underlying premise is false: portraying a community as welcoming to people of all races when it is not; describing a neighborhood as safe when it is not; or claiming that property values are rising when they are not. There is a kernel of truth to people's heuristic-driven beliefs—there are in fact profound inequalities across neighborhoods based on their racial composition, and some neighborhoods are indeed unwelcoming to people of color.

Past and persistent institutional racism has created the conditions that animate these perceived correlations, particularly in terms of neighborhood inequalities. And indeed, here is a case where segregation begets segregation: it was the white flight and subsequent disinvestment in what are now segregated black communities that created the tight linkage between racial composition and neighborhood disadvantage. And it is that linkage that gives some searchers a reason to eliminate those communities from their consideration set. Thus, despite evidence to the contrary that any particular community can provide, so long as our nation is dominated by deeply divided neighborhoods there will continue to be fuel for the use of these heuristics.

To be sure, upending the severe racial inequalities across residential space is a daunting task and requires substantial resources and commitment at all levels. Reinvestment in such communities would not only increase the quality of life for existing residents but also loosen the tight correlation that feeds this segregation cycle. A policy that results in everyone moving out of disadvantaged neighborhoods is untenable; rather, we need to dismantle the "architecture of segregation" itself.[32] Over generations, if discrimination were eliminated and economic differences reduced, progress would be made naturally.

In the meantime, the social structural sorting perspective, which views the problem through the lens of neighborhood selection and housing searches and the information that feeds them, points to some policies that could jump-start the undoing of these correlations—both real and imagined. The handful of diverse communities discussed thus far are again instructive. For example, the reason the OPRHC can be successful at securing affirmative moves among its white clients in particular is that when housing counselors drive their white clients to apartments in Oak Park neighborhoods with a higher percentage of African Americans, the units they see are as nice as those on the "whiter" side of town, if not nicer. And when the counselors are asked about school quality, they can show clients data affirming that all of the elementary schools in Oak Park are both diverse and high-performing. They can also show crime statistics to assure potential residents that they are as safe on one side of town as the other. The OPRHC can truthfully portray Oak Park as a community where race and class characteristics are *not* correlated in part because of intentional efforts by the community both symbolic (for example, the passage of a local fair housing ordinance before the national one) and concrete (such as drawing school zoning boundaries to maintain racial balance in all elementary schools, locating an important municipal building in the more diverse part of Oak Park, and passing ordinances to stave off blockbusting that to this day are upheld informally).[33]

In addition to working with clients looking for apartments, the OPRHC works with landlords to ensure that the apartments available to rent throughout the community are equally attractive and well maintained so that the rental housing market in Oak Park remains robust throughout the community. One concrete tool that works synergistically with the OPRHC housing counseling program is the "multifamily housing incentive grant," which provides grants of up to $10,000 to apartment building owners to improve their building's marketability.[34] In exchange, grantees' must affirmatively market their units through the OPRHC.

The South Orange–Maplewood Community Coalition on Race in New Jersey also takes steps in this direction, with a focus on homeowners. Loans are available to improve the external attractiveness of residents' homes so as to ensure that no single section of their community looks different from another. As the organization states, "Well-maintained homes across the entire community increase the appeal of South Orange and Maplewood NJ as great places to live for current and future residents of all races."[35]

Through such efforts and others, communities can invest in programs that attempt to shape the behaviors of individual potential residents while also deliberately distributing resources throughout a community in a manner that defies the stereotypes and unravels the correlated characteristics that outsiders or potential new residents bring with them.

Of course, a single small town (in terms of both geography and population) faces a smaller set of challenges in creating policies that disrupt and prevent the emergence of the structural imbalances that typify our nation as a whole. But these efforts highlight that it can be done—with intention and commitment—and provide some ideas for doing so.

But more generally, these kinds of local efforts can be either significantly hindered or facilitated by broader policy and legislative efforts. To help, state and federal courts can work to eliminate policies that maintain structural disparities between localities. The Washington State Supreme Court is one such example. In 2014, the court ruled that the heavy reliance on local bonds to pay for K-12 education significantly exacerbated differences in school quality across districts and neighborhoods.[36] The local funding strategies that operate in many places can be seen as an outgrowth of institutional racism: school funding linked to property values perpetuates the dramatic disparities set in motion by decades of discriminatory public policies and private actions to confine people of color to the poorest neighborhoods of most metropolitan areas. Certainly, in Washington State and many other places, the reliance on local bonds has not only helped to bolster racial disparities in access to high-quality education but also reinforced the perception that residential areas containing large populations of color offer only poor services and structural deficiencies. Although the Washington State legislature has been painfully slow in adopting new funding strategies, the state court rulings have helped generate conversations about how to moderate structural inequities across places and, by extension, dissolve the link between racial composition and other characteristics. This link plays out every day when people search for a place to live. The goal of all of these policies is to unbundle racial composition from all these other features to expand the consideration sets of searchers of all races and ethnicities.

Ensure That Information About Affordability Is Accurate

As the social structural sorting perspective highlights, an important aspect of the neighborhood selection and housing search processes is the *perceived* reality of the housing market. Knowledge of communities and their features matters, and one aspect of that knowledge is the perceived affordability of a community. As research has demonstrated, cost concerns permeate a housing search across all stages, and so people's perceptions of the affordability of particular neighborhoods matters a great deal in terms of how their searches unfold.[37] There are important consequences if people erroneously eliminate communities from their consideration set before they even know if their perceptions about affordability are accurate. There is little research on the accuracy of perceptions about housing costs and searchers' perceptions of their ability to afford a neighborhood, so it is unclear whether policies or programs that target these perceptions would be effective. Indeed, it may be that new online search tools have increased the available information about the cost of housing in different areas enough that people now have more accurate knowledge of housing costs. Nevertheless, accessible information about average housing costs in a community and the range of available options there may help deter people from eliminating communities based only on their perceptions of the cost of housing.

Increase the Supply of Affordable Housing in High-Opportunity Areas

The elephant in the room, of course, is that there *is* variability in housing costs, and most people *do* have to screen communities based on some upper limit to what they can afford. Although not unique to housing choice voucher holders, the lessons learned about this population and the policy attempts to encourage opportunity moves are instructive. One clear lesson is that there is a general lack of affordable housing options in high-opportunity areas, particularly in urban areas with "hot" housing markets, such as Seattle. The King County Housing Authority has pursued a number of innovative approaches to overcome the challenges of affordable housing and has been quite successful with the outcomes of its voucher holders.

For example, among the approximately 7,000 households with children served by the KCHA, almost one-quarter have accessed high-opportunity neighborhoods—places with lower levels of poverty and better employment opportunities, quality education, and transportation options. This level of success has been achieved despite multifaceted barriers facing low-income families in King County. In this section, we focus on the barriers of high average rents and limited inventory of rental units, but as we emphasize elsewhere in this discussion, the KCHA has probably been successful because its response has been as multifaceted as the multifaceted barriers that are faced by searchers.

One way in which the KCHA has developed innovative real estate–based strategies to increase affordable housing in high-opportunity areas has been expanding the stock of project-based units in these areas. Through the use of low-income housing tax credits and bonds, the KCHA has expanded ownership of workforce housing to more than 5,000 units, many of which are located in high-opportunity suburbs of Seattle. As of 2015, one out of every three households with a voucher renting in a high-opportunity area was living in a property owned by the KCHA.

Land use policies, because of their effects on the availability of housing of different kinds (and at different prices) throughout a metropolitan area, are another policy arena where the social structural sorting perspective points to possible ways to help break the cycle of segregation. Historically, exclusionary zoning played an important role in perpetuating segregation. Originally this was explicitly racial, but as the researcher Rolf Pendall explains, "Even after racial zoning was found to be unconstitutional by the U.S. Supreme Court, large-lot zoning and other land use controls with the potential to exclude racial minorities remained available to municipalities throughout the United States, often as a very thin cover for racial bias."[38] For example, zoning that limits housing development in certain areas to very low density (which typically rules out anything but detached single-family homes) is associated with higher levels of racial segregation.[39] Conversely, places that allow for higher-density developments have higher rates of racial integration.[40]

Increasingly, policymakers and advocates have turned to inclusionary zoning as a tool for reducing segregation. Inclusionary zoning uses "a range of local policies that tap the economic gains from rising real estate values to create affordable housing, thus tying the creation of homes for low- or moderate-income households to the construction of market-rate residential or commercial development."[41] Often this translates into a requirement that a developer rent or sell a certain percentage of new units to lower-income residents. Due to persistent racial inequality in income, inclusionary policies have the potential for making a community more racially and ethnically integrated by increasing the availability of affordable housing in areas where such housing would not otherwise be located. By enhancing the variety of housing stock within communities, a wider range of (often segregated white) communities become more accessible to both HCV participants and lower-income individuals more generally. Both of these groups disproportionately comprise people of color.

The case of the Ethel Lawrence Homes in Mount Laurel, New Jersey, is instructive in looking at the barriers to affordable housing in high-opportunity areas: it was twelve years after the court order mandating this development (in 1985) before plans were officially accepted (in 1997), and it was another three years before the first residents moved into the completed development (in 2000). The resistance by community residents and leaders was profound and prolonged.[42] Despite the dire warnings leading up to the opening of this development, a comprehensive analysis of the effects on the host community and the residents in the development concluded that the project was highly successful and had positive consequences for the residents and little negative impact on the host community. The development's success has been attributed to careful planning. It is noteworthy that the Ethel Lawrence Homes were unusual in that they were 100 percent affordable housing units within a planned development, whereas inclusionary zoning typically involves some percentage of the new units being set aside for affordable rents or purchase prices.[43]

In the face of the realities of neighborhood selection and housing search processes as articulated in the social structural sorting perspective, care must be taken to shape inclusionary programs in a way that encourages integration, if that is the goal. Specifically, unless we understand how race functions in neighborhood selection and housing search processes, inclusionary zoning may result in economically but not racially inclusive communities. As scholars have observed, inclusionary zoning per se is limited in its ability to make inroads into *racial* residential segregation.[44] At its core, the problem is that the "money in a person's pocket" is not the ⚹ only factor driving residential outcomes. Thus, simply creating affordable housing that is accessible to a wider range of people's housing budgets is not sufficient to break the cycle of racial segregation.

In a comparison between efforts in Mount Laurel, New Jersey (different from the Ethel Lawrence Homes) and Montgomery County, Maryland, Orfield makes this crucial point.[45] In both cases, zoning efforts were undertaken to impact affordability and density, but in only one was integration substantially improved. On the one hand, Mount Laurel's fair share housing—referred to as Mount Laurel I and Mount Laurel II—although not requiring inclusionary zoning, generated widespread implementation of such zoning within New Jersey. As a result, there have been substantial increases in lower-cost housing, but aside from the Ethel Lawrence Homes, those increases have mostly benefited whites and moderate-income people.[46]

By contrast, the efforts in Montgomery County, Maryland, have had a more positive impact on racial integration. The county's success has been attributed to two features: (1) a percentage of the new units were set aside for public housing residents; and (2) the individuals who were able to purchase the affordable units were identified through a lottery.[47] Viewed through the social structural sorting perspective, the effectiveness of the lottery is apparent. In essence, by distributing affordable housing through a lottery, the normal channels through which people "end up living where they do" were disrupted. The law professor Florence Roisman explains how the lottery system works:

> Information about the lottery is distributed widely throughout the County. The long-time former director . . . explains the program's success by reference to long-term support from fair housing groups, education of the industry, demonstrated commitment to enforcement of non-discrimination laws, internal networking within minority communities, and commitment by the program administrators.[48]

In this way, the sources of information about available units in Montgomery County were extended beyond the regular channels, reaching more diverse social networks and information sources, and they stayed focused on avoiding discrimination. The routine process was thus disrupted, and the result was greater racial diversity among the new residents.

As both Roisman and Orfield argue, the implementation of inclusionary zoning is crucial: if zoning policies are implemented in a way that reduces race to class, the impact on racial segregation will be minimal. But when, as the Montgomery County example illustrates, the implementation recognizes how race shapes the neighborhood selection and housing search processes—from information sources to social networks to discrimination—the cycle of segregation can be disrupted. As Orfield explains: "Policies that are not explicitly race-based can advance racial integration if they are carefully administered in the ways that frustrate the typical operation of white privilege."[49] In this case, that would be the white privilege shaping the neighborhood selection and housing search processes. Inclusionary zoning policies provide an important tool because they increase the housing options in what are typically predominantly white communities, for a broader spectrum of individuals, and particularly people of color. But these policies are not sufficient unless they are implemented in a way that recognizes the social processes that shape who benefits from them. The framework offered in this book offers a window into the different ways this can be done. It is worth noting that the 2015 Supreme Court ruling that upheld the standard of disparate impact when determining discrimination is a useful tool for helping to upend these processes.[50] For example, zoning policies that are on the face of it racially neutral may violate the Fair Housing Act if demonstrated to be discriminatory in impact even if not in intent.

Part of the success of the Montgomery County approach hinged on ensuring that consideration sets are broadened through increased knowledge and that fewer places are eliminated from consideration. But the use of broader networks and institutions (housing organizations) to disseminate information about the lottery system draws attention to the fact that what happens at stage 2—when alternatives are identified and evaluated—is crucial to the outcome and also opens up opportunities for possible intervention.

POLICY INTERVENTIONS IN STAGE 2 OF A HOUSING SEARCH

Most of the policies and programs discussed so far pertain to the pre-search or first stage of a housing search, when neighborhoods are being identified and some are eliminated. What possible policy levers exist beyond this stage—when searchers are looking at specific neighborhoods and identifying and evaluating specific units? Earlier chapters highlighted the many reasons why neighborhoods and units get filtered out during stage 2. Are there ways to intervene and override those filters that operate to perpetuate segregation? We again consider the ways in which neighborhoods and units are filtered out at stage 2 and whether the social structural sorting perspective points to opportunities to avoid the elimination of certain types of communities and units.

Ensure That Steering Does Not Filter Out Units and Neighborhoods Under Consideration

Because steering remains one of the most common forms of contemporary housing discrimination, continued enforcement of fair housing laws' prohibitions against steering is essential.[51] Our interview data highlight that sometimes steering is the result of statistical discrimination, when the motive is based on assumptions by real estate agents and landlords that a client who is a racial-ethnic minority cannot afford certain areas. To the extent that this is genuinely a function of inaccurate assumptions, real estate agent training may help.

Eva Rosen's study of Baltimore landlords who specialize in renting to voucher holders provides both strong evidence of the persistence of steering and a compelling demonstration of how pernicious it is. Indeed, although her study focuses on the steering of voucher holders in particular, it is not a great leap to imagine that similar processes operate among low-income searchers who are not voucher holders.[52] She finds that landlords often strategically steered clients to specific types of units in certain neighborhoods, based on client characteristics and using aggressive marketing tactics such as offering security deposit assistance, direct marketing in the offices of the voucher program, and listing only the most challenging-to-rent units at the gosection8.com website. Although the steering was not exclusively based on racial composition (her study was conducted in Baltimore, where 90 percent of voucher holders are African American), she finds evidence that race was a factor, such that white voucher holders were never "sent" to poor black neighborhoods. As Rosen concludes, the approach used by these landlords

> results in rigging the game, where a process of "reverse selection" operates: rather than tenants selecting homes and neighborhoods, landlords are selecting tenants. Taken together, these tactics result in a strategic balkanization of the rental housing market that retains voucher holders where they can be most profitable—in the very neighborhoods policymakers would like to provide them with the opportunity to leave.[53]

Overcome Financial Barriers to Rental Units—
Beyond the Monthly Rent

In chapter 7, we drew attention to the varied ways in which economics can shape outcomes beyond the money available for monthly rent or mortgage payments. For example, even if a person could afford to pay the monthly rent, they may not be able to put together the sometimes substantial security deposit that is required. Mobility programs have recognized this barrier and partnered with other organizations (often private foundations) to address it by providing security deposit assistance for voucher holders who are making opportunity moves.

Applying the lessons learned from the HCV program to other populations, it is likely that low-income renters who do not have the benefit of a voucher face similar challenges in assembling security deposits. These individuals could be targeted for security deposit assistance as an incentive for making moves that affirmatively further fair housing. And of course, programs offering down payment assistance for home-buyers could function in a similar way.

Specific to the Housing Choice Voucher program, Rosen's study of landlords who market HCV properties again provides a cautionary tale. Her results remind us that security deposit assistance is a substantial inducement. Indeed, landlords attempting to secure voucher holders as tenants in lower-quality neighborhoods sometimes use such offers to entice them to rent their units in non-opportunity neighborhoods. The effectiveness of security deposit assistance in both settings—to make both opportunity and non-opportunity areas attractive—is a reminder that security deposits are an important factor in a housing search process, since regardless of whether searchers are being enticed to enter a good or bad neighborhood, such assistance is influential.

Of course, there is also the problem that a searcher cannot afford the monthly rent or mortgage payment for particular units or in certain neighborhoods. This has been a problem with the HCV program's success at facilitating moves to improve its participants' neighborhoods and, by extension, their individual outcomes. The value of a voucher (and therefore the upper limit on what the recipient can afford) is determined by a metropolitan area's average rents, or the so-called fair market rent (FMR). As a practical matter, this upper limit precludes many possible rental units in higher-opportunity areas. HUD has piloted programs that increase the flexibility that public housing authorities can exercise in determining maximum rental levels so that the average reflects a smaller geographic area (the so-called small area fair market rate). For example, in Seattle's multifaceted approach to solving the problems of affordable housing in opportunity areas for its voucher holders, one strategy has been to use a multi-tiered payment standard system that better enables households to afford housing in higher-opportunity areas. This system opens up more possible units across a wider range of high-opportunity areas. Given the population served by the HCV program and the broader aims of the program, efforts to generate a better match between the value of the voucher and the available units in better neighborhoods are necessary—but not sufficient—to increase opportunity moves.

Another challenge faced by voucher holders is that there are simply fewer units in high-opportunity areas whose landlords are willing to rent to them. Indeed, expanding the pool of possible landlords—as the Inclusive Communities Project and the Baltimore Mobility Program have done—is another example of the ways in which mobility programs can relieve some of the housing market–related constraints faced by voucher holders. In recruiting landlords in high-opportunity areas, mobility programs must work to manage the efficiency of the program so as to not discourage these landlords from participating.

Given what Rosen's work has shown about some landlords with units in disadvantaged neighborhoods actively recruiting voucher holders and sometimes even getting higher than "market value" rents from voucher holders, it is critical that the pool of potential landlords be expanded carefully and in a way that increases the volume in high-opportunity areas rather than increasing the rent that landlords in low-opportunity areas can garner.[54]

Overcome the Challenges in Finding Available Units

There are a number of reasons why people have difficulty finding vacancies in their selected neighborhood, including an unreliable source of information on available units, a need to move quickly, and other barriers. Searchers may rely on word of mouth or look for FOR RENT signs in windows, for instance, or a voucher holder may use online Section 8 tools that are primarily the domain of landlords with units in low-opportunity areas.[55] Searchers may need to find a unit quickly because their move is involuntary—perhaps precipitated by an eviction—or they may not be able to access the full range of possible options because of transportation or child care challenges.[56]

Both mobility programs in general and the Oak Park Regional Housing Center in particular recognize that finding units in neighborhoods that represent either opportunity moves or affirmative moves, respectively, can be an impediment, and they provide tools to overcome these obstacles. For example, in the area of affirmative moves, the OPRHC provides an apartment-finding service, free of charge, to anyone interested in renting an apartment in Oak Park.[57] Using this service as they would a for-profit "apartment finder" service, clients who are mainly middle-class and seeking private market apartments tell the OPRHC how much rent they can afford and all of the amenities they seek in an apartment—number of bedrooms and bathrooms, availability of parking and laundry facilities, hardwood floors or carpeting, and so on. The OPRHC provides them with listings of available units, but unlike other apartment-finding services, it gives clients options that would not only meet their requirements but also result in an "affirmative" move—that is, one that would increase the diversity of the apartment building or neighborhood. Through this service, the OPRHC ensures that units in neighborhoods within the village of Oak Park that might otherwise be unknown to the searchers become part of the set of possible units they consider and evaluate.

Recognizing that other factors might deter these searchers from pursuing the units on their lists that fall outside their initial consideration set, staff also take clients personally to the available apartments that meet the affirmative move guidelines. The OPRHC counselor drives the client through the neighborhood for a tour of the immediate area and then shows the client the available apartment. This strategy circumvents any other barriers to active consideration of these units by making the visit to the unit very easy: all the searcher needs to do is get in the counselor's car. In addition, if the client chooses to submit an application, the counselor helps with completing the paperwork and facilitates the rental process.

Mobility programs also go to great lengths to make it easier for voucher holders to gain access to units in opportunity areas. They take groups of clients by bus to selected vacant units and provide them with applications to submit on the spot. They also prescreen units to ensure that the landlords will take vouchers, thus sidestepping another way in which searchers might filter out these units.[58]

This hands-on approach goes beyond simply ensuring that people are aware of units to also address constraints. Mobility programs make sure that accessing the units is easy by providing transportation to the available units, having keys to multiple units so that potential tenants can view them all in a single trip, and assisting clients with the rental application process. Affirmative moves and opportunity moves are often more difficult moves to make, so this assistance helps make such a choice as hassle-free as possible.

Jennifer Darrah and Stefanie Deluca's study of Baltimore Mobility Program participants points to an intervention even more profound than providing access—changing the choice framework so that searchers are able to think about neighborhood features and prioritize them.[59] Their study of the BMP is a compelling example of research that takes seriously the housing search and selection process. They draw attention to many of the core social and contextual factors underlying the social structural sorting perspective; as DeLuca and her colleagues have noted in other work: "Individuals act within [the stratified landscape] to move to neighborhoods on the basis of past experiences, family conditions, landlord connections, local knowledge, and imperfect information."[60]

Help to Reduce the Urgency of Moves

As explored in chapter 7, having an urgent need to move is related to economics (low-income movers are more likely than higher-income movers to have time constraints) and the urgency can impact the outcome of a search. Again, the case of the voucher program is instructive. In the HCV program, there is a built-in (somewhat artificial) time constraint in that voucher holders must "lease up" within ninety days of the receipt of the voucher or they will lose their voucher. Observers have pointed out that the ninety-day limit can be a tremendous barrier to anything but a non-opportunity move because of the time it takes to disseminate information, counsel clients, take them to new communities, and ensure that the property passes the additional set of inspections to qualify. (In high-opportunity areas, landlords are often unfamiliar with the program and the process.) In other words, it takes time to disrupt the way a search would routinely unfold. This time pressure also makes voucher holders targets of unscrupulous landlords who know the short time frames that constrain them and who sometimes take advantage of this to funnel them into low-opportunity areas.[61]

Similarly, it is often easier for searchers who may be thinking about making an affirmative move to rely on networks and not do extra homework to find a diverse neighborhood that meets their criteria. As a result, a white searcher, for example, may take the fallback position of taking a unit in an all-white neighborhood simply because it is easier. Programs like the OPRHC function in similar ways to help searchers break out of these normal processes. In the HCV programs, HUD and public housing authorities are incorporating some flexibility and extensions to the ninety-day limit in order to encourage higher-quality moves and better outcomes for voucher holders. For communities seeking to encourage diverse moves, programs that make moves easier and more efficient can overcome the sometimes lengthier processes involved.

Breaking down the process and understanding what makes opportunity moves and affirmative moves more time-consuming can point to methods

like those used by the OPRHC and mobility programs: taking potential tenants to units they are qualified for and thereby shortening the time
needed to make such a move. Another way of acknowledging that better
moves take more time would be to provide temporary housing solutions
for people faced with an emergency move.

Enforce Fair Housing Laws and Extend
Their Protections to "Source of Income"

Despite the illegality of discrimination on the basis of race-ethnicity, there
is evidence that both exclusionary and non-exclusionary forms of discrimination persist, and that non-exclusionary forms may even be increasing,
as described in chapter 9. Since both types of discrimination can funnel
people toward segregative housing outcomes, the need to address both is
paramount. In addition to the more subtle types of exclusionary discrimination identified by housing audits, there is another kind of housing discrimination that, while not explicitly racial, has disproportionate impact
on people of color.

Landlords regularly practice what is called "source-of-income"
discrimination—that is, because it is legal in most places, they refuse to
rent to a person whose source of income is a voucher. The staff of mobility programs and fair housing advocates have argued that source-of-
income discrimination is a significant barrier to voucher holders' ability
to make opportunity moves, especially to predominantly white communities. Some jurisdictions have succeeded in making source-of-income
discrimination illegal.[62] This is an important step toward ensuring that this
kind of discrimination does not eliminate units that would be integrative
moves for minority voucher holders. For example, in Seattle, the KCHA
has worked with the Washington Low Income Housing Alliance to help
pass local ordinances to end source-of-income discrimination as part of its
multifaceted set of policies aimed at improving the housing of low-income
households.

Work to Eliminate Non-exclusionary
Discrimination

Non-exclusionary discrimination—the kind of discrimination that does
not necessarily deny access but does make the conditions and terms of the
housing different based on a person's race or ethnicity—is alive and well.
Non-exclusionary discrimination may shape present and future mobility
and neighborhood selection processes, and there is evidence that its impacts

are felt across housing markets—among voucher holders, mortgage applicants, and renters alike.

A vivid example is described in an *Atlantic Monthly* article about a U.S. Justice Department fair housing complaint. A voucher holder in California, the writer notes, "was welcomed by her neighbors when she first arrived. But when the neighbors found out that [she] was a participant in the federal Section 8 housing voucher program, she found herself with new worries. She became the target of bullying and harassment—not just from neighborhood residents, but from the police as well." Moreover, as the article reports:

> In the early 2000s, Palmdale and Lancaster began spending "significant resources" to pay for investigators and sheriff's deputies for the sole purpose of aggressively monitoring families in the Section 8 voucher program. . . . As a result, hundreds of black families had investigators randomly show up at their doors, often with a posse of armed sheriffs, to search their homes and interrogate them about their housing status.[63]

This may be an extreme case, but it clearly suggests the challenges faced by racial-ethnic minority voucher holders who *do* succeed in moving into opportunity areas but are treated poorly there. These voucher holders may ultimately decide to leave the new neighborhood to escape this bad treatment.

Non-exclusionary discrimination is not limited to voucher holders, as chapter 9 reminds us. Even when landlords agree to rent to racial-ethnic minorities, they may treat these tenants differently than their white tenants—for example, by attending to unit problems less promptly, providing fewer tenant incentives, being hostile, or differentially enforcing rules and regulations. In addition, neighbors may make life difficult for these tenants. Non-exclusionary discrimination is also substantial in the mortgage industry and again can have implications for how long a person remains in a unit. Denying loans to racial-ethnic minorities has become rare, but what remains commonplace is targeting racial-ethnic minorities (through predatory lending practices and subprime mortgages) for riskier and more expensive loan products that have serious consequences for the homeowners trapped by them. The prevalence and persistence of non-exclusionary discrimination requires that efforts to root it out must be just as vigilant as efforts to address exclusionary discrimination (which tends to be the focus of existing policies), since non-exclusionary discrimination affects both a person's decision to remain in a community and his or her willingness to move into a similar kind of community in the future.

N POLICY CONTEXT

ιcy context, as it relates to fair housing, was affected substantially by HUD's release in June 2015 of new rules that had been years in the making. Communities that receive HUD grants are now obligated to take steps to break down the barriers to fair housing and equal opportunity in their community. This is a step in the direction of undoing the effects of decades of HUD policies that created segregation in the first place. The HUD rules mandate that a community cannot simply demonstrate that it does not discriminate on the basis of all of the protected categories, but must also take steps to break down the barriers to integration. In short, it is no longer sufficient to enforce nondiscrimination laws; explicit steps must now be taken to affirmatively further fair housing. Funding recipients have been obligated to do this ever since the passage of the 1968 Fair Housing Act, but the 2015 ruling on affirmatively furthering fair housing provides clearer guidelines as well as data-based tools to help communities meet this obligation. As communities grapple with the census data that pinpoint where their problems are located, it will be interesting to see what sort of neighborhood selection and housing search processes are implied by the solutions offered.

A more complex and nuanced model with features articulated by the social structural sorting perspective could be used to help point policy-makers and community leaders in the right direction. Beyond testing and enforcement, the implication of the social structural sorting perspective is that we need to understand how neighborhood selection and housing search processes are shaped by lived experiences, social networks, and the media, and also how the perceived realities of the housing market can shape searchers, searches, and outcomes through the multifaceted ways in which preferences, discrimination, and economics shape and are shaped by the residential processes that perpetuate segregation. The goal of efforts to affirmatively further fair housing should be to enrich people's consideration sets in a way that puts back into contention those places that might otherwise be filtered out and that recognizes the many barriers to moves that would, in the aggregate, break down segregation. This would include changing perceptions (and realities) of exclusionary and non-exclusionary discrimination; creating affordable opportunities, in both reality and people's perceptions; disrupting the operation of heuristics that eliminate places based on the perception of correlated characteristics; eliminating the reality of correlated characteristics; and ensuring full consideration of the range of options.

Indeed, the varied and subtle forces that perpetuate segregation as articulated by the social structural sorting perspective call for efforts that extend well beyond enforcement of nondiscrimination laws. Many of the examples of policies and insights in this chapter have focused on voucher recipients. But important as it is to intervene in the search processes of families receiving assistance from a major U.S. housing assistance program, voucher holders represent a very small share of the overall housing market and are not themselves the primary engine of segregation in the United States.[64] It is non-voucher holders—ranging from those with equally severe financial constraints who do not have a voucher to those who could afford to live just about anywhere—whose moves (or decisions not to move) fuel the cycle of segregation. Deliberate policies and programs to intervene in the social context of the mobility process of these groups are rare, with the notable exceptions of the OPRHC, the efforts in Shaker Heights, and New Jersey's Coalition on Race. More balanced and creative policies and programs to reach these larger groups are needed. Indeed, as Jennifer Darrah and Stefanie DeLuca note in the conclusion of their analysis of voucher holders:

> While we have focused on the choice frameworks of voucher participants we hope that future scholarship will also attend to the choice frameworks of dominant groups such as white middle class families. Indeed, structural limitations as well as preferences of dominant groups may play the strongest role in perpetuating segregation. Future research should explore the types of interventions that could modify the residential choice frameworks of white middle class families so that they too might prefer more diverse communities. These dynamics are a critical part of the solution, as research has shown that the residential decisions and preferences of whites, especially to avoid black areas, are among the most important determinants of segregation.[65]

We agree wholeheartedly with this call for additional research, and it is to this point that we turn in the next chapter, where we explore the research implications of the social structural sorting perspective, identify promising research directions, and also spell out how the social processes explored throughout this book set in motion a self-perpetuating system that requires explicit intervention to break down.

Chapter 11 | New Approaches to Understanding Segregation

IN RECENT YEARS, several prominent scholars have argued that growing population diversity, increasing economic resources among minority populations, and a softening of racial animus have ushered in a new age of integration. They point to a decline in the number of neighborhoods occupied exclusively by a single racial group and a general decline in average levels of segregation across metropolitan areas to suggest that the era of segregation is behind us. And given the multitude of detrimental impacts for individuals, families, and communities, the demise of residential segregation would be a welcome development.

Unfortunately, the preponderance of the evidence suggests that residential segregation remains a defining feature of most of our metropolitan areas. Although fast-growing cities with relatively few minorities have seen large declines in segregation in recent decades, suppressing the average across all metros, most areas in which nonwhite populations live in large numbers have remained stubbornly segregated, so that most blacks and Latinos still experience metropolitan spaces that are highly stratified by race. Similarly, even though thousands of neighborhoods have become more diverse in recent decades, substantial integration—especially involving whites and blacks—remains the exception to the general rule of persistent neighborhood isolation. Even more troubling is the fact that this racial isolation persists across the course of individual lives and across generations of families.[1]

Some might view this persistence of segregation as an indication of people's inertia, suggesting that metropolitan areas remain highly segregated because individuals choose to remain rooted in their isolated neighborhoods for long periods of time, undercutting the opportunity for more dramatic integration. But the fact is that most people move multiple times in their lifetime, yet tend to experience remarkable contextual consistency

across their life course. That is, the persistence of residential segr.
is a reflection not so much of individual inertia as of the fact that,
they move, individuals tend to cycle between neighborhoods that are
similar in racial composition and often dominated by members of their
own racial group.

THE THEORETICAL IMPLICATIONS OF
PERSISTENT RESIDENTIAL SEGREGATION

Thus, a central task for scholars of residential stratification is to explain
why segregation is perpetuated across lifetimes defined by multiple individual moves, as well as across time and generations of families. As we
have argued, this has been a serious challenge for traditional explanations
of segregation. At the heart of these arguments are assumptions that individuals approach decisions about when, and to which neighborhoods, to
move with a high level of rationality and with comprehensive knowledge
of all residential options. Under these assumptions, it is possible to consider the process of residential sorting as a clean reflection of some combination of neighborhood preferences, the necessary economic resources
to gain access to desired locations, and the force of discrimination that
excludes some from the neighborhoods they choose.

In laying out the social structural sorting perspective, we have argued
that the assumptions informing traditional research on segregation are
highly questionable and that even the forces implicated in traditional arguments play out in the residential mobility process in more subtle and complex
ways than has been reflected in past research on residential stratification.
Moreover, the individual residential mobility decisions that engender residential consistency across the life course and across generations, and that
continually reinforce and maintain segregation within metropolitan areas,
are informed by social processes that extend well beyond considerations
of economic resources, racial residential preferences, and the exclusionary
forces of housing discrimination. All of these forces are surely important,
but they are neither mutually exclusive nor exhaustive explanations of the
residential processes that drive segregation.

The social structural sorting perspective begins with the core assumption that segregation is now woven into the fabric of metropolitan life in
ways that fundamentally alter individual perceptions of residential spaces ⚡
and shape the context of residential mobility decisions so as to continually reinforce segregation. Recognizing that segregation is maintained
through racially distinct patterns of mobility, it seeks to understand the
momentum of segregation by paying explicit attention to the processes

through which members of different racial and ethnic groups search for, and select from, residential options. This perspective also recognizes that, when considering a move, individuals approach the housing search with biases about specific neighborhoods and limited knowledge about large swaths of metropolitan space. As a result, the residential sorting process does not necessarily reflect a rational selection from among all possible neighborhood options, but rather is the manifestation of social processes that lead individuals to be sorted among the neighborhoods in the limited set that, in their limited knowledge, they view as acceptable. These choices are certainly informed by economic considerations, racial preferences, and experiences of discrimination—although probably in much more subtle ways than has been assumed in past research—but also by a wide range of daily activities, experiences over the life course, and social interactions. By focusing on these social processes, the social structural sorting perspective highlights the ways in which segregation by race has become self-perpetuating, reinforcing itself through social processes and remaining high in many metropolitan areas despite the integrative forces of population diversification, liberalizing social attitudes, and considerable changes in patterns of economic stratification.

Our goals in this final chapter are twofold. Our first goal is to articulate the research implications of this new theoretical perspective. Although available evidence provides considerable support for the basic tenets of the social structural sorting perspective, this evidence is pieced together from disparate sources, often from a small handful of metropolitan areas, and most of it is largely circumstantial. As we will argue, fully testing the basic tenets of the social structural sorting perspective and fleshing out its intricacies will require new approaches to collecting and analyzing more comprehensive data on neighborhood selection processes. The last segment of this chapter is dedicated to the articulation of the types of questions and problems these new data will need to address.

Finally, we pull together the various strands of the social structural sorting perspective to articulate some of the key ways in which segregation has become self-perpetuating in metropolitan America. Here we highlight how segregation not only shapes the mechanisms implicated in traditional segregation arguments but also orders daily activity and residential experiences in ways that create racially disparate patterns of neighborhood knowledge and perceptions. These patterns of neighborhood knowledge have potentially profound effects on how individuals approach housing searches, shaping the residential mobility processes that continually reinforce segregation. In essence, we argue, segregation is continually replicated through its reciprocal relationships with a variety of social and economic processes.

THE RESEARCH IMPLICATIONS OF THE
SOCIAL STRUCTURAL SORTING PERSPECTIVE

We have offered the social structural sorting perspective as a new way of understanding the drivers of residential segregation by race. While considerable, the evidence we have presented in support of this new theoretical argument remains largely circumstantial. We have argued that existing frameworks, at least as traditionally applied, are inadequate for explaining the persistence of residential segregation or underlying patterns of residential stratification, and we have highlighted some clues that point to the importance of social networks, residential knowledge, life course development, and related search processes as important drivers of residential stratification.

But there is much more that needs to be learned about these dynamics. To fully assess the dynamics highlighted in the social structural sorting perspective, we must both utilize existing sources in more effective ways and develop completely new sources of information. A relatively simple first step would be to extend ongoing research to focus more on the subtle ways in which the forces implicated in traditional theoretical arguments affect residential decision-making. For example, rather than simply assessing the impact of racial composition on neighborhood desirability and attempting to separate this effect from the role of nonracial conditions, more work should be dedicated to the ways in which a single feature or features of a neighborhood might lead to a whole slew of assumptions about the broader conditions of the area. Moreover, these studies must move beyond the still common practice of examining general attitudes toward hypothetical neighborhoods to considerations of individuals' assessments of specific neighborhoods and how these assessments are connected to their decisions about whether and where to move.

Much more work is also needed on how economic resources and related conditions shape the context of a move, the tools used to assess neighborhoods and identify suitable units, and the decisions made in the process. To understand the full role of economic resources in maintaining residential stratification, we must not only gather information on group differences in levels of education, income, and wealth but also gain a much better understanding of how these resources translate—perhaps in different ways for members of different groups—into variations in the different stages of the mobility decision process.

Similarly, we need more information about how the anticipation of discriminatory treatment—and not just experiences of explicit discrimination— affects decisions to move, is a factor in determining the set of neighborhoods considered during the housing search, and affects destination decisions for those who do move. These new lines of research should not only attend to how actual and anticipated discrimination play out in the various stages of the housing market but also focus on the life course experiences that shape perceptions of potential discrimination and assess the conditions and individual characteristics that might lead individuals to consider a location despite the anticipation of potential discrimination. Again, attention to these nuances would not only reinvigorate the debate about the relative efficacy of traditional explanations of segregation but also provide a much more realistic depiction of the roles of discrimination, economic conditions, and residential preferences and the interactions between them.

The social structural sorting perspective also highlights the need to extend our investigations beyond these traditional theoretical frames. Understanding the drivers of residential stratification requires the development of new data on racial differences in levels of knowledge about a wide range of neighborhoods within the local housing market and assessment of the implications for group differences in the effective choice set adopted by residential searchers. Existing data provide only rough indicators of individuals' neighborhood knowledge in a single city. (Notably, Maria Krysan and Michael Bader asked respondents to simply indicate which neighborhoods they "don't know anything about.")[2] As a result, we currently know very little about the specific level and content of individuals' knowledge about specific neighborhoods, or the extent to which the reported level of knowledge is associated with particular assumptions about social and economic conditions in these neighborhoods.

Similarly, although previous research examines the role of racial composition in perceptions of neighborhood amenities in one's own neighborhood, we need much better information about residents' perceptions of the characteristics of other communities in their metropolitan area.[3] Collecting data on variations and determinants of neighborhood knowledge and perceptions—not just of one's current neighborhood but of the entire metropolitan region—would allow us to take fuller advantage of increasingly popular statistical strategies for modeling neighborhood choice, which currently rely, like the study of residential stratification more generally, on the unrealistic assumption of full and uniform knowledge of neighborhood options.[4]

At the same time, we must develop ways to examine the factors that shape these patterns of residential knowledge and neighborhood perceptions. Here a more concerted effort to understand historical and contemporary media depictions of specific neighborhoods, and how these depictions are processed and interpreted by members of different groups, would make important contributions to research on residential decision-making. Just as important would be the development of new sources of data on patterns in and repercussions of direct exposure to potential neighborhoods. Recent research on variations in activity space across different groups and neighborhoods and the impact of these behavioral dynamics on life chances points to the development of effective techniques for collecting and assessing data on where individuals spend time on a daily basis.[5] From the perspective of better understanding the processes through which residential stratification is reinforced, employing these types of techniques to assess racial differences in the geographic scope of activity space and the specific neighborhoods to which individuals are exposed as part of their daily round is especially important. Ideally, these data would differentiate between the types of interactions occurring within these neighborhood spaces—for example, identifying one type of interaction as visiting with family and friends in the neighborhood. Such an interaction would generate information that is likely to differ in both quality and quantity from information gathered on a shopping trip to the area.

In a similar way, efforts to understand the role of indirect exposure to specific residential options should be a high priority for future research. Here methods to understand the scope and shape of social networks provide an important starting point to understanding how information about specific housing opportunities and general impressions about the quality and character of potential neighborhoods flow through interpersonal contacts.[6] This would help to build on the implications of promising, but largely suggestive, research on the role of kinship linkages in residential decision-making. Specifically, such research would provide an opportunity to observe the flow of information about specific residential options through broader social systems and to understand the role of racially stratified networks in the reinforcement of residential stratification.

Research focused on understanding the role of social networks in the stratification process should attend to the physical location and social position of members of the network and how these locational features might help to explain racial and ethnic differences in knowledge about, and perceptions of, specific neighborhoods and the geographic scope of the consideration set. Moreover, delineating variations in both the content and efficiency of information flows through networks nodes, as well as the connection of these features to the nature of relationships within the network, will be especially important for understanding the role of social networks in residential mobility processes. At the same time, it will be imperative to understand how these features vary with individual economic resources, experiences of discrimination, and other drivers of residential stratification; the role of social networks in the spatial structures of specific metropolitan areas; and, especially, how social networks are conditioned by specific features of the local housing market. In other words, future research must adopt a more expansive view of the types of social and structural conditions that affect individual neighborhood selection and housing search processes and, by extension, continually shape patterns of residential stratification.

If we are to develop clearer pictures of how residential knowledge and perceptions develop, and how they shape residential trajectories, we need to expand the temporal scope of our analytic strategies. Although there is growing recognition of the fact that residential context tends to be maintained across the life course and even across generations, the bulk of existing research attempts to understand the roots of residential stratification by focusing on the present-time characteristics of individuals and households.[7] This orientation leads us to focus on correlates of current residential location while paying little or no attention to the legacy of past residential experiences. For example, we tend to focus on how current economic resources or residential preferences shape the decision about when and where to move, but we ignore the fact that these current conditions not only shape but are shaped by past residential experiences. Because these residential feedback loops tend to unfold over long periods of time—over the course of generations of individual lives—our traditional approaches to studying residential stratification typically miss them. In this sense, a full understanding of the role of the factors implicated in popular theoretical arguments—socioeconomic characteristics, preferences, and discrimination—in shaping patterns of segregation requires considerably more work on how these characteristics are themselves shaped by segregation.

It is worth noting that these efforts to build more complete models of residential sorting have implications that extend far beyond understanding patterns of residential segregation. The social dynamics of neighborhood selection that we have described certainly complicate the effort to disentangle the effects of neighborhoods on individuals from the dynamics that lead individuals to occupy particular neighborhoods. Certainly, simply controlling for the effects of individual- and family-level characteristics is insufficient, since neighborhood selection processes are themselves a reflection of the effects of the neighborhood context and the social interactions they afford. Developing more complete models of residential selection would allow us to more fully assess the role of reciprocal links between neighborhood selection processes and the processes of socialization and resource deprivation assumed to influence individual outcomes. In other words, developing more complete information about the processes through which residential stratification develops would enable us to move beyond the treatment of residential selection as a source of statistical noise to be controlled away in contextual-effects research in order to develop strategies that incorporate dynamic processes of residential selection as important sources of stratification.[8]

Most glaring in existing research is the tendency to ignore the influence of past residential experiences on subsequent residential choices. As reviewed earlier, new literature suggests a strong continuity of residential outcomes across the life course, with neighborhood experiences early in life serving as strong predictors of neighborhood outcomes later in life. These links between childhood neighborhood exposures and residential location throughout the adult life course provide strong hints about how residential stratification is maintained across generations. However, we currently know very little about the specific mechanisms through which this life course continuity of residential context is maintained. Circumstantial evidence suggests that perceptions of residential options and the development of information about various types of housing options, in anticipation of discrimination, the development of neighborhood preferences, and socioeconomic attainment across the life course may be important mechanisms. However, much more needs to be done to measure the effects of early-life residential experiences on all of these mechanisms, as well as the repercussions for actual mobility decisions.

For now, the high level of dependence of residential attainment on earlier residential experiences should push researchers to move beyond analytic strategies that assume racial differences in residential location and mobility simply reflect contemporary conditions. We must create new tools that can generate new sources of data, while also utilizing existing longitudinal data more effectively, to move beyond the assumption implicit in much research on residential mobility and neighborhood attainment: that each decision related to mobility—each decision to move or not and each destination choice—reflects a fresh, independent foray into the housing market. As we have attempted to argue, people bring with them considerable baggage—past residential experiences, neighborhood perceptions, and market blind spots—that significantly shapes their residential decision-making. Because this baggage accumulates over a lifetime of residential experience, we must do more to model decisions about whether and where to move as part of a sequence of residential decisions. This will require taking better advantage of the full power of the longitudinal data already at our disposal and finding ways to bolster these data to more effectively tap underappreciated factors in the residential decision-making process. Similarly, we should aspire to move beyond the focus on contemporary correlates of residential segregation at the aggregate level to an assessment of the momentum built into broader systems of residential stratification.

F-PERPETUATION OF SEGREGATION

Some servers have argued that the era of pronounced residential segregation is nearing its end, but the bulk of the evidence contradicts this claim. Especially in places with large minority populations, segregation, with its multitude of impacts on neighborhood inequality and broader patterns of social stratification, remains pronounced. In fact, a central challenge for those interested in understanding urban dynamics is to explain why segregation has remained so high despite strong evidence of declining discrimination, liberalizing racial attitudes, and economic progress among at least some members of minority groups.

A central claim of the social structural sorting perspective is that segregation remains high because it is inextricably tied to a set of social dynamics that shape racially disparate mobility patterns. These social processes both shape and are shaped by segregation in ways that have essentially allowed segregation to become self-perpetuating. In fact, residential segregation by race tends to perpetuate itself in a wide variety of ways: by creating residential histories for members of different racial and ethnic groups that intersect only marginally; by circumscribing daily interactions to distinct social spaces; by shaping the geographic location of social networks in ways that limit experiences in, and knowledge about, neighborhoods containing other groups; and by affecting racially distinct opportunity structures. Existing research provides hints about the ways in which these dynamics affect, and are affected by, segregation, but the reciprocal links are rarely articulated. Making these conceptual links explicit is crucial for developing effective strategies to investigate and break the cycle of persistent segregation.

Perhaps the most direct way in which segregation reinforces segregation is by shaping the individual-level characteristics and experiences that, according to the traditional theories, affect racial differences in residential outcomes. Here the reciprocal relationship between segregation and economic resources provides the most straightforward example. Decades of research have highlighted the role of racial segregation in maintaining sharp racial differences in socioeconomic resources. As described in our opening chapter, residential segregation tends to relegate black and Latino residents to high-poverty, low-income neighborhoods with relatively few opportunities for educational attainment, income growth, and wealth accumulation.[9] Black children are exposed, on average, to neighborhoods with educational environments that are very different from those occupied by the average white child; these environments expose them to fewer neighbors who have graduated from high school or completed college.[10] Segregation also affects racial differences in school environments; in comparison to their white counterparts, black and brown children are less likely to attend well-funded schools that provide stable staffing, safe and supportive learning environments, and the latest educational tools.[11] These neighborhood and school characteristics have important impacts on educational attainment at the individual level, and thereby play a central role in the maintenance of sharp racial differences in educational outcomes.[12] In this sense, segregation can be seen as a root cause of large and persistent racial and ethnic gaps in educational attainment.[13]

Segregation is similarly implicated in the maintenance of substantial racial and ethnic differences in the economic resources that shape residential stratification. In metropolitan areas with high levels of residential segregation by race, African Americans tend to be relegated to neighborhoods that are more geographically isolated from job opportunities and provide only limited access to the social networks that are valuable to upward income mobility.[14] Similarly, growing racial gaps in wealth that dwarf even substantial racial differences in earnings have roots in residential segregation by race.[15] Again, segregation's role in exposing members of different groups to fundamentally different neighborhood opportunity structures is the key to these effects on wealth inequality. By confining black and Latino homeowners to neighborhoods with lower housing values, more vacancies, higher rates of foreclosure, and weaker rates of property appreciation, segregation severely limits the key wealth-building capacity of homeownership for these groups.[16]

Not surprisingly, then, segregation has been identified as a key factor in the maintenance of large and growing wealth gaps and has also been linked to higher rates of poverty among African Americans and higher levels of income inequality between racial groups.[17] And there is strong evidence that the disadvantages associated with racial isolation persist across generations.[18] Given the important role of segregation in shaping patterns of family wealth and other resources crucial to the provision of opportunities for children, it should come as no surprise that local levels of segregation are significantly and negatively associated with the likelihood that a child will grow up to meet or surpass the economic standing of her parents.[19]

Thus, segregation plays a critical role in shaping the group differences in economic resources that are often assumed to be the key *drivers* of residential stratification. In fact, as reviewed in chapter 7, the economic roots of segregation are indicated by the fact that segregation tends to be highest in those metropolitan areas with the greatest economic disparities between groups.[20] Similarly, a non-negligible share of the racial differences in neighborhood location and mobility can be attributed to racial differences in education, income, and wealth.[21] Most importantly, economic forces often play an important role in shaping the context of residential moves and the tools used to assess neighborhoods and search for housing.

What is rarely acknowledged in arguments from classical economics is that racial differences in socioeconomic resources are themselves *outcomes* of residential segregation. Segregation limits the ability of black and Latino families to accumulate the resources they need to gain access to the types of neighborhoods occupied by whites. The result is dramatic racial and ethnic differences in patterns of residential mobility and immobility that continually reinforce residential segregation. A complete picture of the processes of residential stratification requires that we acknowledge these important feedback loops, seeing segregation not only as an *outcome* of economic inequality but as a structural *driver* of this inequality. In this sense, our typical strategies for understanding the role of economic stratification in maintaining segregation are woefully inadequate because they have failed to capture a broader range of its impact, in addition to the cyclical nature of segregation.

Similar types of self-perpetuating feedback loops are implicated in other traditional theoretical arguments. For example, patterns of residential segregation may significantly shape experiences and perceptions of discrimination. Almost by definition, the residential color line between white and nonwhite neighborhoods is likely to be considerably more indelible in highly segregated metropolitan areas and may reduce the likelihood that residents of such metropolitan areas will seek out housing in neighborhoods occupied by another group. Similarly, given the role of segregation in maintaining their relative economic advantage, whites living in highly segregated cities may have greater motive and opportunity to maintain segregation through discriminatory actions. In other words, segregation may perpetuate itself, in part, by creating a context in which discrimination is more likely.

Residential segregation may also substantially shape residential preferences in ways that reinforce segregation. A strong body of research—mostly couched in terms of the contact hypothesis—suggests that interpersonal contact with members of out-groups tends to erode racial stereotypes and negative attitudes toward these out-groups.[22] To the extent that racial residential preferences are rooted in racial antipathy, residential contact in early life and in the residential context is likely to shape residential preferences in directions that lead to more integration.[23] Growing up in a racially homogenous area—a typical by-product of living in a highly segregated city—tends to result in limited contact with members of other racial and ethnic groups; under these circumstances, individuals may adopt racial attitudes that lead them to avoid neighborhoods containing members of other groups. In this way, segregation may perpetuate itself by shaping residential preferences that, in turn, shape segregative residential decisions. In addition, by creating material differences in social, economic, and physical conditions between neighborhoods with different racial and ethnic compositions, segregation serves to shape perceptions of, and preferences for, neighborhoods containing members of other groups. In other words, segregation helps to create the "kernel of truth" of structural disadvantage in black and Latino neighborhoods that leads those with resources to avoid living in such areas.

Again, these types of feedback loops in which segregation influences on-the-ground experiences that, in turn, reinforce segregation may be fairly obvious to those who study segregation. However, at least to date, these have not been fully articulated either theoretically or analytically. Rather, existing research tends to approach the explanation of segregation by discussing the present-time features that shape residential options and choices, paying little attention to how these features have themselves been shaped by segregation. Focusing on how residential decision-making is rooted in past residential experiences and neighborhood exposures illuminates another way in which segregation begets segregation.

At the individual level, segregation circumscribes daily activities in ways that foster racially differentiated neighborhood knowledge. Because of racial residential segregation, members of different races not only reside in different neighborhoods but also tend to go to separate schools, belong to separate neighborhood-based social and political organizations, and frequent different establishments in their local areas. Even when they travel outside of their immediate neighborhoods, these separate neighborhoods define distinct centers of gravity for the daily activities of members of different races. Given the clustering of similar neighborhoods in most metropolitan areas, members of different races are likely to access neighborhoods with fairly similar racial compositions unless they venture far away from their residential neighborhood. As a result, many white people are likely to live, work, go to school, go to church, shop, play, and pursue all other regular activities in predominantly white neighborhoods. Similarly, especially in metropolitan areas characterized by high rates of segregation, African Americans may rarely access neighborhoods that are not predominantly black during their daily activities.

Racial differences may also emerge from pronounced racial and ethnic differences in life course experiences, since our knowledge of specific neighborhoods is likely to be shaped by our residential histories—the places where we lived in childhood and adolescence and throughout our adult life. Highly segregated metropolitan areas like Chicago may foster stronger perceptions that certain areas are distinctly black areas and others are distinctly white areas. In contrast, in places like Phoenix and Seattle, where segregation is not as well established and neighborhoods are less likely to be racially defined, individuals may be less likely to define all neighborhoods along racial lines and thus less absolute in excluding some from their consideration set.

The persistence of segregation also figures in the very different neighborhood options to which social networks for members of different racial-ethnic groups provide access and information. In addition, any effort to remain near kin or move toward kin results in a segregative move, since segregation serves to concentrate family members in isolated neighborhoods. For example, in Chicago, where segregation has been a fact of life for decades, there are racial implications to the seemingly "nonracial" desire to stay put—to be close to family and friends or where one grew up. Race can have "nothing to do" with why a person picks a residence, but connections to family members and friends can have segregative consequences where segregation has relegated social networks to racially isolated neighborhood settings. As the sociologist Robert Sampson's work has clearly shown, these social connections play a strong role in shaping flows of migration between racially similar neighborhoods and, by extension, maintaining segregation by race.[24]

CONCLUSION

The summer of 2015—which witnessed high-profile and repeated instances of police violence against African Americans, significant court decisions, and the implementation of new agency rules—was arguably one of the most significant in recent history in terms of casting a spotlight on the issue of housing segregation. By then, the simple solution of the past—that enforcement of antidiscrimination legislation would translate into the disappearance of segregation—had been shown to be obviously inadequate. The Supreme Court, when it recognized disparate impact as a legitimate basis for claims of discrimination, also acknowledged that the simple story was insufficient. The business of the Fair Housing Act, which has historically focused on disparate treatment, remains unfinished: we have not broken down the barriers to a truly integrated society. The challenge today is to seize new tools and muster the will to design policies and programs informed by insights about the forces underpinning the self-perpetuation of segregation. These factors become clearer, we argue, when we ask how people end up living where they do. The lens of that question informs and suggests policies and programs and identifies points where interventions might break the cycle of segregation.

As Justice Anthony Kennedy wrote in the majority opinion that upheld disparate impact in *Texas Department of Housing and Community Affairs v. Inclusive Communities Project:*

> Much progress remains to be made in our Nation's continuing struggle against racial isolation. In striving to achieve our "historic commitment to creating an integrated society," *Parents Involved, supra, at 797 (Kennedy, J., concurring in part and concurring in judgment),* we must remain wary of policies that reduce homeowners to nothing more than their race. But since the passage of the Fair Housing Act in 1968 and against the backdrop of disparate-impact liability in nearly every jurisdiction, many cities have become more diverse. The FHA must play an important part in avoiding the Kerner Commission's grim prophecy that "our Nation is moving toward two societies—one black, one white—separate and unequal." *Kerner Commission Report 1.* The Court acknowledges the Fair Housing Act's continuing role in moving the Nation toward a more integrated society.[25]

It is hopeful and reassuring that the U.S. Supreme Court (with a 5–4 vote) upheld this important tool and in so doing reaffirmed a commitment to an integrated society. At the same time, it is worrisome that we remain where we were fifty years ago, having made only slight progress toward staving off that warning of two societies. We suggest that moving beyond traditional explanations of segregation will allow for the development of new policy tools that, along with renewed commitment to racial equality, will once and for all put the Kerner Commission's warning to rest.

Appendix |

Table A2.1   Core Metropolitan Areas by Segregation Type, 1980 and 2010

	Black-White (D_i)	
Metropolitan Area	1980	2010
Integrating metros (segregation declining faster than average)		
Albuquerque, NM	0.457	0.293
Allentown-Bethlehem-Easton, PA-NJ	0.608	0.459
Altoona, PA	0.618	0.404
Ames, IA	0.474	0.320
Anderson, IN	0.771	0.525
Appleton, WI	0.799	0.340
Asheville, NC	0.660	0.462
Atlanta–Sandy Springs–Marietta, GA	0.768	0.584
Auburn-Opelika, AL	0.498	0.338
Austin–Round Rock–San Marcos, TX	0.649	0.485
Bangor, ME	0.506	0.293
Battle Creek, MI	0.712	0.545
Bellingham, WA	0.349	0.179
Billings, MT	0.509	0.245
Bismarck, ND	0.698	0.235
Boise City–Nampa, ID	0.489	0.246
Boulder, CO	0.413	0.166
Brownsville-Harlingen, TX	0.677	0.320
Cape Coral–Fort Myers, FL	0.884	0.594
Casper, WY	0.690	0.206
Cheyenne, WY	0.497	0.275
Chico, CA	0.554	0.326
College Station–Bryan, TX	0.583	0.426
Corpus Christi, TX	0.698	0.436
Corvallis, OR	0.335	0.199
Crestview–Fort Walton Beach–Destin, FL	0.479	0.308
Dallas–Fort Worth–Arlington, TX	0.783	0.556
Davenport-Moline–Rock Island, IA-IL	0.653	0.479
Deltona–Daytona Beach–Ormond Beach, FL	0.746	0.515
Des Moines–West Des Moines, IA	0.710	0.489
Duluth, MN-WI	0.665	0.419
Eau Claire, WI	0.639	0.339
El Paso, TX	0.419	0.299
Elkhart-Goshen, IN	0.720	0.480
Eugene-Springfield, OR	0.466	0.227
Evansville, IN-KY	0.642	0.500
Fargo, ND-MN	0.511	0.301
Farmington, NM	0.457	0.261

Table A2.1   *Continued*

Metropolitan Area	Black-White (D_i) 1980	2010
Fayetteville-Springdale-Rogers, AR-MO	0.687	0.387
Florence, SC	0.527	0.359
Fond du Lac, WI	0.598	0.352
Fort Collins–Loveland, CO	0.499	0.222
Fort Wayne, IN	0.756	0.577
Glens Falls, NY	0.760	0.489
Grand Forks, ND-MN	0.648	0.340
Grand Junction, CO	0.638	0.211
Great Falls, MT	0.652	0.321
Greeley, CO	0.528	0.356
Green Bay, WI	0.691	0.465
Hagerstown-Martinsburg, MD-WV	0.706	0.394
Harrisonburg, VA	0.473	0.356
Hattiesburg, MS	0.651	0.492
Holland–Grand Haven, MI	0.504	0.337
Huntington-Ashland, WV-KY-OH	0.707	0.504
Jackson, TN	0.636	0.491
Jacksonville, FL	0.669	0.521
Janesville, WI	0.690	0.511
Johnson City, TN	0.609	0.457
Joplin, MO	0.580	0.323
Kansas City, MO-KS	0.777	0.587
Kennewick-Pasco-Richland, WA	0.494	0.299
Kingsport-Bristol-Bristol, TN-VA	0.583	0.403
Knoxville, TN	0.669	0.519
Kokomo, IN	0.732	0.421
La Crosse, WI-MN	0.551	0.318
Lafayette, IN	0.454	0.334
Lakeland–Winter Haven, FL	0.635	0.428
Lancaster, PA	0.679	0.503
Laredo, TX	0.768	0.291
Las Cruces, NM	0.475	0.224
Las Vegas–Paradise, NV	0.625	0.361
Lawton, OK	0.401	0.279
Lebanon, PA	0.563	0.354
Lexington-Fayette, KY	0.594	0.458
Lincoln, NE	0.493	0.371
Longview, TX	0.536	0.376
Longview, WA	0.498	0.233

(Table continues on p. 262.)

Table A2.1   *Continued*

Metropolitan Area	Black-White (D$_i$)	
	1980	2010
Louisville/Jefferson County, KY-IN	0.732	0.563
Lubbock, TX	0.680	0.462
Manchester-Nashua, NH	0.512	0.384
McAllen-Edinburg-Mission, TX	0.566	0.393
Medford, OR	0.702	0.238
Midland, TX	0.829	0.476
Minneapolis–St. Paul–Bloomington, MN-WI	0.692	0.502
Missoula, MT	0.622	0.157
Modesto, CA	0.576	0.312
Monroe, MI	0.730	0.432
Muncie, IN	0.706	0.448
Naples–Marco Island, FL	0.825	0.555
North Port–Bradenton-Sarasota, FL	0.837	0.531
Ocean City, NJ	0.632	0.460
Odessa, TX	0.797	0.393
Ogden-Clearfield, UT	0.588	0.293
Oklahoma City, OK	0.712	0.491
Olympia, WA	0.489	0.302
Omaha–Council Bluffs, NE-IA	0.752	0.583
Orlando-Kissimmee-Sanford, FL	0.713	0.495
Oshkosh-Neenah, WI	0.731	0.391
Owensboro, KY	0.617	0.442
Oxnard–Thousand Oaks–Ventura, CA	0.538	0.368
Palm Bay–Melbourne-Titusville, FL	0.643	0.454
Panama City–Lynn Haven–Panama City Beach, FL	0.643	0.438
Parkersburg-Marietta-Vienna, WV-OH	0.558	0.333
Phoenix-Mesa-Glendale, AZ	0.622	0.414
Pittsfield, MA	0.486	0.371
Pocatello, ID	0.570	0.264
Port St. Lucie, FL	0.819	0.464
Portland-Vancouver-Hillsboro, OR-WA	0.686	0.412
Providence–New Bedford–Fall River, RI-MA	0.691	0.508
Provo-Orem, UT	0.751	0.181
Pueblo, CO	0.501	0.310
Racine, WI	0.675	0.520
Rapid City, SD	0.530	0.262
Reading, PA	0.655	0.468
Redding, CA	0.483	0.262
Reno-Sparks, NV	0.438	0.320
Roanoke, VA	0.700	0.542

Table A2.1   *Continued*

Metropolitan Area	Black-White (D$_i$)	
	1980	2010
Rockford, IL	0.770	0.548
Salem, OR	0.491	0.284
Salt Lake City, UT	0.550	0.342
San Angelo, TX	0.514	0.335
San Antonio–New Braunfels, TX	0.619	0.478
San Diego–Carlsbad–San Marcos, CA	0.634	0.485
San Jose–Sunnyvale–Santa Clara, CA	0.503	0.387
Santa Fe, NM	0.473	0.258
Santa Rosa–Petaluma, CA	0.402	0.308
Savannah, GA	0.660	0.487
Scranton–Wilkes-Barre, PA	0.717	0.495
Seattle-Tacoma-Bellevue, WA	0.646	0.458
Sebastian–Vero Beach, FL	0.669	0.456
Sheboygan, WI	0.645	0.435
Sherman-Denison, TX	0.572	0.444
Sioux City, IA-NE-SD	0.631	0.450
Spokane, WA	0.493	0.292
Springfield, MO	0.629	0.423
St. Joseph, MO-KS	0.493	0.380
Stockton, CA	0.633	0.453
Tampa–St. Petersburg–Clearwater, FL	0.766	0.545
Tucson, AZ	0.534	0.346
Tulsa, OK	0.740	0.541
Visalia-Porterville, CA	0.601	0.328
Warner Robins, GA	0.406	0.244
Wausau, WI	0.731	0.390
Wichita Falls, TX	0.704	0.487
Wichita, KS	0.721	0.547
Yakima, WA	0.585	0.361
York-Hanover, PA	0.746	0.475
Yuba City, CA	0.521	0.263
Yuma, AZ	0.524	0.361
Persistently moderate metros (segregation low or moderate in 1980 and integrating slowly)		
Abilene, TX	0.512	0.432
Anchorage, AK	0.376	0.410
Anderson, SC	0.403	0.407
Ann Arbor, MI	0.490	0.529
Anniston-Oxford, AL	0.536	0.443

(Table continues on p. 264.)

Table A2.1   *Continued*

Metropolitan Area	Black-White (D$_i$)	
	1980	2010
Athens–Clarke County, GA	0.512	0.417
Augusta–Richmond County, GA-SC	0.457	0.447
Bay City, MI	0.504	0.397
Binghamton, NY	0.449	0.488
Blacksburg-Christiansburg-Radford, VA	0.215	0.233
Bloomington, IN	0.439	0.430
Bloomington-Normal, IL	0.425	0.351
Bremerton-Silverdale, WA	0.448	0.368
Burlington, NC	0.404	0.408
Burlington–South Burlington, VT	0.347	0.362
Carson City, NV	0.400	0.462
Cedar Rapids, IA	0.482	0.389
Champaign-Urbana, IL	0.499	0.523
Charleston, WV	0.593	0.569
Charleston–North Charleston–Summerville, SC	0.503	0.409
Charlotte-Gastonia-Rock Hill, NC-SC	0.571	0.531
Charlottesville, VA	0.411	0.321
Clarksville, TN-KY	0.446	0.392
Colorado Springs, CO	0.449	0.373
Columbia, MO	0.425	0.351
Columbia, SC	0.572	0.483
Columbus, GA-AL	0.531	0.548
Cumberland, MD-WV	0.457	0.519
Danville, VA	0.305	0.373
Decatur, AL	0.564	0.578
Dothan, AL	0.562	0.453
Dover, DE	0.275	0.273
Dubuque, IA	0.472	0.483
Durham-Chapel Hill, NC	0.500	0.475
El Centro, CA	0.555	0.555
Elmira, NY	0.595	0.476
Fairbanks, AK	0.476	0.372
Fayetteville, NC	0.366	0.307
Florence–Muscle Shoals, AL	0.474	0.420
Fort Smith, AR-OK	0.585	0.505
Gainesville, FL	0.481	0.408
Goldsboro, NC	0.370	0.399
Greensboro–High Point, NC	0.587	0.541
Greenville-Mauldin-Easley, SC	0.547	0.428
Gulfport-Biloxi, MS	0.479	0.407

Table A2.1   *Continued*

Metropolitan Area	Black-White (D$_i$) 1980	2010
Hanford-Corcoran, CA	0.432	0.398
Hickory-Lenoir-Morganton, NC	0.394	0.409
Honolulu, HI	0.396	0.334
Houma–Bayou Cane–Thibodaux, LA	0.459	0.425
Huntsville, AL	0.546	0.494
Iowa City, IA	0.338	0.383
Jacksonville, NC	0.339	0.274
Kalamazoo-Portage, MI	0.556	0.462
Killeen-Temple–Fort Hood, TX	0.497	0.412
Lafayette, LA	0.544	0.443
Lansing-East Lansing, MI	0.569	0.526
Lawrence, KS	0.292	0.250
Lewiston–Auburn, ME	0.514	0.534
Lynchburg, VA	0.381	0.362
Macon, GA	0.514	0.511
Madera-Chowchilla, CA	0.491	0.559
Madison, WI	0.489	0.466
Merced, CA	0.409	0.325
Morgantown, WV	0.330	0.357
Napa, CA	0.544	0.589
Norwich–New London, CT	0.530	0.490
Pascagoula, MS	0.555	0.514
Pensacola–Ferry Pass–Brent, FL	0.594	0.470
Portland–South Portland–Biddeford, ME	0.557	0.455
Poughkeepsie-Newburgh-Middletown, NY	0.526	0.461
Raleigh-Cary, NC	0.455	0.414
Riverside–San Bernardino–Ontario, CA	0.529	0.442
Rochester, MN	0.498	0.466
Rocky Mount, NC	0.404	0.359
Rome, GA	0.569	0.467
Sacramento–Arden-Arcade–Roseville, CA	0.576	0.546
Salisbury, MD	0.525	0.420
San Luis Obispo–Paso Robles, CA	0.520	0.482
Santa Barbara–Santa Maria–Goleta, CA	0.376	0.373
Santa Cruz–Watsonville, CA	0.312	0.246
Sioux Falls, SD	0.503	0.444
Spartanburg, SC	0.419	0.419
St. Cloud, MN	0.483	0.515
State College, PA	0.516	0.449

(*Table continues on p. 266.*)

Table A2.1   *Continued*

Metropolitan Area	Black-White (D$_i$) 1980	2010
Sumter, SC	0.446	0.348
Tallahassee, FL	0.511	0.439
Texarkana, TX–Texarkana, AR	0.402	0.421
Topeka, KS	0.567	0.493
Tuscaloosa, AL	0.483	0.544
Tyler, TX	0.520	0.485
Vallejo-Fairfield, CA	0.411	0.417
Victoria, TX	0.488	0.414
Vineland-Millville-Bridgeton, NJ	0.418	0.460
Virginia Beach–Norfolk–Newport News, VA-NC	0.584	0.469
Wheeling, WV-OH	0.544	0.492
Wilmington, NC	0.504	0.458
Worcester, MA	0.569	0.493
Legacy metros (highly segregated in 1980 and integrating slowly)		
Akron, OH	0.732	0.579
Albany, GA	0.653	0.519
Albany-Schenectady-Troy, NY	0.634	0.587
Alexandria, LA	0.642	0.595
Amarillo, TX	0.720	0.564
Atlantic City–Hammonton, NJ	0.706	0.567
Bakersfield-Delano, CA	0.632	0.505
Baltimore-Towson, MD	0.739	0.644
Baton Rouge, LA	0.680	0.572
Beaumont–Port Arthur, TX	0.755	0.673
Birmingham-Hoover, AL	0.716	0.652
Boston-Cambridge-Quincy, MA-NH	0.745	0.615
Bridgeport-Stamford-Norwalk, CT	0.685	0.660
Buffalo–Niagara Falls, NY	0.794	0.710
Canton-Massillon, OH	0.653	0.536
Chattanooga, TN-GA	0.719	0.630
Chicago-Joliet-Naperville, IL-IN-WI	0.877	0.753
Cincinnati-Middletown, OH-KY-IN	0.772	0.670
Cleveland-Elyria-Mentor, OH	0.854	0.726
Columbus, OH	0.721	0.600
Danville, IL	0.711	0.680
Dayton, OH	0.780	0.635
Decatur, IL	0.627	0.525
Denver-Aurora-Broomfield, CO	0.696	0.596
Detroit-Warren-Livonia, MI	0.872	0.740

Table A2.1   *Continued*

Metropolitan Area	Black-White (D$_i$)	
	1980	2010
Erie, PA	0.660	0.628
Flint, MI	0.834	0.673
Fresno, CA	0.624	0.498
Gadsden, AL	0.682	0.663
Grand Rapids–Wyoming, MI	0.755	0.614
Harrisburg-Carlisle, PA	0.739	0.630
Hartford–West Hartford–East Hartford, CT	0.709	0.624
Houston–Sugar Land–Baytown, TX	0.733	0.607
Indianapolis-Carmel, IN	0.783	0.645
Jackson, MI	0.730	0.575
Jackson, MS	0.682	0.558
Johnstown, PA	0.680	0.607
Kankakee-Bradley, IL	0.713	0.607
Lake Charles, LA	0.660	0.608
Lima, OH	0.621	0.516
Little Rock–North Little Rock–Conway, AR	0.632	0.580
Los Angeles–Long Beach–Santa Ana, CA	0.810	0.657
Mansfield, OH	0.678	0.591
Memphis, TN-MS-AR	0.687	0.622
Miami–Fort Lauderdale–Pompano Beach, FL	0.818	0.641
Michigan City–La Porte, IN	0.689	0.561
Milwaukee-Waukesha–West Allis, WI	0.838	0.796
Mobile, AL	0.709	0.590
Monroe, LA	0.636	0.634
Montgomery, AL	0.607	0.543
Muskegon-Norton Shores, MI	0.736	0.712
Nashville-Davidson—Murfreesboro—Franklin, TN	0.651	0.550
New Haven–Milford, CT	0.691	0.622
New Orleans–Metairie-Kenner, LA	0.693	0.633
New York–Northern New Jersey–Long Island, NY-NJ-PA	0.810	0.770
Niles–Benton Harbor, MI	0.727	0.693
Ocala, FL	0.604	0.473
Peoria, IL	0.705	0.686
Philadelphia-Camden-Wilmington, PA-NJ-DE-MD	0.767	0.671
Pine Bluff, AR	0.655	0.613
Pittsburgh, PA	0.721	0.631
Richmond, VA	0.627	0.516
Rochester, NY	0.678	0.630
Saginaw–Saginaw Township North, MI	0.825	0.649

(Table continues on p. 268.)

Table A2.1   *Continued*

Metropolitan Area	Black-White (D$_i$)	
	1980	2010
Salinas, CA	0.617	0.516
San Francisco–Oakland-Fremont, CA	0.702	0.597
Sandusky, OH	0.606	0.610
Shreveport–Bossier City, LA	0.645	0.564
South Bend–Mishawaka, IN-MI	0.621	0.515
Springfield, IL	0.674	0.540
Springfield, MA	0.721	0.617
Springfield, OH	0.667	0.555
St. Louis, MO-IL	0.817	0.707
Steubenville-Weirton, OH-WV	0.642	0.522
Syracuse, NY	0.748	0.650
Terre Haute, IN	0.640	0.554
Toledo, OH	0.788	0.632
Trenton-Ewing, NJ	0.706	0.629
Utica-Rome, NY	0.671	0.612
Waco, TX	0.611	0.512
Washington-Arlington-Alexandria, DC-VA-MD-WV	0.692	0.611
Waterloo–Cedar Falls, IA	0.739	0.602
Williamsport, PA	0.625	0.565
Winston-Salem, NC	0.691	0.561
Youngstown-Warren-Boardman, OH-PA	0.770	0.654

Source: Authors' calculations from the 1970–2010 Neighborhood Change Database (Geolytics 2014).

Table A2.2 Metropolitan Population and Housing Characteristics, by Segregation Type, 2010

	Integrating Metros	Persistently Moderate Metros	Legacy Metros
Number of metropolitan areas	149	97	85
Average population	592,944	372,584	1,515,512
Region (percentage)			
Northeast	8.72	10.31	21.18
Midwest	26.85	18.56	38.82
South	33.56	53.61	32.94
West	30.87	17.53	7.06
Average dissimilarity (D_i) scores			
Black-white, 1980	0.62	0.47	0.71
Asian-white, 1980	0.42	0.43	0.47
Latino-white, 1980	0.37	0.35	0.43
Black-white, 2010	0.39	0.44	0.61
Asian-white, 2010	0.29	0.34	0.38
Latino-white, 2010	0.35	0.34	0.42
Average racial composition, 2010			
Percentage Latino	16.02	10.68	9.44
Percentage non-Latino Asian	3.02	3.81	3.19
Percentage non-Latino Black	6.41	14.53	17.31
Percentage non-Latino White	73.12	69.84	69.55
Average percentage of housing units vacant	10.58	10.20	9.88
Average percentage of housing units renter-occupied	29.89	31.52	29.95
Average percentage of housing built in previous ten years	17.39	15.24	8.31
Average percentage moving in last year	16.38	16.86	14.07
Average percentage in manufacturing, 2010	3.96	3.49	4.25
Average percentage in military, 2010	0.14	0.39	0.02
Average percentage employed in government, 2010	7.66	9.54	7.46
Average percentage enrolled in college, 2010	1.01	1.63	0.99

Source: Authors' calculations from the 2010 decennial census and the 2009–2013 American Community Survey.

Notes |

Epigraph: National Committee Against Discrimination in Housing, *How the Federal Government Builds Ghettos* (New York: 1967). Reproduced in *Housing Legislation of 1967: Hearings Before the Subcommittee on Housing and Urban Affairs of the Committee on Banking and Currency*, 90th Cong. (1967) (testimony before the senate).

CHAPTER 1

1. 114 Cong. Rec. 2,280 (1968). Statement of Senator Edward Brooke, quoting from National Committee Against Discrimination in Housing, *How the Federal Government Builds Ghettos* (New York: 1967).
2. Sarat 2001.
3. Crowder, Pais, and South 2012; Sampson 2012.
4. Sharkey 2008.
5. Glaeser and Vigdor 2012; Massey and Denton 1993; Massey, Rothwell, and Domina 2009.
6. Massey and Denton 1993.
7. Hannah-Jones 2012; Hirsch 2000; Rothstein 2014, 2017.
8. Federal Housing Administration 1938.
9. Jackson 1987.
10. Dean 1947.
11. Sugrue 1993.
12. Massey and Denton 1993.
13. President William Clinton, Executive Order 12892, January 17, 1994, 110–14.
14. Yinger 1995.
15. Government Accountability Office 2010.
16. Badger 2015; Garrison 2015.
17. Durrheim and Dixon 2013; *Milliken v. Bradley*, 418 U.S. 717 (1977); *Parents Involved in Community Schools v. Seattle School District No. 1*, 551 U.S. 701 (2007).
18. Turner et al. 2013.
19. Roscigno, Karafin, and Tester 2009.

20. Massey and Rothwell 2009.
21. Rugh and Massey 2010; Hall, Crowder, and Spring 2015.
22. Sampson 2012.
23. Spring, Tolnay, and Crowder 2016; Sharkey 2012.
24. Krysan and Bader 2007; Krysan, Crowder, et al. 2016.
25. Clark 1982; Hempel 1970; Lake 1981.
26. Bruch and Feinberg 2017; Bruch and Swait 2014, 2017; Bruch, Feinberg, and Lee 2016.

CHAPTER 2

1. Glaeser and Vigdor 2012.
2. Iceland 2009; Timberlake and Iceland 2007.
3. We define metropolitan areas using the definitions described by the U.S. Office of Management and Budget in 2003. Our focus on the 331 metropolitan areas appearing in all four decennial censuses since 1980 omits the smallest, newest metropolitan areas that tend to have fairly low concentrations of minority groups. To maintain comparability of neighborhoods over time, we define neighborhoods using 2010 census tract boundaries and utilize census tract data distributed by Geolytics (2014).
4. The index of dissimilarity for two groups, blacks and whites in this example, is calculated as

$$D = 0.5\sum_{i=1}^{n}\left|\frac{w_i}{W_T} - \frac{b_i}{B_T}\right|,$$

where n is the number of tracts in the metropolitan area, w_i is the number of white residents in tract i, W_T is the total white population in the metropolitan area, b_i is the number of black residents in tract i, and B_T is the total black population in the metropolitan area. Despite its limitations, the index of dissimilarity is the most popular measure of residential segregation by race and tends to be highly correlated with other measures of segregation at the metropolitan level.
5. Massey and Denton 1993.
6. Holloway, Wright, and Ellis 2012; Lee, Iceland, and Farrell 2014; Parisi et al. 2015.
7. Between 1980 and 2010, there were 731 tracts that crossed above the 90 percent black threshold and 442 tracts that crossed above the 90 percent white threshold.
8. Scores and trends for these pan-ethnic groups hide a good deal of variation in the segregation experienced by more specific groups. For example,

among Latinos, Mexicans tend to be more highly segregated from whites than Cubans, and among Asians, Southeast Asian groups tend to be more segregated from whites than Japanese Americans in most metropolitan areas.

9. Geolytics 2014.
10. Census data in 1970 contain only rough racial categories.
11. Fasenfest, Booza, and Metzger 2004.
12. Among neighborhoods that were black-white in 1980, 8.6 percent were predominantly white in 2010. Fewer than 1 percent of all other types of tracts became predominantly white during this period.
13. Glaeser and Vigdor 2012.
14. Ibid.
15. Hwang and Sampson 2014.
16. The average percentage decline in the Latino-white dissimilarity index was 1.9 percent between 1980 and 2010, and the median was 2.1 percent.
17. Hall 2013; Lichter et al. 2010.
18. Table A2.1 provides a list of the metropolitan areas included in each type.
19. Across the 331 metropolitan areas, the average rate of black-white segregation decline was 21.96 percent between 1980 and 2010. In this first category, we also include the one metropolitan area—Blacksburg-Christiansburg-Radford, Virginia—in which the level of black-white segregation was already in the low range as of 1980.
20. Massey and Denton 1993.
21. Ibid.
22. Table A2.2 provides average population and housing market characteristics for metropolitan areas in each segregation type.
23. Charles, Dinwiddie, and Massey 2004; Massey et al. 2011.
24. Chetty et al. 2014a; Macartney, Bishaw, and Fontenot 2013.
25. Alexander 2012; Wakefield and Uggen 2010.
26. Adler and Stewart 2010; Kochanek, Arias, and Anderson 2013.
27. Adelman et al. 2001; Crowder and South 2003, 2011.
28. Kneebone and Holmes 2015.
29. Crowder and South 2008; Quillian 2003; Sharkey 2008.
30. Neild and Balfanz 2006; Sampson 2012; Wilson 1987.
31. Kneebone, Nadeau, and Berube 2011; Quillian 2012.
32. Massey and Denton 1993.
33. Logan 2011.
34. Firebaugh and Farrell 2015.
35. Peterson and Krivo 2010a, 33.
36. Sampson 2012.
37. Hall, Crowder, and Spring 2015; Baumer, Wolff, and Arnio 2012; Cui and Walsh 2015.
38. Hipp 2011.

39. Crowder and Downey 2010; Morello-Frosch and Lopez 2006.
40. Bower et al. 2014; Moore and Diez Roux 2006; Peterson and Krivo 2010a; Theall, Drury, and Shirtcliff 2012; Ko et al. 2014; White, Haas, and Williams 2012.
41. Williams 2012; Williams and Collins 2001.
42. Anthopolos et al. 2014; Gibbons and Yang 2014; Greer et al. 2014; Kershaw and Albrecht 2014; LaVeist, Gaskin, and Trujillo 2011; Morello-Frosch and Jesdale 2006; Nuru-Jeter and LaVeist 2011.
43. Yang and Matthews 2015.
44. Ananat 2011; Bayer, Ross, and Topa 2005; Boustan 2013.
45. Ananat 2011; De la Roca, Ellen, and O'Regan 2014; Thomas and Moye 2015.
46. Squires and Kubrin 2005.
47. Oliver and Shapiro 2006; Shapiro, Meschede, and Osoro 2013.
48. Hyra et al. 2013; Rugh and Massey 2010; Hall, Crowder, and Spring 2015.
49. Bayer, Ferreira, and Ross 2013; Bocian, Li, and Ernst 2010; Rugh 2015.
50. Baumer, Wolff, and Arnio 2012; Baxter and Lauria 2000; Capone and Metz 2003; Ellen, Lacoe, and Sharygin 2013; Teasdale, Clark, and Hinkle 2012; Wallace, Hedberg, and Katz 2012; Williams, Galster, and Verma 2014.
51. Shapiro, Meschede, and Osoro 2013.
52. Condron et al. 2013; Massey and Fischer 2006.
53. De la Roca, Ellen, and O'Regan 2014; Orfield and Frankenberg 2014; Orfield, Kucsera, and Siegel-Hawley 2012; Reardon and Owens 2014.
54. Ananat 2011; Card and Rothstein 2007; Quillian 2014. Much of this research shows that the effects of neighborhood context and metropolitan segregation persist even after accounting for residential selection processes and endogeneity of residential segregation.
55. Sharkey 2013.
56. Chetty et al. 2014b.
57. Anderson 2010.
58. Stiglitz 2012.
59. Carmichael and Kent 2014.
60. Dixon, Durrheim, and Tredoux 2005; Durrheim and Dixon 2013; Massey and Denton 1993; Sugrue 2014.
61. Rothwell 2012; Uslaner 2011; Gibbons 2015.
62. Alba and Logan 1993; Logan and Molotch 1987.
63. Alba and Logan 1993; Charles 2003.
64. Massey and Denton 1993; Roscigno, Karafin, and Tester 2009; Ross and Turner 2005; Squires 2007; Yinger 1995.
65. Charles 2006.
66. Clark 2009; Krysan and Bader 2007; Krysan and Farley 2002.
67. Charles 2006; Johnson, Farrell, and Guinn 1997; Wilson and Taub 2006.
68. Charles 2006; Krysan and Bader 2007; Krysan and Farley 2002.
69. For an exception, see Adelman 2005.

70. See, for example, Clark 2009.
71. Crowder, South, and Chavez 2006; Logan et al. 1996.
72. Sampson 2012.

CHAPTER 3

1. Clark 1982; Hempel 1970; Lake 1981.
2. Bruch and Feinberg 2017; Bruch and Swait 2014.
3. Bruch and Feinberg 2017; Bruch, Feinberg, and Lee 2016; Bruch and Swait 2014, 2017.
4. Bruch and Swait 2014; Cahill 1994; Clark and Flowerdew 1982; Clark and Smith 1979; Maclennan and Wood 1982; Talarchek 1982.
5. The decision on whether or not to search has also received attention in housing search research (see, for example, Smith et al. 1979). We focus primarily on the stages of the search related to the selection of residential destinations, since decisions made at these stages have the greatest potential for affecting residential attainment, not only for individuals but also for aggregate patterns of segregation.
6. Maclennan and Wood 1982.
7. Huff 1982.
8. Ibid.; Smith et al. 1979.
9. Although those from outside of the area may be something closer to a blank slate, as we will show, even these housing searchers often come with some knowledge.
10. Hempel 1970, 58.
11. Ibid., 164.
12. Krysan and Bader 2009.
13. Huff 1982; Smith et al. 1979, 9; Talarchek 1982; Maclennan and Wood 1982; Hempel 1970.
14. Holme 2002; Lareau 2014; Weininger 2014.
15. Maclennan and Wood 1982, 151.
16. Ibid., 152.
17. Clark and Flowerdew 1982, 10.
18. Bruch and Feinberg 2017; Bruch, Feinberg, and Lee 2016; Bruch and Swait 2017; DeLuca and Rosenbaum 2003.
19. Bruch and Swait 2017.
20. Bruch, Feinberg, and Lee 2016; Bruch and Swait 2017.
21. Lareau 2014.
22. Gigerenzer and Gaissmaier 2011. For a relevant elaboration of the model, although one outside the realm of housing searches, see Bruch, Feinberg, and Lee 2016.

23. Ibid., 454.
24. Gigerenzer, Czerlinski, and Martignon 1999.
25. Maclennan and Wood 1982; Cahill 1994; Talarchek 1982; Clark and Smith 1979; Clark and Flowerdew 1982; Bruch and Swait 2014.
26. Farley, Krysan, and Couper 2004.
27. The demographics of the respondents were as follows: There were more female (64 percent) than male (36 percent) participants, but in terms of race-ethnicity, renter/owner status, and residence, the sample was evenly divided with eight white, eight black, and nine Latino participants; thirteen owners and twelve renters; and thirteen city residents and twelve suburbanites. The ages of the participants were not systematically gathered, but all were over twenty-five years old, with participants in their twenties, thirties, forties, and fifties. The names used here are pseudonyms.
28. See Krysan et al. 2009.
29. The demographics of the respondents were as follows: There were more female (58 percent) than male (42 percent) participants, but in terms of race-ethnicity, renter/owner status, and residence, the sample was fairly evenly divided: there were eight white, eight black, and eight Latino participants; eleven owners and thirteen renters; and eleven city residents and thirteen suburbanites. The age of the participants ranged from twenty-six to fifty-six, with an average age of thirty-nine years. The names used here are pseudonyms.
30. In the earlier in-depth interviews and focus groups, we relied on fliers distributed in public places and on newspaper ads. In the 2012 study, we used only Craigslist ads.
31. Park 1950; Park, Burgess, and McKenzie 1984.
32. Fowler, Lee, and Matthews 2016.
33. Crowder, Pais, and South 2012.

CHAPTER 4

1. Hempel 1970, 76–77.
2. Ibid., 79.
3. Maclennan and Wood 1982.
4. Unfortunately, the question did not specify the capacity in which searchers used their social networks during their searches. Fifteen percent said that "friends/relatives" were the most important resource in their search. So we cannot be sure whether searchers used their networks to suggest places to search (stage 1) or whether their networks provided actual leads on housing units (stage 2).
5. Talarchek 1982.

6. The most common information source for these features was "previous knowledge of the environment," a finding we consider in more detail in chapter 5.

7. Talarchek 1982.

8. Among respondents in the 2011 and 2013 AHS Recent Mover module, 39 percent of non-Latino blacks and 38 percent of Latinos reported finding their new unit by word of mouth. Interestingly, this percentage is very similar to the share reported by John Goodman (1978) in studies of housing markets in Indiana and Arizona in the mid-1970s: about one-third of home-buyers and renters found their new unit through "friends and relatives."

9. Kimelberg 2014; Pattillo, Delale-O'Connor, and Butts 2014; Weininger 2014.

10. Goodman 1978; Huff 1982.

11. McCarthy 1982.

12. Krysan 2008.

13. Spring et al., forthcoming.

14. Ibid.

15. For a review, see McPherson, Smith-Lovin, and Cook 2001.

16. Ibid.; Smith, McPherson, and Smith-Lovin 2014.

17. Owing to the sampling structure of the PSID, we do not have complete kin networks for both members of married-couple families. Thus, we have a more complete kin network for the spouse connected to a PSID core family than for the spouse who married into a PSID family. In these cases, we use the kin network of the PSID core family member to represent the network for the entire household. Whether the network is that of the male or female spouse in married-couple families is essentially random, but to be sure, we include a control for whether the kin network is that of a male or female. PSID kin networks are also limited to kin who met the rules for being followed by the PSID and who were available for interviews and not lost to follow-up. Therefore, we do not claim to represent individuals' or households' entire kin networks. Despite these limitations, our detailed data on kin relationships and the geographic location of kin go beyond any measures contained in other large-scale studies of residential mobility. Furthermore, it is unlikely that the omission of some kin is systematic in ways that would bias our results. We restrict our measures of kin location to kin who maintain a separate household from the respondent, according to year-specific family identification variables in the PSID. This restriction ensures that our kin measures do not include members of the same household (parents and children, spouses, and so on) who are likely to make joint mobility decisions.

18. Just over 24 percent of PSID householders moved to a different census tract between biennial interviews in the years 1997 to 2013.

19. We found that these associations between the composition of destination tracts and the average composition of kin tracts are slightly stronger in

metropolitan areas with higher levels of segregation, like Chicago, than in metropolitan areas with lower levels of segregation.

20. Sociodemographic controls include the education, age, marital status, and gender of the household head as well as annual family income, wealth, housing tenure, and number of children in the family.

CHAPTER 5

1. Talarchek 1982.
2. This is a reference to Chicago's street numbering system: "00" is the beginning point- the corner of Madison and State street in downtown Chicago.
3. These distances are calculated as the linear distance between centroids of census tracts of origin and destination for mobile PSID householders between 1997 and 2013. As such, this is likely to be a liberal estimate of the average distance moved. For those moving from the edge of one census tract to the adjoining edge of the neighboring tract—moving across the street or to the next block, for example—the distance between tract centroids would drastically overestimate the distance moved.
4. Jones and Pebley 2014.
5. Ibid.; Palmer 2013; Silm and Ahas 2014; Wong and Shaw 2011.
6. Jones and Pebley 2014.
7. Ibid.
8. The average percentage own group in the tract of origin for mobile PSID respondents in the years after 1997 is 70.8 percent, and it is especially high (83.1 percentage) for white movers. The average percentage own group in the tract of destination is just slightly below that in origin neighborhoods, at 70.6 percent.
9. Britton and Goldsmith 2013; Sampson and Sharkey 2008; Sharkey 2013.
10. Very similar results are observed in models predicting neighborhood diversity.
11. All adult residential observations are for years in which the individual had established a separate household from her or his parents and was between the ages of nineteen and fifty-four. Because the longitudinal PSID contains multiple adult observations per individual, and these individuals are clustered within metropolitan areas, we utilize a multilevel modeling strategy. We focus on black and white respondents because the PSID data contain so few members of other groups who were observed throughout adolescence as well as in adulthood. For efficiency of presentation, we show in table 5.1 just those coefficients from these complex models that are most substantively important.
12. The constant in this model is 83.898, indicating that, during the average year of adulthood, white householders live in neighborhoods in which 84 percent of their neighbors are white.

13. Becker 1962; Schultz 1961; Ross and Mirowsky 2010; Mirowsky and Ross 2007.
14. Darrah and DeLuca 2014.
15. Ibid., 363–64.

CHAPTER 6

1. Krysan and Bader 2009.
2. Rosenblatt and DeLuca 2012; Wood 2014.
3. Rosenblatt and DeLuca 2012, 271.
4. Krysan and Bader 2007; Bader and Krysan 2015.
5. Goldstein and Gigerenzer 1999.
6. Ibid.
7. Weininger 2014.
8. See, for example, Ettema and Peer 1996; Martin 2000. On communities' prospects for the future, see Lindgren 2009.
9. Entman 1990, 1992; Gilliam et al. 1996; Gilliam and Iyengar 2000.
10. Klite, Bardwell, and Salzman 1997.
11. Lindgren 2009.
12. For example, Ettema and Peer 1996; Martin 2000.
13. Lindgren 2009.
14. Tukachinsky, Mastro, and Yarchi 2015.
15. Matei, Ball-Rokeach, and Qiu 2001, 455.
16. Ibid., 454.
17. Bruch and Swait 2017.
18. Krysan and Bader 2007; Bader and Krysan 2015.
19. Talarchek 1982.
20. Ibid., 37.
21. Bruch and Swait 2017, 9 (emphasis in original).
22. Talarchek 1982; Bruch and Swait 2017.
23. Talarchek 1982, 40.
24. Bruch and Feinberg 2017; Bruch and Swait 2014, 2017; Bruch, Feinberg, and Lee 2016.
25. Gigerenzer and Goldstein 1999, 76.
26. Ibid., 82.
27. Bruch and Feinberg 2017.
28. Ibid.
29. We appreciate the suggestion of a reviewer of an earlier draft of this manuscript that pointed us to this specific heuristic.
30. Krysan et al. 2009.
31. Krysan, Farley, and Couper 2008.
32. Bonam, Bergsieker, and Eberhardt 2016, 1566.

33. Quillian and Pager 2010, 98–99.
34. Quillian and Pager 2001, 721.
35. Ibid., 749.
36. Krysan and Bader 2007; Bader and Krysan 2015.
37. Krysan and Bader 2007.
38. Bader and Krysan 2015.
39. Bruch and Swait 2017; Bruch and Feinberg 2017.

CHAPTER 7

1. Park 1950; Park, Burgess, and McKenzie 1984.
2. Alba and Logan 1993; Logan and Molotch 1987.
3. Alba and Logan 1993; Charles 2003; Logan et al. 1996.
4. Farley and Frey 1994; Logan, Stults, and Farley 2004.
5. The association between the metropolitan black-white income ratio and seg-regation is diminished but remains statistically significant with controls for: total population in the metropolitan area; the proportion black in the popu-lation; the concentration of local workers employed in manufacturing and government occupations; the concentration of retirees in the metropolitan area; characteristics of the housing market, including the vacancy rate, the concentration of renter-occupied housing units, and the proportion of units built since 1980; the age of the metropolitan area, as measured by the period in which the central city first exceeded 50,000 in population; and the region in which the metropolitan area is located.
6. Compare to Iceland and Wilkes 2006.
7. Spivak, Bass, and St. John 2011.
8. Here we include households that moved to a different neighborhood and those that moved to a different unit within the same neighborhood since both types of move have implications for the maintenance of residential stratification.
9. Supplemental analyses indicate that the effects of socioeconomic characteris-tics on mobility destinations are similar across different types of segregation regimes, although the effect of income on neighborhood destinations appears to be slightly more pronounced in metropolitan areas that have remained moderately segregated than in either fast-changing metropolitan areas or those that have remained highly segregated for decades.
10. Crowder, South, and Chavez 2006.
11. Bayer, McMillan, and Rueben 2004; Harsman and Quigley 1995; Ihlanfeldt and Scafidi 2002; Jargowsky 2013.
12. The coefficient of determination (R^2) for an OLS model predicting black-white segregation (D_i) in 2010 as a function of the black-white income ratio in 2010 (see figure 7.1) is 0.1515.

13. Hempel 1970.
14. Talarchek 1982.
15. Krysan, Farley, and Couper 2008.
16. Crowder and South 2005; Pattillo-McCoy 1999.
17. Massey and Denton 1993.
18. Desmond 2016.
19. The first quintile for recent movers in the AHS includes those in families with incomes of $11,712 and below. Minimum income values for other quintiles are $11,713 for the second, $24,998 for the third, $42,002 for the fourth, and $74,967 for the fifth.
20. These differences between the highest income category and the lowest two income categories in the probability of involuntary movement are statistically significant ($p < 0.000$).
21. Crowder 2000; Desmond 2016; Hall, Crowder, and Spring 2015.
22. Income differences in the use of word of mouth and the use of online resources are statistically significant and remain so even after controlling for gender, age, race, and family composition. These income variations do not differ significantly across metropolitan areas with different historical patterns of segregation.
23. Both education and income are statistically significant predictors of the reasons for ending the search and remain so after controlling for other individual- and household-level characteristics related to housing processes.
24. Rhodes and DeLuca 2014, 161.
25. Rosenblatt and DeLuca 2012.
26. Ibid., 256, 274.
27. Darrah and DeLuca 2014.
28. Rhodes and DeLuca 2014.
29. Crowder 2000; Desmond 2016. About 58 percent of white recent movers in the AHS reported that they stopped looking for housing because they were happy with the unit they found, compared to 47 and 49 percent, respectively, for black and Latino recent movers. Similarly, whereas about 13 percent of whites reported stopping their search because they had to move quickly, 17 percent of blacks and 16 percent of Latinos reported this kind of desperation decision. And in comparison to white recent movers, black and Latino recent movers were more likely to report that they could find no other options. Specifically, just under 0.9 percent of whites, 2.2 percent of blacks, and 3 percent of Latinos reported that they stopped searching because they knew of no other housing options.
30. Among recent movers in the 2011 and 2013 AHS, about 39 percent of black householders and 38 percent of Latino householders found their new unit through word of mouth, compared to 28 percent of white householders. Similarly, in comparison to white movers (8 percent), higher percentages of black (10 percent) and Latino (14 percent) movers found their unit by seeing a sign.

In contrast, whites (28 percent) were much more likely than either blacks (15 percent) or Latinos (17 percent) to find their unit online. All of these differences are greatly attenuated and become statistically nonsignificant after controlling for income, education, and housing tenure.

CHAPTER 8

1. Farley et al. 1978; Farley et al. 1994; Farley 2011.
2. Farley 2011.
3. Farley et al. 1978; Farley et al. 1994; Krysan and Bader 2007.
4. Farley et al. 1994; Krysan and Bader 2007.
5. Bobo and Zubrinsky 1996.
6. Ibid.
7. Ibid.
8. Charles 2000, 2003, 2006.
9. Charles 2000.
10. Charles 2003.
11. Krysan, Carter, and van Londen 2016.
12. The CAS was part of a two-city study that included the Detroit Area Study, and respondents were given the option to populate their ideal neighborhood with not only whites, blacks, Latinos, and Asians but also Arab Americans owing to the large Arab American population in the Detroit metropolitan area.
13. Krysan, Carter and van Londen 2016.
14. Schelling 1971.
15. Clark 1991; Fossett 2006.
16. Bruch and Mare 2006.
17. Bobo et al. 2000.
18. Ihlanfeldt and Scafidi 2002.
19. Ibid.
20. Freeman 2000.
21. Adelman 2005, 226.
22. In this discussion of how the traditional drivers of segregation are not mutually exclusive, we focus on whites and the difficulty of disentangling race from class perceptions. In chapter 9, we make a similar argument about how inextricably linked black racial residential preferences are with another driver of segregation: perceptions of discrimination. Although black preferences may also be connected to perceptions of social class characteristics, existing studies suggest that the link is weaker and that the more salient issue relates to perceptions of discrimination.
23. Bobo and Zubrinsky 1996; Charles 2006; Harris 1999, 2001; Krysan et al. 2009; Taub, Taylor, and Dunham 1984.
24. Harris 1999, 2001; Taub, Taylor, and Dunham 1984.
25. Harris 1999, 2001.
26. Crowder 2000; Crowder and South 2008; Swaroop and Krysan 2011.

27. Emerson, Yancey, and Chai 2001; Krysan et al. 2009; Lewis, Emerson, and Klineberg 2011.
28. Krysan, Farley, and Couper 2008; Quillian and Pager 2010.
29. Krysan, Farley, and Couper 2008, 20.
30. Although in-depth interview participants of all races could recite a set of correlated neighborhood characteristics, the connection between neighborhood racial composition and social class characteristics tended to be more nuanced for black and Latino respondents than for white respondents. Blacks and Latinos in our in-depth interviews had a more disaggregated picture of how race and class are connected, perhaps because they were generally more experienced with, and exposed to, neighborhoods with higher percentages of Latinos or African Americans. Armed with this knowledge, blacks and Latinos recognize more subtle differences between neighborhoods that are similar on some features, and so they may assume a weaker correlation between the race- and class-related characteristics of neighborhoods. As a result, the assumption of correlated characteristics probably has a stronger connection to the construction of whites' consideration sets than to the consideration sets of African Americans and Latinos. Our evidence is only suggestive on this point; studies that explore this question in more detail are needed to establish its validity.
31. Quillian and Pager 2010.
32. Darrah and DeLuca 2014; DeLuca and Rosenbaum 2003, 335.
33. Havekes, Bader, and Krysan 2016.
34. This table is a modified version of "Percentage (Mis)match Between Percentage Own Racial/Ethnic Group in Ideal Neighborhood, Search Locations, and Current Neighborhood by Race/Ethnicity" by Esther Havekes, Michael Bader, and Maria Krysan, licensed under Creative Commons Attribution 4.0 International License (http://creativecommons.org/licenses/by/4.0/).
35. Darrah and DeLuca 2014.
36. Ibid.; Rosenblatt and DeLuca 2012.
37. Bruch and Swait 2017; Bruch and Feinberg 2017.
38. Hempel 1970.
39. Bruch and Swait 2017; Bruch and Feinberg 2017.
40. Hempel 1970, 131.
41. Ibid., 130.
42. Ibid.
43. Ibid., 134.
44. Bruch and Swait 2017.
45. Krysan and Bader 2007; Bader and Krysan 2015.
46. Adelman 2005; Havekes, Bader, and Krysan 2016.
47. In 2010, Maywood was 74.4 percent black and 12.6 percent white; Bellwood was 75.5 percent black and 13.9 percent white; and Hinsdale was 1.3 percent black and 90 percent white.
48. Hempel 1970.
49. Havekes, Bader, and Krysan 2016.

CHAPTER 9

1. For one such criticism, see Heckman 1998.
2. Turner et al. 2013.
3. Ibid.
4. Purnell, Idsardi, and Baugh 1999; Massey and Lundy 2001.
5. Squires and Chadwick 2006.
6. Ewens, Tomlin, and Wang 2014.
7. Hanson and Hawley 2011.
8. Yinger 1995.
9. Ross et al. 2008; Ross and Yinger 2002. For an example of the latter, see Munnell et al. 1992.
10. Pager and Shepherd 2008.
11. This is consistent with the distinction made by Vincent Roscigno, Diane Karafin, and Griff Tester (2009) between non-exclusionary and exclusionary discrimination: discrimination can be reflected in either denial of access (to a unit or a mortgage) or treatment that makes the conditions of a unit or mortgage different based on race-ethnicity.
12. Apgar, Calder, and Fauth 2004; Williams, Nesiba, and McConnell 2005.
13. Anacker and Carr 2011; Rugh, Albright, and Massey 2015; Rugh and Massey 2010.
14. Williams, Nesiba, and McConnell 2005, 182.
15. Anacker and Carr 2011; Rugh, Albright, and Massey 2015; Rugh and Massey 2010; Williams, Nesiba, and McConnell 2005.
16. Roscigno et al. 2009, 52.
17. Ibid.
18. Ibid.
19. Ondrich, Stricker, and Yinger 1999.
20. Hanson and Hawley 2011.
21. Ondrich, Ross, and Yinger 2003.
22. Fischer and Massey 2004, 231 (emphasis in original).
23. Galster and Godfrey 2005.
24. Ibid., 258.
25. Rosen 2014, 335.
26. Ibid., 333 (emphasis in original).
27. Galster and Keeney 1988.
28. South and Crowder 1998.
29. Lake 1981.
30. Clark 1991; Patterson 1997; Thernstrom and Thernstrom 1997.
31. Charles 2006; Krysan and Farley 2002; Krysan, Carter, and von Londen 2016.
32. Roscigno et al. 2009.

33. Krysan and Farley 2002.
34. Turner et al. 2013; Roscigno et al. 2009; Yinger 1995.
35. Here and throughout, it is important to clarify that we cannot be certain that the bad treatment was due to racial-ethnic discrimination. As we focus on whether or not the expectation of discrimination had the intended effect, the important point is that this is how bad treatment was perceived by the searcher.
36. Kwate et al. 2013.
37. Silverman 2011.
38. Note that much of our argument about the impact of social class on discrimination relies on studies of African Americans; few studies of Latinos (of this sort) have been conducted, and so we cannot draw conclusions about the processes for Latinos. We would expect, however, that there are similarities.
39. Page 1995.
40. Massey and Lundy 2001.
41. Hanson and Hawley 2011.
42. Williams, Nesiba, and McConnell 2005.
43. Rugh and Massey 2010.
44. Bocian et al. 2011; Immergluck and Wiles 1999.
45. Rugh, Albright, and Massey 2015, 190; Anacker and Carr 2011; Anacker, Carr, and Pradhan 2012; see also Brown, Webb, and Chung 2013.
46. Rugh, Albright, and Massey 2015, 206.
47. Ondrich, Ross, and Yinger 2003; Page 1995.
48. Quillian 2006. Other forms of statistical discrimination rely on assumptions about preferences. For example, real estate agents may assume that black clients prefer to live in racially mixed neighborhoods and steer their clients to such places. Or they may steer black clients away from whiter neighborhoods because they make assumptions about the preferences of existing white residents. There is plenty of historical evidence of this form of statistical discrimination, though more recent experimental studies show stronger support for a form of statistical discrimination that relies on assumptions about the financial capacity of black and Latino clients (Zhao 2005; Page 1995).
49. Ondrich, Ross, and Yinger 2003.
50. Ibid., 870.
51. Feagin and Sikes 1994; Lacy 2007.

CHAPTER 10

1. Apel 2014; Eligon 2015; Rothstein 2014, 2017.
2. Kerner Commission 1968.
3. Eligon 2015.
4. Ibid.
5. U.S. Department of Housing and Urban Development, n.d. (authors' emphasis).

6. Eligon 2015.
7. In the 1990s, HUD funded a large-scale randomized social experiment in Baltimore, Boston, Chicago, Los Angeles, and New York City to determine if voucher holders who moved to opportunity areas fared better than their counterparts who did not. The results of this Moving To Opportunity (MTO) demonstration project were mixed and depended on the age of the child who moved as well as the outcome of interest. (Employment outcomes were not largely affected, but health and happiness were.) Nevertheless, an important lesson learned from this experiment was the difficulty of intervening in the search process to ensure that individuals moved into opportunity areas—and stayed there when they did. In addition, Patrick Sharkey (2012) reports that the experimental group in Chicago was no more likely to move to a high-opportunity area than the control group. Another striking finding is that the high-opportunity moves often did not stick—one or two years after the initial move, the voucher holders often ended up living back in the kinds of high-poverty neighborhoods they were living in before they received a voucher (Turner et al. 2011). Although the goal of improving the neighborhoods in which voucher holders live is only minimally incorporated into the priorities of the traditional HCV, it is a core focus of so-called mobility programs. Often an outcome of lawsuits against HUD (for example, *Walker v. HUD* in Dallas and *Thompson v. HUD* in Baltimore), mobility programs have at their core the goal of assisting voucher holders in making a move into a community that offers better opportunities. There is evidence that housing voucher holders make moves that maintain segregation. For example, Kirk McClure (2008) reports that voucher holders and equally disadvantaged non-voucher holders lived in low-poverty neighborhoods at about the same levels (about one-quarter). Moreover, McClure finds that black and Hispanic HCV participants were less likely than white participants to reside in low-poverty areas.
8. DeLuca and Rosenbaum 2003; Rosenblatt and DeLuca 2012.
9. Badger 2015.
10. Maly 2008.
11. In the 1960s, Oak Park was facing the prospect of white flight and racial turnover, which had begun to occur in the bordering Chicago neighborhood of Austin. Today Oak Park is racially integrated (22 percent African American, 7 percent Latino, and 68 percent white), while neighboring Austin is 85 percent black. Staving off racial turnover was the outcome of a series of deliberate actions by advocates and local officials that are chronicled in Carole Goodwin's (1979) excellent analysis and description.
12. Maly 2008, 222.
13. See the South Orange–Maplewood Community Coalition on Race website at: www.twotowns.org; and City of Shaker Heights, "Moving to Shaker,"

at: http://www.shakeronline.com/city-services/moving-to-shaker (accessed August 28, 2017).

14. Berdahl-Baldwin 2015.
15. Engdahl 2009, 16.
16. Darrah and DeLuca 2014, 363.
17. Rosen 2014; DeLuca and Rosenbaum 2003; Rosenblatt and DeLuca 2012.
18. DeLuca and Rosenbaum 2003, 336.
19. Darrah and DeLuca 2014, 373–74.
20. Ibid.
21. Rosen 2014.
22. Ibid., 333.
23. Darrah and DeLuca 2014.
24. Fischer 2009.
25. Ibid., 8.
26. Bruch and Swait 2017; Bruch and Feinberg 2017; Gigerenzer, Todd, and ABC Research Group 1999.
27. Orfield 2005, 149.
28. Ibid., 150.
29. Nyden, Maly, and Lukehart 1997.
30. Orfield 2005, 152.
31. In the interest of full disclosure, Maria Krysan has served as an unpaid member of the Board of Directors of the OPRHC since 2004.
32. Jargowsky 2015.
33. Goodwin 1979.
34. Village of Oak Park, "Village Services: Housing Programs," available at: http://www.oak-park.us/village-services/housing-programs (accessed August 28, 2017).
35. South Orange–Maplewood Community Coalition on Race, "Why Integration?" available at: http://www.twotowns.org/neighborhoods/home-maintenance-loan-program/ (accessed August 28, 2017).
36. O'Sullivan and Brunner 2015.
37. Talarchek 1982.
38. Pendall 2000, 125.
39. Massey and Rothwell 2009; Pendall 2000.
40. Massey and Rothwell 2009.
41. Jacobus 2015, 7.
42. For a detailed history, see Massey et al. 2013.
43. Ibid.
44. Orfield 2005; Roisman 2001.
45. Orfield 2005.
46. Ibid., 130.
47. Roisman 2001.

48. Ibid., 107–8.
49. Orfied 2005, 141.
50. *Texas Department of Housing and Community Affairs et al. v. Inclusive Communities Project, Inc. et al.*, 135 S. Ct. 2507 (2015).
51. Turner et al. 2013.
52. Rosen 2014.
53. Ibid., 310.
54. Ibid.
55. Ibid.
56. Desmond 2016.
57. Oak Park Regional Housing Center, "Looking for the Best Apartments in Oak Park? Start at the Oak Park Regional Housing Center," available at: www.liveinoakpark.com (accessed August 28, 2017).
58. Scott et al. 2013.
59. Darrah and DeLuca 2014.
60. Rosenblatt and DeLuca 2012, 275.
61. Rosen 2014.
62. See Poverty and Race Research Action Council 2013.
63. Mock 2015, 1–3.
64. Schwartz 2014.
65. Darrah and DeLuca 2014, 375.

CHAPTER 11

1. Britton and Goldsmith 2013; Sharkey 2013.
2. Krysan and Bader 2009.
3. Quillian and Pager 2001; Sampson and Raudenbush 2004.
4. Bruch and Mare 2012; Quillian 2015.
5. Browning, Cagney, and Boettner 2016; Cagney et al. 2013; Krivo et al. 2013; Browning and Soller 2014.
6. Berkowitz 2013; Cotterell 2013.
7. Sharkey 2013.
8. Hedman and van Ham 2012.
9. Firebaugh and Farrell 2015.
10. Boardman and Saint Onge 2005; Crowder and South 2011.
11. Aud, Fox, and KewalRamani 2010; Berg et al. 2013; Bottiani, Bradshaw, and Mendelson 2016; Massey 2007.
12. Crowder and South 2003, 2011; Leventhal, Dupéré, and Shuey 2014; Nieuwenhuis and Hooimeijer 2016; Rumberger and Lim 2008; Wodtke, Harding, and Elwert 2011; Quillian 2014; Lewis and Diamond 2015.
13. Condron et al. 2013.
14. Ananat 2011; Bayer, Ross, and Topa 2005; Boustan 2013.

15. Shapiro, Meschede, and Osoro 2013.
16. Thomas et al. 2014.
17. Denton 2000; Shapiro, Meschede, and Osoro 2014; Ananat 2011; de la Roca, Ellen, and O'Regan 2014; Thomas and Moye 2015.
18. Sampson and Sharkey 2008; Sharkey 2008, 2013.
19. Chetty et al. 2014a.
20. Logan, Stults, and Farley 2004.
21. Crowder and South 2005; Quillian 2002; South, Crowder, and Pais 2011.
22. Pettigrew and Tropp 2006; Sigelman and Welch 1993.
23. Charles 2006.
24. Sampson 2012.
25. *Texas Department of Housing and Community Affairs et al. v. Inclusive Communities Project, Inc. et al.*, 135 S. Ct. 2507 (2015), 24.

References

Adelman, Robert M. 2005. "The Roles of Race, Class, and Residential Preferences in the Neighborhood Racial Composition of Middle-Class Blacks and Whites." *Social Science Quarterly* 86(1): 209–28.

Adelman, Robert M., Hui-shien Tsao, Stewart E. Tolnay, and Kyle D. Crowder. 2001. "Neighborhood Disadvantage Among Racial and Ethnic Groups." *Sociological Quarterly* 42(4): 603–32.

Adler, Nancy E., and Judith Stewart. 2010. "Health Disparities Across the Lifespan: Meaning, Methods, and Mechanisms." *Annals of the New York Academy of Sciences* 1186(1): 5–23.

Alba, Richard D., and John R. Logan. 1993. "Minority Proximity to Whites in Suburbs: An Individual-Level Analysis of Segregation." *American Journal of Sociology* 98(6): 1388–1427.

Alexander, Michelle. 2012. *The New Jim Crow: Mass Incarceration in the Age of Colorblindness.* New York: New Press.

Anacker, Katrin B., and James H. Carr. 2011. "Analysing Determinants of Foreclosure Among High-Income African-American and Hispanic Borrowers in the Washington, D.C., Metropolitan Area." *International Journal of Housing Policy* 11(2): 195–220.

Anacker, Katrin B., James H. Carr, and Archana Pradhan. 2012. "Analyzing Foreclosures Among High-Income Black/African American and Hispanic/Latino Borrowers in Prince George's County, Maryland." *Housing and Society* 39(1): 1–28.

Ananat, Elizabeth Oltmans. 2011. "The Wrong Side(s) of the Tracks: The Causal Effects of Racial Segregation on Urban Poverty and Inequality." *American Economic Journal: Applied Economics* 3(2): 34–66.

Anderson, Elizabeth. 2010. *The Imperative of Integration.* Princeton, N.J.: Princeton University Press.

Anthopolos, Rebecca, Jay S. Kaufman, Lynne C. Messer, and Marie Lynn Miranda. 2014. "Racial Residential Segregation and Preterm Birth: Built Environment as a Mediator." *Epidemiology* 25(3): 397–405.

Apel, Dora. 2014. " 'Hands Up, Don't Shoot': Surrendering to Liberal Illusions." *Theory and Event* 17(3). Available at: https://muse.jhu.edu/article/559367 (accessed March 22, 2016).

Apgar, William C., Allegra Calder, and Gary Fauth. 2004. "Credit, Capital, and Communities: The Implications of the Changing Mortgage Banking Industry for Community Based Organizations."Cambridge, Mass.: Joint Center for Housing Studies, Harvard University.

Aud, Susan, Mary Ann Fox, and Angelina KewalRamani. 2010. *Status and Trends in the Education of Racial and Ethnic Groups.* Washington: U.S. Department of Education.

Bader, Michael D. M., and Maria Krysan. 2015. "Community Attraction and Avoidance in Chicago: What's Race Got to Do with It?" *Annals of the American Academy of Political and Social Science* 660(1): 261–81.

Badger, Emily. 2015. "Obama Administration to Unveil Major New Rules Targeting Segregation Across U.S." *Washington Post,* July 8.

Baumer, Eric P., Kevin T. Wolff, and Ashley N. Arnio. 2012. "A Multicity Neighborhood Analysis of Foreclosure and Crime." *Social Science Quarterly* 93(3): 577–601.

Baxter, Vern, and Mickey Lauria. 2000. "Residential Mortgage Foreclosure and Neighborhood Change." *Housing Policy Debate* 11(3): 675–99.

Bayer, Patrick, Fernando Ferreira, and Stephen L. Ross. 2013. "The Vulnerability of Minority Homeowners in the Housing Boom and Bust." Working Paper 19020. Cambridge, Mass.: National Bureau of Economic Research (May). Available at: http://www.nber.org/papers/w19020 (accessed March 22, 2016).

Bayer, Patrick, Robert McMillan, and Kim S. Rueben. 2004. "What Drives Racial Segregation? New Evidence Using Census Microdata." *Journal of Urban Economics* 56(3): 514–35.

Bayer, Patrick, Stephen Ross, and Giorgio Topa. 2005. "Place of Work and Place of Residence: Informal Hiring Networks and Labor Market Outcomes." Working Paper 11019. Cambridge, Mass.: National Bureau of Economic Research (January). Available at: http://www.nber.org/papers/w11019 (accessed February 21, 2016).

Becker, Gary S. 1962. "Investment in Human Capital: A Theoretical Analysis." *Journal of Political Economy* 70(5): 9–49.

Berdahl-Baldwin, Audrey. 2015. "Housing Mobility Programs in the United States 2015." Washington, D.C.: PRRAC. Available at: http://prrac.org/pdf/HousingMobilityProgramsInTheUS2015.pdf (accessed August 18, 2017).

Berg, Mark T., Eric A. Stewart, Endya Stewart, and Ronald L. Simons. 2013. "A Multilevel Examination of Neighborhood Social Processes and College Enrollment." *Social Problems* 60(4): 513–34.

Berkowitz, Stephen David. 2013. *An Introduction to Structural Analysis: The Network Approach to Social Research.* Burlington, Vt.: Elsevier.

Boardman, Jason D., and Jarron M. Saint Onge. 2005. "Neighborhoods and Adolescent Development." *Children, Youth, and Environments* 15(1): 138–64.

Bobo, Lawrence, James Johnson, Melvin Oliver, Reynolds Farley, Barry Bluestone, Irene Browne, Sheldon Danziger, Gary Green, Harry Holzer, Maria Krysan, Michael Massagli, and Camille Zubrinsky Charles. 2000. *Multi-City Study of Urban Inequality, 1992–1994: Household Survey Data (3rd ICPSR Version)*. Ann Arbor: University of Michigan, Inter-University Consortium for Political and Social Research.

Bobo, Lawrence, and Camille L. Zubrinsky. 1996. "Attitudes on Residential Integration: Perceived Status Differences, Mere In-Group Preference, or Racial Prejudice?" *Social Forces* 74(3): 883–909.

Bocian, Debbie Gruenstein, Wei Li, and Keith S. Ernst. 2010. "Foreclosures by Race and Ethnicity: The Demographics of a Crisis." Durham, N.C.: Center for Responsible Lending (June 18). Available at: http://www.responsiblelending.org/mortgage-lending/research-analysis/foreclosures-by-race-and-ethnicity.pdf (accessed March 22, 2016).

Bocian, Debbie Gruenstein, Wei Li, Carolina Reid, and Roberto G. Quercia. 2011. *Lost Ground, 2011: Disparities in Mortgage Lending and Foreclosures*. Durham, N.C.: Center for Responsible Lending (November). Available at: http://www.responsiblelending.org/mortgage-lending/research-analysis/Lost-Ground-2011.pdf (accessed March 20, 2016).

Bonam, Courtney M., Hilary B. Bergsieker, and Jennifer Eberhardt. 2016. "Polluting Black Space." *Journal of Experimental Psychology: General* 145(11): 1561–82.

Bottiani, Jessika H., Catherine P. Bradshaw, and Tamar Mendelson. 2016. "Inequality in Black and White High School Students' Perceptions of School Support: An Examination of Race in Context." *Journal of Youth and Adolescence* 45(6): 1–16.

Boustan, Leah Platt. 2013. "Racial Residential Segregation in American Cities." Working Paper 19045. Cambridge, Mass.: National Bureau of Economic Research (May). Available at: http://www.nber.org/papers/w19045 (accessed March 16, 2016).

Bower, Kelly M., Roland J. Thorpe, Charles Rohde, and Darrell J. Gaskin. 2014. "The Intersection of Neighborhood Racial Segregation, Poverty, and Urbanicity and Its Impact on Food Store Availability in the United States." *Preventive Medicine* 58(1): 33–39.

Britton, Marcus L., and Pat Rubio Goldsmith. 2013. "Keeping People in Their Place? Young-Adult Mobility and Persistence of Residential Segregation in U.S. Metropolitan Areas." *Urban Studies* 50(14): 2886–2903.

Brown, Lawrence A., Michael D. Webb, and Su-Yeul Chung. 2013. "Housing Foreclosure as a Geographically Contingent Event: Columbus Ohio 2003–2007." *Urban Geography* 34(6): 764–94.

Browning, Christopher R., Kathleen A. Cagney, and Bethany Boettner. 2016. "Neighborhood, Place, and the Life Course." In *Handbook of the Life Course,* edited by Michael J. Shanahan, Jeylan T. Mortimer, and Monica Kirkpatrick Johnson. London: Springer.

Browning, Christopher R., and Brian Soller. 2014. "Moving Beyond Neighborhood: Activity Spaces and Ecological Networks as Contexts for Youth Development." *Cityscape* 16(1): 165–96.

Bruch, Elizabeth E., and Fred Feinberg. 2017. "Decision Making Processes in Social Contexts." *Annual Review of Sociology* 43: 207–27.

Bruch, Elizabeth, Fred Feinberg, and Kee Yeun Lee. 2016. "Extracting Multistage Screening Rules from Online Dating Activity Data." *Proceedings of the National Academy of Sciences of the United States of America* 113(38): 10530–35.

Bruch, Elizabeth E., and Robert D. Mare. 2006. "Neighborhood Choice and Neighborhood Change." *American Journal of Sociology* 112(3): 667–709.

———. 2012. "Methodological Issues in the Analysis of Residential Preferences, Residential Mobility, and Neighborhood Change." *Sociological Methodology* 42(1): 103–54.

Bruch, Elizabeth E., and Joffre Swait. 2014. "All Things Considered? Cognitively Plausible Models of Neighborhood Choice." Paper presented to the annual meetings of the Population Association of America. Boston (May 1–3).

———. 2017. "All Things Considered? How Decision Strategies Shape Neighborhood Sorting." Unpublished manuscript. Ann Arbor: University of Michigan.

Cagney, Kathleen A., Christopher R. Browning, Aubrey L. Jackson, and Brian Soller. 2013. "Networks, Neighborhoods, and Institutions: An Integrated 'Activity Space' Approach for Research on Aging." In *New Directions in the Sociology of Aging,* edited by Linda J. Waite and Thomas J. Plewes. Washington, D.C.: National Academies Press.

Cahill, Dennis J. 1994. "A Two-Stage Model of the Search Process for Single-Family Houses: A Research Note." *Environment and Behavior* 26(1): 38–48.

Capone, Charles A., and Albert Metz. 2003. "Mortgage Default and Default Resolutions: Their Impact on Communities." Paper presented to the Federal Reserve Bank of Chicago "Conference on Sustainable Community Development." Washington, D.C. (March 27). Available at: https://www.chicagofed.org/~/media/others/events/2003/seeds-of-growth/2003-conf-paper-session2-capone-pdf.pdf (accessed March 22, 2016).

Card, David, and Jesse Rothstein. 2007. "Racial Segregation and the Black-White Test Score Gap." *Journal of Public Economics* 91(11): 2158–84.

Carmichael, Jason T., and Stephanie L. Kent. 2014. "The Persistent Significance of Racial and Economic Inequality on the Size of Municipal Police Forces in the United States, 1980–2010." *Social Problems* 61(2): 259–82.

Charles, Camille Zubrinsky. 2000. "Neighborhood Racial-Composition Preferences: Evidence from a Multiethnic Metropolis." *Social Problems* 47(3): 379–407.

———. 2003. "The Dynamics of Racial Residential Segregation." *Annual Review of Sociology* 29: 167–207.

———. 2006. *Won't You Be My Neighbor? Race, Class, and Residence in Los Angeles.* New York: Russell Sage Foundation.

Charles, Camille Z., Gniesha Dinwiddie, and Douglas S. Massey. 2004. "The Continuing Consequences of Segregation: Family Stress and College Academic Performance." *Social Science Quarterly* 85(5): 1353–73.

Chetty, Raj, Nathaniel Hendren, Patrick Kline, and Emmanuel Saez. 2014a. "Where Is the Land of Opportunity? The Geography of Intergenerational Mobility in the United States." Working Paper 19843. Cambridge, Mass.: National Bureau of Economic Research. Available at: http://www.nber.org/papers/w19843 (accessed February 22, 2016).

———. 2014b. "Where Is the Land of Opportunity? The Geography of Inter-generational Mobility in the United States." Working Paper 19843. Cambridge, Mass.: National Bureau of Economic Research (January). Available at: http://www.nber.org/papers/w19843.pdf (accessed March 16, 2016).

Clark, William A. V., ed. 1982. *Modelling Housing Market Search.* New York: St. Martin's Press.

———. 1991. "Residential Preferences and Neighborhood Racial Segregation: A Test of the Schelling Segregation Model." *Demography* 28(1): 1–19.

———. 2009. "Changing Residential Preferences Across Income, Education, and Age Findings from the Multi-City Study of Urban Inequality." *Urban Affairs Review* 44(3): 334–55.

Clark, William A. V., and Robin Flowerdew. 1982. "A Review of Search Models and Their Application to Search in the Housing Market." In *Modelling Housing Market Search,* edited by William A. V. Clark. New York: St. Martin's Press.

Clark, William A.V., and Terence R. Smith. 1979. "Modeling Information Use in a Spatial Context." *Annals of the Association of American Geographers* 69(4): 575–88.

Condron, Dennis J., Daniel Tope, Christina R. Steidl, and Kendralin J. Freeman. 2013. "Racial Segregation and the Black/White Achievement Gap, 1992 to 2009." *Sociological Quarterly* 54(1): 130–57.

Cotterell, John. 2013. *Social Networks in Youth and Adolescence.* New York: Routledge.

Crowder, Kyle. 2000. "The Racial Context of White Mobility: An Individual-Level Assessment of the White Flight Hypothesis." *Social Science Research* 29(2): 223–57.

Crowder, Kyle, and Liam Downey. 2010. "Inter-Neighborhood Migration, Race, and Environmental Hazards: Modeling Micro-Level Processes of Environmental Inequality." *American Journal of Sociology* 115(4): 1110–49.

Crowder, Kyle, Jeremy Pais, and Scott J. South. 2012. "Neighborhood Diversity, Metropolitan Constraints, and Household Migration." *American Sociological Review* 77(3): 325–53.

Crowder, Kyle, and Scott J. South. 2003. "Neighborhood Distress and School Dropout: The Variable Significance of Community Context." *Social Science Research* 32(4): 659–98.

———. 2005. "Race, Class, and Changing Patterns of Migration Between Poor and Nonpoor Neighborhoods." *American Journal of Sociology* 110(6): 1715–63.

———. 2008. "Spatial Dynamics of White Flight: The Effects of Local and Extralocal Racial Conditions on Neighborhood Out-Migration." *American Sociological Review* 73(5): 792–812.

———. 2011. "Spatial and Temporal Dimensions of Neighborhood Effects on High School Graduation." *Social Science Research* 40(1): 87–106.

Crowder, Kyle, Scott J. South, and Erick Chavez. 2006. "Wealth, Race, and Inter-Neighborhood Migration." *American Sociological Review* 71(1): 72–94.

Cui, Lin, and Randall Walsh. 2015. "Foreclosure, Vacancy, and Crime." *Journal of Urban Economics* 87(C): 72–84.

Darrah, Jennifer, and Stefanie DeLuca. 2014. " 'Living Here Has Changed My Whole Perspective': How Escaping Inner-City Poverty Shapes Neighborhood and Housing Choice." *Journal of Policy Analysis and Management* 33(2): 350–84.

Dean, John P. 1947. "Only Caucasian: A Study of Race Covenants." *Journal of Land and Public Utility Economics* 23(4): 428–32.

De la Roca, Jorge, Ingrid Gould Ellen, and Katherine M. O'Regan. 2014. "Race and Neighborhoods in the Twenty-First Century: What Does Segregation Mean Today?" *Regional Science and Urban Economics* 47: 138–51.

DeLuca, Stefanie, and James E. Rosenbaum. 2003. "If Low-Income Blacks Are Given a Chance to Live in White Neighborhoods, Will They Stay? Examining Mobility Patterns in a Quasi-Experimental Program with Administrative Data." *Housing Policy Debate* 14(3): 305–45.

Denton, Nancy A. 2000. "The Role of Residential Segregation in Promoting and Maintaining Inequality in Wealth and Property." *Indiana Law Review* 34(4): 1199–1213.

Desmond, Matthew. 2016. *Evicted: Poverty and Profit in the American City.* New York: Broadway Books.

Dixon, John, Kevin Durrheim, and Colin Tredoux. 2005. "Beyond the Optimal Contact Strategy: A Reality Check for the Contact Hypothesis." *American Psychologist* 60(7): 697–711.

Durrheim, Kevin, and John Dixon. 2013. *Racial Encounter: The Social Psychology of Contact and Desegregation.* New York: Routledge.

Eligon, John. 2015. "A Year After Ferguson, Housing Segregation Defies Tools to Erase It." *New York Times,* August 8.

Ellen, Ingrid Gould, Johanna Lacoe, and Claudia Ayanna Sharygin. 2013. "Do Foreclosures Cause Crime?" *Journal of Urban Economics* 74(C): 59–70.

Emerson, Michael O., George Yancey, and Karen J. Chai. 2001. "Does Race Matter in Residential Segregation? Exploring the Preferences of White Americans." *American Sociological Review* 66(6): 922–35.

Engdahl, Lori. 2009. "New Homes, New Neighborhoods, New Schools: A Progress Report on the Baltimore Housing Mobility Program." Baltimore: Baltimore Regional Housing Campaign and Poverty and Race Research Action Council.

Available at: http://www.prrac.org/pdf/BaltimoreMobilityReport.pdf (accessed April 14, 2016).

Entman, Robert M. 1990. "Modern Racism and the Images of Blacks in Local Television News." *Critical Studies in Media Communication* 7(4): 332–45.

———. 1992. "Blacks in the News: Television, Modern Racism, and Cultural Change." *Journalism and Mass Communication Quarterly* 69(2): 341–61.

Environmental Protection Agency (EPA). 2012. "Toxic Release Inventory." [Machine-readable database]. Available online at: https://www.epa.gov/toxics-release-inventory-tri-program/tri-data-and-tools (accessed August 24, 2017).

Ettema, James S., and Limor Peer. 1996. "Good News from a Bad Neighborhood: Toward an Alternative to the Discourse of Urban Pathology." *Journalism and Mass Communication Quarterly* 73(4): 835–56.

Ewens, Michael, Bryan Tomlin, and Liang Choon Wang. 2014. "Statistical Discrimination or Prejudice? A Large Sample Field Experiment." *Review of Economics and Statistics* 96(1): 119–34.

Farley, Reynolds. 2011. "The Waning of American Apartheid?" *Contexts* 10(3): 36–43.

Farley, Reynolds, and William H. Frey. 1994. "Changes in the Segregation of Whites from Blacks During the 1980s: Small Steps Toward a More Integrated Society." *American Sociological Review* 59(1): 23–45.

Farley, Reynolds, Maria Krysan, and Mick P. Couper. 2004. Detroit Area Study and Chicago Area Study. ICPSR23820-V2. Ann Arbor, Mich.: Inter-University Consortium for Political and Social Research. DOI: 10.3886/ICPSR23820.v2.

Farley, Reynolds, Howard Schuman, Suzanne Bianchi, Diane Colasanto, and Shirley Hatchett. 1978. "Chocolate City, Vanilla Suburbs: Will the Trend Toward Racially Separate Communities Continue?" *Social Science Research* 7(4): 319–44.

Farley, Reynolds, Charlotte Steeh, Maria Krysan, Tara Jackson, and Keith Reeves. 1994. "Stereotypes and Segregation: Neighborhoods in the Detroit Area." *American Journal of Sociology* 100(3): 750–80.

Fasenfest, David, Jason Booza, and Kurt Metzger. 2004. *Living Together: A New Look at Racial and Ethnic Integration in Metropolitan Neighborhoods, 1990–2000.* Washington, D.C.: Brookings Institution.

Feagin, Joe R., and Melvin P. Sikes. 1994. *Living with Racism: The Black Middle-Class Experience.* Boston: Beacon Press.

Federal Housing Administration (FHA). 1938. *Underwriting Manual: Underwriting and Valuation Procedure Under Title II of the National Housing Act with Revisions to February, 1938.* Washington, D.C.: FHA.

Firebaugh, Glenn, and Chad R. Farrell. 2015. "Still Large, but Narrowing: The Sizable Decline in Racial Neighborhood Inequality in Metropolitan America, 1980–2010." *Demography* 53(1): 1–26.

Fischer, Mary J., and Douglas S. Massey. 2004. "The Ecology of Racial Discrimination." *City and Community* 3(3): 221–41.

Fischer, Paul. 2009. "Evaluation of the Regional Portability Pilot Program." Chicago: Housing Choice Partners (August 20). Available at: http://www.metroplanning. org/uploads/cms/documents/Evaluation_of_the_Portability_Pilot_Program. pdf (accessed August 28, 2017).

Fossett, Mark. 2006. "Ethnic Preferences, Social Distance Dynamics, and Residential Segregation: Theoretical Explorations Using Simulation Analysis." *Journal of Mathematical Sociology* 30(3): 185–273.

Fowler, Christopher S., Barrett A. Lee, and Stephen A. Matthews. 2016. "The Contributions of Places to Metropolitan Ethnoracial Diversity and Segregation: Decomposing Change Across Space and Time." *Demography* 53(6): 1955–77.

Freeman, Lance. 2000. "Minority Housing Segregation: A Test of Three Perspectives." *Journal of Urban Affairs* 22(1): 15–35.

Galster, George, and Erin Godfrey. 2005. "By Words and Deeds: Racial Steering by Real Estate Agents in the U.S. in 2000." *Journal of the American Planning Association* 71(3): 251–68.

Galster, George C., and W. Mark Keeney. 1988. "Race, Residence, Discrimination, and Economic Opportunity Modeling the Nexus of Urban Racial Phenomena." *Urban Affairs Review* 24(1): 87–117.

Garrison, Trey. 2015. "HUD's Social Engineering Is Coming to Your Neighborhood." *HousingWire,* July 8. Available at: http://www.housingwire.com/blogs/1-rewired/post/34414-huds-social-engineering-is-coming-to-your-neighborhood (accessed August 28, 2017).

Geolytics. 2014. "Neighborhood Change Database (NCDB) Tract Data from 1970–2010." Available at: http://www.geolytics.com/USCensus,Neighborhood-Change-Database-1970-2000,Products.asp (accessed August 18, 2017).

Gibbons, Joseph. 2015. "Does Racial Segregation Make Community-Based Organizations More Territorial? Evidence from Newark, N.J., and Jersey City, N.J." *Journal of Urban Affairs* 37(5): 600–619.

Gibbons, Joseph, and Tse-Chuan Yang. 2014. "Self-Rated Health and Residential Segregation: How Does Race/Ethnicity Matter?" *Journal of Urban Health* 91(4): 648–60.

Gigerenzer, Gerd, Jean Czerlinski, and Laura Martignon. 1999. "How Good Are Fast and Frugal Heuristics?" In *Decision Science and Technology: Reflections on the Contributions of Ward Edwards,* edited by James Shanteau, Barbara A. Mellers, and David A. Schum. New York: Springer Science+Business Media.

Gigerenzer, Gerd, and Wolfgang Gaissmaier. 2011. "Heuristic Decision Making." *Annual Review of Psychology* 62: 451–82.

Gigerenzer, Gerd, and Daniel G. Goldstein. 1999. "Betting on One Good Reason: The Take the Best Heuristic." In *Simple Heuristics That Make Us Smart*, edited by Gerg Gigerenzer, Peter M. Todd, and the ABC Research Ground. New York: Oxford University Press.

Gigerenzer, Gerd, Peter Todd, and ABC Research Group. 1999. *Simple Heuristics That Make Us Smart.* New York: Oxford University Press.

Gilliam, Franklin D., and Shanto Iyengar. 2000. "Prime Suspects: The Influence of Local Television News on the Viewing Public." *American Journal of Political Science* 44(3): 560–73.

Gilliam, Franklin D., Shanto Iyengar, Adam Simon, and Oliver Wright. 1996. "Crime in Black and White: The Violent, Scary World of Local News." *Harvard International Journal of Press/Politics* 1(3): 6–23.

Glaeser, Edward, and Jacob Vigdor. 2012. *The End of the Segregated Century: Racial Separation in America's Neighborhoods, 1890–2010.* New York: Manhattan Institute for Policy Research.

Goldstein, Daniel G., and Gerd Gigerenzer. 1999. "The Recognition Heuristic: How Ignorance Makes Us Smart." In *Simple Heuristics That Make Us Smart,* edited by Gerd Gigerenzer, Peter M. Todd, and the ABC Research Group. New York: Oxford University Press.

Goodman, John L., Jr. 1978. "Urban Residential Mobility: Places, People, and Policy." Washington, D.C.: Urban Institute. Available at: http://eric.ed.gov/?id=ED189199 (accessed September 23, 2015).

Goodwin, Carole. 1979. *The Oak Park Strategy: Community Control of Racial Change.* Chicago: University of Chicago Press.

Government Accountability Office (GAO). 2010. "Housing and Community Grants: HUD Needs to Enhance Its Requirements and Oversight of Jurisdictions' Fair Housing Plans." GAO-10-905. Washington, D.C.: GAO (September 14). Available at: http://www.gao.gov/products/GAO-10-905 (accessed August 28, 2017).

Greer, Sophia, Michael R. Kramer, Jessica N. Cook-Smith, and Michele L. Casper. 2014. "Metropolitan Racial Residential Segregation and Cardiovascular Mortality: Exploring Pathways." *Journal of Urban Health* 91(3): 499–509.

Hall, Matthew. 2013. "Residential Integration on the New Frontier: Immigrant Segregation in Established and New Destinations." *Demography* 50(5): 1873–96.

Hall, Matthew, Kyle Crowder, and Amy Spring. 2015. "Neighborhood Foreclosures, Racial/Ethnic Transitions, and Residential Segregation." *American Sociological Review* 80(3): 526–49.

Hannah-Jones, Nikole. 2012. *Living Apart: How the Government Betrayed a Landmark Civil Rights Law.* New York: ProPublica.

Hanson, Andrew, and Zackary Hawley. 2011. "Do Landlords Discriminate in the Rental Housing Market? Evidence from an Internet Field Experiment in U.S. Cities." *Journal of Urban Economics* 70(2): 99–114.

Harris, David R. 1999. " 'Property Values Drop When Blacks Move In, Because . . .': Racial and Socioeconomic Determinants of Neighborhood Desirability." *American Sociological Review* 64(3): 461–79.

——. 2001. "Why Are Whites and Blacks Averse to Black Neighbors?" *Social Science Research* 30(1): 100–116.

Harsman, Björn, and John M. Quigley. 1995. "The Spatial Segregation of Ethnic and Demographic Groups: Comparative Evidence from Stockholm and San Francisco." *Journal of Urban Economics* 37(1): 1–16.

Havekes, Esther, Michael Bader, and Maria Krysan. 2016. "Realizing Racial and Ethnic Neighborhood Preferences? Exploring the Mismatches Between What People Want, Where They Search, and Where They Live." *Population Research and Policy Review* 35(1): 101–26.

Heckman, James J. 1998. "Detecting Discrimination." *Journal of Economic Perspectives* 12(2): 101–16.

Hedman, Lina, and Maarten van Ham. 2012. "Understanding Neighbourhood Effects: Selection Bias and Residential Mobility." In *Neighbourhood Effects Research: New Perspectives,* edited by Maarten Van Ham, David Manley, Nick Bailey, Ludi Simpson, and Duncan Maclennan. New York: Springer.

Hempel, Donald J. 1970. *A Comparative Study of the Home Buying Process in Two Connecticut Housing Markets.* Storrs: University of Connecticut, School of Business Administration, Center for Real Estate and Urban Economic Studies.

Hipp, John R. 2011. "Spreading the Wealth: The Effect of the Distribution of Income and Race/Ethnicity Across Households and Neighborhoods on City Crime Trajectories." *Criminology* 49(3): 631–65.

Hirsch, Arnold. 2000. "Planned Destruction: The Interstates and Central City Housing." In *From Tenements to the Taylor Homes: In Search of an Urban Housing Policy in Twentieth-Century America,* edited by John F. Bauman, Roger Biles, and Kristin M. Szylvian. State College: Pennsylvania State Press.

Holloway, Steven R., Richard Wright, and Mark Ellis. 2012. "The Racially Fragmented City? Neighborhood Racial Segregation and Diversity Jointly Considered." *The Professional Geographer* 64(1): 63–82.

Holme, Jennifer Jellison. 2002. "Buying Homes, Buying Schools: School Choice and the Social Construction of School Quality." *Harvard Educational Review* 72(2): 177–206.

Huff, James O. 1982. "Spatial Aspects of Residential Search." In *Modelling Housing Market Search,* edited by William A. V. Clark. New York: St. Martin's Press.

Hwang, Jackelyn, and Robert J. Sampson. 2014. "Divergent Pathways of Gentrification: Racial Inequality and the Social Order of Renewal in Chicago Neighborhoods." *American Sociological Review* 79(4): 726–51.

Hyra, Derek S., Gregory D. Squires, Robert N. Renner, and David S. Kirk. 2013. "Metropolitan Segregation and the Subprime Lending Crisis." *Housing Policy Debate* 23(1): 177–98.

Iceland, John. 2009. *Where We Live Now: Immigration and Race in the United States.* Berkeley: University of California Press.

Iceland, John, and Rima Wilkes. 2006. "Does Socioeconomic Status Matter? Race, Class, and Residential Segregation." *Social Problems* 53(2): 248–73.

Ihlanfeldt, Keith R., and Benjamin Scafidi. 2002. "Black Self-Segregation as a Cause of Housing Segregation: Evidence from the Multi-City Study of Urban Inequality." *Journal of Urban Economics* 51(2): 366–90.

Immergluck, Daniel, and Marti Wiles. 1999. *Two Steps Back: The Dual Mortgage Market, Predatory Lending, and the Undoing of Community Development.* Chicago: Woodstock Institute.

Jackson, Kenneth T. 1987. *Crabgrass Frontier: The Suburbanization of the United States.* Oxford: Oxford University Press.

Jacobus, Rick. 2015. *Inclusionary Housing: Creating and Maintaining Equitable Communities.* Cambridge, MA: Lincoln Institute of Land Policy. Available at: https://www.honolulu.gov/rep/site/ohou/ohou_docs/Inclusionary_Housing_Jacobus_09-15.pdf (accessed August 28, 2017).

Jargowsky, Paul A. 2013. "Concentration of Poverty in the New Millennium: Changes in Prevalence, Composition, and Location in High Poverty Neighborhoods." New York and New Brunswick, N.J.: Century Foundation and Rutgers Center for Urban Research and Education.

———. 2015. "Architecture of Segregation: Civil Unrest, the Concentration of Poverty, and Public Policy." New York: Century Foundation (August 7). Available at: https://tcf.org/content/report/architecture-of-segregation/ (accessed March 10, 2016).

Johnson, James H., Walter C. Farrell, and Chandra Guinn. 1997. "Immigration Reform and the Browning of America: Tensions, Conflicts, and Community Instability in Metropolitan Los Angeles." *International Migration Review* 31(4): 1055–95.

Jones, Malia, and Anne R. Pebley. 2014. "Redefining Neighborhoods Using Common Destinations: Social Characteristics of Activity Spaces and Home Census Tracts Compared." *Demography* 51(3): 727–52.

Kerner Commission. 1968. *Report of the National Advisory Commission on Civil Disorders.* New York: Bantam Books.

Kershaw, Kiarri N., and Sandra S. Albrecht. 2014. "Metropolitan-Level Ethnic Residential Segregation, Racial Identity, and Body Mass Index Among U.S. Hispanic Adults: A Multilevel Cross-Sectional Study." *BMC Public Health* 14(1): 283–92.

Kimelberg, Shelley McDonough. 2014. "Middle-Class Parents, Risk, and Urban Schools." In *Choosing Homes, Choosing Schools,* edited by Annette Lareau and Kimberly Goyette. New York: Russell Sage Foundation.

Klite, Paul, Robert A. Bardwell, and Jason Salzman. 1997. "Local TV News Getting Away with Murder." *Harvard International Journal of Press/Politics* 2(2): 102–12.

Kneebone, Elizabeth, and Natalie Holmes. 2015. "The Growing Distance Between People and Jobs in Metropolitan America." Washington, D.C.: Brookings Institution. Available at: http://www.brookings.edu/research/reports2/2015/03/24-people-jobs-distance-metropolitan-areas-kneebone-holmes (accessed March 16, 2016).

Kneebone, Elizabeth, Carey Nadeau, and Alan Berube. 2011. "The Re-emergence of Concentrated Poverty: Metropolitan Trends in the 2000s." Washington, D.C.:

Brookings Institution (November 3). Available at: http://www.brookings.edu/research/papers/2011/11/03-poverty-kneebone-nadeau-berube (accessed March 16, 2016).

Ko, Michelle, Jack Needleman, Kathryn Pitkin Derose, Miriam J. Laugesen, and Ninez A. Ponce. 2014. "Residential Segregation and the Survival of U.S. Urban Public Hospitals." *Medical Care Research and Review* 71(3): 243–60.

Kochanek, Kenneth D., Elizabeth Arias, and Robert N. Anderson. 2013. "How Did Cause of Death Contribute to Racial Differences in Life Expectancy in the United States in 2010?" NCHS Data Brief 125. Washington: U.S. Department of Health and Human Services, National Center for Health Statistics (July).

Krivo, Lauren J., Heather M. Washington, Ruth D. Peterson, Christopher R. Browning, Catherine A. Calder, and Mei-Po Kwan. 2013. "Social Isolation of Disadvantage and Advantage: The Reproduction of Inequality in Urban Space." *Social Forces* 92(1): 141–64.

Krysan, Maria. 2008. "Does Race Matter in the Search for Housing? An Exploratory Study of Search Strategies, Experiences, and Locations." *Social Science Research* 37(2): 581–603.

Krysan, Maria, and Michael Bader. 2007. "Perceiving the Metropolis: Seeing the City Through a Prism of Race." *Social Forces* 86(2): 699–733.

———. 2009. "Racial Blind Spots: Black-White-Latino Differences in Community Knowledge." *Social Problems* 56(4): 677–701.

Krysan, Maria, Courtney Carter, and Marieke van Londen. 2016. "The Diversity of Integration in a Multiethnic Metropolis: Exploring What Whites, African Americans, and Latinos Imagine." *Du Bois Review: Social Science Research on Race*, DOI:10.1017/S1742058X16000291.

Krysan, Maria, Mick P. Couper, Reynolds Farley, and Tyrone Forman. 2009. "Does Race Matter in Neighborhood Preferences? Results from a Video Experiment." *American Journal of Sociology* 115(2): 527–59.

Krysan, Maria, Kyle Crowder, Molly M. Scott, Carl Hedman, Sade Adeeyo, Somala Diby, and Sierra Latham. 2016. *Research Report: Racial/Ethnic Differences in Housing Search.* Washington, D.C.: Urban Institute.

Krysan, Maria, and Reynolds Farley. 2002. "The Residential Preferences of Blacks: Do They Explain Persistent Segregation?" *Social Forces* 80(3): 937–80.

Krysan, Maria, Reynolds Farley, and Mick P. Couper. 2008. "In the Eye of the Beholder: Racial Beliefs and Residential Segregation." *Du Bois Review: Social Science Research on Race* 5(1): 5–26.

Kwate, Naa Oyo A., Melody S. Goodman, Jerrold Jackson, and Julen Harris. 2013. "Spatial and Racial Patterning of Real Estate Broker Listings in New York City." *Review of Black Political Economy* 40(4): 401–24.

Lacy, Karyn. 2007. *Blue Chip Black: Race, Class, and Status in the New Black Middle-Class.* Berkeley: University of California Press.

Lake, Robert W. 1981. *The New Suburbanites: Race and Housing in the Suburbs.* New Brunswick, N.J.: Transaction Publishers.

Lareau, Annette. 2014. "Schools, Housing, and the Reproduction of Inequality." In *Choosing Homes, Choosing Schools,* edited by Annette Lareau and Kimberly Goyette. New York: Russell Sage Foundation.

LaVeist, Thomas A., Darrell Gaskin, and Antonio J. Trujillo. 2011. "Segregated Spaces, Risky Places: The Effects of Racial Segregation on Health Inequalities." Washington, D.C.: Joint Center for Political and Economic Studies. Available at: http://jointcenter.org/sites/default/files/Segregated%20Spaces%20Fact%20 Sheet.pdf (accessed February 7, 2016).

Lee, Barrett A., John Iceland, and Chad R. Farrell. 2014. "Is Ethnoracial Residential Integration on the Rise? Evidence from Metropolitan and Micropolitan America Since 1980." In *Diversity and Disparities: America Enters a New Century,* edited by John R. Logan. New York: Russell Sage Foundation.

Leventhal, Tama, Véronique Dupéré, and Elizabeth A. Shuey. 2014. "Children in Neighborhoods." In *Handbook of Child Psychology and Developmental Science,* edited by Richard M. Lerner, M. H. Bornstein, and Tama Leventhal. Hoboken, N.J.: John Wiley & Sons.

Lewis, Amanda, and John Diamond. 2015. *Despite the Best Intentions: How Racial Inequality Thrives in Good Schools.* New York: Oxford University Press.

Lewis, Valerie A., Michael O. Emerson, and Stephen L. Klineberg. 2011. "Who We'll Live With: Neighborhood Racial Composition Preferences of Whites, Blacks and Latinos." *Social Forces* 89(4): 1385–1407.

Lichter, Daniel T., Domenico Parisi, Michael C. Taquino, and Steven Michael Grice. 2010. "Residential Segregation in New Hispanic Destinations: Cities, Suburbs, and Rural Communities Compared." *Social Science Research* 39(2): 215–30.

Lindgren, April. 2009. "News, Geography, and Disadvantage: Mapping Newspaper Coverage of High-Needs Neighbourhoods in Toronto, Canada." *Canadian Journal of Urban Research* 18(1): 74–97.

Logan, John R. 2011. "Separate and Unequal: The Neighborhood Gap for Blacks, Hispanics, and Asians in Metropolitan America." US2010 Project (July). Available at: https://s4.ad.brown.edu/Projects/Diversity/Data/Report/report0727.pdf (accessed March 16, 2016).

Logan, John R., Richard D. Alba, Tom McNulty, and Brian Fisher. 1996. "Making a Place in the Metropolis: Locational Attainment in Cities and Suburbs." *Demography* 33(4): 443–53.

Logan, John R., and Harvey Luskin Molotch. 1987. *Urban Fortunes: The Political Economy of Place.* Berkeley: University of California Press.

Logan, John R., Brian J. Stults, and Reynolds Farley. 2004. "Segregation of Minorities in the Metropolis: Two Decades of Change." *Demography* 41(1): 1–22.

Macartney, Suzanne, Alemayehu Bishaw, and Kayla Fontenot. 2013. "Poverty Rates for Selected Detailed Race and Hispanic Groups by State and Place: 2007–2011." American Community Survey Brief 11-17. Washington: U.S. Department of Commerce, U.S. Census Bureau (February). Available at: https://www.census. gov/prod/2013pubs/acsbr11-17.pdf (accessed March 22, 2016).

Maclennan, Duncan, and Gavin Wood. 1982. "Information Acquisition: Patterns and Strategies." In *Modelling Housing Market Search,* edited by William A. V. Clark. New York: St. Martin's Press.

Maly, Michael. 2008. *Beyond Segregation: Multiracial and Multiethnic Neighborhoods.* Philadelphia: Temple University Press.

Martin, Deborah G. 2000. "Constructing Place: Cultural Hegemonies and Media Images of an Inner-City Neighborhood." *Urban Geography* 21(5): 380–405.

Massey, Douglas S. 2007. *Categorically Unequal: The American Stratification System.* New York: Russell Sage Foundation.

Massey, Douglas S., Len Albright, Rebecca Casciano, Elizabeth Derickson, and David N. Kinsey. 2013. *Climbing Mount Laurel: The Struggle for Affordable Housing and Social Mobility in an American Suburb.* Princeton, N.J.: Princeton University Press.

Massey, Douglas S., Camille Z. Charles, Garvey Lundy, and Mary J. Fischer. 2011. *The Source of the River: The Social Origins of Freshmen at America's Selective Colleges and Universities.* Princeton, N.J.: Princeton University Press.

Massey, Douglas S., and Nancy A. Denton. 1993. *American Apartheid: Segregation and the Making of the Underclass.* Cambridge, Mass.: Harvard University Press.

Massey, Douglas S., and Mary J. Fischer. 2006. "The Effect of Childhood Segregation on Minority Academic Performance at Selective Colleges." *Ethnic and Racial Studies* 29(1): 1–26.

Massey, Douglas S., and Garvey Lundy. 2001. "Use of Black English and Racial Discrimination in Urban Housing Markets: New Methods and Findings." *Urban Affairs Review* 36(4): 452–69.

Massey, Douglas S., and Jonathan Rothwell. 2009. "The Effect of Density Zoning on Racial Segregation in U.S. Urban Areas." *Urban Affairs Review* 44(6): 779–806.

Massey, Douglas S., Jonathan Rothwell, and Thurston Domina. 2009. "The Changing Bases of Segregation in the United States." *Annals of the American Academy of Political and Social Science* 626(1): 74–90.

Matei, Sorin, Sandra J. Ball-Rokeach, and Jack Linchuan Qiu. 2001. "Fear and Misperception of Los Angeles Urban Space: A Spatial-Statistical Study of Communication-Shaped Mental Maps." *Communication Research* 28(4): 429–63.

McCarthy, Kevin. 1982. "An Analytical Model of Housing Search." In *Modelling Housing Market Search,* edited by William A. V. Clark. New York: St. Martin's Press.

McClure, Kirk. 2008. "Deconcentrating Poverty with Housing Programs." *Journal of the American Planning Association* 74(1): 90–99.

McPherson, Miller, Lynn Smith-Lovin, and James M. Cook. 2001. "Birds of a Feather: Homophily in Social Networks." *Annual Review of Sociology* 27: 415–44.

Mirowsky, John, and Catherine E. Ross. 2007. "Life Course Trajectories of Perceived Control and Their Relationship to Education." *American Journal of Sociology* 112(5): 1339–82.

Mock, Brentin. 2015. "How Los Angeles County Furthered Racist 'Fair-Housing' Practices." *Atlantic Monthly: City Lab,* July 28. Available at: http://www.citylab.com/housing/2015/07/how-los-angeles-county-furthered-racist-fair-housing-practices/399731/ (accessed March 29, 2016).

Moore, Latetia V., and Ana V. Diez Roux. 2006. "Associations of Neighborhood Characteristics with the Location and Type of Food Stores." *American Journal of Public Health* 96(2): 325–31.

Morello-Frosch, Rachel, and Bill M. Jesdale. 2006. "Separate and Unequal: Residential Segregation and Estimated Cancer Risks Associated with Ambient Air Toxics in U.S. Metropolitan Areas." *Environmental Health Perspectives* 114(3): 386–93.

Morello-Frosch, Rachel, and Russ Lopez. 2006. "The Riskscape and the Color Line: Examining the Role of Segregation in Environmental Health Disparities." *Environmental Research* 102(2): 181–96.

Munnell, Alicia H., Lynne E. Browne, James McEneaney, and Geoffrey Tootell. 1992. *Mortgage Lending in Boston: Interpreting HMDA Data.* Boston: Federal Reserve Bank of Boston.

Neild, Ruth Curran, and Robert Balfanz. 2006. "An Extreme Degree of Difficulty: The Educational Demographics of Urban Neighborhood High Schools." *Journal of Education for Students Placed at Risk* 11(2): 123–41.

Nieuwenhuis, Jaap, and Pieter Hooimeijer. 2016. "The Association Between Neighbourhoods and Educational Achievement: A Systematic Review and Meta-Analysis." *Journal of Housing and the Built Environment* 31(2): 321–47.

Nuru-Jeter, Amani M., and Thomas A. LaVeist. 2011. "Racial Segregation, Income Inequality, and Mortality in U.S. Metropolitan Areas." *Journal of Urban Health* 88(2): 270–82.

Nyden, Philip, Michael Maly, and John Lukehart. 1997. "The Emergence of Stable Racially and Ethnically Diverse Urban Communities: A Case Study of Nine U.S. Cities." *Housing Policy Debate* 8(2): 491–534.

Oliver, Melvin L., and Thomas M. Shapiro. 2006. *Black Wealth, White Wealth: A New Perspective on Racial Inequality.* New York: Taylor & Francis.

Ondrich, Jan, Stephen Ross, and John Yinger. 2003. "Now You See It, Now You Don't: Why Do Real Estate Agents Withhold Available Houses from Black Customers?" *Review of Economics and Statistics* 85(4): 854–73.

Ondrich, Jan, Alex Stricker, and John Yinger. 1999. "Do Landlords Discriminate? The Incidence and Causes of Racial Discrimination in Rental Housing Markets." *Journal of Housing Economics* 8(3): 185–204.

Orfield, Gary, and Erica Frankenberg. 2014. "Increasingly Segregated and Unequal Schools as Courts Reverse Policy." *Educational Administration Quarterly* 50(5): 718–34.

Orfield, Gary, John Kucsera, and Genevieve Siegel-Hawley. 2012. *E Pluribus . . . Separation: Deepening Double Segregation for More Students.* Los Angeles: The

Civil Rights Project (September). Available at: http://civilrightsproject.ucla.edu/research/k-12-education/integration-and-diversity/mlk-national/e-pluribus . . . separation-deepening-double-segregation-for-more-students/orfield_epluribus_revised_omplete_2012.pdf (accessed March 16, 2016).

Orfield, Myron. 2005. "Land Use and Housing Policies to Reduce Concentrated Poverty and Racial Segregation." *Fordham Urban Law Journal* 33(3): 101–59.

O'Sullivan, Joseph, and Jim Brunner. 2015. "School Funding Back on Table as Court Fines State $100,000 a Day." *Seattle Times,* August 13.

Page, Marianne. 1995. "Racial and Ethnic Discrimination in Urban Housing Markets: Evidence from a Recent Audit Study." *Journal of Urban Economics* 38(2): 183–206.

Pager, Devah, and Hana Shepherd. 2008. "The Sociology of Discrimination: Racial Discrimination in Employment, Housing, Credit, and Consumer Markets." *Annual Review of Sociology* 34: 181–209.

Palmer, John R. B. 2013. "Activity-Space Segregation: Understanding Social Divisions in Space and Time." PhD diss., Princeton University.

Panel Study of Income Dynamics (PSID). 2016. Public use dataset and restricted use data. Ann Arbor, Mich.: Survey Research Center, Institute for Social Research, University of Michigan.

Parisi, Domenico, Daniel T. Lichter, Michael C. Taquino, Jesper Sørensen, and Stephen L. Morgan. 2015. "The Buffering Hypothesis: Growing Diversity and Declining Black-White Segregation in America's Cities, Suburbs, and Small Towns?" *Sociological Science* 2(8): 125–57.

Park, Robert Ezra. 1950. *Race and Culture.* New York: Free Press.

Park, Robert E., Ernest W. Burgess, and Roderick D. McKenzie. 1984. *The City.* Chicago: University of Chicago Press.

Patterson, Orlando. 1997. *The Ordeal of Integration: Progress and Resentment in America's "Racial" Crisis.* Washington, D.C.: Basic Civitas Books.

Pattillo-McCoy, Mary. 1999. *Black Picket Fences: Privilege and Peril in the Black Middle Class Neighborhood.* Chicago: University of Chicago Press.

Pattillo, Mary, Lori Delale-O'Connor, and Felicia Butts. 2014. "High-Stakes Choosing." In *Choosing Homes, Choosing Schools,* edited by Annette Lareau and Kimberly Goyette. New York: Russell Sage Foundation.

Pendall, Rolf. 2000. "Local Land Use Regulation and the Chain of Exclusion." *Journal of the American Planning Association* 66(2): 125–42.

Peterson, Ruth D., and Lauren J. Krivo. 2010a. *Divergent Social Worlds: Neighborhood Crime and the Racial-Spatial Divide.* New York: Russell Sage Foundation.

———. 2010b. "National Neighborhood Crime Study (NNCS), 2000: Version 1." Ann Arbor, Mich.: Interuniversity Consortium for Political and Social Research. DOI: 10.3886/ICPSR27501.

Pettigrew, Thomas F., and Linda R. Tropp. 2006. "A Meta-analytic Test of Intergroup Contact Theory." *Journal of Personality and Social Psychology* 90(5): 751–83.

Poverty and Race Research Action Council (PRRAC). 2013. "Appendix B: State, Local, and Federal Laws Barring Source-of-Income Discrimination." Washington, D.C.: PRRAC (July). Available at: www.prrac.org/pdf/Expanding_Choice_ Appendix_B_Updated.pdf (accessed August 28, 2017).

Purnell, Thomas, William Idsardi, and John Baugh. 1999. "Perceptual and Phonetic Experiments on American English Dialect Identification." *Journal of Language and Social Psychology* 18(1): 10–30.

Quillian, Lincoln. 2002. "Why Is Black-White Residential Segregation So Persistent? Evidence on Three Theories from Migration Data." *Social Science Quarterly* 31(2): 197–229.

———. 2003. "How Long Are Exposures to Poor Neighborhoods? The Long-Term Dynamics of Entry and Exit from Poor Neighborhoods." *Population Research and Policy Review* 22(3): 221–49.

———. 2006. "New Approaches to Understanding Racial Prejudice and Discrimination." *Annual Review of Sociology* 32: 299–328.

———. 2012. "Segregation and Poverty Concentration: The Role of Three Segregations." *American Sociological Review* 77(3): 354–79.

———. 2014. "Does Segregation Create Winners and Losers? Residential Segregation and Inequality in Educational Attainment." *Social Problems* 61(3): 402–26.

———. 2015. "A Comparison of Traditional and Discrete-Choice Approaches to the Analysis of Residential Mobility and Locational Attainment." *Annals of the American Academy of Political and Social Science* 660(1): 240–60.

Quillian, Lincoln, and Devah Pager. 2001. "Black Neighbors, Higher Crime? The Role of Racial Stereotypes in Evaluations of Neighborhood Crime." *American Journal of Sociology* 107(3): 717–67.

———. 2010. "Estimating Risk Stereotype Amplification and the Perceived Risk of Criminal Victimization." *Social Psychology Quarterly* 73(1): 79–104.

Reardon, Sean F., and Ann Owens. 2014. "60 Years After Brown: Trends and Consequences of School Segregation." *Annual Review of Sociology* 40: 199–218.

Rhodes, Anna, and Stefanie DeLuca. 2014. "Residential Mobility and School Choice Among Poor Families." In *Choosing Homes, Choosing Schools,* edited by Annette Lareau and Kimberly Goyette. New York: Russell Sage Foundation.

Roisman, Florence Wagman. 2001. "Opening the Suburbs to Racial Integration: Lessons for the 21st Century." *Western New England Law Review* 23(1): 65–113.

Roscigno, Vincent J., Diana L. Karafin, and Griff Tester. 2009. "The Complexities and Processes of Racial Housing Discrimination." *Social Problems* 56(1): 49–69.

Rosen, Eva. 2014. "Rigging the Rules of the Game: How Landlords Geographically Sort Low-Income Renters." *City and Community* 13(4): 310–40.

Rosenblatt, Peter, and Stefanie DeLuca. 2012. " 'We Don't Live Outside, We Live in Here': Neighborhood and Residential Mobility Decisions Among Low-Income Families." *City and Community* 11(3): 254–84.

Ross, Catherine E., and John Mirowsky. 2010. "Gender and the Health Benefits of Education." *Sociological Quarterly* 51(1): 1–19.

Ross, Stephen L., and Margery Austin Turner. 2005. "Housing Discrimination in Metropolitan America: Explaining Changes Between 1989 and 2000." *Social Problems* 52(2): 152–80.

Ross, Stephen L., Margery Austin Turner, Erin Godfrey, and Robin R. Smith. 2008. "Mortgage Lending in Chicago and Los Angeles: A Paired Testing Study of the Pre-Application Process." *Journal of Urban Economics* 63(3): 902–19.

Ross, Stephen L., and John Yinger. 2002. *The Color of Credit: Mortgage Discrimination, Research Methodology, and Fair-Lending Enforcement.* Cambridge, Mass.: MIT Press.

Rothstein, Richard. 2014. "The Making of Ferguson: How Decades of Hostile Policy Created a Powder Keg." *American Prospect Longform,* October 15. Available at: http://prospect.org/article/making-ferguson-how-decades-hostile-policy-created-powder-keg (accessed March 16, 2016).

———. 2017. *The Color of Law: The Forgotten History of How Our Government Segregated America.* New York: Liveright Publishing.

Rothwell, Jonathan T. 2012. "The Effects of Racial Segregation on Trust and Volunteering in U.S. Cities." *Urban Studies* 49(10): 2109–36.

Rugh, Jacob S. 2015. "Double Jeopardy: Why Latinos Were Hit Hardest by the U.S. Foreclosure Crisis." *Social Forces* 93(3): 1139–84.

Rugh, Jacob S., Len Albright, and Douglas S. Massey. 2015. "Race, Space, and Cumulative Disadvantage: A Case Study of the Subprime Lending Collapse." *Social Problems* 62(2): 186–218.

Rugh, Jacob S., and Douglas S. Massey. 2010. "Racial Segregation and the American Foreclosure Crisis." *American Sociological Review* 75(5): 629–51.

Rumberger, Russell W., and Sun Ah Lim. 2008. *Why Students Drop Out of School: A Review of 25 Years of Research.* Santa Barbara: University of California, California Dropout Research Project (August). Available at: http://www.cdrp.ucsb.edu/dropouts/researchreport15.pdf (accessed March 29, 2016).

Sampson, Robert J. 2012. *Great American City: Chicago and the Enduring Neighborhood Effect.* Chicago: University of Chicago Press.

Sampson, Robert J., and Stephen W. Raudenbush. 2004. "Seeing Disorder: Neighborhood Stigma and the Social Construction of 'Broken Windows.' " *Social Psychology Quarterly* 67(4): 319–42.

Sampson, Robert J., and Patrick Sharkey. 2008. "Neighborhood Selection and the Social Reproduction of Concentrated Racial Inequality." *Demography* 45(1): 1–29.

Sarat, Austin. 2001. *Cultural Pluralism, Identity Politics, and the Law.* Ann Arbor: University of Michigan Press.

Schelling, Thomas C. 1971. "Dynamic Models of Segregation." *Journal of Mathematical Sociology* 1(2): 143–86.

Schultz, Theodore W. 1961. "Investment in Human Capital." *American Economic Review* 51(1): 1–17.

Schwartz, Alex F. 2014. *Housing Policy in the United States.* New York: Routledge.

Scott, Molly M., Mary Cunningham, Jennifer Biess, Jennifer Lee O'Neil, Phil Tegeler, Ebony Gayles, and Barbara Sard. 2013. "Expanding Choice: Practical Strategies for Building a Successful Housing Mobility Program." Washington, D.C.: Urban Institute and Poverty and Race Research Action Council.

Shapiro, Thomas, Tatjana Meschede, and Sam Osoro. 2013. "The Roots of the Widening Racial Wealth Gap: Explaining the Black-White Economic Divide." Research and Policy Brief. Waltham, Mass.: Brandeis University, Institute on Assets and Social Policy (February). Available at: http://www.naacpldf.org/files/case_issue/Shapiro%20racialwealthgapbrief.pdf (accessed February 21, 2016).

———. 2014. "The Widening Racial Wealth Gap: Why Wealth Is Not Color Blind." In *The Assets Perspective,* edited by Reid Cramer and Trina R. Williams Shanks. New York: Palgrave Macmillan.

Sharkey, Patrick. 2008. "The Intergenerational Transmission of Context." *American Journal of Sociology* 113(4): 931–69.

———. 2012. "Residential Mobility and the Reproduction of Unequal Neighborhoods." *Cityscape* 14(3): 9–31.

———. 2013. *Stuck in Place: Urban Neighborhoods and the End of Progress Toward Racial Equality.* Chicago: University of Chicago Press.

Sigelman, Lee, and Susan Welch. 1993. "The Contact Hypothesis Revisited: Black-White Interaction and Positive Racial Attitudes." *Social Forces* 71(3): 781–95.

Silm, Siiri, and Rein Ahas. 2014. "Ethnic Differences in Activity Spaces: A Study of Out-of-Home Nonemployment Activities with Mobile Phone Data." *Annals of the Association of American Geographers* 104(3): 542–59.

Silverman, Robert Mark. 2011. "Black Real Estate Professionals' Perceptions of Career Opportunities: The Economic Detour Redux." *Review of Black Political Economy* 38(2): 145–63.

Smith, Jeffrey A., Miller McPherson, and Lynn Smith-Lovin. 2014. "Social Distance in the United States: Sex, Race, Religion, Age, and Education Homophily Among Confidants, 1985 to 2004." *American Sociological Review* 79(3): 432–56.

Smith, Terence R., William A. V. Clark, James O. Huff, and Perry Shapiro. 1979. "A Decision-Making and Search Model For Intraurban Migration." *Geographical Analysis* 11(1): 1–22.

South, Scott J., and Kyle Crowder. 1998. "Housing Discrimination and Residential Mobility: Impacts for Blacks and Whites." *Population Research and Policy Review* 17(4): 369–87.

South, Scott J., Kyle Crowder, and Jeremy Pais. 2011. "Metropolitan Structure and Neighborhood Attainment: Exploring Intermetropolitan Variation in Racial Residential Segregation." *Demography* 48(4): 1263–92.

Spivak, Andrew L., Loretta E. Bass, and Craig St. John. 2011. "Reconsidering Race, Class, and Residential Segregation in American Cities." *Urban Geography* 32(4): 531–67.

Spring, Amy, Elizabeth Ackert, Kyle Crowder, Scott J. South, and Ying Huang. Forthcoming. "Impacts of Proximity to Kin on Residential Mobility and Destination Choice: Examining Local Movers in Metropolitan Areas." *Demography*.

Spring, Amy, Stewart E. Tolnay, and Kyle Crowder. 2016. "Moving for Opportunities? Changing Patterns of Migration in North America." In *International Handbook of Migration and Population Distribution*, edited by Michael J. White. New York: Springer.

Squires, Gregory D. 2007. "Demobilization of the Individualistic Bias: Housing Market Discrimination as a Contributor to Labor Market and Economic Inequality." *Annals of the American Academy of Political and Social Science* 609(1): 200–214.

Squires, Gregory D., and Jan Chadwick. 2006. "Linguistic Profiling: A Continuing Tradition of Discrimination in the Home Insurance Industry?" *Urban Affairs Review* 41(3): 400–415.

Squires, Gregory D., and Charis E. Kubrin. 2005. "Privileged Places: Race, Uneven Development, and the Geography of Opportunity in Urban America." *Urban Studies* 42(1): 47–68.

Stiglitz, Joseph. 2012. *The Price of Inequality*. New York: W. W. Norton & Co.

Sugrue, Thomas J. 1993. "The Structures of Urban Poverty: The Reorganization of Space and Work in Three Periods of American History." In *The "Underclass" Debate: Views from History*, edited by Michael B. Katz. Princeton, N.J.: Princeton University Press.

———. 2014. *The Origins of the Urban Crisis: Race and Inequality in Postwar Detroit*. Princeton, N.J.: Princeton University Press.

Swaroop, Sapna, and Maria Krysan. 2011. "The Determinants of Neighborhood Satisfaction: Racial Proxy Revisited." *Demography* 48(3): 1203–29.

Talarchek, Gary M. 1982. "Sequential Aspects of Residential Search and Selection." *Urban Geography* 3(1): 34–57.

Taub, Richard P., D. Garth Taylor, and Jan D. Dunham. 1984. *Paths of Neighborhood Change: Race and Crime in Urban America*. Chicago: University of Chicago Press.

Teasdale, Brent, Lynn M. Clark, and Joshua C. Hinkle. 2012. "Subprime Lending Foreclosures, Crime, and Neighborhood Disorganization: Beyond Internal Dynamics." *American Journal of Criminal Justice* 37(2): 163–78.

Theall, Katherine P., Stacy S. Drury, and Elizabeth A. Shirtcliff. 2012. "Cumulative Neighborhood Risk of Psychosocial Stress and Allostatic Load in Adolescents." *American Journal of Epidemiology* 176(7): S164–74.

Thernstrom, Stephan, and Abigail Thernstrom. 1997. *America in Black and White: One Nation, Indivisible*. New York: Simon & Schuster.

Thomas, Hannah, Tatjana Meschede, Alexis Mann, Allison Stagg, and Thomas Shapiro. 2014. *Location, Location, Location: The Role Neighborhoods Play in Family Wealth and Well-being*. Waltham, Mass.: Institute on Assets and Social Policy

(October). Available at: https://iasp.brandeis.edu/pdfs/2014/Location.pdf (accessed February 21, 2016).

Thomas, Melvin, and Richard Moye. 2015. "Race, Class, and Gender and the Impact of Racial Segregation on Black-White Income Inequality." *Sociology of Race and Ethnicity* 1(4): 490–502.

Timberlake, Jeffrey M., and John Iceland. 2007. "Change in Racial and Ethnic Residential Inequality in American Cities, 1970–2000." *City and Community* 6(4): 335–65.

Tukachinsky, Riva, Dana Mastro, and Moran Yarchi. 2015. "Documenting Portrayals of Race/Ethnicity on Primetime Television over a 20-Year Span and Their Association with National-Level Racial/Ethnic Attitudes." *Journal of Social Issues* 71(1): 17–38.

Turner, Margery Austin, Jennifer Comey, Daniel Kuehn, and Austin Nichols. 2011. *Helping Poor Families Gain and Sustain Access to High-Opportunity Neighborhoods.* Washington, D.C.: Urban Institute.

Turner, Margery Austin, Rob Santos, Diane K. Levy, Doug Wissoker, Claudia Aranda, and Rob Pitingolo. 2013. *Housing Discrimination Against Racial and Ethnic Minorities 2012.* Washington, D.C.: U.S. Department of Housing and Urban Development. Available at: http://www.huduser.gov/portal/Publications/pdf/HUD-514_HDS2012.pdf (accessed August 28, 2017).

U.S. Department of Housing and Urban Development (HUD). N.d. "Housing Choice Voucher Program Section 8: Housing Choice Vouchers Fact Sheet." Available at: http://portal.hud.gov/hudportal/HUD?src=/topics/housing_choice_voucher_program_section_8 (accessed March 29, 2016).

Uslaner, Eric M. 2011. "Trust, Diversity, and Segregation in the United States and the United Kingdom." *Comparative Sociology* 10(2): 221–47.

Wakefield, Sara, and Christopher Uggen. 2010. "Incarceration and Stratification." *Annual Review of Sociology* 36: 387–406.

Wallace, Danielle, E. C. Hedberg, and Charles M. Katz. 2012. "The Impact of Foreclosures on Neighborhood Disorder Before and During the Housing Crisis: Testing the Spiral of Decay." *Social Science Quarterly* 93(3): 625–47.

Weininger, Elliot B. 2014. "School Choice in an Urban Setting." In *Choosing Homes, Choosing Schools*, edited by Annette Lareau and Kimberly Goyette. New York: Russell Sage Foundation.

White, Kellee, Jennifer S. Haas, and David R. Williams. 2012. "Elucidating the Role of Place in Health Care Disparities: The Example of Racial/Ethnic Residential Segregation." *Health Services Research* 47(3, pt. 2): 1278–99.

Williams, David R. 2012. "Miles to Go Before We Sleep: Racial Inequities in Health." *Journal of Health and Social Behavior* 53(3): 279–95.

Williams, David R., and Chiquita Collins. 2001. "Racial Residential Segregation: A Fundamental Cause of Racial Disparities in Health." *Public Health Reports* 116(5): 404–16.

Williams, Richard, Reynold Nesiba, and Eileen Diaz McConnell. 2005. "The Changing Face of Inequality in Home Mortgage Lending." *Social Problems* 52(2): 181–208.

Williams, Sonya, George Galster, and Nandita Verma. 2014. "Home Foreclosures and Neighborhood Crime Dynamics." *Housing Studies* 29(3): 380–406.

Wilson, William Julius. 1987. *The Truly Disadvantaged: The Inner City, the Underclass, and Public Policy.* Chicago: University of Chicago Press.

Wilson, William Julius, and Richard P. Taub. 2006. *There Goes the Neighborhood: Racial, Ethnic, and Class Tensions in Four Chicago Neighborhoods and Their Meaning for America.* New York: Random House.

Wodtke, Geoffrey T., David J. Harding, and Felix Elwert. 2011. "Neighborhood Effects in Temporal Perspective: The Impact of Long-Term Exposure to Concentrated Disadvantage on High School Graduation." *American Sociological Review* 76(5): 713–36.

Wong, David W. S., and Shih-Lung Shaw. 2011. "Measuring Segregation: An Activity Space Approach." *Journal of Geographical Systems* 13(2): 127–45.

Wood, Holly. 2014. "When Only a House Makes a Home: How Home Selection Matters in the Residential Mobility Decisions of Lower-Income, Inner-City African American Families." *Social Service Review* 88(2): 264–94.

Yang, Tse-Chuan, and Stephen A. Matthews. 2015. "Death by Segregation: Does the Dimension of Racial Segregation Matter?" *PloS One* 10(9): 1–26.

Yinger, John. 1995. *Closed Doors, Opportunities Lost: The Continuing Costs of Housing Discrimination.* New York: Russell Sage Foundation.

Zhao, Bo. 2005. "Does the Number of Houses a Broker Shows Depend on a Homeseeker's Race?" *Journal of Urban Economics* 57(1): 128–47.

Index

Boldface numbers refer to figures and tables.

crime: racial composition of a
community and perceptions of, 122;
residential segregation and, 30
Crowder, Kyle, 56

Darrah, Jennifer, 105, 222–23, 238, 243
data: Chicago as research focus, 57,
61–62; demographics of respondents,
276n27, 276n29; qualitative, 56–59;
secondary analysis of large-scale
national data sets, 62–65; sources of,
55–56. *See also* methodology; names
of studies
decision-making, residential. *See*
residential selection process
DeLuca, Stefanie: assumption of
immutable preferences, lack of
support for, 163; Baltimore Mobility
Program, study of, 222–23, 238–39;
lived experiences, constrained
contexts and, 145; low-income
African Americans, study of, 148;
outcomes and preferences, relationship of, 161; voucher holders, study
of, 49, 105, 144, 243
Denton, Nancy, 7, 18–19, 26, 29, 138
Desmond, Matthew, 138–39
Detroit Area Study (DAS), 57, 282n12
discrimination: anticipation of,
187–97; community, assumptions
regarding, 190–94; community,
reputation for, 188–90; complexity
of, the social structural sorting
perspective and, 211; the consideration set and, 186–97; contemporary segregation, role in, 10–11;
exclusionary and non-exclusionary,
distinction between, 284n11; intersection of preferences, social class,
and, 208–11; in the mobility process, 55; non-exclusionary (*see* non-
exclusionary discrimination);

patterns and prevalence of,
research on, 177–80; perceived
social class and, 206–8; racial steering, 10, 55, 175, 181–85, 197–202,
207–8, 211, 225, 235; research needs
on anticipated, 247–48; residential
segregation, impact on, 180–86;
social class and, 204–11; source-of-
income, 240; stage two, responses
to, 200–204; statistical, 206–8,
285n48; as traditional explanation
for residential segregation, 5, 33–34,
176, 186, 204
disparate impact, 234, 256–57

economic resources: affordability,
real and perceived concerns with,
133–38; association between family
income and residential destinations
for mobile PSID householders in
core metropolitan areas, 1997–2013,
131; black-white segregation as a
function of income stratification in
core metropolitan areas, 2010, **129**;
constrained contexts due to, choices
within, 144–48; the context of a
residential move and, 138–44;
future research needs regarding,
247; how recent movers first heard
about the current unit, by family
income quintile, 2011–2013, **142**;
racial segregation, implications for,
148–50; reasons for moving
reported by recent movers, by family income quintile, 2011–2013, **140**;
reasons given by recent movers for
stopping the housing search, by
income quintile, 2011–2013, **143**;
residential segregation and, 29,
31–32, 253–54; standard model
of residential segregation and,
127–33; as traditional explanation